APPLIED ANTHROPOLOGY

A Career-Oriented Approach

Margaret A. Gwynne

State University of New York at Stony Brook

Boston   New York   San Francisco
Mexico City   Montreal   Toronto   London   Madrid   Munich   Paris
Hong Kong   Singapore   Tokyo   Cape Town   Sydney

Editor: Jennifer Jacobson
Editorial Assistant: Elizabeth Lee
Marketing Manager: Taryn Wahlquist
Editorial-Production Administrator: Deborah Brown
Editorial Production Service: Susan McNally
Composition Buyer: Linda Cox
Manufacturing Buyer: Andrew Turso
Design and Electronic Composition: Denise Hoffman
Cover Administrator: Kristina Mose-Libon
Photo Researchers: Kate Cook, Liz Wood, Margaret Gwynne

For related titles and support materials, visit our online catalog at www.ablongman.com.

Between the time Website information is gathered and then published, it is not unusual for some sites to have closed. Also, the transcription of URLs can result in unintended typographical errors. The publisher would appreciate notification where these errors occur so that they may be corrected in subsequent editions.

Library of Congress Cataloging-in-Publication Data

Gwynne, Margaret Anderson.
    Applied anthropology : a career-oriented approach / Margaret A. Gwynne
       p.   cm.
    Includes bibliographical references and index.
    ISBN 0–205–35866–7
      1. Applied anthropology.   2. Ethnology—Vocational guidance.   I. Title.
  GN397.5 .G99 2003
  301—dc21

                           2002027754

Printed in the United States of America
10 9 8 7 6 5 4 3 2 1   VHP   06 05 04 03 02

For Tom,
who makes everything I do possible.

CONTENTS

◇ ◇ ◇

3 THE HISTORY OF APPLIED CULTURAL ANTHROPOLOGY   53

4 THE ETHICS OF APPLIED CULTURAL ANTHROPOLOGY   79

P R E F A C E

This book addresses a concern of immediate and practical importance to college juniors and seniors: choosing a career field. Students at this level are eager for practical information on the career possibilities for which their studies—until now, purely academic—have prepared them. Most, however, have little understanding of the possibilities for the real-world application of anthropological method and theory to development, business, social work, law enforcement, public health, medicine, or other career fields. My goal in writing this book has been to provide advanced undergraduate readers with an informative, accessible, and comprehensive text that they will find directly relevant to their own concerns.

PLAN OF THE BOOK

Part One of this book introduces applied cultural anthropology (Chapter 1) and provides background information on the theories and techniques used by applied anthropologists (Chapter 2), the emergence and growth of the subdiscipline (Chapter 3), and ethical considerations surrounding the practice of anthropology (Chapter 4). This section is followed by eight chapters (5–12), each of which describes a major domain of application in the areas of development (Part Two), social services (Part Three), business and marketing (Part Four), and health care (Part Five). In keeping with a major theme of the book, the final section, Part Six ("Next Steps"), contains practical information for students on finding a job as an applied anthropologist.

THEMES

Several themes permeate these chapters. The first and most important is the depth and breadth of anthropology's practical applications. The book consistently emphasizes the diversity and the rewards of the various career paths open to college students who have studied anthropology.

A second consistent theme is globalization and the benefits and problems it has engendered. In my experience, the majority of undergraduate anthropology students are genuinely concerned about global social problems such as poverty, ill health, and overpopulation. Many of my students tell me they do not want to become bankers, merchants, or stockbrokers; they want to help make the world a better place. Thus this book strongly emphasizes the potential contributions of applied anthropologists to the solution of specific global problems. Because my students find the idea of working abroad very appealing, I have emphasized international job possibilities for applied anthropologists as strongly as domestic ones.

A third theme is cultural relativism. The book consistently promulgates the idea that for applied anthropologists to find workable, sustainable solutions to global problems, they must evaluate each culture or subculture in terms of its own values rather than those of any other culture.

Finally, the book takes a balanced view of its subject. Over the years, applied anthropology has often been criticized, both from within and outside its parent discipline. Some critics have questioned whether social scientists are justified in forsaking the objectivity that characterizes other sciences, including other social sciences. Others have challenged what they perceive to be an inherent attitude of paternalism in applied cultural anthropology, especially in development work. Still others, with some justification, have pointed to instances in which applied anthropological work has failed to meet its goals. This book presents an evenhanded treatment of its subject, mentioning such criticisms where appropriate. I have striven for another kind of balance as well: my illustrative materials, including the portraits of applied anthropologists at work, are quite intentionally evenly balanced by sex.

FEATURES

Pedagogical Options

Because applied anthropology is offered at different levels and for different constituencies at different colleges and universities, I have provided instructors with several options for tailoring the material included in the book to their needs. They may choose among these options to suit the level of expertise of their students, the particular domains of application they wish to cover, and the quantity of material they wish to assign. Three of the chapters (2–4) in Part One contain theoretical, methodological, historical, and moral and philosophical background information typically, but not universally, covered in introductory applied anthropology courses. These are stand-alone chapters, for assignment by instructors who wish to include these topics in their courses. Instructors who wish to omit one or more of them (perhaps because their students have been exposed to them at another level or because these topics tend to be less interesting, to most students, than specific domains of application) can do so without compromising their students' understanding of the material presented in the rest of the book. For instructors whose students lack the basics of anthropology or require a review of basic materials, the book includes two background appendices entitled "Review: Anthropology's Four Traditional Fields" and "Review: Theory and Method in Cultural Anthropology." Some instructors will choose to assign these; some not, depending on their students' prior exposure to and familiarity with anthropology. For instructors whose applied anthropology courses include applications of anthropology in subdisciplines other than cultural anthropology, the book includes two additional appendices, describing career possibilities in applied physical anthropology and cultural resources management (applied archaeology). Again, some instructors will want to assign these appendices to support their classroom presentations; others will not. Finally, since the number of class hours or semester weeks required per course varies somewhat among academic institutions, instructors may want to assign more or less of the material contained in this book. I have included thirteen chapters plus four chapter-length appendices. By choosing among these seventeen selections, instructors will be able to tailor their reading assignments to fit their own calendars and requirements.

"An Applied Anthropologist at Work" Boxes

In my experience, students respond positively to examples of the work of real-life applied anthropologists. Each of the "domain" chapters of this book contains a description of the career path of a successful practitioner whose professional life has been especially interesting or meaningful.

"Food for Thought" Boxes

It is my strong feeling that college-level textbooks should not only inform their student readers; they should also challenge students to think creatively. This book therefore contains a series of discussion questions, set off from the text in boxes entitled "Food for Thought." Each box presents a problematic scenario that requires students to interpret the factual information presented in the relevant chapter in the light of social values or personal ethics.

Additional Features

This book is student-friendly: the writing style is clear and conversational, topics and subtopics are clearly distinguished, and no chapter is so long that it cannot be read thoroughly at a single sitting (about forty-five minutes is ideal, according to my students). All terms that may be unfamiliar to student readers are set in boldface type and defined in the text. A list of these terms, with their definitions, appears at the end of each chapter.

ACCOMPANYING SUPPLEMENTS

Anthropology Career Resources Handbook

To help students pursue their interests in specific careers, the *Anthropology Career Resources Handbook* is available to accompany this book. The handbook contains comprehensive lists, organized by career field, of suggested further readings, relevant journals, practitioners and other organizations (including addresses, phone numbers, and web addresses), advanced academic programs (at both the Master's and Ph.D. levels), and relevant websites. All ten domains of application covered in the textbook and its appendices are included in the handbook, as well as numerous other domains, such as applied environmental anthropology, appropriate technology and technology transfer, museum work, applied educational anthropology, and applied anthropological linguistics.

Instructor's Manual and Testbank

To assist instructors with their lesson plans and evaluation responsibilities, I have prepared an *Instructor's Manual and Testbank* to accompany this text. Each section of the manual contains an expanded outline of the corresponding book chapter; a summary of the main points discussed in the chapter; a list of chapter-specific suggestions that can be used for lectures or term paper assignments; a list of chapter-relevant reference materials that can also be used for developing classroom presentations or assigning student papers; a list of available chapter-relevant videos, with complete ordering information; and a test bank containing chapter-specific essay, short answer, and multiple-choice test questions.

ACKNOWLEDGMENTS

It has been my good fortune, over many years, to enjoy two kinds of professional experience: doing applied cultural anthropology and teaching it. Consequently I am indebted, for the inspiration behind this book and for many of the ideas it contains, both to professional colleagues and to students. I thank the many host-country counterparts with whom I have been privileged to work on various international health projects, mostly in Eastern Caribbean countries: economists, medical doctors and nurses, statisticians, employees of ministries of health and finance, and most especially my field informants. The warmth, generosity, insights, and patience of these colleagues are responsible for the eagerness with which I have returned again and again to the field. I also acknowledge, with gratitude, the formative influence of my many applied anthropology students at SUNY/Stony Brook, both undergraduate and graduate. Without the opportunity to teach as well as to learn from them, this book would not have been possible.

Many generous colleagues and friends have contributed to these pages, in both direct and indirect but universally significant ways. These contributors include Bill Arens, David Bernstein, Nancy Blaine, Fred Bloom, Christopher Brown, Michael Clatts, Pat Crawford, Emma Crewe, Joel Freehling, Mitzi Goheen, Adnan Hyder, Llewellyn Gill, Fred Grine, Lily and Neeraj Kak, Wendie Wahlstrom Lapham, Tom May, Leila Porter, Munro Proctor, Leslie Raneri, Merrill Singer, Kennedy Roberts, Bob Robertson, Vivian Rorhl, Ritu Sharma, John Shea, John Sherry, Susan Squires, Soheir Stolba, Dan Varisco, and Barry Wint. I owe a special debt of gratitude to my mentor in the field of international health and development, the late Dieter K. Zschock.

For helpful reviews of draft versions of these chapters, I gratefully acknowledge the assistance of Sharlotte Neely, Northern Kentucky University; Wayne Allen, Minnesota State University, Mankato; W. Penn Handweker, University of Connecticut; Jeanne Simonelli, Wake Forest University; O. William Farley, University of Utah; Kathleen Nadeau, California State University, San Bernardino; and Miriam Sealock, Towson University.

My editor at Allyn and Bacon, Jennifer Jacobson, could not have been more supportive, encouraging, cheerful, or prompt, and I was delighted to discover that she and I are removed from one another by only three rather than the usual six degrees of separation. Also at Allyn and Bacon, editorial assistants Tom Jefferies and Elizabeth Lee, no doubt burdened with other writers' manuscripts as well as mine, were consistently patient and helpful. Both Mr. Jefferies and development editor Mary Ellen Lepionka, herself an anthropologist, provided thoughtful criticism of parts of the manuscript. I also thank the production team Deborah Brown, Susan McNally, and Denise Hoffman for their hard work and attention to detail.

Finally, for their rock-solid personal support, encouragement, and patience with my eccentricities and preoccupations throughout the several years it took me to write this book, I salute, with love and appreciation, Tom, Cathy, Thad, Elizabeth, Thomas, Ellen, Nik, Jay, Laila, Meg, Chris, and even baby Mary.

I alone, of course, am responsible for any conceptual or semantic sins of omission or commission this book may contain.

Margaret A. Gwynne
Stony Brook, New York
February, 2002

CHAPTER

1 INTRODUCTION: USES OF CULTURAL ANTHROPOLOGY

INTRODUCTION

One of the many functions of higher education is to prepare graduates to use the knowledge gained through academic study in useful, personally satisfying, and (one hopes) income-producing ways. This book is about the many ways in which one kind of knowledge—the kind gained from the intensive academic study of cultural anthropology—can be put to practical, professional use. It describes how and why an understanding of the precepts of cultural anthropology is relevant to a range of interesting and rewarding careers in business, economic and human development, the law, health care, and many other arenas.

What Is Applied Anthropology?

Applied anthropology is the use of ideas, techniques, and data, drawn from any of the four traditional fields of anthropology, in the attempt to contribute to solutions to real-world problems. It is thus mainly practical rather than theoretical in intent. It is also collaborative: in most of the professional domains in which anthropological ideas, techniques, and data are put to practical use, "applying anthropology" means that anthropologists work together with people whose problems are amenable to anthropological solutions, in order to identify and solve those problems. Degree-holding professionals who engage in this kind of problem-solving anthropology, either part-time or full-time, inside or outside of the academic community, are called **applied anthropologists.**

A distinction is sometimes drawn between the terms *applied anthropologist* and *practicing anthropologist,* based on whether the anthropological work in question is being undertaken by an academic or a nonacademic anthropologist, or whether its expected outcome is more theoretical or practical. Applied anthropology, to some, suggests work done by academic anthropologists, usually for specifically practical rather than theoretical purposes (for example, van Willigen 1987:1). Practicing anthropology can suggest specifically non-academic employment (van Willigen 1987:1) but can also refer, more broadly, to the use of anthropological skills in any setting or area of endeavor (for example, Wallace 1997:2; Baba 1994:174). This broader definition is the one endorsed by the **National Association for the Practice of Anthropology,** or **NAPA,** the arm of the American Anthropological Association representing anthropologists whose goals and interests are weighted toward the practical rather than the theoretical. NAPA defines practicing anthropologists as "professionally trained anthropologists, regularly employed or retained by clients such as social service organizations, non-profit organizations, government agencies, business and industrial firms, and public educators, who apply their specialized knowledge to problem solving" (NAPA 2002).

A third term, *professional anthropology,* is sometimes used as a synonym for practicing anthropology in its more restricted, nonacademic sense. Since these distinctions are neither clear enough nor significant enough to be meaningful for purposes of this book, the term *applied anthropology* (the most commonly encountered of the three terms) is used consistently throughout this book, in a broadly inclusive sense.

Applied anthropology is not an isolated, bounded, monolithic discipline, distinct from all others, but rather a heterogeneous field that overlaps with others and consists of numerous domains of application. Its many different kinds of practitioners have different backgrounds, interests, and ideas, and engage in different professional practices. The majority of today's applied anthropologists work in nonacademic settings, but applied anthropology can by no means be characterized as nonacademic, since a substantial minority of practitioners are part-time or even full-time academics.

What all applied anthropologists, academic or nonacademic, share in common is the attempt, using anthropological ideas and techniques, to help individuals, families, communities, corporations, and even whole nations address their needs and wants. Applied anthropologists help cities to provide adequate social services, hospitals to improve health, businesses to make money, schools to teach immigrant students, states to ensure compliance with cultural resources laws, governments to identify their war dead, and international aid organizations to feed the poor in developing nations. In addition to such practical accomplishments, applied anthropologists also contribute, through their research, to anthropology's knowledge base, although they are not *primarily* engaged in the search for knowledge for its own sake (see Chapter 2).

Each of the four traditional branches of anthropology (see Appendix 1, p. 317) includes applied anthropologists. Thus the term *applied anthropologist* appropriately describes certain cultural anthropologists (working in areas as diverse as medicine, social services, manufacturing, marketing, and law enforcement), certain biological anthropologists (working, for example, in the area of forensics), some anthropological linguists (working, for example, in bilingual education), and some archaeologists (working, for example, in cultural resources management) (see Walker 1997: 50). In each case, the accumulated knowledge and methods of data collection and analysis associated with a particular field of anthropology are "applied," or put to some practical, real-world use. The primary subject of this book is the first of these realms of application: applied cultural anthropology. (Career opportunities in branches of anthropology other than cultural anthropology are discussed in Appendices 3 and 4, p. 335 and p. 345 respectively.)

Applied anthropology has experienced rapid growth over the past few decades (see Chapter 3). A generation ago, in 1972, only an estimated 2 percent of professional anthropologists described themselves as nonacademic applied anthropologists; most of the remainder were teachers (Dunkel 1992:10). Today, more than half of all anthropologists work, full-time or part-time, in some applied subfield of anthropology (Hamada 1999:2), and the range of future jobs from which anthropology students can choose continues to grow. As one applied anthropologist recently put it, "Professional anthropology . . . is becoming more evident with each passing year" (Anderson 1998:40).

The "Fifth Field" Debate

For most of the history of their traditionally four-field discipline, anthropologists did not consider applied anthropology to be a separate branch or field; each variety of applied anthropology was viewed as a subfield (generally a minor subfield) within its parent branch. Among the past generation of anthropologists, however, that view—although it has not been completely reversed (see, for example, Bennett 1996)—has changed profoundly. Many (perhaps even most) anthropologists now see applied anthropology as a distinct fifth subfield of their discipline (Baba 1994; Fiske and Chambers 1995; see Figure 1.1).

The reasons for the attitudinal shift are both quantitative and qualitative. First is the growing number of anthropologists, many of them relatively recent degree-earners, now engaged in applied work, either part-time or full-time (Baba 1994: 174). Second and more important, applied anthropology has made significant theoretical contributions to its parent discipline (see "Theories of Practice," Chapter 2). Both of these factors have encouraged a new view of applied anthropology as a separate subfield that has produced a discrete body of new knowledge that does not replicate the knowledge base of any of the other four subfields (Baba 2000:28). The

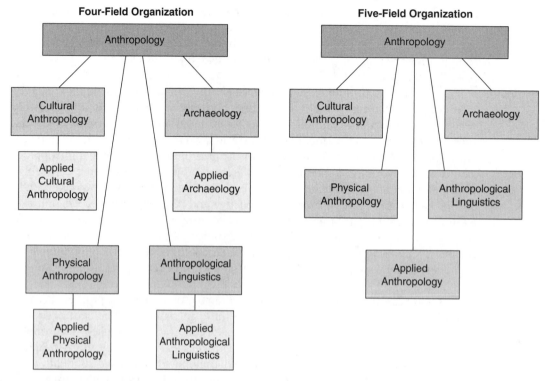

◊ **FIGURE 1.1**   **Four-Field vs. Five-Field Organization of Anthropology**

American Anthropological Association recognized this shift in outlook in 1983, when it created the National Association for the Practice of Anthropology specifically to address the needs and interests of applied anthropologists (see Chapter 3).

Yet even though applied work has grown greatly in numbers of practitioners in recent years, has established itself theoretically as distinct from the other four subfields of anthropology, and has been officially recognized by the American Anthropological Association as a separate "dimension" of anthropology, there is still some lingering debate about whether this collective career area is, or should be, considered an official fifth field. For example, one anthropologist, writing as recently as 1999, still referred to anthropology's "four-going-on-five major subfields" (Wolcott 1999:221).

One reason for the remaining resistance to the acceptance of applied anthropology as a separate field is that each of anthropology's four traditional fields—cultural anthropology, archaeology, physical anthropology, and anthropological linguistics—has a long and respected history as a recognized area of academic inquiry, complete with iconic figures, now-classic works, common-interest organizations, journals, and time-honored undergraduate and graduate curricula. Applied anthropology lacks this lengthy track record. The idea behind applied anthropology is by no means new; in fact, some of the earliest anthropological research was prompted by practical concerns (see Chapter 3). But apart from a flurry of applied activity around the time of World War II, the frequent, formalized, and well-publicized application of anthropological precepts to practical problems by academically trained anthropologists is a relatively recent phenomenon within the discipline (see Chapter 3). Some representatives of the four traditional fields feel that applied anthropology per se has not yet existed long enough to earn the title of "fifth field."

An additional reason why applied anthropology has yet to win universal acclaim as a fifth field of anthropology may result from the ongoing debate about anthropology's status as a **science:** an objective body of knowledge gained from studying, learning about, and testing phenomena and ideas within a particular subject area, using agreed-upon data-collection and testing methods.[1] Since science has generally been acknowledged as anthropology's "dominant parental strain" (Kuklick 1997:47), anthropologists have generally viewed themselves as objective observers of humans and human behavior. Cultural anthropology, whose object of interest is living people, is obviously a somewhat different kind of science from astronomy or molecular biology; cultural anthropologists characterize their discipline as a "social" science, distinct from the physical sciences in that its object of interest is living people. Many, however, see it as a science nonetheless—similar to other sciences in basic philosophy and intent. (Others view cultural anthropology as embodying principles more akin to those of the humanities than the sciences.)

Some of these "scientific" anthropologists may feel that applied cultural anthropology's explicit commitment to beneficial social change is incompatible with a key element in most definitions of science—objectivity (see, for example, D'Andrade 1995; Lett 1997) and thus that this kind of applied anthropology cannot appropriately be considered part of a scientific anthropology. Academic anthropologist Jeanne Simonelli, for example, was told in graduate school that her pursuit of applied studies in her local community was "not *real* anthropology" (Simonelli 2001: 48).[2] Based on the number of academic departments of anthropology that now include applied cultural anthropology in their undergraduate and graduate curricula, this view is waning.

FOOD FOR THOUGHT   Anthropologist David Cleveland writes that "the great strength of anthropology, including applied anthropology, lies in its potential to lead the way in bringing together humanistic and scientific approaches for understanding humans" (Cleveland 2000:371). Do you agree? Does it matter whether applied cultural anthropology is considered a science or not? Why?

Despite the ongoing "fifth field" debate, most anthropologists today would probably agree that applied anthropology in any of its manifestations is a distinct and important dimension of general anthropology. Since 1983, the year in which the American Anthropological Association granted official recognition to applied anthropology with the creation of NAPA, the debate has been largely semantic. For the record, in this book applied anthropology is considered to be a fifth field of anthropology—generative of its own techniques and theory, represented by its own common-interest organizations, and often taught separately from general anthropology on both the undergraduate and graduate levels.

What Is Applied Cultural Anthropology?

Applied cultural anthropology is the use of ideas, techniques, and data derived from the field of cultural anthropology in the attempt to contribute to solutions to social problems—problems encountered by human beings as members of social groups. These problems range from the general to the specific, and their solutions usually involve social change. In general terms, applied cultural anthropologists are interested in achieving as broad as possible an understanding of pan-human concerns such as poverty, illness, overpopulation, and inequality, with a view to contributing to policies that may eventually ameliorate these conditions. More narrowly, much applied work in cultural anthropology attempts to contribute to solutions to specific problems affecting particular neighborhoods, communities, institutions, municipalities, or nations—for example, a conflict between police officers and the residents of an inner-city neighborhood, a corporation's less-than-fully-productive workforce, the rapid spread of a sexually transmitted disease in a particular city, the failure of mothers in a certain state to ensure that their children are fully immunized, or a country's need to increase agricultural production. In any case, general or specific, the precepts of cultural anthropology inform efforts to understand the problem and to identify and implement changes that may alleviate it.

Just as varied as the range of human problems of interest to applied cultural anthropologists are the kinds of practitioners who address these issues and the ways in which they go about it. Some of those who work outside of academe apply anthropological ideas and techniques to real-world problems as **consultants**: independent contractors, with expertise in one or more geographical or topical areas, who are hired on a temporary basis, either short-term or long-term (Wilson 1998). Some are full-time employees of businesses, governments, or public or private aid organizations. These anthropologists are likely to work on specific problems identified by their employers. Others are full-time academics, who may provide theoretical background on specific social problems. Still others, mainly but not exclusively academics, may be employed part-time as temporary consultants, charged with contributing informed ideas on how specific human problems might be addressed. Even academics who do not consider themselves applied cultural anthropologists at all may find that their theoretical research into particular social problems may inform applied efforts to alleviate those problems. There is no clear dividing line between theoretical and applied anthropological research, and often no clear distinction between applied and academic cultural anthropologists.

Cultural anthropology has included a significant applied component ever since its establishment as a discrete academic discipline in the middle of the nineteenth century. Indeed, some of the earliest cultural anthropological fieldwork was undertaken primarily for applied purposes—for example, the efficient colonial governance of subject peoples (see Chapter 3). However, the number of cultural anthropologists doing applied work, and the range of problems addressed, are both greater now than ever before. Today, applied cultural anthropology is the largest of the applied subfields of anthropology, in terms of relative numbers of degree-holding practitioners.

Much of the reason for this increase in applied cultural anthropology is related to **globalization,** the growing interconnectedness among all of Earth's inhabitants. The term encompasses phenomena such as recent improvements in transportation

◇ *Applied cultural anthropology draws on anthropological theories, methods, and data to help find solutions to societal problems. Working as a consultant, an applied cultural anthropologist (second from left) meets with health officials in a Caribbean country in a collaborative attempt to improve health care in the country.*

and communications, which permit rapid—even instantaneous—contact between people living in disparate areas around the globe; the supranational political conflicts, global economy, and new and reemerging diseases all of us increasingly share; and the global effects of local environmental degradation (Cleveland 2000). Recent, profound, worldwide changes in technology, information management, communications, geopolitics, and the global economy have solved many human problems, but (along with important twentieth-century demographic and environmental changes) have created others. Cultural anthropological information, insights, and expertise are increasingly drawn on in the search for specific solutions to these problems and for overarching policies to alleviate them.

BASIC ROLES: RESEARCH, POLICY DEVELOPMENT, AND INTERVENTION

Broadly speaking, applied cultural anthropologists address human problems in three important ways. The first of these, **applied research,** is research undertaken for purposes of gaining the knowledge or information needed to address specific needs or goals. One applied cultural anthropologist, for example, researched how mothers in a small Caribbean country felt about the public health services available to their children, in order to help the country's Ministry of Health establish policies that would promote more effective health care (Zschock et al. 1991:119–121). Another investigated how the Boeing Company's team-based approach to building aircraft affected shop floor mechanics—information needed to increase productivity (Benson 2000:26–27.) Applied research is vital to the identification of those problems for which solutions are possible, the formulation of policies that will encourage positive social change (see especially Hackenberg and Hackenberg 1999), the development and implementation of change strategies, and the evaluation of ongoing or completed attempts to implement positive change.

The second way in which applied cultural anthropologists help address human problems is through policy development: the establishment, analysis, or revision of the policies that govern people's lives. Policies in this context range from informal social prescriptions to institutional regulations to national and international laws. Cultural anthropologists are particularly well placed to understand the complex factors that influence how groups of people arrive at, and sometimes change, the fundamental guidelines that govern their social, economic, and political lives.

Finally, applied cultural anthropologists help address human problems through **intervention,** the explicit, hands-on attempt to foster positive social, economic, or political change through direct action. An intervention might consist, for example, of the establishment of a storefront health services center in an urban neighborhood, the preparation of an educational videotape on ways to reduce racial and sexual discrimination in the workplace, or a house-to-house vaccination campaign in a poor community in a Central American country. Interventions can be undertaken at the local, regional, national, or supranational levels. Ideally they are collaborative, involving their intended beneficiaries and other participants in addition to applied cultural anthropologists.

◊ *Interviews to promote positive social change are frequently health-related. The establishment of a walk-in health clinic in an urban neighborhood enables local residents to better protect their health.*

The first of these three basic roles, applied research, is common to the other two; it is essential to both policy development and intervention. But the extent to which an applied anthropologist plays either of the other two roles depends largely on his or her professional status. Full-time academic cultural anthropologists and academics who serve outside of academe as occasional consultants are more likely to confine their applied research to policy-related issues; nonacademic applied cultural anthropologists are often involved in both policy development and intervention. No matter what the specific problem or the scope of the individual anthropologist's involvement, however, the fundamental goal is to help people with social problems to achieve positive social change.

Over the years, applied cultural anthropology has often been criticized for not always achieving its intended goal (a criticism that will be addressed in Chapter 3). As with any profession, there have been successes and failures, rewards and disappointments. There is no guarantee that any given applied cultural anthropologist will be effective, nor that anthropological research, or the policy development or direct intervention that anthropological research supports, will result in either immediate or long-term improvements to people's health or legal affairs or success in business or the way they interact with their natural environment, although that is certainly the usual intent. One applied anthropologist thus describes the field of applied cultural anthropology, with unusual candor, as "a set of opportunities that some people with anthropology degrees pursue out of hunger or genuine social dedication or both" (Bennett 1996:S48). This book will make it abundantly clear that those who are motivated more by hunger than by social dedication should pursue careers other than applied cultural anthropology.

ACADEMIC AND APPLIED CULTURAL ANTHROPOLOGY: A COMPARISON

Even though the professional endeavors of applied anthropologists are sufficiently distinct from those of their exclusively academic colleagues to provoke debate over whether or not these efforts should collectively be considered a separate field of the discipline, the distinction between theoretical and applied anthropologists is far from black and white. To a great extent, academic and applied anthropologists share the same theories, methods, ethical mandates, and knowledge base. As applied anthropologist Marietta Baba (2000:28) points out, "we are all part of the same anthropology" (see also Cernea 1995:345).

Thus, applied cultural anthropology differs from its academic counterpart not so much in terms of fundamental precepts but of certain philosophical and practical distinctions. First, applied cultural anthropologists' immediate *objectives* often differ from those of their academic colleagues. (The methodological differences mandated by these different objectives are discussed in Chapter 2.) Second, the *philosophical perspectives* of academic and applied cultural anthropologists—perhaps most especially on the key issue of change-oriented engagement with research populations—are sometimes different. Finally, applied and academic cultural anthropologists sometimes cite different *motivations* for their work.

Objectives

Much of the research undertaken by college- or university-based scholars, no matter what their academic discipline, is done for the purpose of contributing to human knowledge. This kind of research, termed "theoretical" (or "basic," or "pure") research, is more speculative than results-oriented in intent. It may have some useful payoff, either immediately or over the long term, but practical results are not its primary goal. Likewise, theoretical research may or may not result in a contribution to theory. It demands no further justification than its potential to enhance humankind's understanding of a particular subject. Theoretical anthropologists' main goal is to understand and explain the existence, development, appearance, behavior, and beliefs of human beings—not necessarily to address specific human problems or to attempt to promote beneficial social change.

Applied anthropologists are not at all averse to theoretical research, and applied cultural anthropology, like the other applied subfields of anthropology, is by no means atheoretical. Indeed, as pointed out earlier, it is impossible to draw a clear distinction between theoretical and applied work; many applied anthropologists are academicians who work in one or more applied subfields part-time. Neither are the goals of theoretical and applied work mutually incompatible. Theoretical research may be undertaken primarily to test hypotheses and contribute theories about human beings' existence, development, appearance, behavior, and beliefs, but at the same time it may also contribute to the accomplishment of practical goals beyond the production of knowledge. Likewise, applied research may be primarily directed at the achievement of specific, practical goals or the solution of particular problems, but—as one applied anthropologist recently put it—"practice generates theory" as well (Hill 2000:3; see also Bernard 1998:696; Baba 2000). (Examples of the feedback relationship between practice and theory are provided in Chapter 2, in the section entitled "Theory Development in the Course of Practice.")

However, the immediate objectives of most applied cultural anthropologists are more practical and results-oriented than theoretical. Their primary goal is to address and help solve specific, real-world social, economic, and political problems, through research and data analysis that lead to policy recommendations or to the implementation of specific change strategies. This goal may be pursued with varying degrees of emotional investment; some applied cultural anthropologists see themselves as "neutral experts," others as "engaged advocates" (Winthrop 1997:41). With the possible exception of business anthropology (Chapter 9), however, the goal is usually intentionally philanthropic, aimed at helping people (especially poor people) improve their quality of life—to help them substitute healthy behaviors for unhealthy ones, for example, or improve their educational levels or increase their employment opportunities.

Philosophical Perspectives

Academic and applied cultural anthropologists sometimes hold different views about the extent to which their personal values should influence their professional efforts. It is probably safe to say that most academic cultural anthropologists, despite their scientific intellectual heritage, give frequent and serious thought to the problems inherent in applying the dogma of rigorous scientific objectivity to the study of human beings. Their relationships with their research populations are almost always conducted at a more humane level than that scientific ideal would suggest. At the same time, however, most academic cultural anthropologists avoid overt attempts to impose their ideas and values on the people they study. Applied cultural anthropologists are quite different in this regard. If academic cultural anthropology is (ideally) value-neutral, applied cultural anthropology is "value-explicit" (van Willigen 1993).

One reason for this difference can be attributed to anthropology's historical inclusion among the sciences, discussed above. Since most cultural anthropologists have thought of themselves as scientists, they have historically avoided (insofar as is possible) intentionally introducing change into the communities of people they study, even as other kinds of scientists conscientiously avoid biasing their data. For applied cultural anthropologists, however, the main purpose of their work is to help people determine if and how intentional change should take place, and then to help them achieve it.

Another reason why academic cultural anthropologists have historically attempted to maintain a value-neutral stance, vis-à-vis the people they study, results from their understanding of relationships of power and authority in human interaction. "Imposing the values of [a] more powerful culture—Western or European—on [a] smaller and less powerful culture often leads to a serious disruption of that culture" (Gert 1995:30). Cultural anthropology has done much to illuminate what happens when the values of more powerful groups are imposed on less powerful ones. The decision on the part of some cultural anthropologists to learn from, but to refrain from influencing, those they study is thus a logical response to the universal existence among humans of unbalanced structures of power and authority, and anthropologists' wish to avoid contributing to social disruption.

The value-neutral/value-explicit debate has important implications for the legitimacy and potential of applied cultural anthropology, with its clear-cut goal of change for the better. Some applied cultural anthropologists justify imposing their own values on others by citing the notion of universal values—those embraced by all cultures (Gert 1995:30). (This concept is discussed in Chapter 4.) Others argue that applied cultural anthropology, by definition, involves "a commitment to action" that takes moral precedence over theory formulation and demands the pursuit of "value-laden goals" (Scheper-Hughes 1995; Baba 2000:22–28). (This ethical perspective is discussed in Chapters 4 and 5.)

FOOD FOR THOUGHT

Suppose you are an academic cultural anthropologist, living and working in Ethiopia in order to study the social repercussions of starvation on a pastoralist group. As you pursue your ethnographic fieldwork among members of this impoverished group, should you feel compelled to help alleviate their hunger? Why or why not? If so, are you concerned that your sympathy for the pastoralists might bias your research? Explain your answer.

Motivations

Nonacademic applied anthropologists cite many reasons for seeking employment outside academe, beyond the immediate availability of jobs in the two different arenas. One important factor is the sense that applied work has greater immediacy and relevance. Some applied cultural anthropologists derive great satisfaction from helping to search for solutions to some of humanity's most challenging problems, such as poverty, overpopulation, or AIDS, through research, policy development, or direct intervention. Some strongly believe that it is no longer enough for cultural anthropologists to observe, describe, and analyze people in social groups; they have a moral obligation to take action for the betterment of humankind. In any case, the perception of relevance strongly motivates many applied cultural anthropologists.

Other applied cultural anthropologists say they enjoy the greater intellectual variety that applied work affords. They take pride in the fact that their efforts not only test but actually contribute to anthropological theory (see Chapter 2), but they are also rewarded by the opportunity to wrestle with the question of how best to help others. They particularly welcome applied anthropology's creative, problem-solving orientation.

Still other applied cultural anthropologists choose this subdiscipline because it affords them the opportunity to work with others rather than alone, as is more common for full-time academic cultural anthropologists (see Erickson and Stull 1998). Depending on the nature of a given applied project, the "others" with whom applied cultural anthropologists work often include the project's intended beneficiaries, and the whole gamut of professional expertise, including academic as well as non-academic colleagues (see "The Collaborative Nature of Applied Work," Chapter 2).

FOOD FOR THOUGHT   Do any of the motivations mentioned above make applied cultural anthropology appealing to you personally? Which one(s)? Why? Do any seem meaningless to you personally? Which one(s)? Why?

CAREERS IN APPLIED CULTURAL ANTHROPOLOGY

The Range of Possibilities

Parts Two through Five of this book describe eight career areas in which applied cultural anthropologists are actively involved in research, policy development, intervention, or all three. These areas are development, advocacy, social work, the law and law enforcement, business, social marketing, medicine, and international health. (Appendices 3 and 4 describe two additional career areas for applied anthropologists in fields other than cultural anthropology: archaeology and physical anthropology.) Each chapter describes the fundamental concepts associated with a particular career area, the kinds of problems encountered by applied cultural anthropologists working in that area, the specific roles these anthropologists play, the responsibilities they shoulder, and related issues of professional ethics and policy development. Some of the careers described are in the public sector and others in the private sector;[3] some involve living abroad while others do not; some are profit-driven and others more philanthropic.

This book by no means exhausts the range of possibilities for employment as an applied cultural anthropologist. Other fields in which applied cultural anthropologists have found rewarding jobs include education, technology development, agricultural development, and natural resources management. Students interested in exploring areas of applied anthropology other than those described in this book and its appendices will find the National Association for the Practice of Anthropology, as well as the **Society for Applied Anthropology** (or **SfAA,** the largest and oldest anthropological practitioner organization in the United States, established in 1941), helpful. Contact information for these organizations is provided in the accompanying *Anthropology Career Resources Handbook.*

Important Considerations

When one is choosing a lifetime career, personal inclinations are paramount: a prospective career field should be of intense and sustainable interest, should be remunerative enough to assure that one's financial requirements are met, and should offer the promise of a high level of personal satisfaction. But a number of additional, more practical matters should be considered as well. These include what kind of employer to work for; whether or not additional education or training (expensive in terms of both time and money) will be required to establish, maintain, or enhance a career in a given area; what level of job security a given career can be expected to offer, over the course of one's working years; and what kind of lifestyle—mobile or stationary, affluent or modest, relaxed or stressful—can be expected.

Employers and Workplaces.   Academic anthropologists must fulfill teaching and other service obligations to the colleges and universities that employ them, but in terms of research, they essentially work for themselves. They usually choose their own research topics, often find their own funding, write at their own pace, and publish their work whenever and wherever they wish. In contrast, applied anthropologists, whether part-time or full-time, work for others. They pursue research topics of interest to their employers, who also fund their research; they submit written reports by deadlines established by their employers and publish the results of their research only with the permission of (and often under the auspices of) their employers.

Most employment in applied cultural anthropology takes place in nonacademic institutions, whether private or public, national or international, profit-making or not-for-profit. The most common kinds of organizations employing applied cultural anthropologists are:

- *Governments (usually a specific branch of government).* An example is the United States Agency for International Development (USAID). State and local governments also hire applied cultural anthropologists.

- *International aid agencies.* Many of these multilateral organizations are branches of the United Nations. Examples include the World Health Organization (WHO) and the United Nations Development Programme (UNDP).
- *Non-governmental organizations (NGOs).* These non-profit institutions, which may be local, national, or international, are sometimes funded privately and sometimes funded (wholly or in part) by government. An example is the Washington-based Center for Development and Population Activities (CEDPA).
- *Private foundations.* These are frequently funded through the generosity of wealthy individuals. Examples include the Ford, Rockefeller, and Kellogg Foundations.
- *Private businesses.* These employing applied cultural anthropologists tend to be large, publicly traded, multinational corporations, such as General Motors, Xerox, and Coca-Cola.
- *Private charitable organizations.* While some of these (such as Catholic Relief Services) are religious organizations, many (such as Habitat International) are non-sectarian.
- *Consulting firms.* These may be either for-profit or nonprofit. Typically they receive public funds, earmarked for specific purposes, through competitive bidding, and—depending on the work involved—hire consultants to carry it out.

Additional Educational Requirements. Merely to be employed by one of the organizations above does not necessarily require a high level of education, but establishing a career as an applied cultural anthropologist in any of them usually requires training or education beyond the undergraduate level. Occasionally, someone who has majored in cultural anthropology at this level is able to apply the knowledge gained in pursuing a B.A. degree to the resolution of practical problems immediately after graduating from college. One fortunate cultural anthropology major, for example, took an entry-level job as a "gal Friday" for a Washington-area consulting firm immediately after graduating from college, and within a year was working in Honduras as an applied cultural anthropologist, on a USAID-funded health research project. Most college graduates holding B.A. degrees, however, discover that they must supplement their undergraduate anthropological expertise with advanced training.

One logical choice for career preparation is an advanced degree in applied anthropology,[4] but even individuals with graduate degrees in applied anthropology may find they not only want but need an additional degree or further training in a specialty area. In the best of all possible worlds, the optimal combination of degrees for a career as an applied cultural anthropologist would probably be a B.A. with a cultural anthropology major, an M.A. in applied anthropology, plus a third degree— a business or law degree, or a Ph.D. in a specialty area such as public health, economics, community development, or international relations. Occasionally, a college graduate who cannot immediately afford the advanced degree(s) needed for a particular career path is fortunate enough to find an employer who will help him or her, as a valued employee, to gain further training or education by agreeing to underwrite some or all of the costs or by allowing time off for studies.

Job Security.   Some applied cultural anthropologists work as full-time employees of government or international agencies, NGOs, charities, or businesses. Others are consultants who work—usually serially—for a variety of employers, as the need for their services arises. They may sign either short-term contracts (usually lasting from a few weeks to a few months) or long-term contracts (usually lasting for a year or more), but it is understood that their services are temporary. For some consultants, consulting work is their only employment, and they devote their full time to it. Others, such as academics who undertake consulting work only occasionally, are part-timers, in which case their consultancies are apt to be short-term.

Applied cultural anthropologists working as permanent employees enjoy more job security than consultants. Not only are they hired for the long term; they are also likely to work in the public sector, where jobs tend to be relatively secure (a disproportionate number of all jobs in applied cultural anthropology are in the public rather than the private sector). Consultants, whether full-time or part-time, must always consider what they might be doing next month or next year. In addition, job-related benefits such as health coverage and pension plans, especially for short-term consultants, are few or nonexistent. On the other hand, consultants enjoy a greater amount of job flexibility, a wider variety of experiences, and usually more travel than their permanently employed colleagues do.

Lifestyle.   A major consideration in deciding on a future career is lifestyle: whether to live and work in one's home state, another state, or a foreign country; whether one will be able to live affluently or only modestly; whether one will be mainly sedentary or highly mobile; whether one's professional life will be mainly solitary or will involve meeting and working with others.

◇ *Applied cultural anthropology often involves work in international settings. At right, an American anthropologist (second from right, in baseball cap) meets with Maasai pastoralists in Tanzania, Africa.*

Residence.   Much of the work done by applied cultural anthropologists, especially in career areas such as development anthropology or public health, is international in scope. Thus, even though domestic jobs are readily available, a substantial proportion of all applied cultural anthropologists live and work abroad, for some or even most of their careers. One not-uncommon career pattern is a series of long-term consultancies that take the anthropologist to various parts of the world, for several years at a time. Many applied cultural anthropologists see this mobility as a definite advantage of their career field. Others, for reasons of personal preference or family obligation, prefer to remain permanently close to home. A career that combines academics with a series of short-term consultancies may provide the best of both alternatives.

Income.   Public sector jobs in any career area, including anthropology, are apt to pay less well than equivalent jobs in the private sector. Public sector jobs in cultural anthropology tend to appeal to altruistic individuals who derive greater satisfaction from helping others than they would from accumulating financial wealth. Perhaps because of this, and also perhaps because of the relative availability of jobs in the two sectors, fewer applied cultural anthropologists work in the private sector. Of those who do, most work for major corporations, and their incomes tend to be somewhat higher than those of public sector employees; by mid-career, most are earning the equivalent of middle-management salaries. But the lower lifetime earning potential of public sector employees may be offset by the many intangible rewards of their jobs.

Mobility.   Whether long-term or short-term, international jobs, almost by definition, involve relatively more mobility than employment by domestic employers. An applied cultural anthropologist employed by a major aid organization (such as the World Health Organization, a branch of the United Nations), a private charitable organization that is international in scope, or a major corporation doing business in several different countries can expect to spend many years of his or her professional life living and working abroad. Since many of these organizations are headquartered in First World countries, frequent travel from one's work site to headquarters can be anticipated. On the opposite side of the coin, employment by a local or state law enforcement agency or educational system, a social services agency, or a health care facility almost guarantees a relatively sedentary existence.

Collegiality.   Finally, careers in applied cultural anthropology usually involve working with colleagues, as part of a group. Applied research, policy development, and intervention all tend to be collaborative efforts, in which the applied cultural anthropologist works closely with others—usually not with other applied cultural anthropologists, but rather with intended beneficiaries and professionals in other fields. Many applied cultural anthropologists view this, too, as among the great advantages of their chosen career field. They may particularly enjoy the opportunity to learn the methods and vocabularies of other disciplines and to translate their own anthropological methods and vocabulary into terms that practitioners of other disciplines can understand (Cernea 1995).

FOOD FOR THOUGHT

Put the following in order, from most important to least important, based solely on your personal preferences:

- High income level
- High status among peers
- Job security
- Permanence of residence
- Living and working in the United States as opposed to a foreign country
- A 40-hour work week with little compulsory overtime
- Working independently

TWO CASE STUDIES IN APPLIED CULTURAL ANTHROPOLOGY

The following case studies, describing two recent applied projects that included applied cultural anthropology, focus on whole projects rather than the specific work of particular anthropologists (profiles of individual applied cultural anthropologists are found in boxed features, entitled An Applied Cultural Anthropologist at Work, in Chapters 5–12). Together the two cases cannot be said to be representative of all applied work. Rather, they are intended to convey a general idea of what kinds of endeavors require anthropological expertise, what kinds of goals are set, what kinds of roles applied anthropologists are called upon to play in reaching these goals, and what kinds of expertise and time commitments anthropologists are expected to contribute.

The first case study describes a research project requiring short-term cultural anthropological expertise, contributed on a consulting basis, to help it get started. The second describes a program of intervention involving long-term cultural anthropological input. While both projects included substantial applied research, the first was oriented toward policy development, and the second toward direct intervention.

Despite these differences, however, there are two important similarities between the two projects. First, the goal of both projects was to find a solution to a specific problem affecting a particular group of people. Second, in both cases achieving this goal required exploring and defining the knowledge, beliefs, values, needs, and behavior of people in a particular group.

Case Study 1: A Short-Term Independent Consultancy

In 1987, the World Health Organization established a Global Programme on AIDS (GPA, later to become UNAIDS), to address what had by then become a global health crisis. The goal of the GPA was to provide technical and financial support for national and international efforts to prevent the spread of HIV/AIDS while the world's scientists attempted to find a cure. Because this disease can be addressed from a behavioral as well as a medical perspective, the GPA established the Social and Behavioural Studies and Support (SBSS) Unit to research the behaviors that contribute to the spread of the disease and—based on this research—to help articulate policies that would ultimately save lives.

Disease prevention was a major focus of the Global Programme on AIDS. Thus, when a new contraceptive and disease-prevention device called the "female condom" appeared on the market, the GPA was eager to know whether women around the world could and would make use of it to protect themselves against HIV infection. GPA therefore decided to develop a long-term research project that would put the female condom to the test. A project steering committee, consisting of SBSS Unit members and AIDS specialists from Latin America, Africa, and Southeast Asia, was quickly formed. The committee proposed identifying groups of women, anywhere in the world, who might benefit from knowing about and having access to the female condom, and then providing these women with female condoms and information about how to use them. The women's rates of HIV/AIDS infection would be monitored, over a period of years, to see whether or not the device was effective.[5]

To get the project started, the steering committee needed someone who could review and synthesize the available literature on male/female sex roles and relationships in general, and the female condom specifically, and then design a research strategy that would test the acceptability and efficacy of the female condom in different countries and cultures. A cultural anthropologist with an understanding of the roles and relationships of males and females in different cultures would be ideal. Since the actual implementation of the study could be done, under WHO supervision, by health care professionals in various countries, anthropological expertise would be required only for the development phase of the project. Thus what the steering committee needed was a short-term consultant, or (in WHO terms) a "temporary technical advisor."

As is customary in consulting work, appropriate candidates for this task were identified mainly through word of mouth. The chosen consultant, a cultural anthropologist with a background in gender studies and medical anthropology, brought two important kinds of expertise to the job: a broad knowledge of culture, gender theory, and medical anthropology, and specialized knowledge about the sociocultural and economic contexts in which people's perceptions about sex, HIV/AIDS, and health risks are forged.

A detailed contract, specifying the anthropologist's scope of work over a period of three months, was drawn up, and the consultancy commenced as soon as the anthropologist's spring-semester academic obligations had ended. She began at her home university by undertaking a comprehensive literature search, using the Internet and her institution's library. This done, she traveled to WHO headquarters in Geneva, Switzerland, to meet with the steering committee and to discuss a number of complex questions with its members. Who would be likely to benefit from the female condom—single women? married women? prostitutes (often termed "commercial sex workers")? teenagers? urban or rural women? poor or middle-class women?[6] Which would be the best countries in which to test the device? Could a research protocol be devised that would work cross-culturally? How might appropriate study participants be recruited? How could potential users best be educated about the female condom? What culture-specific barriers to the acceptance and use of the device might exist? How would a study of the female condom complement other related WHO/GPA projects and the work of other health-related organizations and projects?

Back home at her university after the meeting, the anthropologist began to design a project that would introduce the female condom to various groups of women in different cultures, and then follow up on them to see whether or not having access to this device had made a difference. Because earlier studies had shown that the provision of health information alone was ineffective in achieving sustainable, health-related behavior change, the anthropologist decided to base the study on the "peer health education" model. In this model, study participants are given the opportunity to engage in mutual problem solving, which has been shown to enhance self-esteem and feelings of empowerment on which sustained behavioral change is likely to be contingent. Carefully selected groups of women, in several different countries, would be invited to peer education sessions where they would be provided with free condoms, information about their use, and the interpersonal skills necessary to use their new knowledge effectively.

Three months later, the research design was complete (Gwynne 1992). Again the consultant flew to Geneva to meet with the steering committee. After final discussions and last-minute additions and changes, the research design was approved. Her short-term consultancy completed, the anthropologist returned to her university in time to meet her fall classes.

Case Study 2: A Long-Term Multidisciplinary Project

In 1991, local health officials in Tegucigalpa, the capital of Honduras, became increasingly concerned about chronic poor health among the residents of an impoverished city neighborhood. The specific problem was the lack of adequate sanitation in the neighborhood. Residents lacked indoor toilets, showers, and sinks; indeed, many homes had neither running water nor sewer hookups for the disposal of waste. These deficiencies were contributing to a high rate of illness and a low standard of living for community residents (Ocasio 1995).

The officials turned for help to a private, nonprofit, U.S.-based organization, the Cooperative Housing Foundation (CHF), which specializes in helping the poor in densely populated urban areas around the world attain basic needs such as housing and sanitary facilities. As is typical of such projects, the CHF employees and outside consultants who worked together on this project represented multiple disciplines, not just cultural anthropology.[7]

The first step was background research. Working together, the project's participants, already familiar with the people and culture of Tegucigalpa's poor neighborhoods (called *barrios marginales*), first researched waste management technologies and strategies for community health education appropriate for poor urban settings. They followed up this library research with a **KAP survey,** a data-collection technique aimed at determining the knowledge, attitudes, and practices of a specific group of people regarding a specific topic. The purpose of the KAP survey was to determine what residents believed and understood about the need for sanitation, what sanitation improvements they felt were needed, what they saw as the obstacles preventing them from obtaining their needs, and what they would be willing to do to reach the goal of improved sanitation.

Next came the planning phase of the project, informed by the research that had preceded it. The overall plan that emerged consisted of multiple stages with different goals, but would ultimately make affordable and appropriate sanitation technologies available to the needy. Neighborhood residents who agreed to participate in the project would first be educated about existing health threats and the need for environmental sanitation. A low-interest loan program would then be established to put basic sanitary facilities—latrines, outdoor showers, and laundry facilities—within the reach of any poor family that wanted them. After the new facilities were installed, project members would provide instructions on how to use, clean, and maintain them, and then follow up for six months to answer questions and to reinforce health education (Ocasio 1995:26–29).

The most visible part of the project was the intervention phase, or actual implementation of the plan. This consisted of two parts, conducted by different members of the project team. The first was educational: raising awareness about actual and potential health problems by educating any and all interested community members about environmental sanitation. The second was economic: setting up the banking program to make low-interest loans available to poor families.

◇ *In many countries, residents of poor, overcrowded, urban neighborhoods suffer ill health due in part to inadequate sanitation. Dilapidated houses blanket a hillside in one such neighborhood in Tegucigalpa, Honduras.*

The final phase of the project was an evaluation of its success. (Evaluation as a part of applied cultural anthropologists' basic research strategy is discussed in Chapter 2.) This assessment showed that the program was highly successful in improving health conditions in Tegucigalpa. There was a "marked increase in awareness of issues related to health and hygiene" among the intended beneficiaries of the project. Almost a thousand families took out project loans, and the sanitation units constructed using program money were well maintained (Ocasio 1995:31). The project is still ongoing, and has recently been expanded to include poor areas outside Tegucigalpa (ibid.:32).

CONCLUSION

This book describes and discusses the work of applied cultural anthropologists, professionals with academic degrees in cultural anthropology who use theories, perspectives, research methods, and data developed within cultural anthropology to understand and help solve practical problems faced by communities of people. Some of the most compelling of these problems, such as poverty, disease, overpopulation, and inequality, are encountered in both international and domestic settings and constitute global crises. Others are domestic problems arising in fields such as business, education, health care, and the law.

In addition to describing the kinds of problems applied cultural anthropologists help solve, this book also addresses a concern of immediate and practical importance to most students: choosing a career field. It introduces a number of different career paths open to those who have studied cultural anthropology, as well as a number of individuals, portrayed in An Applied Cultural Anthropologist at Work vignettes, who are currently enjoying satisfying careers in which they use their backgrounds in cultural anthropology. Some of the individuals profiled are full-time applied cultural anthropologists who identify themselves as such; some are part-timers, mainly academics who do applied research from time to time as consultants. A few are professionals who do not identify themselves as either full-time or part-time applied cultural anthropologists, but who nevertheless contribute, theoretically or practically or both, to the solution of human problems.

This book is not a training manual; understanding the theories, perspectives, methodologies, and policy implications surrounding the application of cultural anthropology in any of the career areas described in Chapters 5–12 requires study and training far beyond what a single book, much less a single chapter, can convey. The intent of this book is rather to suggest the wide range of possibilities for interesting and rewarding careers for applied cultural anthropologists in a number of vocational fields, and to point out specific ways in which an undergraduate major or graduate degree in cultural anthropology would be relevant to each career. For students with anthropological training who are willing to go on for further study, the opportunities to apply cultural anthropological expertise professionally are virtually limitless.[8]

KEY TERMS

applied anthropologist   a degree-holding professional who undertakes applied work in anthropology

applied anthropology   the use of anthropological ideas, techniques, and data in the attempt to contribute to solutions to people's real-world problems

applied cultural anthropology   the use of ideas, techniques, and data derived from cultural anthropology to find solutions to problems encountered by human beings as members of social groups

applied research   research for purposes of gaining the knowledge or information needed to address a specific goal

consultant   an independent contractor with special expertise who works for an employer on a temporary basis

globalization   the growing interconnectedness among all people

intervention   the attempt of an applied cultural anthropologist to foster positive social, economic, or political change through direct action

KAP survey   a data-collection technique aimed at determining the knowledge, attitudes, and practices of a specific group of people regarding a specific topic

National Association for the Practice of Anthropology (NAPA)   an arm of the American Anthropological Association, created in 1983 to represent applied anthropologists

nongovernmental organization (NGO)   a local, national, or international nonprofit institution, funded either privately or (wholly or partially) by government

private sector   the sector of the economy in which goods and services are produced, for a profit, by private individuals or businesses

public sector   the sector of the economy in which goods and services are produced, as a public service, by some branch of government

science   an objective body of knowledge gained from studying, learning about, and testing phenomena and ideas within a particular subject area, using agreed-upon data-collection and testing methods

Society for Applied Anthropology (SfAA)   the largest and oldest anthropological practitioner organization in the United States, established in 1941

NOTES

1. For thorough discussions of whether anthropology is a science or not, see Kuznar 1997; Endicott and Welsch 2001.
2. In recent years, postmodernist anthropologists have criticized the positivist science approach, providing a "needed correction" in anthropology (Price 2001:57), but in anthropology, as in other realms, old ideas are slow to change. See "The Question of Scientific Detachment" in Chapter 4 for further discussion of this point.
3. The **public sector** is the sector of the economy in which goods and services are produced, as a public service, by some branch of government. The **private sector** is the sector of the economy in which goods and services are produced, for a profit, by private individuals or businesses.
4. Although some graduate programs still do not include applied anthropology, and only one major graduate program (at the University of South Florida) requires it (Price 2001), the number of

such programs is increasing yearly. The *Anthropology Career Resources Handbook* lists the institutions that do offer degree programs in applied anthropology.

5. Funding for this project was provided by the Global Programme on AIDS of the World Health Organization. The study was carried out over a period of several years, in three of the world's poorer and less industrialized countries. Final research results are not yet available.

6. In many countries, it is not the poorest women but rather women of middle-level socioeconomic status, both married and unmarried, who are at the most significant risk of HIV infection, since they are the most likely to have multiple partners or to have sex with men who do.

7. Funding and other support for this project were supplied by the United States Agency for International Development (USAID), the United Nations Children's Fund (UNICEF), and local nongovernmental organizations (see Chapter 5 for a discussion of these agencies).

8. Readers who discover one or more professional arenas of particular interest should consult the accompanying *Anthropology Career Resources Handbook*, which contains ideas for following up on specific career possibilities.

REFERENCES

Anderson, Penny
1998. "A Note from the NAPA President." *Anthropology Newsletter* 39 (2):40.

Baba, Marietta L.
1994. "The Fifth Subdiscipline: Anthropological Practice and the Future of Anthropology." *Human Organization* 53 (2):174–186.

2000. "Theories of Practice in Anthropology: A Critical Appraisal." In *The Unity of Theory and Practice in Anthropology: Rebuilding a Fractured Synthesis* (NAPA Bulletin 18), edited by Carole E. Hill and Marietta L. Baba, 17–44. Washington, DC: NAPA.

Bennett, John
1996. "Applied Anthropology: Ideological and Conceptual Aspects." *Current Anthropology* 36:S23–S53.

Benson, Judith
2000. "Challenging a Paradigm in Two Directions: Anthropologists in Business and the Business of Practicing Anthropology." In *Careers in Anthropology: Profiles of Practitioner Anthropologists* (NAPA Bulletin no. 20), edited by Paula L. W. Sabloff, 23–27. Washington, DC: American Anthropological Association.

Bernard, H. Russell (ed.)
1998. *Handbook of Methods in Cultural Anthropology*. Walnut Creek, CA: Altamira Press.

Cleveland, David A.
2000. "Globalization and Anthropology: Expanding the Options." *Human Organization* 59:370–374.

Cernea, Michael M.
1995. "Social Organization and Development Anthropology" (1995 Malinowski Award lecture to the SfAA). *Human Organization* 54 (3):340–352.

D'Andrade, Roy
1995. "Moral Models in Anthropology." *Current Anthropology* 36 (3):399–408.

Dunkel, Tom
1992. "A New Breed of People Gazers." *Insight,* Jan. 13, 10–13.

Endicott, Kirk M., and Robert Welsch (eds.)
2001. "Should Cultural Anthropology Model Itself on the Natural Sciences?" in *Taking Sides: Clashing Views on Contemporary Issues in Anthropology,* edited by Kirk M. Endicott and Robert Welsch, pp. 178–199. Guilford CT: McGraw-Hill/Dushkin.

Erickson, Ken, and Donald Stull
1998. *Doing Team Ethnography: Warnings and Advice*. Thousand Oaks, CA: Sage Publications.

Fiske, Shirley, J., and Erve Chambers
1995. "The Inventions of Practice." *Human Organization* 55 (1):1–12.

Gert, Bernard
1995. "Universal Values and Professional Codes of Ethics." *Anthropology Newsletter* 36 (7):30–31.

Gwynne, Margaret A.
1992. "Proposal for a Cross-Cultural Study of Women's Role in Sexual Negotiation and the Potential Impact of the Female Condom." Geneva, Switzerland: WHO/GPA.

Hackenberg, R. A., and B. H. Hackenberg
1999. "You CAN Do Something! Forming Policy from Applied Projects, Then and Now." *Human Organization* 58 (1):1–15.

Hamada, Tomoko
1999. "Practicing Anthropology in Business Organizations." *Practicing Anthropology* 21 (4):2–4.

Hill, Carole E.
2000. "Strategic Issues for Rebuilding a Theory and Practice Synthesis." In *The Unity of Theory and Practice in Anthropology: Rebuilding a Fractured Synthesis* (NAPA Bulletin 18), edited by Carole E. Hill and Marietta L. Baba, 1–16. Washington, DC: NAPA.

Kuklick, Henrika
1997. "After Ishmael: The Fieldwork Tradition and its Future." In *Anthropological Locations: Boundaries and Grounds of a Field Science*, edited by Akhil Gupta and James Ferguson, 47–65. Berkeley: University of California Press.

Kuznar, Lawrence A.
1997. *Reclaiming a Scientific Anthropology*. Walnut Creek, CA: Altamira Press.

Lett, James
1997. *Science, Reason, and Anthropology*. Lanham, MD: Rowman and Littlefield Publishers, Inc.

NAPA (National Association for the Practice of Anthropology)
2002. NAPA website: www.aaanet.org/napa/index.htm

Ocasio, Raymond, Theresa A. Kilbane, and Judith A. Hermanson
1995. "An Urban Environmental Sanitation Loan Program in Honduras." In *Down to Earth: Community Perspectives on Health, Development and the Environment*, edited by Bonnie Bradford and Margaret A. Gwynne, 23–34. West Hartford, CT: Kumarian Press.

Price, Laurie J.
2001. "The Mismatch Between Anthropology Graduate Training and the Work Lives of Graduates." *Practicing Anthropology* 23 (1):55–60.

Scheper-Hughes, Nancy
1995. "The Primacy of the Ethical: Propositions for a Militant Anthropology." *Current Anthropology* 36 (3):409–420.

Simonelli, Jeanne
2001. "Mainstreaming the Applied Track: Connections, Guides, and Concerns." *Practicing Anthropology* 23 (1):48–49.

van Willigen, John
1987. *Becoming a Practicing Anthropologist: A Guide to Careers and Training Programs in Applied Anthropology* (NAPA Bulletin No. 3). Washington, DC: American Anthropological Association.
1993. *Applied Anthropology: An Introduction*. Westport, CT: Bergin and Garvey.

Walker, Christopher H.
1997. "Reflections of an 'Outsider' Anthropologist." In *Practicing Anthropology in the South*, edited by James M. T. Wallace, 48–53. Athens, GA: University of Georgia Press.

Wallace, James M. T.
1997. "Putting Anthropology into Practice in the 1990s." In *Practicing Anthropology in the South*, edited by James M. T. Wallace, 1–12. Athens, GA: University of Georgia Press.

Wilson, Ruth P.
1998. "The Role of Anthropologists as Short-Term Consultants." *Human Organization* 57 (2):245–252.

Winthrop, Robert
1997. "The Real World: Advocates, Experts, and the Art of Being Useful." *Practicing Anthropology* 19 (3):41–42.

Wolcott, Harry F.
1999. *Ethnography: A Way of Seeing*. Walnut Creek, CA: Altamira Press.

Zschock, Dieter K., et al.
1991. *Comparative Health Care Financing in St. Lucia, Grenada, and Dominica*. Needham Heights, MA: Ginn Press.

CHAPTER

2 METHOD AND THEORY IN APPLIED CULTURAL ANTHROPOLOGY

INTRODUCTION

Most readers of this book will already be familiar with three different kinds of "tools" commonly used by academically oriented cultural anthropologists. The first is a body of seminal ideas (usually referred to as anthropological "theories") that guide cultural anthropological research and analysis. The culture concept is a primary example of an anthropological "theory." Second, cultural anthropologists make use of a number of different philosophical approaches or viewpoints, each offering a different perspective on anthropological data; structural-functionalism and postmodernism are two well-known examples. Finally, cultural anthropologists have developed a body of methods that they routinely use for collecting, analyzing, and comparing data; participant observation is undoubtedly the best-known example. These familiar ideas and techniques are briefly reviewed in Appendix 2.

Applied cultural anthropologists, like their academic counterparts, make frequent use of these now-standard "theories," approaches, and techniques. Indeed, some of them were developed, during the infancy of cultural anthropology, specifically for applied purposes. Participant observation, for example, emanated from the requirement of nineteenth-century governments for information on which to base their administration of indigenous peoples.[1] Even as they make use of standard cultural anthropological tools, however, applied cultural anthropologists call upon additional ideas and techniques specifically relevant to the search for practical solutions to real-world problems.

This chapter first compares the basic research strategy used in applied cultural anthropology with classic or traditional cultural anthropological research. Next, it describes two principles fundamental to contemporary applied cultural anthropology: community participation and sustainability. These principles are largely irrelevant to traditional academic cultural anthropology because it lacks the explicit social change orientation of applied work; directed social change has historically been considered neither necessary nor even desirable in purely academic research. The chapter then describes a number of data-gathering and data-analysis methods commonly (if not exclusively) used by applied cultural anthropologists. Some of these methods were formulated within the specific context of applied cultural anthropology; some were borrowed from other disciplines, with or without being altered to suit applied anthropologists' goals. Finally, the chapter describes applied cultural anthropologists' theoretical contributions to their parent discipline and discusses the two-way relationship between theory and actual practice in applied cultural anthropology.

A BASIC STRATEGY FOR APPLIED RESEARCH

For the traditional, scientifically inclined, academic cultural anthropologist, the study of the behavior of human beings as members of social groups is motivated primarily by the desire to contribute to anthropological theory and ideally involves four activities.

1. The anthropologist, typically working alone rather than as part of a larger group, devises a hypothesis to explain some aspect of human social behavior.
2. He or she tests the validity of the hypothesis during a protracted period of ethnographic fieldwork.
3. The resulting data are analyzed, and the original hypothesis is revised and retested (if necessary) in the light of what has been learned.
4. The anthropologist compares what he or she has learned with data from other societies, in order to contribute to a wider understanding of the existence, development, appearance, behavior, and beliefs of human beings.

Today, although the scientific approach is still considered an important model for scholarly work in cultural anthropology, this traditional scenario may be more ideal than real. Theoretical research in cultural anthropology changed considerably over the course of the twentieth century and today is undertaken using a variety of approaches. The research of today's postmodern, and hence more humanistically oriented, cultural anthropologists may be far less rigid, more reflexive, and more interpretive than that of their earlier counterparts. In any case, however, the primary goal is still to learn something about human behavior for its own sake, rather than (or sometimes in addition to) achieving some practical end.

In contrast, applied research is primarily motivated by the desire to address a specific social problem, not by the desire to build theory. It is likely to involve representatives of other disciplines; the anthropologist rarely works alone. Rather than being more or less fixed and sequential, the applied cultural anthropologist's activities are apt to vary: policy research requires certain steps, intervention research requires others, direct intervention requires still others, and the amount of time available for each depends on the specific project at hand. Thus, although applied work in cultural anthropology is characterized, like classic theoretical work, by a series of well-defined activities, they are not the same activities that typify most academic cultural anthropology.

In the ideal (albeit not universally representative) scenario, the first step in a directed social change project is the identification of a specific problem that appears amenable to solution. This step is unlikely to be undertaken by an applied anthropologist himself or herself. Much more commonly, an organization—a government, an aid organization, or a charitable foundation—decides on a social change project. (More rarely, this step may be undertaken by a community of people hoping to benefit from directed change.)

Organizations sponsoring directed social change projects often wish to promote specific policy and/or action agendas, but rather than designing and implementing projects themselves, they may call upon applied cultural anthropologists to help them develop projects that are realistic for particular cultural contexts. An applied anthropologist may be asked, for example, to do a needs assessment (an appraisal of what is needed in a specific context; see p. 39), or to assess whether a specific policy or intervention will prove culturally acceptable to those who are intended to benefit from it. Once a project has been decided upon, an applied cultural anthropologist may be called on to undertake a social impact assessment: a determination of the potential effects of a new policy or intervention on the population intended to benefit from it (see p. 39; social impact assessment is also discussed in Chapter 4, in the context of the ethical considerations behind the national laws, policies, and agency regulations that mandate it).

After identifying a problem to which a solution may realistically be found, the applied cultural anthropologist conducts research—documentary, ethnographic, or both—to learn as much as possible about the problem, the setting, the actors, and what may already have been done or tried, in terms of both policy and direct intervention, to ameliorate the situation. This research phase need not take a great deal of time; employers typically hire applied cultural anthropologists who are already familiar with the theoretical and ethnographic context in which a given problem exists (Wilson 1998:45–46). Additionally, when ethnographic fieldwork is required, the anthropologist often employs specialized techniques that speed the process (see "Rapid Ethnographic Assessment," p. 37). Depending on the problem, the research may provide the background for policy recommendations (which may in turn result in future intervention), the development and implementation of a specific plan for positive change, or both (see Shore and Wright 1997; Hackenberg and Hackenberg 1999).

The third step in a directed change effort depends on what kind of change is intended. If the end goal is policy formulation, the third step is usually undertaken collectively by the applied cultural anthropologist, other project employees, the agency that is funding the project, and representatives of the agency or organization responsible for implementing policy reforms. The collected data are analyzed, sometimes over a considerable period of time, and policies are developed and formalized. If, on the other hand, the end goal is to take some direct action, the third step consists of development of a concrete plan, including a timetable, budget, and personnel roster, for addressing the problem. Again, this step is usually undertaken collectively by the applied cultural anthropologist, other project employees, and representatives of the agency that is funding the project.

The heart of many applied projects is intervention, defined in Chapter 1, in which specific action is taken to address a problem or problems identified in the project's first phase. Ideally, the applied cultural anthropologist as "intervener" (Dudley 1993) works in concert with members of the community of people whom the project is intended to benefit. In reality, it may be difficult or impossible to obtain the full participation of those who are meant to benefit from a directed change effort. (The ethics of this problem are discussed in Chapter 4.) No matter what the extent to which beneficiaries are actively involved, the anthropologist is likely to work during this stage with others who have professional expertise in fields related to the problem—for example (depending on the project), businesspeople, economists, or medical professionals—and with representatives of the funding agency. A project involving direct intervention was described in Chapter 1, pp. 19–21. Chapters 5–12 of this book contain many additional examples of interventions.

Finally, applied cultural anthropologists are frequently called upon to determine the success of a project. An **evaluation** is a formal assessment to determine whether or not a problem is currently being addressed appropriately or—if the project or program has been completed—has been solved satisfactorily (Rossi and Freeman 1989; Chelimsky and Sadish 1997). Typically, the evaluator is charged with judging the problem-solving efforts of others, although a relatively new form of evaluation, self-evaluation, undertaken by project stakeholders, is sometimes used. Evaluation is a mandatory part of many applied projects, since the organizations and agencies that fund applied research and intervention, whether public, private, or charitable, understandably want to know whether or not their money and other resources have been deployed effectively.

Of the several different kinds of evaluation, process evaluation and summative evaluation are probably the most frequently encountered. **Process evaluation** (alternatively termed **formative evaluation** when used early in an intervention to increase its potential for success) is carried out while an intervention is underway, in order to determine whether progress toward specific goals is being made in a timely and efficient fashion. Frequently this kind of intervention is ongoing throughout the life of a project. **Summative evaluation** (also called **outcome evaluation**) is carried out at the end of an intervention, in order to determine whether previously specified goals have been met.

In either type of evaluation, the evaluator is responsible for devising measurable indicators of a project's goals, for collecting reliable data on these indicators, and for comparing these data against the project's original goals. Alternatively, some evalua-

tions involve the collection of similar data from a control group that has not participated in the intervention, and the comparison of these data with data from the intervention group. The data collected may be either qualitative or quantitative. In some
specialized cases, highly mathematical techniques such as meta-analysis, a set of procedures for quantifying intervention results, are used (Cooper and Lindsay 1998). A
voluminous literature describes these and other evaluation methodologies.[2]

FOOD FOR THOUGHT   The government of a southern U.S. state funded a five-year project, now
completed, to discourage pre-teens from smoking. Suppose you have been
selected as an outside consultant to undertake a summative evaluation of
this project. Identify three ways in which the degree of success of the project
might be measured.

This idealized script is of course subject to all the exigencies of venue, time,
and varying social, economic, and political agendas, but its individual steps—problem identification, research, policy formulation or project planning, intervention,
and evaluation—do, in some combination, typify much applied cultural anthropological work.[3] Again, the overarching *raison d'être* behind these steps, whether or
not they are all taken or taken sequentially, is social betterment via directed change.
Table 2.1 compares the research strategies used most typically in theoretical and applied work in cultural anthropology.

◇ TABLE 2.1   Comparison of Basic Strategies: Theoretical and Applied

	Classic Theoretical Research	Applied Research
1. Primary motivation	Desire to contribute to anthropological theory	Desire to address a specific social problem
2. Collaboration with others	Usually no	Usually yes
3. Steps taken	More or less fixed and sequential	Variable, depending on project
4. Most common research methods	Participant observation	Specialized techniques, such as rapid ethnographic assessment and focus groups
5. Typical activities	▪ Devise hypothesis ▪ Test validity of hypothesis through ethnographic fieldwork ▪ Analyze data collected ▪ Revise and retest hypothesis (if necessary) ▪ Compare data with data from other societies	▪ Identify a problem amenable to solution ▪ Rapidly conduct policy or intervention research ▪ Analyze research data ▪ Formulate policy *or* implement intervention ▪ Evaluate project
6. Time frame	Long term (often a year or more)	Short term (often a few weeks or months)

THE UNDERLYING PRINCIPLES OF APPLIED RESEARCH

Two fundamental principles underlie applied research: community participation and sustainability. These principles are perhaps most strongly associated with international development (see Chapter 5), but apply equally to any social change effort, international or domestic.

Community Participation

The successful accomplishment of applied cultural anthropology's primary goal of directed social change requires a great deal more than well-meaning attempts on the part of outsiders to promote various socially beneficial ideas. It also requires that the desires, needs, and capabilities of those with whom, and on whose behalf, applied cultural anthropologists attempt to encourage beneficial change are taken into account. The term **community participation** refers to the active involvement of the intended beneficiaries in every step of the change process, from planning to research to implementation to evaluation.

The idea of community participation dates to the 1920s and 1930s, when a few enlightened colonial administrators began to argue for greater involvement and self-direction on the part of indigenous populations (Dudley 1993:159). It was later expressed in the "action anthropology" of Sol Tax in the 1950s, subsequently called "participatory action research" (see p. 36). Today, community participation is considered crucial to projects whose goal is directed social change (see, for example, Ryan and Robinson 1996; Gardner and Lewis 1996:110ff.). Ensuring effective community participation virtually mandates anthropological expertise, since its success rests heavily on ethnographic research to determine what local people think and want (Pottier 1993:1).

In the absence of community participation, attempts to promote socially beneficial goals are sometimes imposed on aid recipients by outsiders—individuals or organizations who are undoubtedly well-meaning but who may be ignorant of a given target population's actual requirements and preferences. Whether in the form of ideas, money, facilities, equipment, or technical assistance, such aid, termed **top-down assistance,**[4] is often inadequate and ineffectual. Not surprisingly, projects based on the top-down approach often fail because the "help" provided does not match the actual wants, needs, or capabilities of those who are meant to benefit from it.

A simple example comes from the small Eastern Caribbean island nation of St. Lucia. In the late 1980s, the St. Lucian national hospital, where patient records were written by hand on filing cards, was given a state-of-the art computer by a foreign aid agency. Unfortunately, however, no one at the hospital knew how to use the computer, and after a few months of disuse in the humid Caribbean climate, its keys began to stick, making it completely useless (see Trisolini et al. 1992). Had hospital staff—the intended beneficiaries in this case—had appropriate input into the process by which the computer was chosen as a donation, they would obviously have informed the aid agency that the computer would be useful only if hospital staff were trained to use, maintain, and repair it.

Ideally, when community participation is appropriately implemented, aid recipients identify their own problems and needs, initiate requests for assistance, and participate fully in the preparation of research proposals and the implementation and evaluation of funded projects. These project steps may appear relatively straightforward and easily accomplished, but they incorporate a number of potential problems. Perhaps the knottiest is that communities are never homogeneous, but rather fragmented and often stratified as well, by sex, age, caste, ethnicity, and so on. In some cultures, for example, women's involvement in extra-domestic affairs is either frowned upon or taboo. The existence of local social distinctions and hierarchies means that community members are never equal; instead, "aspirations towards participation, however genuine, take place in the context of existing relations of power and hierarchy" (Crewe and Harrison 1998:184). All participation, by definition, subtly embodies these power differentials. Thus, for example, when local people identify their own needs, the opinions of the more powerful among them may prevail.

There are other complicating issues as well. A change that improves the lives of members of one group may actually be deleterious to the members of another. Nor is it always clear who could or should participate in a social change project. Defining what kind of participation is expected may be difficult; often the roles that participants could or should play in project design, implementation, and evaluation are far from obvious (Cernea 1985:357). Defining the extent of participants' involvement, while also taking into account that those meant to benefit from applied research always have other demands on their time and energy, can also be challenging (Uphoff 1985). In some cases, local people may resist community participation, since "true participation is a threat to powerful vested interests" (Dudley 1993:7). Sometimes participation means "little more than consultation within a predetermined paradigm" (Crewe and Harrison 1998:112). Finally, there is always a power differential between helper and beneficiary (see, for example, ibid.:1; see also "Power and Authority," Chapter 4, p. 85).

FOOD FOR THOUGHT As an applied cultural anthropologist working for an international aid agency, you learn that a lack of electric power is a major factor contributing to conditions of extreme poverty, malnutrition, and ill health in a rural region of Bangladesh. However, neither the local people nor local government officials have requested assistance from any aid agency. What, if anything, do you do? Would suggesting help constitute top-down assistance?

Despite these problems, however, community participation, successfully implemented, not only helps ensure that social change projects achieve their intended results, but also empowers individuals and communities, and bonds their members together. Today, based on lessons from the recent past, the concept goes even further, including the notion of comprehensive indigenous participation and empowerment as well as several even broader ideas. One of these is that development workers should seek to learn from community members, not just teach them. Another is that community participation should explicitly promote seeking solutions and raising consciousness, "helping people to understand their circumstances" (Dudley 1993:163). Finally, assistance projects should include representatives of all potential stakeholders, not just the immediate "target" beneficiaries of a project.

Today, the idea of community participation incorporates a strong human rights perspective. As a matter of human rights, the intended beneficiaries of projects have the right either to accept or to reject innovations, and ultimately to determine the pace and direction of change within their communities. For an example of community participation at work, see the description of the Kenya Water for Health Organization on page 37.

Sustainability

Broadly speaking, **sustainability** is the idea that the results or effects of projects intended to promote beneficial change should be able to be carried forward, by their beneficiaries, into the indefinite future—after outside assistance has ended. Although the basic idea is both simple and sensible, there has been considerable debate in recent years about how best to ensure sustainability.

The idea of sustainability arose after the beneficial effects of numerous development projects, implemented prior to and during the 1980s, evaporated after the funding for these projects came to an end. In particular, a major rural development program, inaugurated in 1970 by the World Bank and implemented in many different countries with little input from local people, ultimately proved to be a "gigantic failure"; in 1987, the Bank acknowledged that many of the projects undertaken under this program had proven unsustainable (Keare 2001:160). In some cases, the intended beneficiaries of these and similar projects were ultimately left worse off than they had been before (see, for example, Johnson 1994).

A project in the early 1980s, in the small Philippine village of Casiguran, provides an example. Some of the farmers in this village of coconut, corn, and cassava growers were producing enough food to be considered well off, but others—many of them tenant farmers—literally did not have enough to eat. In 1984, the Philippine government, concerned about poverty and economic inequality in much of the nation, asked the United States Agency for International Development for help with an agricultural reform project intended to help low-income farmers increase their productivity (Clatts 1991). A pilot project, intended to foster economic development by introducing new agricultural technologies to poor tenant farmers, was developed, and Casiguran was chosen as the site where it would be implemented. The project's planners—Filipino government officials and USAID employees—believed that teaching the poorest farmers to raise new and different crops, such as coffee and pineapples, would earn them much-needed income, and also reduce the economic disparities between the poor farmers and the rest of the community. Casiguran's poor farmers were provided with the necessary seeds and agricultural technologies.

After only two years, it had become obvious that the intended benefits of the project were unsustainable. In the long run, most of the tenant farmers had not seen any significant increase in either agricultural production or household income and had reverted to their old crops and agricultural methods. In this as in similar instances, the reasons for the project's failure were complex and included the planners' failure to take into account the low demand for the new crops in the local market, the farmers' inability to commit sufficient additional time to the new labor-intensive farming technologies, and the important role of local women—who were not taught the new technologies—in farming. In the end, the project actually intensified the economic inequalities it was intended to reduce.

In the late 1980s, the idea of sustainability was thoroughly discussed, dissected, and reconstituted by applied cultural anthropologists and others involved in the promotion of beneficial social change. As a result, what had originally been a rather simple idea has taken on more complex meanings. Today, sustainability refers very specifically to several different aspects of directed change projects: the social, the technological, and the environmental.

Socially, the term *sustainability* not only implies the broad but ill-defined goal of a continuation of benefits in the absence of outside help, but it also explicitly mandates the continued involvement of local people, based on the realization that "to a great extent, acceptance of new methods by local people depends on the degree of their involvement in problem identification and solving" (Bragg and Schultz 1991:110). And project beneficiaries should not merely stay involved; they are also responsible for ensuring that whatever social structures, relationships, and policies are needed for long-term management of project benefits are in place. For example, the matter of rights to access a new village well must be determined equitably and permanently at the local level.

Technologically, the material benefits of development should be locally maintainable. If, for example, a hospital in a developing country is given a computer through a development project, hospital personnel should be instructed in how to operate it, how to train others to use it, how to secure supplies and replacement parts for it, and how to repair it. If a donor organization provides poor Pakistani farmers with a new variety of rice, capable of doubling the yield of traditional varieties, the farmers must be able to afford to buy more seed, plus any fertilizers or irrigation equipment or harvesting equipment necessary to ensure a good crop, after the donor organization has left (Smillie 1991:99–100). If the technology is a small-scale hydroelectric plant intended to supply lighting for a local school in Papua New Guinea, replacement parts must be available in New Guinea so they do not have to be imported, at high cost, from elsewhere (Arata 1979:397).

Environmentally, sustainability incorporates the broad dictum that nonrenewable natural resources should be conserved throughout the development process. Any technological changes must explicitly rely on renewable natural resources (such as solar or water power) and conserve nonrenewable natural resources (such as oil and naturally fertile soil). If, for example, an agricultural intensification project successfully increases crop yields, the increase should not ultimately result in soil depletion.

METHODS

Applied cultural anthropologists frequently call upon a set of techniques that are little used in academic research. Some of these are adaptations of standard anthropological data-gathering and data-analysis methods, tailored for greater suitability for applied purposes. Others have been borrowed from other disciplines (see Denzin and Lincoln 2000).

Why Are Specialized Techniques Required?

Applied cultural anthropologists' use of specialized techniques is necessitated by three factors. First, the goals of applied work differ from those of purely academic work. Research in applied cultural anthropology frequently focuses on a particular problem or action undertaken in a specific cultural context, rather than a broad-based assessment of a cultural milieu. Thus applied cultural anthropologists' goals are often more narrowly defined than those of their academic colleagues. Second, due both to funding limitations and the urgency of needed reforms, applied research is often done under time constraints, necessitating methods that permit the collection of the greatest amount of data in the shortest amount of time. Third, responsible applied cultural anthropology often requires its practitioners to develop traditional interviewer–informant relationships into something more resembling working partnerships with those whose problems are the focus of research or who are intended to benefit from intervention.

 FOOD FOR THOUGHT Cultural anthropology incorporates a number of highly useful perspectives, such as cultural relativism and the emic point of view (see Appendix 2). These perspectives are as important to applied cultural anthropologists as they are to academic researchers. However—unlike many of the methods applied researchers use—these perspectives have not required alteration to make them appropriate for applied work. Why not?

The Collaborative Nature of Applied Work

In the field, applied cultural anthropologists work with and collect data from informants, just as academic anthropologists do. But they also work closely with two other groups of people. The first group consists of other professionals, often hired on a consulting basis, whose particular expertise is required to accomplish the goals of the program or project at hand. In addition to these experts, this group may also include one or more representatives of the agency, organization, or institution that set the agenda and/or provided the funding for the work. These individuals may represent several or many different disciplines (Erickson and Stull 1998:5) but are unlikely to be other cultural anthropologists. The second group consists of representatives of the intended beneficiaries of the program or project. Applied cultural anthropologists' greater number of more varied working relationships represents a

◇ *Applied cultural anthropology usually involves collaborative research and action, in which professionals representing several or many different disciplines—not just cultural anthropology—participate.*

significant departure from academic cultural anthropology, in which researchers are much more apt to work with their informants alone, on research agendas of their own choosing.

An applied research project undertaken recently in the Eastern Caribbean island nation of Dominica provides an example. The project, sponsored by a U.S.-based charitable foundation, was intended to provide the government of Dominica with policy options for the reorganization of its public health system for greater efficiency (Zschock et al. 1991).

The applied cultural anthropologist who participated in this project gathered valuable data from local informants, in much the same manner as in academic fieldwork. The informants were ordinary citizens of Dominica, who were interviewed in their homes or at health care facilities for their knowledge and opinions about traditional medicine, Western-style biomedicine, or both. In addition to these informants, however, the applied anthropologist also worked closely with two different teams of professional colleagues. During the project's planning phase, these colleagues included experts in several health-related fields: an American health economist, a Jamaican medical doctor, a health insurance specialist, and a representative of the Pan American Health Organization, a regional branch of the World Health Organization.

Later, in Dominica during the research phase of the project, the applied anthropologist worked closely with the chief medical officer, permanent secretary, and principal nursing officer of the Dominican Ministry of Health. The Dominican project participants were chosen not only for their broad cultural expertise (as are many of the informants from whom academic anthropologists get their data) but for several other reasons as well: their specific knowledge about local health-related matters (such as the adequacy of public versus private ambulatory care facilities in Dominica); their placement within social networks advantageous to the goals of the project; and their potential to benefit—as citizens of Dominica, representatives of the existing health system, and potential stakeholders in health system reform—from the project.

Although the members of both of these groups were experts in their respective fields, none of them had had any training in cultural anthropology. Not surprisingly, the fieldworker's relationships with them were fundamentally different from traditional anthropologist–informant interactions. In part for this reason, applied cultural anthropologists frequently substitute the terms *collaborators, counterparts,* or *partners* for the term *informants,* still commonly used in academic field research.

Some Useful Field Methods

This section briefly describes the best known and most frequently used of the techniques employed by applied cultural anthropologists to gather and analyze data in the field. It does not attempt to synthesize, much less to substitute for, the vast literature on applied methods, but rather to convey a general idea of the types of specialized techniques used in applied research.[5]

Surveys.   Surveying a group of people to discover their ideas, values, beliefs, opinions, or needs is a technique historically associated more strongly with sociological than with anthropological research, but it can provide applied cultural anthropologists with large amounts of broad-ranging and relatively quickly acquired data. The technique relies on quantitative instruments such as pre-prepared questionnaires. Surveys are particularly appropriate in complex communities, in which there is no single "native" point of view, because they facilitate the collection of a breadth of ideas and opinions (Finan and van Willigen 2002:63). Researchers using this technique must often make difficult trade-offs between resource investment and results: a longer-term effort, involving more survey respondents, will produce more information; a shorter-term effort will cost less. A major advantage of the technique is that when certain standardized sampling procedures are followed, the research results may carry the added weight of statistical significance.

In an example of this technique, one applied cultural anthropologist used surveys to assist the Ministries of Health of several Eastern Caribbean countries to resolve some of their health care financing problems. In each country, adult consumers of health services, selected so as to reflect the population both demographically and socioeconomically, responded to pre-prepared questionnaires that first covered basic demographic information and then solicited respondents' opinions, values, and expectations regarding the quality of public and private health services, the availability and affordability of health insurance, respondents' willingness to pay for improved health services under a social insurance plan, and related issues (Zschock et al. 1991:119–123). The data were used to inform subsequent policy decisions about health care financing.

Participatory Action Research.   Some applied cultural anthropologists (along with others in the so-called helping professions), while acknowledging the inevitable power differential between change agent and beneficiary referred to above, have viewed the existence of this differential as an immutable fact of their practice. Others have consciously tried to lessen its effects. **Participatory action research**

(PAR) is a behavioral change strategy in which members of local communities initiate, carry out, and assume complete and permanent "ownership" of projects intended to result in locally beneficial social change (see Whyte 1991; Scrimshaw and Gleason 1992; Ryan and Robinson 1996; Perez 1997; Bernard 1998:69; Greenwood and Levin 1998; Trotter and Schensul 1998:73–74; Ervin 2000:199–210). The applied cultural anthropologist's role is usually confined to facilitation and guidance; direct involvement is precluded.

The strategy originated in Sol Tax's human development and advocacy work with Native Americans during the 1950s (when it was termed *action anthropology;* see Tax 1958; Bennett 1996) and was further elaborated in Paolo Freire's work in popular education in Latin America (Freire 1970). PAR is based on the premise that sustained behavioral change is unlikely to occur unless those who would benefit from it develop a sense of self-determination and empowerment, as well as the belief that they can exert control over their own lives and destinies. Thus, participatory action research is conducted not from the top down, by applied cultural anthropologists or others, but from the bottom up, by its potential beneficiaries. They help to educate each other and to develop a joint plan of action.[6]

FOOD FOR THOUGHT   Imagine that you are an applied cultural anthropologist employed by a large, multiethnic, urban school district. Part of your job is to help ensure that what children learn in school is relevant to the wider culture beyond the public educational system. As an advocate of participatory action research, whom would you choose as your collaborators on this project? How would you go about implementing PAR?

Members of grass-roots organizations are the most likely participants in, and beneficiaries of, participatory action research. In Africa, for example, the Kenya Water for Health Organization (KWAHO) has been highly successful in using PAR to help over a million mostly rural Kenyans gain access to clean water (Mwangola 1995). When communities needing water projects approach KWAHO, the organization supplies anthropological consultants and other trained facilitators but also encourages community representatives to "set specific goals, form committees, identify resources, collect funds, and select a specific technology" (Mwangola 1995:86). Once a water pump has been installed in a village, community members must maintain it. The process is empowering: "a *harambee* ("pull together") spirit develops, and often leads to . . . wider health and education efforts" (ibid.). As the head of KWAHO observes, "When the potential beneficiaries of a water supply project are not themselves involved in running and maintaining the scheme, it is likely to end long before the pump itself breaks down . . . ownership is crucial" (ibid.:87).[7]

Rapid Ethnographic Assessment.   An important way in which applied cultural anthropologists have tailored classic anthropological techniques to their own requirements is by making certain changes to the traditional fieldwork process. These changes are both necessitated and permitted by the fact that the steps ideally involved in applied cultural anthropology—problem identification, research, planning, intervention, and evaluation—do not always require total immersion in a culture. Applied cultural anthropologists have therefore adapted some ethnographic techniques used in more theoretical studies to suit their own needs. These techniques include participant observation, the use of both key and casual informants, and others, together comprising a new kind of fieldwork called **rapid ethnographic assessment,** or REA. This method (alternatively termed *rapid assessment procedures,* or RAP) is better suited to applied cultural anthropologists' specific goals (Scrimshaw and Gleason 1992; Beebe 1995, 2001; Trotter and Schensul 1998:717–718; Handwerker 2001).

Rapid ethnographic assessment requires much less time than traditional anthropological fieldwork. The anthropologist is already well versed in the literature on both problem and venue (Wilson 1998:46), often speaks the local language, and has had prior field experience in the region. The method involves interviewing relatively few but carefully chosen collaborators in the field, eliminating the wide-ranging "fishing expedition" field interview technique in favor of addressing only the specific problem under study, and sometimes making use of sampling techniques, focus groups (see below), and pre-prepared and easily quantifiable survey instruments such as questionnaires.

Anthropologist Margaret Casey (Casey 1993) used this technique in Indonesia, where the government (with support from the British foreign aid agency and the European Economic Community) was implementing a project to improve agricultural production, and farmers' lives, by drilling wells, constructing irrigation systems, and forming water management associations (Casey 1993:110). Brought in to evaluate the project as it neared completion, Casey spent only four weeks in Indonesia, one in each of four villages. Interviews with women in these villages

✧ *Rapid ethnographic assessment often involves the use of narrowly-focused, pre-prepared survey instruments. In New Delhi, India, residents of a poor neighborhood respond to specific questions, the answers to which are readily quantifiable.*

revealed that although women were important players in local agricultural production and decision making, they had been neglected by the project's implementers. The data Casey collected on interpersonal relations, gender roles, authority figures, and local politics may result in future project modifications and help ensure both short-term success and long-term sustainability.

Not all applied cultural anthropologists feel that rapid ethnographic assessment is a viable data-collection method. It has been criticized for generating "sloppy assessments" and for "neglecting the collection of long time-series data" (Cernea 1995:348).[8]

Needs Assessment.   A standard component of public policy research and program design (Kozaitis 2000:58), **needs assessment** is an appraisal of what is required to alleviate one or more specific problems in a specific context. The "needs" referred to—sometimes termed "perceived" or "felt" needs in order to distinguish them from supposed needs attributed to a group based on others' perceptions or values—are apt to be basic requirements in areas such as health, sanitation, or education, the fulfillment of which would improve the quality of life of members of a needy group. Several different methods for determining needs have been developed (McKillip 1998).

Ideally, applied cultural anthropologists undertake needs assessments in close collaboration with those who are intended to benefit from some change, since they can most accurately identify their own wants and requirements. The process, which begins in the planning stage but may continue throughout the life of an applied project, is more complex than merely asking people what they lack. One complicating factor is the fact that people are not always aware of what their needs are; for example, if sexually active teenagers do not feel they are at risk of contracting HIV/AIDS, they will not perceive that they need AIDS education. Another is that the same perceived needs sometimes call for different solutions for two different populations. A third is that even the most pressing needs, among extremely needy groups, may have to be prioritized due to funding or time constraints. Because of the complexity of the issues involved, some applied cultural anthropologists have become specialists in needs assessment.[9]

Social Impact Assessment (SIA).   **Social impact assessment** is an appraisal of the potential effects, on individuals, communities, or even nations, of proposed research or a proposed intervention. This can be determined beforehand in a formal, systematic way (Goldman 2000; see also van Willigen 1993:171; Kozaitis 2000:58).

Most often used in a context of large-scale governmental or international development projects, whether or not applied cultural anthropologists are involved, SIA derives from (and is in some cases mandated by) various national laws, policies, and agency regulations. In the United States, these include the National Environmental Policy Act of 1969 (NEPA 1969), which requires consideration of the impact of proposed development or change on the social as well as natural environment, and the "social soundness guidelines" developed by the United States Agency for International Development (USAID) in 1975 to guide its international development work.

There is no single set of agreed-upon steps or standards to guide an SIA (van Willigen 1993:177). One authority lists ten separate steps (Wolf 1983). Preister (1987:50) simplifies the process by describing only the most fundamental steps:

- Develop an understanding of the status quo in the social environment in which a project may be implemented.
- Identify the target group's current concerns relating to the project.
- Collect social and economic data relating to the project, and analyses of the social and economic effects of various project alternatives.
- Promote ample and effective communication among all stakeholders.
- Resolve any conflicts existing among those concerned.

The participation of applied cultural anthropologists is not a requirement of SIAs, and many SIAs are undertaken without them, but their participation greatly facilitates the process because of their ability to "enter into a community, understand cultural dynamics, and translate cultural understanding to decision-makers" (Preister 1987:50).[10]

Focus Group Research.   Focus group research, another field technique more frequently used by applied than academic cultural anthropologists, will already be familiar to many readers because of its widespread use in contexts such as public opinion polling and commercial marketing. A **focus group** is a small group (6–8 persons) convened, under a leader, to focus on and discuss, and thereby to illuminate, a particular topic. The subject might be what homeless people like or dislike about public shelters, what motivates parents to purchase particular toys for their children, or how people feel about increased medical insurance premiums in return for greater benefits.

Whatever the subject, it is usually not addressed directly. The focus group leader may steer the conversation toward the subject but is at pains not to influence the discussion, either in direction or content. The reason is that by letting the conversation and the interaction among participants "float," information that may not have been anticipated beforehand as being relevant may be revealed (Bryant and Bailey 1991:5). This interaction among the participants, and especially the ideas they stimulate in each other, are considered more important than the opinion of any individual participant. Various props to stimulate thought and discussion are often used, and sessions are typically taped and analyzed at length later on, since not only the participants' choice of specific words, but also their actions, may reveal their attitudes toward the subject. Ideally, at the end of a focus group session, whoever assembled the group has a more thorough understanding of people's thoughts, feelings, and attitudes about the subject at hand.

As an example of the use of focus groups, applied medical anthropologist Merrill Singer and his colleagues conducted a series of focus groups with people living with AIDS (PWAs) as part of a needs assessment to define the kinds of resources and support PWAs require. In some of the focus groups, involving clients of social services agencies that provided specific services to PWAs, the participants were unknown to each other. Other focus groups consisted of PWAs who already knew each

◇ *Focus group sessions are sometimes more revealing of people's ideas, attitudes, and feelings than one-on-one interviews. At right, members of a focus group discuss the packaging of a new product.*

other as members of support groups; for these participants, talking about AIDS was already part of their "natural social world." Interestingly, the two kinds of focus groups provided the researchers with different kinds of information, "the former being more 'task oriented' and the latter being more freewheeling" (Singer 2002: 91).

The use of focus groups for applied research is somewhat controversial. They have been criticized as unproductive and faddish, and by no means all applied cultural anthropologists use them. For those who do, however, focus groups have two major advantages over more traditional one-on-one interviewing. First, they can save considerable time, since the ethnographer is able to elicit ideas and information from a number of people at once. Second, the interaction of group members may produce insights that one-on-one discussion cannot.[11]

Social Network Analysis. Social structure, consisting of all the ways in which people both divide themselves into groups and bind themselves together as members of groups, holds enormous interest for cultural anthropologists for the light it sheds on how societies are constituted and maintained, and how they change. **Social network analysis,** used by sociologists as well as cultural anthropologists, is a way of gathering and organizing information about social structure by focusing on individuals or small groups and their relationships with others. The goal of social network analysis is to establish patterns of association among people, to assess the effects of such patterns on social organization, and ultimately to further our understanding of human motivation and behavior (Mitchell 1984; Marsden 1990; Trotter and Schensul 1998; Scott 2000).

Social networks may be of three kinds. Probably the least useful to applied cultural anthropologists are the broadest and most inclusive, **set-centered networks,** which assume the existence, in any society, of groups ("sets") of individuals—ranging from cliques of friends to kin groups to common-interest groups—with contacts or links with one another. Participant observation has long been considered the best way to get information on set-centered networks. However, this method is too time-consuming to be commonly used by applied cultural anthropologists, whose research goals and intervention activities are usually much more narrowly focused. (A previously existing set-centered network analysis of a particular community would, of course, be of great benefit to an applied cultural anthropologist interested in researching one or more specific sets of people within that community.)

Ego-centered networks focus on a particular individual ("ego") and include all the links between this person and other individuals in a community under investigation. Data are typically gathered in individual interviews. Ego-centered network analysis is useful to applied cultural anthropologists since it sheds light on the kinds of influences exerted on given individuals and suggests what social support systems exist for them. This information can then be used to create effective interventions (Trotter and Schensul 1998:71). For example, researchers working on an AIDS-prevention project in Denver used ego-centered networks to trace patterns of exposure to AIDS by linking specific crack-addicted women to their sexual partners. Some of the women's partners were gang members who sold drugs. The research led to the expansion of the prevention program to target both crack users and gang members (Singer 2002:97).

Specialized networks are networks of individuals who share particular interests or sets of beliefs, or engage in particular behaviors (for example, a network of individuals linked by their use of a particular drug). Exploring specialized networks has proven especially useful to applied cultural anthropologists developing health-related interventions (see Needle et al. 1995), since most people's health-related beliefs and behaviors are forged in informal contexts such as families, groups of friends, or common-interest associations.[12] One applied anthropologist, for example, was able to bring homeless teenagers into a storefront clinic in New York for medical examinations and counseling by drawing upon the teenagers' informal networks based on friendship and drug use (M. Clatts, pers. comm.).

 FOOD FOR THOUGHT The "environmental justice movement" brings environmentalists, educators, applied cultural anthropologists, and local people together to identify and rectify environmental rights abuses. As the applied anthropologist on a project to determine the extent of such abuses in your state, which of the techniques described above—surveys, participatory action research, rapid ethnographic assessment, needs assessment, social impact assessment, focus group research, and social network analysis—would you use? Why?

"The Toolkit of a Good Professional Anthropologist"

Recently, the National Association for the Practice of Anthropology, recognizing that the ideas, techniques, and knowledge base required for responsible applied cultural anthropology had never been formally defined, established a "Toolkit Committee" to identify the specific tools—perspectives, methods, skills, and so on—needed for responsible applied work (García Ruiz 2000). According to former NAPA president and Toolkit Committee member Niel Tashima, "Professional anthropologists must have the ability to be clear about the value our methods bring to the study of current societal problems" (García Ruiz 2000:45).

The committee developed "The Toolkit of a Good Professional Anthropologist" (see Table 2.2) only after much discussion and outside review. Committee members stress that it should be considered a work in progress, which will undoubtedly be refined in the future. In its present form, the chart sums up and augments the material presented in this section on methods and provides additional food for thought.[13]

A WORD ABOUT THE "NEW ETHNOGRAPHY"

The "new ethnography," a set of field techniques designed to produce an understanding of cultural categories and distinctions meaningful to the members of a given society and to yield very accurate, language-based, numerically quantifiable field data (see Appendix 2), has found adherents among some applied cultural anthropologists. The great value of this and other cognitive field methods is that they help cultural anthropologists to reduce, if not eliminate, their own cultural biases. The anthropologist invites his or her interviewees to construct their own cultural categories, rather than making presuppositions about the ways in which they categorize their world. The free listing technique (see Appendix 2), for example, helps the anthropologist avoid the cultural bias that would inevitably be projected with direct questions, which—no matter how carefully formulated—are often tantamount to "leading the witness." Cognitive methods can greatly help in the development of an emic perspective on a specific topic, although they cannot substitute for other, more traditional, methods.

The techniques of the new ethnography, including the use of explanatory models and various taxonomic methods (see Appendix 2), are appealing to applied cultural anthropologists for two reasons. First, they produce large amounts of quantifiable data, which are readily accepted as relevant by the other kinds of scientists with whom applied cultural anthropologists often work on their projects. And second, they save fieldwork time by going directly to the heart of a specific problem in a quick and efficient manner. Thus, they are compatible with the aims of REA.[14]

THEORY DEVELOPMENT IN THE COURSE OF PRACTICE

The Relationship Between Theory and Practice

Chapter 1 noted that academic anthropology is primarily a theoretical discipline, and contributing to human knowledge is the primary motivation behind the work of most academic anthropologists. No matter what their particular field of anthro-

◇ **TABLE 2.2   The Toolkit of a Good Professional Anthropologist**

PERSPECTIVE (Our Core Approach)	METHODS (What We Own/Use—Italicized If We Own It)	SKILLS (How We Do It)	ANTHROPOLOGICAL ATTRIBUTES (Informs Use of Methods)	PROFESSIONAL ATTRIBUTES (Needed To Be Effective)	EXAMPLES OF APPLICATIONS (What We Do)	CHALLENGES (To Enhance Our Professionalism)
Holistic	*Ethnography*	Finding themes and patterns	Ability to work in teams as collaborators	Ability to work in teams as collaborators	Time-limited, focused, product-oriented work	Engagement and disengagement
Systemic	*Interactive, systematic participation in observing*	Cultural brokering*	Adaptability	Can-do orientation	Advocacy research	Social skills
Integrative	Structured, systematic observation	Translating	Advocacy orientation	Entrepreneurial	Analyst	Good work habits
Contextual	Analysis	Teaching	Approachability	Multidisciplinary orientation	Administration	Public relations
Comparative	Focus groups	Interpreting and presenting others' views	Multiple lenses	Understanding of quantitative methods	Policy making	Positive professional presentation of selves
Cross-cultural	Rapid assessments	Speaking and writing clearly	Flexibility	Business skills	Planning	Borders with other disciplines
People-oriented	Interviewing	Building trust	Risk-taker	Technology skills	Training	Lines/boundaries of our work
Relativistic	Evaluation	Storytelling	Good work habits		Program services and research design	Fieldwork experience in all professional training
Emic and Etic valuation	Testing analysis with informants	Narrating	Participatory		Service provision	Disseminating our methods and outcomes
Recognition of complexity	Qualitative and Quantitative research	Facilitating	Listening skills		Therapy	Developing support networks
Focus on process	Iterative approach to research	Integrating disparate parts into a whole	Respectful		Product R&D	
Collaborative	Secondary and archival research	Systematizing/using complex information	Learner		Program evaluation	
We ask what the questions are before we ask for answers	Research design	Inductive and deductive reasoning	Curious, inquisitive		Sales and Marketing	
Theoretically informed	Data collection	Marketing ideas or projects	Nonjudgmental		Teaching	
	Data management				Mediation	

*Defined in Chapter 6.
Source: NAPA/AAA.[13]

pology, the professional lives of academic anthropologists are very largely spent collecting information and developing ideas about human beings of the past or present; using this information and these ideas to devise premises that might help explain the existence, development, appearance, behavior, and beliefs of human beings; and then testing and revising their premises in the light of what they have found.

It is a common academic conceit that important ideas in any field are formulated and tested by theoreticians working in academic contexts; these ideas are subsequently dispersed into nonacademic contexts, where they are put to use (Ferguson 1997:150). This intellectual transfer has often occurred in applied cultural anthropology, but so has the opposite: applied work has also contributed to theory (Kozaitis 2000:55). Nevertheless, applied cultural anthropology has been criticized both for the extent to which its theoretical basis is not its own and for its failure to generate theories of practice.

Part of the reason for this criticism is that applied cultural anthropologists have neglected to emphasize their theoretical contributions—so much so that "anthropologists who are not engaged in applied research have been known to comment that the place of theory in applied anthropology is modest, if not absent" (Wilson 1998:46). Yet it is important to remember that academic anthropology has generated few, if any, hard-and-fast theories, and also that contributions to theory can include "theoretical products" such as "concepts, propositions, methodologies for purposeful action, hypotheses, models, etc." (Cernea 1995:348).

As an example of how theoretical work can contribute to the accomplishment of practical goals beyond the production of knowledge, cultural anthropologist James Peacock describes how his academic fieldwork in Indonesia later influenced a specific political outcome (Peacock 2000:104ff.). During his study of an Indonesian Muslim political movement, Peacock became acquainted with a supporter of the movement, with whom he continued to correspond and exchange views through the years. The acquaintance eventually became the movement's leader and was recently instrumental in removing the Indonesian president from office. Peacock points out that most cultural anthropologists can similarly trace the influence of their theoretical work on specific people and events (Peacock 2000:105).

On the opposite side of the coin, when anthropological concepts are applied "across the grain of practical experience" (Anglin 1997:33), contributions to theory can result. In fact, "the research objects of applied anthropology generally have no less intrinsic potential to generate theory than the research objects of academic anthropology" (Cernea 1995:348). As an example, applied business anthropologist Tomoko Hamada (see Chapter 9) recently reexamined the "multiple and vague" meanings associated with the culture concept as part of a study of a Japanese multinational corporation (Hamada 2000:79ff.). Calling into question the utility of several models of culture currently being used in the analysis of businesses, Hamada argues that rapid global change demands new ideas about the culture of business organizations. She devised the notion of "quality culture," which embraces earlier models in which culture is viewed as dynamic rather than static, but allows greater possibility for individual human agency (Hamada 2000:95). Hamada argues that business anthropology is "an immensely fertile ground for anthropological theory building" (Hamada 2000:99–100).

"Theories of Practice"

Applied anthropologist Marietta Baba notes that "applied anthropology need not and should not be expected to give birth to and nurture its 'own' theories of humanity, separate and apart from those of general anthropology, as if practitioners worked with a different species of human on a different planet" (Baba 2000:8). Nevertheless, she has identified four distinct "theories of practice" in applied anthropology (see Table 2.3), defined as explanations of the relationships that necessarily exist between theoretical knowledge and using that knowledge (Baba 2000:19–20). For Baba, ideas that "describe and explain the value of practice and its potential role in the discipline" together constitute the "theory of applied anthropology" (Baba 2000:8).

FOOD FOR THOUGHT   Do you agree with applied cultural anthropologist Marietta Baba that applied anthropology has no need of its own body of theory, separate from academic anthropology's "theories"? If so, how would you defend your position? If you feel that applied work is different enough from academic work to require the establishment of a separate body of theory, do you think the "underlying principles" described earlier in this chapter are of sufficient importance to be added to Baba's list of theories in Table 2.3?

Another example of how applied cultural anthropology has contributed to anthropological theory is the influence of applied work on anthropological ideas about

◇ **TABLE 2.3   Some Anthropological Theories of Practice**

Theory	Basic Idea
Linear theory	The idea that the value of applied anthropology derives from basic anthropological theory
Feedback theory	The idea that practice and theory have an "exchange relationship," with each contributing to the development of the other
Policy theory	The idea that feedback also exists between practice and policy, and that application should contribute to the betterment of humanity by informing policy
Praxis theory	The idea that there is a "way of knowing" termed *praxis* (defined not merely as practice, but as "a commitment to action") that is superior to theory and demands the "pursuit of value-laden goals"

Source: Baba 2000:22–28.

social change. Over the years, numerous ideas about how the process of change actually occurs have been proposed. Applied cultural anthropologists, whose work involves directed, beneficial social change, have been uniquely positioned to test and revise these ideas and to suggest new ones, since "ideas about change influence the goals, planning, methods, and outcomes of efforts to implement policies and programs" (Barger and Reza 1987:55).

One applied project, for example, involved improving the living and working conditions of migrant farm laborers, most of them Mexican Americans, working seasonally on farms in the U.S. Midwest. These socially and economically disenfranchised laborers had little control over their working conditions, much less any input into the laws that regulated their work. Applied cultural anthropologists working with them to rectify this situation developed and tested a theory of change, which they termed an "adaptive systems model," incorporating the idea that "the content and direction of changes are governed by the interaction of different forces within an integrated system" (Barger and Reza 1987:56). They determined that this change model "has the greatest potential for understanding change, and . . . offers the best guidelines for applied change" (Barger and Reza 1987:72).

CONCLUSION

Although the different goals and time frames of academic and applied cultural anthropologists may necessitate the use of somewhat different techniques and the implementation of different principles, fundamental similarities exist between the two kinds of cultural anthropology. Both academic and applied cultural anthropologists are trained to probe for the emic perspective; both approach their understanding of people in societies or groups other than their own from a holistic viewpoint; both are committed to the comparative method; both conscientiously employ the concept of cultural relativism in order to reach objective and non-ethnocentric conclusions. Finally, both academic and applied cultural anthropologists are specialists in cross-cultural translation; they are experts at making sense of the culture of a given group of people and explaining it in terms that can be understood by the members of other groups.

K E Y T E R M S

community participation   the active involvement of the intended beneficiaries of directed change in every step of the change process

ego-centered network   a social network centering on a particular individual and including all the links between this person and others in his or her community

evaluation   an assessment to determine whether or not a problem is currently being addressed appropriately or has been solved satisfactorily

focus group   a small group of people convened to focus on and discuss, and thereby to illuminate, a particular topic

formative evaluation   a type of process evaluation used early in an intervention to increase its potential for success

needs assessment   an appraisal of what needs to be done to alleviate one or more specific problems in a specific context

outcome evaluation   an alternate term for summative evaluation

participatory action research (PAR)   a behavioral change strategy in which members of local communities initiate, carry out, and assume responsibility for projects intended for their benefit

process evaluation   an assessment, carried out while an intervention is underway, in order to determine whether progress toward specific goals is being made in a timely and efficient fashion

rapid ethnographic assessment (REA)   a set of field methods that involve shortcutting classic anthropological techniques in order to address specific problems quickly and precisely

set-centered network   a social network based on groups of individuals linked to one another

social impact assessment   a determination of the impact of an applied project on the population intended to benefit from it

social network analysis   a way of gathering and organizing information about social structure by focusing on individuals or small groups and their relationships with others

specialized network   a social network involving individuals who share particular interests or sets of beliefs, or engage in particular behaviors

summative evaluation   an assessment carried out at the end of an intervention, in order to determine whether previously specified goals have been met

sustainability   the idea that the results or effects of successful applied anthropological work should be able to be sustained by those who benefit from the work

top-down assistance   attempts at problem solving imposed on intended beneficiaries from the outside

NOTES

1. See Chapter 3. Bronislaw Malinowski is sometimes credited with being the "father of participant observation," but this field method predates Malinowski's early-twentieth-century fieldwork by many years. As early as 1879, anthropologist Frank Hamilton Cushing was living and conducting applied research among the Zuni of the American southwest at the behest of the U.S. Bureau of American Ethnology.

2. Comprehensive discussions of project and program evaluation can be found in Patton 1990 and Chelimsky and Sadish 1997.

3. See Bernard 1998:69ff. for a different perspective. Bernard divides the activities of applied cultural anthropologists into five distinct types of research: policy research, evaluation research, cultural intervention research, advocacy or action research, and participatory action research.

4. Top-down assistance is discussed in Chapter 5.
5. Some of the techniques mentioned in this section are elaborated elsewhere in this book, in the context of specific professional arenas. For example, social impact assessment is further discussed in the chapter on ethics (Chapter 4); action anthropology, mentioned in this chapter in the context of participatory action research, is further discussed in the chapter on cultural advocacy (Chapter 6). Other methods, treated briefly in this chapter, are described exhaustively elsewhere (see, for example, Bickman and Rog 1998; Trotter and Schensul 1998, Ervin 2000).
6. Bottom-up approaches are criticized in Keare 2001; see Chapter 5 for discussion.
7. Further information about participatory action research, with additional examples, can be found in this book, in the discussions of community participation in Chapter 5, cultural advocacy in Chapter 6, and peer education in Chapter 11.
8. A comprehensive discussion of REA can be found in Scrimshaw and Gleason 1992.
9. A comprehensive discussion of needs assessment can be found in McKillip 1998.
10. A comprehensive discussion of social impact assessment can be found in Preister 1987.
11. Comprehensive discussions of the use of focus groups can be found in Bryant and Bailey 1991, Agar and MacDonald 1995, Morgan 1997, Morgan and Kreuger 1997, Stewart and Shamdasani 1998, and Krueger and Casey 2000.
12. A comprehensive discussion of network analysis can be found in Scott 2000.
13. The "Toolkit of a Good Professional Anthropologist" originally appeared in *Anthropology News* 41 (3):44, March 2000. The members of NAPA's "Toolkit Committee" are Niel Tashima, Cathleen Crain, Susan Squires, Mitchell Allen, Brian Byrne, Ken Price, Kathleen Quirk, and Eliot Lee. The "Toolkit" is reproduced here with the permission of NAPA/AAA.
14. For exhaustive compendia of the methods used in cultural anthropology in general, see Bernard 1998; see also Schensul and LeCompte 1999, especially vols. 6 and 7, which are most relevant to applied work.

REFERENCES

Agar, Michael, and James MacDonald
1995. "Focus Groups and Ethnography." *Human Organization* 54 (1):78–87.

Anglin, Mary K.
1997. "Activist Praxis and Anthropological Knowledge." In *Practicing Anthropology in the South*, edited by James M.T. Wallace, 33–42. Athens, GA: University of Georgia Press.

Arata, Ed
1979. "Papua New Guinea: Micro-Hydroelectric Projects for Rural Development." In *Appropriate Technology for Development: A Discussion and Case Histories*, edited by Donald D. Evans and Laurie Nogg Adler, 397–409. Boulder, CO: Westview Press.

Baba, Marietta L.
2000. "Theories of Practice in Anthropology: A Critical Appraisal." In *The Unity of Theory and Practice in Anthropology: Rebuilding a Fractured Synthesis* (NAPA Bulletin 18), edited by Carole E. Hill and Marietta L. Baba, 17–44. Washington, DC: NAPA.

Barger, W. K., and Ernesto Reza
1987. "Community Action and Social Adaptation: The Farmworker Movement in the Midwest." In *Collaborative Research and Social Change: Applied Anthropology in Action*, edited by Donald D. Stull and Jean J. Schensul, 56–75. Boulder, CO: Westview Press.

Beebe, James
1995. "Basic Concepts and Techniques of Rapid Appraisal." *Human Organization* 54 (1):4–51.
2001. *Rapid Assessment Process: An Introduction*. Walnut Creek, CA: Altamira Press.

Bennett, John
1996. "Applied and Action Anthropology: Ideological and Conceptual Aspects." *Current Anthropology* 36:S23–S53.

Bernard, H. Russell (ed.)
1998. *Handbook of Methods in Cultural Anthropology*. Walnut Creek, CA: Altamira Press.

Bickman, Leonard, and Debra J. Rog (eds.)
1998. *Handbook of Applied Social Research Methods*. Thousand Oaks, CA: Sage Publications.

Bragg, Wayne G., and Eugene B. Schultz Jr.
1991. "Rootfuel: A New Strategic Approach to the Fuelwood Scarcity Problem in Third World Drylands." In *Urban and Rural Development in Third World Countries: Problems of Populations in Developing Nations*, edited by Valentine James, 106–111. Jefferson, NC: McFarland and Co.

Bryant, Carol A., and Doraine F. C. Bailey
1991. "The Use of Focus Group Research in Program Development." In *Soundings: Rapid and Reliable Research Methods for Practicing Anthropologists*, edited by John van Willigen and Timothy L. Finan, 4–39. Washington, DC: American Anthropological Association.

Casey, Margaret
1993. "Development in Madura: An Anthropological Approach." In *Practising Development: Social Science Perspectives*, edited by Johan Pottier, 110–137. London: Routledge.

Cernea, Michael (ed.)
1985. *Putting People First: Sociological Variables in Rural Development*. New York: Oxford University Press.

Chelimsky, Eleanor, and William R. Sadish (eds.)
1997. *Evaluation for the 1st Century: A Handbook*. Thousand Oaks, CA: Sage Publications.

Clatts, Michael C.
1991. *Order and Change in a Southeast Asian Community: An Ethnographic Perspective on Development Initiatives*. Ph.D. Dissertation, Department of Anthropology, SUNY/Stony Brook.

Cooper, Harris M., and James J. Lindsay
1998. "Research Synthesis and Meta-analysis." In *Handbook of Applied Social Research Methods*, edited by Leonard Bickman and Debra J. Rog, 315–337. Thousand Oaks, CA: Sage Publications.

Crewe, Emma, and Elizabeth Harrison
1998. *Whose Development? An Ethnography of Aid*. London: Zed Books.

Denzin, Norman K., and Yvonna S. Lincoln
2000. *Handbook of Qualitative Research* (2nd ed.) Thousand Oaks, CA: Sage Publications.

Dudley, Eric
1993. *The Critical Villager: Beyond Community Participation*. London: Routledge.

Erickson, Ken, and Donald Stull
1998. *Doing Team Ethnography: Warnings and Advice*. Thousand Oaks, CA: Sage Publications.

Ervin, Alexander M.
2000. *Applied Anthropology: Tools and Perspectives for Contemporary Practice*. Boston: Allyn and Bacon.

Ferguson, James
1997. "Anthropology and Its Evil Twin: 'Development' in the Constitution of a Discipline." In *International Development and the Social Sciences*, edited by Frederick Cooper and Randall Packard, 150–175. Berkeley: University of California Press.

Finan, Timothy J., and John van Willigen
2002. "The Pursuit of Social Knowledge: Methodology and the Practice of Anthropology." In *The Applied Anthropology Reader*, edited by James McDonald, 62–70. Boston: Allyn and Bacon.

Freire, Paolo
1970. *Pedagogy of the Oppressed*. New York: Seabury Press.

Garcia Ruiz, Carmen
2000. "Toolkit for Professional Anthropologists." *Anthropology News* 41 (3):44–45.

Gardner, Katy, and David Lewis
1996. *Anthropology, Development, and the Post-Modern Challenge*. London: Pluto Press.

Goldman, Laurence R.
2000. *Social Impact Analysis: An Applied Anthropology Manual*. Oxford, UK: Berg Publishers.

Greenwood, Davydd J., and Morten Levin
1998. *Introduction to Action Research: Social Research for Social Change*. Thousand Oaks, CA: Sage Publications.

Hackenberg, R. A., and B. H. Hackenberg
1999. "You CAN Do Something! Forming Policy from Applied Projects, Then and Now." *Human Organization* 58 (1):1–15.

Hamada, Tomoko
2000. "Anthropological Praxis: Theory of Business Organization. In *The Unity of Theory and Practice in Anthropology: Rebuilding a Fractured Synthesis* (NAPA Bulletin 18), edited by Carole E. Hill and Marietta L. Baba, 79–103. Washington, DC: NAPA.

Handwerker, W. Penn
2001. *Quick Ethnography*. Walnut Creek, CA: Altamira Press.

Johnson, Barbara Rose
1994. *Who Pays the Price?* Washington, DC: Island Press.

Keare, Douglas H.
2001. "Learning to Clap: Reflections on Top-Down vs. Bottom-Up Development." *Human Organization* 60 (2):159–165.

Kozaitis, Kathryn A.
2000. "The Rise of Anthropological Praxis." In *The Unity of Theory and Practice in Anthropology: Rebuilding a Fractured Synthesis* (NAPA Bulletin 18), edited by Carole E. Hill and Marietta L. Baba, 45–66. Washington, DC: NAPA.

Krueger, Richard A., and Mary Anne Casey
2000. *Focus Groups: A Practical Guide for Applied Research* (3rd ed.). Thousand Oaks, CA: Sage Publications.

Marsden, P. V.
1990. "Network Data and Measurement." *Annual Review of Sociology* 16:435–463.

McDonald, James H.
2002. *The Applied Anthropology Reader.* Boston: Allyn and Bacon.

McKillip, Jack
1998. "Needs Analysis: Process and Techniques." In *Handbook of Applied Social Research Methods*, edited by Leonard Bickman and Debra J. Rog, 61–84. Thousand Oaks, CA: Sage Publications.

Mitchell, J. Clyde
1984. "Social Network Data." In *Ethnographic Research: A Guide to General Conduct*, edited by Roy F. Ellen, 67–7. (ASA Research Methods in Social Anthropology, No. 1.) London: Academic Press.

Morgan, David L.
1997. *Focus Groups as Qualitative Research* (2nd ed.). Thousand Oaks, CA: Sage Publications.

Morgan, David L., and Richard A. Kreuger (eds.)
1997. *The Focus Group Kit* (Vols. 1–6). Thousand Oaks, CA: Sage Publications.

Mwangola, Margaret
1995. "Bringing Clean Water to Kenyan Households." In *Down to Earth: Community Perspectives on Health, Development and the Environment*, edited by Bonnie Bradford and Margaret A. Gwynne, 85–91. West Hartford, CT: Kumarian Press.

Needle, Richard H., S. L. Coyle, S. G. Genser, and R. T. Trotter
1995. "The Social Network Paradigm." In *Social Networks, Drug Abuse and HIV Transmission*, edited by R.H. Needle et al., 1–2 (NIDA Research Monograph 151). Rockville, MD: U.S. Department of Health and Human Services.

Patton, Michael Q.
1990. *Qualitative Evaluation and Research Methods.* Newbury Park, CA: Sage Publications.

Peacock, James L.
2000. "Theory and Practice by Anthropologists: A Case Study." In *The Unity of Theory and Practice in Anthropology: Rebuilding a Fractured Synthesis* (NAPA Bulletin 18), edited by Carole E. Hill and Marietta L. Baba, 104–118. Washington, DC: NAPA.

Perez, Carlos A.
1997. "Participatory Research: Implications for Applied Anthropology." *Practicing Anthropology* 19 (3): 2–7.

Pottier, Johan (ed.)
1993. *Practising Development: Social Science Perspectives.* London: Routledge.

Preister, Kevin
1987. "Issue-Centered Social Impact Assessment." In *Anthropological Praxis: Translating Knowledge into Action*, edited by Robert M. Wulff and Shirley J. Fiske, 39–55. Boulder, CO: Westview Press.

Rossi, Peter H., and Howard E. Freeman
1989. *Evaluation: A Systematic Approach* (4th ed.). Newbury Park, CA: Sage Publications.

Ryan, Joan, and Michael Robinson
1996. "Community Participatory Research: Two Views From Arctic Institute Practitioners." *Practicing Anthropology* 18 (4):7–12.

Scott, John
2000. *Social Network Analysis: A Handbook* (2nd ed.). Thousand Oaks, CA: Sage Publications.

Schensul, Jean J., and Margaret D. LeCompte (eds.)
1999. *Ethnographers Toolkit.* Walnut Creek, CA: Altamira Press.

Scrimshaw, N.S., and G.R. Gleason (eds.)
1992. *Rapid Assessment Procedures: Qualitative Methodologies for Planning and Evaluation of Health-Related Programs.* Boston: International Nutrition Foundation for Developing Countries.

Shore, Chris, and Susan Wright (eds.)
1997. *Anthropology of Policy: Critical Perspectives on Governance and Power.* London: Routledge.

Singer, Merrill
2002. "Toward the Use of Ethnography in Health Care Program Evaluation." In *The Applied Anthropology Reader*, edited by James H. McDonald, 88–104. Boston: Allyn and Bacon.

Smillie, Ian
1991. *Mastering the Machine: Poverty, Aid and Technology.* Boulder, CO: Westview Press.

Stewart, David W., and Prem N. Shamdasani
1998. "Focus Group Research: Exploration and Discovery." In *Handbook of Applied Social Research Methods*, edited by Leonard Bickman and Debra J. Rog, 505–556. Thousand Oaks, CA: Sage Publications.

Tax, Sol
1958. "The Fox Project." *Human Organization* 17: 17–19.

Trisolini, Michael, S. Russell, M. Gwynne, and D. Zschock
1992. "Methods for Cost Analysis, Cost Recovery, and Cost Control for a Public Hospital in a Developing Country: Victoria Hospital, St. Lucia." *International Journal of Health Planning and Management* 7:103–113.

Trotter, Robert T., and Jean J. Schensul
1998. "Methods in Applied Anthropology." In *Handbook of Methods in Cultural Anthropology,* edited by H. Russell Bernard, 691–735. Walnut Creek, CA: Altamira Press.

Uphoff, Norman
1985. "Fitting Projects to People." In *Putting People First,* edited by Michael M. Cernea, 359–395. New York: Oxford University Press.

van Willigen, John
1993. *Applied Anthropology: An Introduction* (rev. ed.). Westport, CT: Bergin and Garvey.

Wilson, Ruth P.
1998. "The Role of Anthropologists as Short-Term Consultants." *Human Organization* 57:245–252.

Whyte, William F. (ed.)
1991. *Participatory Action Research.* Newbury Park, CA: Sage Publications.

Wolf, C. P.
1983. "A Methodological Overview." In *Social Impact Assessment Methods,* edited by Kurt Finsterbusch, L.G. Llewellyn, and C. P. Wolf, 15–35. Beverly Hills, CA: Sage Publications.

Zschock, Dieter K., M. A. Gwynne, B. Wint, and J. C. Robayo
1991. *Comparative Health Care Financing in St. Lucia, Grenada, and Dominica.* Needham Heights, MA: Ginn Press.

CHAPTER 3

THE HISTORY OF APPLIED CULTURAL ANTHROPOLOGY

INTRODUCTION

In a sense, applied cultural anthropology has always existed. It has not, of course, always been recognized by that name, but it appears that human beings have been universally and perpetually interested both in learning about the customs and cultures of people in societies other than their own, and in putting what they learn about "others" to some practical use—sometimes for purposes of beneficial social change, often not. History is replete with examples of adventurers, missionaries, merchants, and soldiers who traveled to exotic locations, lived among and observed the peoples they encountered, collected information about them, and used this information to achieve specific economic, political, or religious goals. Many of these examples distantly predate both the establishment of anthropology as an academic discipline and the emergence of applied cultural anthropology as a career field (Adams 1998).

The Greek historian Herodotus (*ca.* 485–425 B.C.E.) explored the lands bordering the Mediterranean Sea in the fifth century B.C.E., collecting information about the peoples and cultures he encountered. He offered this information to his government to help guide its political relationships with foreign countries, which may qualify him for the title of the world's first applied anthropologist, or at least its first literate one. The armies of Alexander the Great, Roman legionnaires, Arabian traders, Norse explorers, and European crusaders followed in his wake. However, the idea of accumulating useful data about "the other" was not pursued in any systematic way until the Renaissance, when European scholars began to compile interesting facts about the "queer customs of savage peoples" as a part of what has been referred to as their "collecting mania" (Adams 1998:195).

Through the next several hundred years, the collection of ethnographic data, for reasons of either curiosity or practical application, became increasingly commonplace, although no one seems to have had the idea of doing ethnographic research for applied purposes "at home," among familiar people. In the sixteenth and seventeenth centuries, *conquistadores* and explorers such as Amerigo Vespucci, Hernán Cortés, Samuel de Champlain, and Louis Joliet produced useful written accounts of their discoveries. In the eighteenth century, Captain James Cook explored the South Pacific, and Father Lafitau, a Jesuit priest who lived with the Mohawk of New York State primarily to convert them to Christianity, used ethnographic data to develop a commercial trade in ginseng, a local herb with medicinal properties. The first person recruited specifically to collect ethnographic data may have been an early-nineteenth-century French scholar, François Peron, who accompanied French explorers on an 1802 voyage to America (Adams 1998:58).

Today, most of these individuals—and the many others who lived among and studied people in unfamiliar cultures centuries ago, putting what they learned to use—are mere footnotes in anthropological history. Yet their travels, ethnographic interests, artifact collections, intercultural experiences, and practical achievements, whether inspired by political, economic, missionary, or military intent, can be viewed as mileposts along the way toward the eventual development of applied cultural anthropology.

This chapter examines historical events and processes, both within the discipline of cultural anthropology and outside it, that permitted and encouraged the birth and growth of today's applied cultural anthropology. Like that of its parent discipline, applied cultural anthropology's history is a story of "discomfiture, of turning away and then back again" (Des Chene 1997:55). Some of the "discomfiture" persists to this day. Many contemporary anthropologists see the events and processes described in this chapter as having ultimately resulted in the emergence of a new, distinct, officially sanctioned dimension of academic anthropology, well qualified to take its place alongside cultural anthropology, archaeology, biological anthropology, and anthropological linguistics as the fifth member of the family of anthropological subdisciplines (see "The 'Fifth Field' Debate," Chapter 1). For others, however, the jury is still out.

DEVELOPMENTAL PERIODS

The history of applied cultural anthropology can be divided into six developmental periods (Table 3.1). Anthropological and non-anthropological developments in each of these periods contributed to the establishment of applied cultural anthropology as it is understood and practiced today. Although there is nothing official about these

◇ **TABLE 3.1   Developmental Periods in Applied Cultural Anthropology**

Period	Milestones
1. The nineteenth and early twentieth centuries	European political envoys, merchants, and missionaries, following earlier travelers, collect ethnographic data about "others." Academic anthropology programs and professional organizations are established. North American ethnographers study American Indians for purposes of administration, trade, or religious conversion. A few academic anthropologists, including Franz Boas, undertake part-time applied work.
2. The Great Depression: 1930–1940	Jobs for U.S. anthropologists are created under the New Deal. U.S. anthropologists research Native American cultures, industrial management issues, land use, community development, and nutrition. European anthropologists continue to contribute to colonial administration. Cultural anthropology's focus widens to include contemporary societies.
3. World War II: 1940–1945	U.S. anthropologists support and contribute heavily to war effort. Society for Applied Anthropology founded (1941).
4. Midcentury: 1945–1960	Following World War II, academic anthropology expands greatly as many anthropologists leave government service for academe. Foreign assistance to western European and (later) other countries presages development anthropology. Applied anthropology's first code of ethics written (1949). Cold War and McCarthyism spur applied work of a few anthropologists, but overall, applied anthropology wanes.
5. The 1960s	Anthropologists criticize U.S. involvement in Vietnam War and avoid government service. Project Camelot canceled amid criticism by social scientists. Establishment of USAID and Peace Corps helps to cast idea of foreign assistance in a positive light. AAA drafts first ethics statement to guide anthropologists' involvement in government and business (1967).
6. Modern times: 1970 to the present	As college enrollments decline, applied anthropology revives. New federal legislation mandates anthropological involvement in historical, environmental, and social arenas. NAPA created (1983). Number and percentage of applied anthropologists both reach new highs.

time periods, they do provide one framework for understanding how applied cultural anthropology was born, evolved, and finally emerged as an important component of twenty-first-century anthropology.[1]

Beginnings

The Nineteenth and Early Twentieth Centuries.   The desire to collect useful information about non-Western peoples and cultures took on a new immediacy as the age of exploration gave way to the colonial period, and by the middle of the nineteenth century, European political leaders, merchants, and missionaries had become dependent on reliable ethnographic information for purposes of religious conversion, mercantilism, or colonial administration. Thus, for example, the Scottish physician and missionary David Livingstone was dispatched to central and southern Africa in the mid–nineteenth century to collect geographic and ethnographic data and to preach the Christian gospel. The government of the Netherlands sent trained ethnographers to its vast colony in Indonesia in 1905, with both governance and profit in mind. Britain and Belgium soon followed suit, dispatching ethnographers to South Africa, the Anglo-Egyptian Sudan, and the Belgian Congo for the same purposes. The results of their work were sometimes enlightened, sometimes not.

Perhaps not entirely coincidentally, in this context of administrative, economic, ecclesiastical, and intellectual interest in "the other," mid-nineteenth-century scholars such as Lewis Henry Morgan in the United States and E. B. Tylor in Britain were laying the groundwork for the academic discipline of anthropology. The first departments of anthropology were established at European universities; American universities soon followed suit. Shortly afterwards, in both parts of the world, the first professional anthropological membership associations were founded. In Britain, the Royal Anthropological Society of Great Britain and Ireland, precursor of today's Royal Anthropological Institute, was established in 1869. The American Anthropological Association (AAA), today the largest and most important group of anthropologists in the Americas, was created in 1902 to represent and encourage the interests of anthropologists in all four of the new discipline's fields.

Some of the members of these new organizations were doing practical, goal-oriented research (which today would be termed applied research), and there was explicit recognition on the part of early scholars, such as W. H. R. Rivers (a medical doctor who accompanied anthropologist A. C. Haddon on an anthropological expedition to the Torres Straits) and Bronislaw Malinowski (an anthropologist who undertook protracted fieldwork in the Trobriand Islands), that anthropological ideas could be of use to colonial governments (see Stocking 1992, especially Chapter 6). At the time, however, neither the Royal Anthropological Society nor the AAA viewed applied anthropology as constituting a separate field of the discipline.

"Indianology."   The beginnings of applied cultural anthropology in America differed somewhat from the European pattern. In Europe, nineteenth- and early-twentieth-century anthropologists were obliged to travel to exotic locales to pursue their work as independent data-collectors or employees of colonial governments. North American cultural anthropologists, however, had no need to leave home, since North America still contained numerous groups of indigenous peoples.

Thus, in America, the nineteenth century saw the birth of **"Indianology"** (see Adams 1998, Chapter 5) and the creation of a number of American administrative agencies and ethnological societies, the various goals of which included governing, containing, converting, employing, absorbing, or assisting Native Americans, engaging them in trade, or studying them for what they could contribute to scholarship. In the United States, Congress created the Bureau of Indian Affairs (BIA) in 1824, and the Bureau of American Ethnology (BAE, administratively a part of the Smithsonian Institution) in 1879. Both organizations hired individuals to research Native American cultures for purposes not only of gathering information but also of establishing administrative policies. These fieldworkers were precursors of today's American applied cultural anthropologists (Adams 1998:249).

FOOD FOR THOUGHT

Given that a few colonies still remain in the world (for example, several of the Eastern Caribbean islands), how do you feel about colonial governments (for example, the government of France) hiring applied cultural anthropologists to study and interpret the cultures and customs of people living in their colonies, for purposes of more efficient colonial administration? Would you feel differently if you were a resident of one of these colonies? Why or why not?

A notable example of the work of these early applied cultural anthropologists was the investigation of the "Ghost Dance" of the Plains Indians, carried out with the support of the BAE by anthropologist James Mooney in 1895. A few years prior to Mooney's study, in 1889, in the context of concerted Native American resistance to government policies, the leader of a Plains millennial cult had convinced his followers that their repeated performance of a ritual called the Ghost Dance would result in the overthrow of the Native Americans' oppressors and the restoration of their dead ancestors to life. Just a year later, in 1890, the infamous massacre at Wounded Knee on South Dakota's Pine Ridge Reservation effectively brought an end to the Native Americans' anti-government resistance. Nevertheless, the Native Americans continued to perform the emotionally charged Ghost Dance—much to the consternation of the government, which was worried that the ritual might encourage another uprising. Mooney, in a now-famous example of late-nineteenth-century American applied cultural anthropology, was charged with advising the U.S. Department of War how best to defuse this possibility (Mooney 1896).

A good example of an "Indianologist" par excellence was Frank Hamilton Cushing, one of the early anthropologists employed by the Bureau of American Ethnology to collect information and artifacts from Native American groups. Without formal training in anthropology, a subject not yet taught in American universities, Cushing was dispatched by the BAE in 1879 to collect ethnographic data among the Zuni of the southwestern United States. Hardly an invited guest, Cushing nevertheless found acceptance among the Zuni, immersing himself completely in Zuni life and living among these Native American people for years. Not only did he observe the customs of the Zuni and diligently record great quantities of information about them, but eventually he also came to participate in their daily lives as an

◇ *Nineteenth-century applied cultural anthropologist Frank Hamilton Cushing (1857–1900), at right in Zuni dress, became so thoroughly immersed in studying the Zuni that he became an accepted member of their society.*

accepted member of their society. The ethnographic information that Cushing (and others like him) collected was admirable from a scholarly point of view, yet there is no doubt that some of this information was later used by the U.S. government to inform federal policies that resulted in the disenfranchisement and segregation of Native Americans.

Cushing was typical of a number of early anthropologists who were motivated primarily by curiosity about other cultures, but who were willing at the same time to collect anthropological data for government or industry, for reasons—it would later develop—of political control or economic exploitation. It is ironic that the results of Cushing's research were, in a broad sense, detrimental to the very people to whom he devoted such affection and so much of his anthropological career.

Boas and Other Academic Part-Timers.   The practical application of anthropological interest continued into the twentieth century. In the 1920s, for example, one of the most important figures in academic anthropology, Columbia University professor Franz Boas, was also a part-time applied anthropologist. Best known for his historical particularist viewpoint, his determined efforts to salvage cultural data, and his firm anti-racist convictions, Boas applied his skill in anthropometry (the study and comparison of measurements of the human body) for the purpose of disproving the theory that new immigrants into the United States had smaller brains than earlier settlers did and would thus eventually weaken the American gene pool.

Despite considerable practical interest in ethnographic research in the nineteenth and early twentieth centuries, however, the idea that academically trained anthropologists could develop full-time, extra-academic careers by using anthropological ideas and methods to promote directed social change was still not widespread. Most "applied anthropologists" were academics, like Boas, who engaged in applied work only part-time, and their work was much more apt to be related to policy formulation and administrative problems than to social welfare efforts or private economic interests (two areas that involve many of today's applied cultural anthropologists). Applied anthropology would have to wait until the 1930s, many years after the mid-nineteenth-century birth of anthropology as a recognized academic discipline, to discover more specific applications in areas such as education, nutrition, agricultural development, and economic development.

The Great Depression: 1930–1940

In the United States, the event most responsible for promoting the growth and specialization of applied cultural anthropology (if there was a single event, as opposed to a historical process such as the development of "Indianology") was the stock market crash of 1929. Within two years of that historic October day, more than one quarter of all Americans of working age were unemployed, and the Great Depression was in full swing. The result, from the point of view of cultural anthropology, was to "put poverty and social issues on the anthropological map" (Gupta and Ferguson 1997:22).

The New Deal.   To stem the downward economic spiral, President Franklin D. Roosevelt commissioned an array of innovative federal programs and agencies collectively known as the "New Deal" (1933–1938), one of the major goals of which was the creation of jobs—including jobs for anthropologists. Under various New Deal programs and projects, numerous cultural anthropologists were employed, for the first time, outside of colleges and universities on a full-time basis. Some went to work in the public sector, to address domestic social problems; others found jobs in the private sector, encouraged by Roosevelt's belief that efficient, cost-effective private enterprise could stimulate much-needed social and economic reform.

One of the areas for which anthropological training was especially appropriate was the treatment of Native Americans, many of whom by now lived impoverished, demoralized lives on reservations established and overseen by the government. Thus, in 1932, President Roosevelt appointed anthropologist John Collier as Commissioner of Indian Affairs and head of the Bureau of Indian Affairs. Collier was well known for his appreciation of Native American culture and tradition (Adams 1998:236). He hired a number of other anthropologists, including well-known scholars such as Julian Steward and Clyde Kluckhohn, to research Native American cultures and to advise the BIA on enlightened Indian policy. Although later criticized for paternalism, Collier was ultimately instrumental in winning the reversal of government policies, established previously, that restricted Native Americans' rights and cultural expression, and in establishing a health care system for Native Americans.

Collier's efforts, as well as those of other applied anthropologists hired by the BIA, resulted in the passage, in 1934, of the Indian Reorganization Act (Stocking 1992:163; van Willigen 1993:23). The purpose of this legislation was to protect and benefit Native Americans. Under its provisions, they were empowered to form tribal governments, take out inexpensive government loans, start businesses, and regain land that had earlier been seized from them. The Indian Reorganization Act represented "the first intensive application of modern cultural anthropological concepts and methods to the problems of governmental administration" (Eddy and Partridge 1987:25). At the same time, other anthropologists were working in other branches of the government, such as the Department of Agriculture, helping to solve Depression-related problems in the areas of industrial management, land use, community planning and administration, and nutrition (see van Willigen 1993:24).

Anthropology and the Private Sector.   The business world was slower to make use of cultural anthropology's nonacademic potential. Compared with the number of cultural anthropologists working for some branch of government during the years of the Great Depression, only a few were employed in the private sector. However, a number of academic anthropologists were becoming increasingly interested in the structure, work environment, and management of industrial organizations. Most of them studied the effects of the workplace environment on the productivity of office and factory workers—a connection that seems quite obvious today.

One of the earliest of these few studies was later to be viewed as an important ground-breaker. In 1932, the Western Electric Company entered into collaboration with several academic researchers in a study of worker productivity at one of its plants, the Hawthorne Works in Chicago (Baba 1986:4). When the study began to yield interesting and unexpected results, a cultural anthropologist, W. Lloyd Warner, was called in. Together, Warner and the other researchers not only showed that workers in their places of work could be analyzed according to anthropological principles, but also made some important discoveries about the conditions that stimulate worker output. The project, which lasted for several years, represented the birth of "industrial anthropology" (see Chapter 9) as a subfield of applied cultural anthropology (Baba 1986:5).

Warner and several other anthropologists then expanded their interest in the anthropology of modern social and work environments to the study of community relations. In a New England town dubbed "Yankee City," they analyzed class structure and social networks as reflected in business organizations and voluntary associations (Warner and Lunt 1941). Thanks to Warner and other cultural anthropologists who followed in his footsteps (among them Conrad Arensberg, Ralph Linton, and Margaret Mead), anthropology's focus was greatly widened to include modern industrial societies and their problems. This important research established a theoretical and methodological ground floor for subsequent work in applied cultural anthropology.

European Colonial Interests.   In Europe, meanwhile, a number of cultural anthropologists continued to be employed outside academia. Most Western European countries still had overseas colonies, and almost all European cultural anthropologists doing applied research still worked for national governments, helping

them to administer their colonies, rather than for businesses. Perhaps the most fa-
mous of the government-sponsored ethnographers of the 1930s was Sir E. E. Evans-
Pritchard, who studied the Nuer, cattle pastoralists of East Africa, at the behest of the
British government.

As in the United States, some of the applied cultural anthropologists who
worked for European governments (including Evans-Pritchard) were criticized,
both at the time and later, for being self-interested, paternalistic, nonscientific, biased in favor of their own countries and cultures, or mere tools of colonial
regimes—or all of these. Indeed, it has been suggested that European cultural anthropology, during this period, existed essentially as the handmaiden of colonialism,
an allegation that can be disputed on two points. First, European anthropologists
had sought ethnographic data long before the colonial era. Second, the ethnographers involved were often critical of colonial administrations (Adams 1998:365).

FOOD FOR THOUGHT Today's soldiers, sailors, and airmen are government employees whose
jobs involve activities for which they are sometimes criticized because they
may harm others. In the past, some applied cultural anthropologists, also
government employees, were similarly criticized for what were perceived
to be harmful activities. Is there a moral distinction between the two kinds
of jobs? Would you be comfortable in a job requiring you to supply information about "others" to your government? Why or why not?

It is important to point out that these European anthropologists were doing
applied cultural anthropology for what they surely perceived at the time to be all the
right reasons—most notably, to ensure the effective, efficient, and compassionate
administration, by colonial regimes, of indigenous peoples. Evans-Pritchard's primary loyalty, for example, lay genuinely and resolutely with the Nuer. But colonial
governments hardly needed any philosophical justification based on humane
ethnographic work (Adams 1998:365). Their policies were explicitly predicated on
self-interest and notions of Manifest Destiny.

World War II: 1940–1945

Cultural anthropologists' interests in business organizations and their efforts on behalf of national governments in the 1930s paved the way for a tremendous increase in
applied cultural anthropology during World War II, especially in the United States.
With the country at war with both Germany and Japan, understanding the cultures—
and hence the motivations—of the political leaders and citizens of these countries, as
well as allied countries, became crucially important to the U.S. government. Institutes
of regional studies were established at a number of universities for the express purpose of examining and understanding the cultures and lifeways of foreign peoples.
Diplomats, politicians, and representatives of the military attended these institutes
to learn more about the areas of the world in which they were politically interested or
to which they might be posted. Meanwhile, industrial anthropologists turned their

interest and expertise in worker productivity toward helping to increase efficiency and output in war-related industries.

American anthropology was united in supporting U.S. participation in the war (Stocking 1992:165). In 1941, the American Anthropological Association formally endorsed the participation of its members in the war effort, and an astonishing proportion of American anthropologists, including leading lights such as Margaret Mead, Ruth Benedict, Julian Steward, Clyde Kluckhohn, Fred Eggan, and Ralph Linton, became involved (Stocking 1992:165–166). According to one estimate, of the 303 professional anthropologists in the United States at the time, no fewer than 295 became either part- or full-time applied anthropologists by contributing in some way toward winning the war (Mead 1977:149).

Despite this unity and heavy involvement, the AAA did not as yet recognize applied anthropology as a separate, official branch of the discipline. A number of individual "practicing" anthropologists, however, realized the long-term value of using anthropological ideas and methods to help solve practical problems. In the same year as the AAA endorsement of the war effort, a group of practitioners—among them Margaret Mead and Ruth Benedict—established the Society for Applied Anthropology (SfAA) at Harvard University (see Chapter 1), in order to establish a professional network, share information and experiences, and draw recognition to their applied work. The SfAA has since become the largest of the anthropological practitioner organizations, and its major publication, *Human Organization,* is widely recognized as the premier journal in the field. At the time of its establishment in 1941, however, the membership of the SfAA was small and reflected only a modest proportion of the applied work being done. The earliest SfAA members typically split their time between academic and applied cultural anthropology.

A number of these newly part-time academic anthropologists, including Mead and Benedict, were hired by the federal government to research the cultures of various countries for the Office of Strategic Services (OSS, the precursor of the Central Intelligence Agency) or the Bureau of Overseas Intelligence of the government's Office of War Information (OWI). Their main assignment was to provide information to support effective military planning. Some of them, including Mead, also served on a government committee to research the problem of maintaining American morale during the war (Mead 1979). Others served as translators of foreign language documents or facilitated the U.S. military occupation of Pacific islands wrested from Japanese control during the war.

A few anthropologists, including Ruth Benedict, undertook "national character studies," which sought to shed light on the motivations behind the group behavior of enemies and allies alike, through understanding the role of culture in the development of personality. The results of these studies were decidedly mixed. For example, thanks to Benedict's understanding of his symbolic importance to the Japanese people, the emperor of Japan was permitted to remain on the throne after the war to facilitate the postwar reconstruction of his country. At the same time, the national character of the Japanese was mistakenly attributed, at least in part, to early toilet training practices.

Some of the anthropologists who participated in the war effort would later be criticized, both from within and outside the discipline. An example is those anthro-

 During World War II, famed American anthropologist Margaret Mead (1901–1978) contributed significantly to the war effort, and helped to establish the Society for Applied Anthropology. Mead is pictured here in 1942.

pologists who helped to organize and administer "war relocation centers," internment camps in which some 110,000 Japanese Americans were detained for the duration of the war. This episode is now widely viewed as an ignominious one in American history. However, it should be noted in fairness to the applied anthropologists involved that they were successful in improving living conditions for the incarcerated Japanese Americans and believed they were helping to prevent even greater wrongs. And at the time, the anthropological community was in general agreement that government service on the part of anthropologists was both ethical and appropriate under the circumstances (see Moos 1995:34).

FOOD FOR THOUGHT Both the American public in general and anthropologists in particular were fervent supporters of their government during World War II. During the Vietnam War, however—especially in its later years—there was widespread criticism of U.S. involvement from both the general public and from anthropologists. What historical, intellectual, or other factors might have been responsible for this dramatic difference? If you had been an anthropology student during the Vietnam War years, would your study of anthropology have influenced your opinion of the war? How?

Midcentury: 1945–1960

The Resurgence of Academic Anthropology.
With the end of World War II, applied cultural anthropologists pulled back from government service, although not from their involvement in the private sector. Most cultural anthropologists who had been involved in war-related work for the government returned to their academic institutions. A few, including well-known scholars such as Homer Barnett

and Ward Goodenough, continued to work for the federal government, mostly in connection with the U.S. occupation of Japan or the administration of the Pacific islands collectively called the U.S. Trust Territories. Others continued to do important applied work in the private sector. However, the number of available nonacademic jobs, especially in government service, had dwindled. In general, "[d]uring the crisis of World War II, vital links between anthropological research and policy applications existed, but as the crisis subsided, the linkage was broken" (Eddy and Partridge 1987:45). In the years immediately following the war, the United States made a number of important foreign policy decisions and commitments, both in the Pacific and in war-torn European countries, but cultural anthropologists did not play a major role in these decisions. Once again, anthropology's "center of gravity" was academe (Stocking 1992:167).

What had happened to bring about such a dramatic change in applied cultural anthropologists' employment opportunities, especially in the public sector, in such a short time? One factor was undoubtedly the pointed criticism, from within the discipline, of some of the applied anthropological work done during the war (such as the internment of Japanese Americans) and immediately afterwards (such as the administration of the Pacific Trust Territories) (Willis 1974). More broadly, an attitudinal shift was occurring in American society as a whole. By the time the Korean War began in 1950, the single-minded patriotic vision that had sustained Americans through World War II was disintegrating, and "some Americans—including anthropologists—now decided that not only was warfare dubious, but in any war or conflict the side chosen by the United States was unethical, if not outright evil" (Moos 1995:34). This view exacerbated the skepticism of some within the anthropological community about government efforts to study and understand foreign peoples, and also about the morality of past anthropological involvement in these efforts. Academic anthropology in the immediate postwar years became "either ambivalent or antagonistic" toward applied efforts in support of government (Chambers 1989:90).

A second important reason for the overall decline in the number of applied cultural anthropologists after World War II was that thousands of veterans who had postponed or interrupted their higher education in order to participate in the war effort were now returning to school, paying their tuition with advantageous government loans under the Servicemen's Readjustment Act of 1944 (the "GI bill"). This rush to enroll or reenroll filled college and university classes—including anthropology classes—to capacity in the immediate postwar years. As the demand for professors of anthropology increased, new academic positions were created. Anthropologists whose jobs in government agencies had evaporated had little trouble finding positions on college and university campuses. Given the healthy job market, these teachers naturally trained their students for academic rather than applied work.

The Birth of "Development Anthropology."   But even as many former applied anthropologists were returning to their academic posts, the seeds of a fertile employment field for future applied cultural anthropologists—"development anthropology"—were being sown (see Chapter 5; see also Gardner and Lewis 1996:6ff.). The proximate cause was the devastation the war had wrought in Europe.

In many European countries, the infrastructure—roads, bridges, hospitals, schools—had been damaged or completely destroyed during the war. Moreover, postwar agricultural output and industrial production were falling far short of demand. Many Europeans were literally starving.

In 1944, the United Nations had established a global lending institution, the International Bank for Reconstruction and Development (IBRD), creating a future need for anthropological expertise in choosing the countries and development projects this agency would support, and in carrying out its projects. In 1946, with the war now over and Europe in a state of crisis, the United States instituted its own financial assistance program, the European Recovery Plan (ERP). More commonly termed the Marshall Plan (after the then U.S. secretary of state, George C. Marshall), the plan was established not only to assist war-torn European nations, but also to advance U.S. foreign policy interests. (The European recipients of U.S. assistance under the Marshall Plan would later become donor nations themselves, for the same reasons.)

The U.S. government recognized that helping Europe to rebuild would serve America well in the long run. For example, European countries might someday provide a lucrative market for American-made goods. Additionally, the United States was anxious to prevent western European countries, under political pressure from the USSR, from becoming socialist or Communist. But in addition to these considerations, the Marshall Plan reflected a genuinely humanitarian impetus. Many Americans felt the United States had a moral obligation to aid its suffering European cousins. In distributing some $13 billion under the Marshall Plan, much of it in the form of cash, food, buildings, and equipment, to European countries (mainly Britain, France, Italy, and West Germany), the United States was establishing a precedent that would later have important ramifications for applied cultural anthropological work in foreign countries.

FOOD FOR THOUGHT In your opinion, is it acceptable for a national government to extend much-needed foreign aid for political as well as humanitarian purposes? What about for political purposes only? Explain your answer.

Development assistance was so successful in the immediate postwar period that a few years later, in 1949, the United Nations extended the idea to other areas of the world, establishing the Expanded Program of Technical Assistance for Economic Development of Under-Developed Countries. Soon the IBRD was loaning millions of dollars for development projects that were intended to raise living standards in sixteen non-industrialized countries. A few applied cultural anthropologists participated in implementing these projects, and the industry they helped create has employed many thousands of cultural anthropologists ever since.

Responding to the idea of anthropological involvement in foreign aid and—by extension—foreign policy issues, the Society for Applied Anthropology, which had been founded in 1941, began to debate the ethical considerations involved. At particular issue was whether American foreign policy, which had seemed so altruistic and magnanimous in the immediate postwar years, was really "directed more toward a kind of economic imperialism than to promoting the interests of other peoples" (Chambers 1985:56). These discussions led directly to the establishment of applied anthropology's first code of ethics (Mead, Chapple, and Brown 1949). Initially drawn up in 1949, the SfAA code, now entitled "Professional and Ethical Responsibilities," has since been revised twice, in 1963 and again in 1983 (see Chapter 4).

The Cold War Era.   In the United States, based largely on the success of the Marshall Plan in achieving its economic and political objectives and on the precedent set by the IBRD, Congress decided that foreign aid should be extended to include the developing world as well as Europe. It thus created the Technical Cooperation Administration (TCA) in 1950 to administer a program labeled Point Four (so called because a description of this proposed new program was the fourth point made by President Truman in his inaugural address in 1949). The program was ostensibly devoted to fostering economic and social development in what by then had come to be called the Third World,[2] much of it in the areas of agricultural development, education, and health. Its objectives, however, were guided by the politics of the "Cold War," the post–World War II ideological struggle between the Americans and the Soviets.

To some extent, the Cold War spurred anthropological involvement in economic and human development efforts. Cultural anthropologists had been providing data and policy recommendations to various governments for a century or more, but the complexities of international relations in the late 1940s and throughout the 1950s meant that anthropological insights were in ever greater demand. The U.S. Department of State, the military, and the Central Intelligence Agency (CIA) all employed social scientists, including applied cultural anthropologists. Think tanks and university-based policy research centers also hired cultural anthropologists as consultants (Sharpless 1997:184).[3] As the 1950s progressed, individuals, charitable organizations, and finally nations warmed increasingly to the idea of foreign assistance for humanitarian as well as political purposes. While relatively few cultural anthropologists were involved at first, a future niche for applied cultural anthropologists in the foreign policy and international development arenas was gradually being carved out.

One anthropologist involved in development work during this time was Allan Holmberg, a professor of anthropology at Cornell University. In the firm belief that anthropological ideas and methods could help promote much-needed economic and social development among impoverished Third World peoples, Holmberg embarked on a major study of community change on a worldwide scale. In 1952, as part of this project, Holmberg (together with colleagues from Cornell and local institutions and the government of Peru) instituted the now-famous Cornell Peru project, more commonly termed the Vicos project (Holmberg 1958).

Vicos was a hacienda, a huge farm worked by peasant laborers, located in a valley of the Andes mountains in Peru. Like many other Latin American haciendas, it was owned by wealthy absentee landlords; the actual tillers of the land were renters who paid their landlords three days of work each week in exchange for a house, a small garden plot, and some domestic animals. This tenant farming arrangement was an unhappy one for the 1,700 peasants of Vicos. Their gardens were small, their crops frequently failed, their nutrition and health were poor, their formal education was almost nonexistent, and they were constantly in debt to their landlords.

Holmberg and his colleagues developed a five-year project whose short-term goal was to raise the peasants' standard of living by introducing specific technical and social changes (Mangin 1979:65; see also Doughty 1987). Eventually, they hoped, the peasants' health, education, and economic decision-making abilities would improve, their self-esteem and community spirit would increase, and they would gradually assume control of the hacienda. Holmberg called his strategy for achieving this ambitious goal "participant intervention." He would not simply live among and observe the peasants while overseeing the project, but would actively intervene in their lives to help bring about both economic and social improvements.

Under the Vicos project, the hacienda's tenant farmers were given needed income-producing items (for example, high-yield seeds) and taught new skills (for example, how to operate sewing machines). Education and cooperative credit programs were established; a model garden was created; and community discussions, in which the peasants learned to seek cooperative solutions to common problems, were held. The community prospered, and a few years later the tenant farmers—better fed, better housed, and far better educated than they had been under the old system—purchased the hacienda from its absentee owners (Mangin 1979:66).

The Vicos project was clearly a remarkable exception rather than a typical applied anthropological project of its time, and it was criticized on this and other grounds. In general, American anthropology was not in favor of intervention in foreign countries, and this feeling continued throughout the 1950s. But the importance of the Vicos project to the future of applied cultural anthropology would be hard to overestimate. It was the first major economic development project in which

⬦ *In the 1950s, applied cultural anthropologists contributed to the Vicos Project, a social change effort aimed at helping to improve the lives of Peruvian sharecroppers (see here cultivating corn). Eventually these tenant farmers were able to purchase the Vicos farm from its absentee landlords.*

the principles of cultural anthropology were successfully employed to improve the lifestyle, sense of self-worth, and rights of impoverished peasants (Doughty 1987: 458–459). In a more general way, the project demonstrated that—at least in certain circumstances—cultural anthropology (together, as Mangin [1979:82] and others pointed out, with initiative, energy, and enthusiasm on the part of the intended beneficiaries) could provide the ideas and methods required to make significant contributions toward the resolution of apparently intractable economic and social development problems.

In the domestic sphere, McCarthyism provided an impetus to nonacademic employment, as cultural anthropologists who had been "blacklisted" forged research opportunities in other arenas, such as businesses, communities, the educational system, and the family. As they pursued their studies of various aspects of American culture, Jules Henry, Margaret Mead, Hortense Powdermaker, Lloyd Warner, and others faced challenges from within the discipline over whether or not what they were doing was really anthropology (Wolcott 1999:35). However, like their counterparts in international work, they helped set the stage for several of the applied subdisciplines described later in this book.

In addition, a few applied anthropologists continued to work with Native Americans. Notable among them was Sol Tax, who encouraged the Fox to identify their own problems and to participate in every aspect of solving them. Action anthropology, his term for this indigenous involvement (later to be termed "participatory action research"), was a major contribution to development anthropology (see Chapter 2).

While the Cold War stimulated applied work among some cultural anthropologists, it simultaneously encouraged an academic focus on the part of the majority. Thanks in large part to the ideological contest between "superpowers," the 1950s witnessed a veritable explosion of technical developments in both the physical and social sciences. The United States found itself in a space race with the Soviet Union, which in 1957 launched the first space satellite, *Sputnik,* to the amazement of the world and to the chagrin of American scientists. In part due to the threatening military implications of the Soviet Union's new technological expertise and in part due to national pride, the United States poured financial and human resources into scientific endeavors. Perhaps the most notable of these was aerospace research, but the renewed national emphasis on scientific advancement spilled over into the social sciences, including anthropology. With research funding plentiful, academic cultural anthropologists tackled difficult theoretical problems and created new anthropological specialties, such as cultural evolutionary studies and legal anthropology. The consequences for applied cultural anthropology were predictable; overall, interest in the practical application of the theories and methods of cultural anthropology waned.

The 1960s: Rethinking Applied Anthropology

A relatively small number of anthropologists continued to do applied work in international contexts into the 1960s,[4] but the post–World War II skepticism on the part of many academic anthropologists toward anthropological involvement in foreign affairs continued. Critics, wary of anything that smacked of social engineering, felt that the role of the anthropologist should be restricted to research, specifically excluding involvement in decision making or serving as "change agents" (Chambers 1989:89). This skepticism was exacerbated by U.S. interests in the political affairs of South Vietnam—interests that would soon lead to America's entanglement in another prolonged and bloody war. By the time the United States entered the Vietnam War militarily in 1964, with the passage by Congress of the Gulf of Tonkin Resolution, many American academics believed that the real enemy was not Communism but rather the U.S. government (Moos 1995:34). Among them were a number of academic anthropologists who

> *began to take it as self-evident that those of their colleagues who worked with—or worse yet, for—the U.S. government had forfeited their claim to academic freedom, and could not be viewed as championing the rights of "the people" . . . they concluded that putting one's skills and life to use in actual policy formation or policy execution for the United States was so unethical and unprofessional as to be anthropologically dishonorable.* (Moos 1995:34)

USAID and the Peace Corps.   Neither the American government nor the public at large mirrored anthropologists' skepticism about foreign involvement. In 1961, the U.S. Congress, impressed at the success of the Technical Cooperation Administration and the Point Four program (and perhaps aware of the dramatic improvements in the lives of Peruvian peasants brought about by the Vicos project), passed the Foreign Assistance Act, under which a new U.S. foreign aid organization, the **U.S. Agency for International Development (USAID),** was established. In the same year, President John F. Kennedy created the **Peace Corps,** which sent skilled Americans abroad, at the request of needy foreign countries, to help implement improvements in the areas of economic development, education, health, and agriculture. Political and economic gain were by no means the only objectives of such assistance; many Americans (if few anthropologists) felt that the richest nation on earth had a moral obligation to help less fortunate countries. Although neither of the new institutions explicitly incorporated applied cultural anthropology, several anthropologists, including Henry F. Dobyns and Paul L. Doughty, contributed to Peace Corps program design and evaluation.

FOOD FOR THOUGHT   Imagine that you are a college graduate who majored in cultural anthropology and are now serving as a Peace Corps volunteer in a Third World country. What kinds of work would be interesting, feasible, appropriate, and productive for you to do, based on what you know so far (from Chapters 1 and 2) about the goals and methods of applied cultural anthropology?

"Project Camelot."   In 1965, two years after the assassination of President Kennedy, a research project devised by the U.S. Department of Defense provoked a maelstrom of controversy over the ethics of social scientific research that was far more vitriolic than the ethical debates of the late 1940s (Horowitz 1967; Wax 1978). The idea behind "Project Camelot" (so designated in honor of the fallen President) was to enlist social scientists, including cultural anthropologists, to study the conditions underlying social unrest in foreign countries, beginning in several Latin American countries. The information provided by these consultants would be used to help national leaders who supported the United States to suppress opposition groups. Many anthropologists viewed this plan not so much as political support for allies as interference on the part of one national government in the internal affairs of others—if not outright spying.

Largely in response to the angry protests of the very social scientists who had been envisioned as implementing it, Project Camelot was canceled in 1965. Soon afterward, in response to this failed project as well as to allegations that anthropologists had been improperly involved in clandestine research in Southeast Asia (Fluehr-Lobban 1998:182), the American Anthropological Association embarked on a series of much-needed steps designed to prevent further controversies of this kind. An inquiry into the relationship between anthropological consultants and the organizations that hired them was commissioned; the Committee on Research Problems and Ethics was established to study the complicated ethical issues involved; and in 1967 the AAA's first formal statement on ethics, "Statement on Problems of Anthropological Research," was drafted (Fluehr-Lobban 1998:175; Ackroyd 1984: 135).[5] AAA members agreed that applied cultural anthropologists should reject any work whose results could not be made public, which automatically eliminated a great deal of applied research in both government and business.

At the end of the decade, U.S. involvement in the war in Vietnam drew ever more scathing criticism from most cultural anthropologists (as it did from much of the U.S. population). Anthropologists' strong antigovernment political stance was naturally accompanied by the widespread rejection of the idea of government service of any kind, foreign or domestic. At the same time, anthropologists themselves continued to be taken to task for previous government involvement—for example, by Native American writer Vine Deloria. A Sioux who had been born on the Pine Ridge Reservation in South Dakota, near the site of the notorious Wounded Knee massacre of 1890, Deloria published his influential book *Custer Died for Your Sins* (the first of a number of books on Native American life) in 1969. The book denounced both the U.S. government's policies toward Native Americans and the meddling of anthropologists—"ideological vultures" (Deloria 1969:95)—in Native Americans' lives.

Business Anthropology.   Meanwhile, the area of business anthropology saw a continuation of the postwar slide originally precipitated by the ready availability of academic jobs. Certainly the ethical opprobrium attached to nonacademic anthropology in general affected business anthropology as well. Most cultural anthropologists with interests in business pursued these interests within academia, where they tended to focus more on the theoretical than the practical aspects of businesses as social organizations. A few studied occupational subgroups, using standard anthropological ideas and methods to analyze, for example, miners or truck drivers. But academics in general—including anthropologists—took a rather superior, ivory-tower view of anything so crass as attempting to make money. Relatively few anthropologists were actually employed by businesses during these years.

One area of applied cultural anthropology that burgeoned during the 1960s was educational anthropology, in which the ideas and techniques of cultural anthropology are called upon to help find solutions to educational problems. Some applied cultural anthropologists, for example, researched the values and beliefs of minority students so that educational programs could better target their needs. Others undertook research in bilingual education or alternative education (such as occupational training and nontraditional education). Outside academe, most of the work of these early educational anthropologists took place within conventional Western-style public or private educational systems. The Council on Anthropology and Education was formed in 1968 as a membership and advocacy organization for what was by now a growing number of educational anthropologists.

Modern Applied Cultural Anthropology: 1970 to the Present

The 1970s: A Revival. In 1971, the AAA at last adopted an official code of ethics, entitled "Principles of Professional Responsibility," to guide the conduct of its members (AAA 1971; see also AAA 1998; Chapter 4). Among other things, this code provided assurance, much needed both within the discipline and outside it, that henceforth cultural anthropologists would not participate in inappropriate attempts at social engineering or intervene in foreign countries' affairs. Meanwhile, the unpopular Vietnam War was winding down (although the last U.S. troops would not be withdrawn until 1973). Applied cultural anthropology's fortunes began to revive.

At about the same time, a demographic shift occurred that spurred applied cultural anthropology's revival. The "baby boomers"—the large cohort of Americans who had been born in the years following World War II and who had swelled college enrollments in the late 1960s—had completed their college educations, and (except for a relatively small number of Korean War returnees) there were few veterans earning college degrees under the GI bill. Most Vietnam veterans did not take advantage of the educational opportunities offered under the bill, for two reasons: first, college students were exempt from the draft during the Vietnam era, so those who did serve consisted largely of men and women who were uninterested in college education or who had already graduated from college; and second, the program now limited the period of time during which servicemen and women could take advantage of the education benefit. Not surprisingly, college and university anthropology departments saw their enrollments begin to drop. Soon the number of newly minted anthropologists graduating from American colleges and universities began to exceed the number needed to fill academic positions, and teaching jobs became increasingly hard to find.

Fortunately for 1970s job-seekers, the U.S. government had passed several laws requiring anthropological expertise in the 1960s and early 1970s (see Table 3.2). As a result of this new federal legislation, as well as a general feeling among anthropologists that government employment was now acceptable, more and more anthropologists were able to find nonacademic employment in the areas of international development, housing and urban development, historic preservation, environmental policy, occupational health and safety, and community planning and management.

◇ **TABLE 3.2   A Sampling of 1960s and Early 1970s U.S. Federal Legislation Requiring Anthropological Expertise**

1961 (amended 1973). **Foreign Assistance Act.** Created USAID, the arm of the federal government charged with overseeing economic and humanitarian assistance programs in less developed countries around the world. USAID also provides disaster relief, food aid, emergency humanitarian aid, health care programs, and family-planning services in foreign countries.

1965. Housing and Urban Development Act. Created the Department of Housing and Urban Development (HUD), the government agency that oversees urban renewal projects, provides housing subsidies and public housing for low-income families; helps find appropriate housing for the homeless, the elderly, and the disabled; and ensures against discrimination in housing. HUD also oversees the construction and maintenance of low-income public housing specifically for Native Americans.

1966. National Historic Preservation Act. Established a program for the preservation of the "historical and cultural foundations of the Nation." Included were the creation of state historic preservation offices, a program to "assist Indian tribes in preserving their particular historic properties," and increased preservation training opportunities for federal, state, tribal, and local government workers and students.

1969. National Environmental Policy Act of 1969 (NEPA). Required that experts be called upon to assess the impact of development projects on "the environment," which is broadly interpreted to include not only the natural but also the cultural environment. Before a dam can be built or a pipeline dug, experts must assess the project's social and economic impact as well as its impact on plants and animals, air and water.

1970. Occupational Safety and Health Act. Created the Occupational Safety and Health Administration (OSHA) to promote safety for American workers by establishing and enforcing safety regulations and implementing employee health programs.

Two additional developments in the 1970s also opened up jobs for applied anthropologists: Southeast Asian immigration into the United States in the aftermath of the Vietnam War, and the women's movement. Many of the era's new Ph.D.'s, who had assumed, during their years of graduate education, that they would become academics, wound up instead in satisfying and productive jobs assisting with the enculturation, education, and health care of Southeast Asian refugees, or helping local, state, or national government begin to redress the country's long history of discrimination against women.

Despite the increase in applied cultural anthropology, business anthropology continued to languish in the early and middle 1970s; in general, anthropologists still saw themselves as somehow above the profit motive. Then, in 1975, the idea that businesses could provide not only useful but also respectable employment for cultural anthropologists got a helping hand from an unlikely source: Conrad Arensberg, a distinguished academic anthropologist whose career, following his participation in

W. Lloyd Warner's Yankee City study, had centered on traditional ethnographic work. Arensberg was ahead of his time in that his wide range of anthropological interests also included businesses. "We need more insight into the dynamics of large-scale business organization(s) for many reasons," said Arensberg, "for managing [them], for teaching management to manage [them], for efficiency, for taming business organizations for human use and social responsibilities, and for coming to terms with the powerful force and steady growth shown by large-scale business organizations in national and international life" (Arensberg 1975; see also Arensberg 1987).

This well-publicized statement of support, coming from a highly regarded ethnographer and theorist, seems to have given business anthropology a shot in the arm. Within the next few years, this area of applied cultural anthropology had gained not only anthropological endorsement but many new practitioners as well. There has been a slow but steady increase in business anthropology ever since (Hafner 1999:G1).

The 1980s: Official Recognition. By the early 1980s, hundreds if not thousands of applied cultural anthropologists were employed not only in the private sector and international development agencies, but also domestically in areas such as health care, social welfare, education, and the law. Indeed, "during the 1980s the word 'anthropologist' became one of the key signs which marked a project proposal as 'progressive'" (Dudley 1993:113). There was some criticism, especially of the policies and projects of certain large and highly visible **bilateral** ("two-sided") **organizations** (the foreign assistance agencies of individual governments) and **multilateral** ("many-sided") **organizations** (aid organizations made up of a number of member countries; the United Nations, consisting of almost all the countries in the world, is by far the largest of these). From time to time, for example, the U.S. Agency for International Development and the World Bank were taken to task for not having achieved their stated goals and even for having done more harm than good (see, for example, Ferguson 1990; Escobar 1995; Johnson 1994; see also Chapter 5 for a discussion of these critiques). In general, however, there was no longer much doubt within anthropology about the value of responsible applied work.

FOOD FOR THOUGHT Over the years, applied cultural anthropology has tended to wax and wane in popularity and numbers of practitioners, depending on historical, demographic, and other factors. Based on such factors, what do you think the state of applied cultural anthropology will be in 2005? What if the First World recessionary economic trend of 2001 returns, or the stagnation of 2002 continues? What if the Western powers become involved in a formally declared armed conflict?

Under the circumstances, members of the American Anthropological Association felt that the time had come for official recognition of applied anthropology within the overall discipline. In 1983, the National Association for the Practice of

Anthropology (NAPA) was at last established as an official branch of the American Anthropological Association. An umbrella group, NAPA was designed to foster interest in applied anthropology, to support applied anthropologists, and to represent their interests. (Its membership considerably overlapped that of the SfAA, which had split with the AAA in the early 1980s during organizational restructuring.) Further contributing to the acceptability of applied work as ethically acceptable, the AAA reconsidered its earlier dictum prohibiting the publication of applied research results. It now endorsed proprietary research with the proviso that research populations should not be harmed in any way.

Applied anthropology's heyday had begun. Over the course of the decade of the 1980s, the percentage of newly graduated anthropology Ph.D.'s who took nonacademic jobs grew from 32 percent in 1984 to 42 percent in 1986 to 54 percent in 1988 (AAA 1997).

The 1990s and Beyond. The relative percentages of new Ph.D.'s choosing nonacademic employment dropped off slightly in the 1990s; a 1997 survey undertaken by the American Anthropological Association indicated that about a third of all anthropologists earning a Ph.D. that year (the most recent year for which figures are available) went to work outside of academics, usually for government branches, not-for-profit organizations and charitable institutions, or businesses (AAA 1997). Throughout the 1990s, however, applied anthropology continued, in the words of the AAA, to be "a growth industry" (ibid.) in terms of the increasing number of professional arenas in which applied anthropologists were involved.

Today the complexion of applied cultural anthropology is quite different from what it was in the past. First, the number of applied anthropologists—presently an estimated one half of all anthropologists (Hafner 1999:G1)—is greater than ever before. Second, many of these anthropologists are full-time employees of branches of government, not-for-profit organizations, charitable institutions, or businesses for which they work—a very different situation from that of a generation or two ago, when most applied anthropologists were part-timers doing applied work as a sideline to their academic jobs. A third difference between then and now is a new educational emphasis on applied anthropology. A substantial and increasing number of academic institutions are now offering master's degree programs in applied anthropology (see the *Anthropology Career Resources Handbook*).

As the new millennium began, applied cultural anthropology had reached unprecedented heights, not just in terms of the numbers of practitioners but also in terms of scope and legitimacy. Today there are literally thousands of applied cultural anthropologists. They are bringing their anthropological expertise to an ever-increasing array of career fields, and their work is recognized, both within and outside academic anthropology, as valid, significant, and worthy of high esteem.

FOOD FOR THOUGHT In 1997, anthropologist James Ferguson wrote: "Applied work in nearly any field suffers from a relatively low academic status, as against loftier theoretical pursuits" (Ferguson 1997:157). What factors might have precipitated this remark?

It remains to be seen whether today's high relative proportion of applied to academic anthropologists will continue. As of mid-2001, unemployment in both the United States and Canada was relatively low, resulting in job openings in many academic areas (including the social sciences), but a recessionary trend and the historic events of late 2001 depressed American employment in general. Nevertheless, the demand for professors seems to be steady or even increasing, for several reasons: the offspring of the baby boomers are beginning to reach college age; college education is becoming more and more important in establishing a satisfying and financially rewarding career; and Ph.D.'s who began their college teaching careers in the last big "hiring binge," which lasted from 1955 to 1972, are retiring (Hafner 1999:G1).

CONCLUSION

The academic discipline of cultural anthropology, because of its origins in the collection of data on indigenous or foreign peoples and cultures for both self-serving and altruistic reasons, has always included an applied component of sorts. However, the impetus behind applied work has changed significantly over the years, along with the proportion of cultural anthropologists engaged in this kind of work. No longer a tool most heavily employed for political or economic advantage, applied cultural anthropology today has many additional objectives. Frequently it serves the humanitarian goals of world bodies, national governments, nongovernmental agencies (NGOs), or charitable organizations. Even when it supports purely commercial objectives, today's applied cultural anthropology is governed by stringent ethical guidelines (see Chapter 4).

In any case, applied cultural anthropology appears to have found a permanent, recognized, and valued niche within its parent discipline. Most applied cultural anthropologists today believe "we are all part of the same anthropology" (Hill and Baba 2000:28), a discipline to which applied anthropology is making significant contributions.

K E Y   T E R M S

anthropometry   the study and comparison of measurements of the human body

bilateral organization   the foreign assistance agency of a country's government

"Indianology"   nineteenth-century studies of Native Americans, many of them commissioned by government agencies and ethnological societies

multilateral organization   an aid organization made up of a number of member countries

Peace Corps   an agency of the U.S. government created in 1961 to send trained Americans to foreign countries, at their request, to work in the areas of economic development, education, health, and agriculture

U.S. Agency for International Development (USAID)   the foreign assistance arm of the U.S. government

NOTES

1. For alternative developmental frameworks, see van Willigen 1993 and Ervin 2000.
2. Dudley (1993:9) concisely defines the term *Third World* as "countries which, in material terms, are less well off." The "first" and "second" worlds are the Western democracies and the former Soviet bloc, respectively.
3. These efforts are reflected in several important books published in the 1950s, most notably Edward H. Spicer's *Human Problems in Technological Change* (1952), Margaret Mead's *Cultural Patterns and Technological Change* (1955), and Homer Barnett's *Anthropology and Administration* (1956).
4. See Ward Goodenough's *Cooperation in Change* (1963), Conrad Arensberg and Arthur Niehoff's *Introducing Social Change* (1964), and George Foster's *Applied Anthropology* (1969).
5. This statement was formally adopted in 1971; see Chapter 4.

REFERENCES

Ackroyd, Anne V.
1984. "Ethics in Relation to Informants, the Profession, and Governments." In *Ethnographic Research: A Guide to General Conduct*, edited by Roy F. Ellen, 133–154. (ASA Research Methods in Social Anthropology No. 1.) London: Academic Press.

Adams, William Y.
1998. *The Philosophical Roots of Anthropology.* Stanford, CA: Center for the Study of Language and Information.

American Anthropological Association (AAA)
1971. *Principles of Professional Responsibility.* Washington, DC: American Anthropological Association.
1997. *AAA Survey of Anthropology PhDs.* http://www.ameranthassn.org/97SURVEY.HTM
1998. "Code of Ethics of the American Anthropological Association." *Anthropology Newsletter* 39 (6): 19–20.

Arensberg, Conrad M.
1975. "Discussion of C. Steward Sheppard: The Role of Anthropology in Business Administration." In *Anthropology and Society*, edited by Bela C. Maday, 71–75. Washington, DC: Anthropological Society of Washington.
1987. "Theoretical Contributions of Industrial and Development Studies." In *Applied Anthropology in America* (2nd ed.), edited by Elizabeth M. Eddy and William L. Partridge, 59–88. New York: Columbia University Press.

Arensberg, Conrad M., and Arthur Niehoff
1964. *Introducing Social Change: A Manual for Americans Overseas.* Chicago: Aldine.

Baba, Marietta L.
1986. *Business and Industrial Anthropology: An Overview* (NAPA Bulletin No. 2). Washington, DC: American Anthropological Association.
2000. "Theories of Practice in Anthropology: A Critical Appraisal." In *The Unity of Theory and Practice in Anthropology: Rebuilding a Fractured Synthesis* (NAPA Bulletin 18), edited by Carole E. Hill and Marietta L. Baba, 17–44. Washington, DC: NAPA.

Barnett, Homer
1956. *Anthropology and Administration.* New York: Harper and Row.

Chambers, Erve
1989 (orig. 1985). *Applied Anthropology: A Practical Guide.* Prospect Heights, IL: Waveland Press.

Deloria, Vine, Jr.
1969. *Custer Died for Your Sins: An Indian Manifesto.* London: Macmillan.

Des Chene, Mary
1997. "Locating the Past." In *Anthropological Locations: Boundaries and Grounds of a Field Science*, edited by Akhil Gupta and James Ferguson, 66–85. Berkeley: University of California Press.

Doughty, Paul L.
1987. "Vicos: Success, Rejection, and Rediscovery of a Classic Program." In *Applied Anthropology in America* (2nd ed.), edited by Elizabeth M. Eddy and William L. Partridge, 433–459. New York: Columbia University Press.

Dudley, Eric
1993. *The Critical Villager: Beyond Community Participation.* London: Routledge.

Eddy, Elizabeth M., and William L. Partridge (eds.)
1987. *Applied Anthropology in America* (2nd ed.). New York: Columbia University Press.

Ervin, Alexander M.
2000. *Applied Anthropology: Tools and Perspectives for Contemporary Practice*. Boston: Allyn and Bacon.

Escobar, Arturo
1995. *Encountering Development: The Making and Unmaking of the Third World*. Princeton, NJ: Princeton University Press.

Ferguson, James
1990. *The Anti-Politics Machine: Development, Depoliticization, and Bureaucratic Power in Lesotho*. Cambridge, UK: Cambridge University Press.

1997. "Anthropology and Its Evil Twin: 'Development' in the Constitution of a Discipline." In *International Development and the Social Sciences*, edited by Frederick Cooper and Randall Packard, 150–175. Berkeley: University of California Press.

Fluehr-Lobban, Carolyn
1998. "Ethics." In *Handbook of Methods in Cultural Anthropology*, edited by H. Russell Bernard, 173–202. Walnut Creek, CA: Altamira Press.

Foster, George
1969. *Applied Anthropology*. Boston: Little Brown.

Gardner, Katy, and David Lewis
1996. *Anthropology, Development, and the Post-Modern Challenge*. London: Pluto Press.

Goodenough, Ward
1963. *Cooperation in Change*. New York: Russell Sage Foundation.

Gupta, Akhil, and James Ferguson (eds.)
1997. *Anthropological Locations*. Berkeley: University of California Press.

Hafner, Katie
1999. Coming of Age in Palo Alto. *New York Times*, June 10, 1999, G1–G8.

Hill, Carole E., and Marietta L. Baba (eds.)
2000. *The Unity of Theory and Practice in Anthropology: Rebuilding a Fractured Synthesis* (NAPA Bulletin 18). Washington, DC: NAPA.

Holmberg, Allan R.
1958. "The Research and Development Approach to the Study of Change." *Human Organization* 17: 12–16.

Horowitz, I. L.
1967. *The Rise and Fall of Project Camelot: Studies in the Relationship between Social Science and Practical Politics*. Cambridge, MA: MIT Press.

Johnson, Barbara Rose (ed.)
1994. *Who Pays the Price? The Sociocultural Context of Environmental Crisis*. Washington, DC: Island Press.

Mangin, William
1979. "Thoughts on Twenty-four Years of Work in Peru: The Vicos Project and Me." In *Long-Term Field Research in Social Anthropology*, edited by George M. Foster et al., 65–84. New York: Academic Press.

Mead, Margaret
1955. *Cultural Patterns and Technological Change*. New York: Mentor.

1977. "Applied Anthropology: The State of the Art." In *Perspectives on Anthropology 1976* (American Anthropological Association Special Publication No. 10), edited by A. F. C. Wallace et al., 142–161. Washington, DC: American Anthropological Association.

1979. "Anthropological Contributions to National Policies During and Immediately After World War II." In *The Uses of Anthropology*, edited by Walter Goldschmidt, 145–158. Washington, DC: American Anthropological Association.

Mead, Margaret, Eliot D. Chapple, and G. Gordon Brown
1949. "Report of the Committee on Ethics." *Human Organization* 8 (2):20–21.

Mooney, James
1896. *The Ghost Dance Religion and the Sioux Outbreak of 1890*. Washington, DC: Bureau of American Ethnology.

Moos, Felix
1995. "Anthropological Ethics and the Military." *Anthropology Newsletter* 36 (9):34.

Sharpless, John
1997. "Population Science, Private Foundations, and Development Aid." In *International Development and the Social Sciences*, edited by Frederick Cooper and Randall Packard, 176–200. Berkeley: University of California Press.

Spicer, Edward H.
1952. *Human Problems in Technological Change: A Casebook*. New York: Sage Publications.

Stocking, George W., Jr.
1992. *The Ethnographer's Magic and Other Essays in the History of Anthropology*. Madison, WI: University of Wisconsin Press.

van Willigen, John
1993. *Applied Anthropology* (rev. ed.). Westport, CT: Bergin and Garvey.

Warner, W. Lloyd, and Paul S. Lunt
1941. *The Social Life of a Modern Community*. New Haven: Yale University Press.

Wax, Murray L.
1978. "Once and Future Merlins: The Applied Anthropologists of Camelot." *Human Organization* 37: 400–408.

Willis, William S., Jr.
1974. "Skeletons in the Anthropological Closet." In *Reinventing Anthropology*, edited by Dell Hymes, 284–312. New York: Vintage Books.

Wolcott, Harry F.
1999. *Ethnography: A Way of Seeing*. Walnut Creek, CA: Altamira Press.

CHAPTER

4

THE ETHICS OF APPLIED CULTURAL ANTHROPOLOGY

INTRODUCTION

Recently, while working on a public health project, applied medical anthropologist and AIDS researcher Dr. Fred Bloom conducted an in-depth interview with an HIV-positive gay man who offered a rich description of a key incident—a high-risk sexual encounter—that embodied important implications for Dr. Bloom's research. The incident involved the interviewee's failure to use a condom during this encounter and his concern about possibly having exposed his sex partner to the virus that causes AIDS.

The interviewee's description of the context and meaning of this encounter was highly significant to Dr. Bloom's research; therefore he felt it was essential to present the narrative text of the interview as accurately as possible when reporting his findings. To change it would weaken the methodological rigor of the research and to risk altering the meaning of the interviewee's words. At the same time, he was aware that, even if he disguised names and places, there was a remote possibility that certain readers of his final research report might recognize the interviewee—for example, through the inclusion of some turn of phrase that the interviewee often used in conversation. Dr. Bloom faced an ethical quandary: how could he protect his interviewee's right to confidentiality and still convey the full import of his words?

All anthropological researchers, both academic and applied, must face and resolve ethical questions throughout their professional lives. These questions may be particularly troublesome for applied cultural anthropologists, since applied work in cultural anthropology is intentionally interventionist and likely to focus on issues that directly affect people's lives, such as their economic status, work relationships, or health. Applied cultural anthropologists may thus have to confront ethical problems more often, and with more immediacy, than their academic colleagues do, and how they solve these ethical dilemmas may have a direct impact on the lives of people they study or among whom they promote directed change (Gilbert et al. 1991:201; Sieber 1998:127).[1]

The extent to which this is true depends, of course, on the realm of application. No field of applied cultural anthropology is immune to ethical quandaries, but in some—cultural advocacy, medical anthropology, and business anthropology, for example—ethical problems are an inevitable component of even the most straightforward situations. Cultural advocates (see Chapter 6) must wrestle with their consciences when groups of indigenous people make unwise choices about the use of local environmental resources. Medical anthropologists involved in clinical trials of potentially useful drugs (see Chapter 11) must grapple with the morality of offering some patients only a placebo. Business anthropologists (see Chapter 9) may find that their suggestions to management for improved efficiency may jeopardize their informants' jobs. Indeed, "matters of ethics are an ordinary, not extraordinary, part of anthropological practice" (Fluehr-Lobban 1998:173). In many instances, there are no clear-cut solutions. Thus, applied cultural anthropologists are frequently confronted with the need to make "ethical compromises" (Irvine 1998:167) and "choices among apparently incompatible values" (AAA 1998:1).

Most applied cultural anthropologists would probably agree that ethical issues have yet to be sufficiently addressed within their subdiscipline (Hill 2000:4), much less resolved. This chapter is intended not to furnish definitive answers, but only to introduce the kinds of ethical considerations all applied cultural anthropologists face, and to describe the guidelines available to help them find acceptable solutions. Subsequent chapters will raise more specific ethical issues in areas of applied anthropology such as health, the environment, business, and law.

IS APPLIED CULTURAL ANTHROPOLOGY MORALLY JUSTIFIED?

A useful distinction is sometimes drawn between *morals* and *ethics*, two closely related terms that are used virtually synonymously in everyday conversation. Morals can be defined as standards of appropriate conduct. These standards can be set either by individuals, as standards of personal conduct, or by society, as a body of obligations required of individual members of society. (In some cases, a society's morals derive from religious belief; in others, they are imposed by the state.) An individual's personal moral standards are, of course, heavily influenced by those of his or her society. *Ethics* is usually defined as the study and evaluation of human conduct according to the prevailing moral code, whether personal or societal. In the following section, the term *morality* refers to standards of conduct deemed appropriate by Western society as a whole, as opposed to the standards of individual cultural anthropologists. Likewise, whether something is designated *ethical* or *unethical* is based on what Western society, not any individual cultural anthropologist, deems morally acceptable and appropriate. Note that non-Western anthropologists *may* have different perspectives, although Western culture, and hence Western ethics, is anthropology's predominant cultural influence.

The Question of Interference

The most fundamental question facing all applied cultural anthropologists is whether or not they are ever really justified in their attempt to intervene in the lives of others, as admirable and humane as their goals may be (see, for example, Wolcott 1999:288ff.). At first glance, it may appear that an affirmative answer to this question is self-evident with the addition of one simple qualification: cultural anthropologists are indeed justified in their attempt to promote beneficial change and improve the lives of others *if* the people involved want, and have requested, anthropological intervention. Indeed, some cultural anthropologists believe that under these circumstances it would be unethical *not* to intervene (see, for example, Scheper-Hughes 1995).

Unfortunately, this simplistic response merely raises other, more difficult, ethical questions. Is anthropological intervention—or the research on which intervention will be based—justified if the potential beneficiaries of an applied project are divided on whether intervention is desirable or not? Is it justified if the potential beneficiaries believe intervention will benefit them but do not fully understand its potential outcomes? If, due to lack of education, a given group of people is incapable of envisioning beneficial anthropological intervention, and hence does not request it, should either research or intervention be pressed on the group's members "for their own good"? Do anthropologists (or anyone else, for that matter) have the right to decide what kind or amount of intervention is "for their own good"? Can either research or intervention be justified in cases in which the instigator of potential social change is a national foreign aid agency—part of a government whose goal is not only altruistic but also political (see Chapter 5)?

Perhaps the most difficult question is this: because, in the past, some interventions on the part of applied cultural anthropologists have been misguided, does this suggest that further attempts should not be made?[2] No consensus among applied cultural anthropologists has been achieved on any of these questions, although a few cultural anthropologists (see, for example, Scheper-Hughes 1995; Moos 1995:34) have argued that anthropological researchers of any kind, theoretical or applied, should feel obliged to intervene whenever and wherever human beings are disenfranchised.

Recall the example, in Chapter 2, of the unsustainable development project undertaken in the Philippine village of Casiguran. Among the project's goals was to reduce existing economic inequalities among the villagers, but the project actually had the opposite effect. Given that Casiguran's poor had said they needed and wanted outside help, was the failed attempt justified? As a disappointed villager, would you welcome a second attempt? Why or why not?

The Question of Scientific Detachment

It was pointed out in Chapter 1 that academic anthropologists have historically viewed their discipline as a science: an objective field of inquiry that seeks out truths about the existence, development, appearance, behavior, and beliefs of human beings, through the use of methods intended to produce unbiased research results. Cultural anthropology is a "social" science, to be sure—manifestly different from physical science in that its object of inquiry is people, not things—but a science nonetheless. In conformity with this view, most academic fieldworkers, over the course of anthropology's history, have contented themselves with studying, understanding, and appreciating members of their research populations exactly as they were, taking care (as best they could) not to visit change upon them. This does not mean that they did not bring qualities of empathy, generosity, and charity with them into the field, but it does mean that—as scientists—most have refrained from intentionally promoting social change in research populations.

Postmodernism notwithstanding, many cultural anthropologists today continue to view their discipline in these terms. Others, however, question whether a "scientific" cultural anthropology is either possible or desirable. The resulting debate is not so much about whether cultural anthropology is a true science or not, but about what "science" means in terms of appropriate anthropological conduct. One view is that cultural anthropology, to be "taken seriously" as a science (D'Andrade 1995), should be "value free" (see, for example, Gert 1995:30); fieldworkers should thus remain "intrinsically detached" from the objects of their research (Wax 1987: 4). According to this view, the goal of a "scientific" anthropologist is to craft a "neutral" account of a culture under study, while "refraining from . . . interfering with it in any way" (Salmon 2001:364). Several arguments are cited in defense of this view: for example, that anthropologists' intentionally affective or philanthropic engagement with research populations would inevitably have a modifying, and hence disruptive, effect on the cultures under study, and thus bias the research. (Critics of this stance point out that this point of view may afford the academic researcher "immunity against criticism for lack of action"; see Ringberg 1995:48).

The other viewpoint is that a scientific cultural anthropology neither demands nor even sanctions "neutrality" and "detachment." According to this view, cultural anthropologists can be objective—for example, by employing methods designed to provide unbiased research results—without being either neutral or detached. Some would go so far as to claim that "the possibility of an ethically neutral or completely value-free science of human behavior now seems . . . both unattainable and undesirable" (Salmon 2001:365).

Applied cultural anthropologists, in contrast to theoreticians, are intentionally and explicitly change-oriented, and hence manifestly *not* "completely value-free." This has led to the charge that applied cultural anthropology is unscientific. Like the question of interference, the issue of the "scientific" validity of applied cultural anthropology—if, indeed, adherence to the principles of science is called for—defies any universally acceptable resolution. Many applied cultural anthropologists believe that their work incorporates the best aspects of scientific research (the search for truth using methods intended to produce objective results) with humanitarianism (the attempt to help change people's lives for the better).

The Question of Cultural Relativism

A related question concerns cultural relativism, an important anthropological perspective defined and discussed in Appendix 2. For some, this term now has a wider meaning than it did when Franz Boas, early in the last century, first argued that cultures should be studied and evaluated in their own cultural contexts, rather than in terms of others' precepts and values; it has subsumed the notion that every culture should be evaluated in terms of its own shared moral values, not those of any other culture. Thus Boas's prescient statement of the value of what would now be called an emic perspective is today often conflated with *ethical* relativism, an admonition to withhold *moral* evaluation of cultural practices. Critics of cultural relativism, redefined in these terms, have complained that an anthropologist who takes the perspective literally would have to endorse even the most heinous behavior (the Holocaust perpetrated by the Nazis is often cited as an example) on the grounds that we must be tolerant of all behaviors. Defenders of the concept respond with reference to the notion of universal rights (for example, the universal human right to freedom

◇ *The influential American anthropologist Franz Boas (1858–1942), pictured here in 1906, was among the first to promulgate the principle of cultural relativism.*

from harm) and values (for example, the universal human value that pain avoidance is desirable), which are embraced by all cultures (Gert 1995:30; Handwerker 1997).[3] The Nazis' practices, they would argue, did not represent "the ultimate moral standard for that culture" (Salmon 2001:364).

Regardless of whether the concept of cultural relativism is viewed in its original or its more inclusive sense, most academic cultural anthropologists would probably agree with ethicist Bernard Gert that—with the possible exception of universal rights and values, if indeed they exist—"it is incorrect for any society to impose its values on another, and particularly inappropriate for anthropologists to try to influence any culture or society they are studying" (Gert 1995:30). This viewpoint presents a problem for applied cultural anthropology: while its goals are entirely compatible with the simple admonition to view things through others' eyes, at the same time these goals often do require that applied cultural anthropologists very explicitly "try to influence" the culture of others, which sometimes translates into the attempt to promote certain Western values. International development projects (see Chapter 5), for example, sometimes promote the establishment of democratic institutions.

Most applied cultural anthropologists see no incompatibility between what they do and the anthropological ideal of cultural relativism, with or without overtones of ethical relativism. Their argument is based on the understanding that responsible applied cultural anthropologists conscientiously refrain from making ethnocentric value judgments, instead working toward culturally appropriate changes that are satisfactory to the people with whom they work, and hence compatible with these peoples' moral values. There has as yet been no resolution, among either academic cultural anthropologists or their applied colleagues, of this issue.

FOOD FOR THOUGHT Suppose you are an applied cultural anthropologist working on an international health project to promote safe motherhood among poorly educated, rural women in a Central American country. You discover that immediately after giving birth, these women use cattle dung to stop the flow of blood from the baby's umbilical cord. This custom has been practiced for as long as the women can remember, and they believe it to be safe and effective. Do you attempt to discourage the practice? If not, why not? If so, can you justify this decision on the basis of universal human rights or values?

ETHICAL RELATIONSHIPS

Historically, responsible academic cultural anthropologists conducted their research under two major strictures: they were obliged to refrain from harming the people with whom they worked, and they were obliged to work within (while attempting to expand) the previously established theoretical framework and methodological norms of their discipline. Professional strictures are both more numerous and more complicated in the case of applied cultural anthropologists. As the various formal ethical codes governing applied cultural anthropology make clear (see below), the applied cultural anthropologist must not only avoid harm and adhere to various sets of professional standards but must at the same time pursue relationships with, and discharge obligations to, multiple individuals, groups, and agencies. The most important of these relationships, for present purposes, are with applied anthropologists' research subjects and/or intended beneficiaries, their employers, and their colleagues.[4]

Applied Cultural Anthropologists and Research Subjects or Beneficiary Groups

All cultural anthropologists, both academic and applied, develop relationships with the people among whom they do research or (in the case of applied cultural anthropologists) those they hope to benefit (see Jorgenson 1971). Not surprisingly, these relationships are apt to become intense and personal (Gilbert et al. 1991:202). Moreover, all responsible cultural anthropologists recognize weighty ethical responsibilities to their research populations—responsibilities that supersede even the eminently worthy goal of contributing to human knowledge.

The foremost of these responsibilities is to do no "harm or wrong" (AAA 1998: III-A-1). Cultural anthropologists have a moral obligation to ensure that their impact on any and all **stakeholders**—defined as anyone and everyone with any interests in any given anthropological research effort—is positive rather than negative. Thus cultural anthropologists are admonished, via the ethical codes established by their various membership organizations, to conduct their research openly, never to misrepresent their identities or intentions, to obtain prior agreement from all study participants, to protect research participants' right to confidentiality, and to give credit where it is due.

In this regard, cultural anthropologists are unlike some other social scientists, who "under certain stated conditions . . . mislead informants, whom they label *subjects*" (Kutsche 1998:8). The informants from whom academic cultural anthropologists collect data (today commonly called collaborators or partners, especially in applied cultural anthropology) are less like the research subjects of other disciplines and more like teachers, from whom anthropologists, like students, learn; "they know their cultures; we go to learn those cultures" (ibid.).

Power and Authority.   In the relationships between those who wish to help others and their intended beneficiaries, images of "expert" donors and "unsophisticated" recipients may exist on both sides of the equation (Downe 1999:23). The ineffectiveness of the huge amounts of foreign aid provided recently by the Untied States to Haiti, for example, has been "buttressed by 'aiders' constructions of the 'aided'" (Smith 2001:31). These images of "aiders" and "the aided," familiar to applied cultural anthropologists, reflect the existence of an inherent imbalance of power and authority in the change agent–beneficiary relationship. Despite the concerted efforts of most applied cultural anthropologists, counteracting this imbalance often proves to be a difficult and complex task.

The ideal solution to the problem of an imbalance in power and authority, of course, is full and equal community participation, now considered crucial to projects involving applied cultural anthropologists whose goal is directed social change (see Chapter 2), but truly participatory research and action are often elusive. Among other considerations that might stand in the way of potential beneficiaries' willingness to enter into a full and equal partnership are privacy concerns, a distrust of "others," self-interest, fear of retaliation from others who may disapprove, or simply a desire to "let laying dogs sleep" (Perez 1997:5).

A related problem is that some beneficiaries, desiring the benefits of assistance but reluctant to become full partners, simply tell outside social change agents what they want to hear. The only way to solve this problem is to establish trust "through relatively long social interaction between researchers and villagers" (Perez 1997:5).

Partnership and Trust.   Whether the impetus behind research in cultural anthropology is academic or applied, the relationship between anthropologist and research subject or beneficiary group requires partnership and mutual trust. In the case of applied cultural anthropology specifically, this is as true when applied cultural anthropologists are collecting data from collaborators as part of applied research as it is when they are working to implement specific changes among groups of intended beneficiaries.

Applied cultural anthropologists must be constantly aware that their collaborators, as they contribute opinions, information, and ideas via interviews, focus groups, or casual conversation, are taking a calculated risk. For example, an applied researcher who later publicly attributes a collaborator's statements, perhaps by repeating them to peers or including them in research reports or other published documents, puts the collaborator at risk of criticism, embarrassment, loss of standing in the community, or loss of self-esteem (Stake 1998:102).

The applied research of Dr. Fred Bloom, which began this chapter, exemplifies this potential problem. Dr. Bloom's research involves interviewing HIV-positive gay men, with the ultimate goal of understanding their behavior and motivations in order to devise strategies for disease prevention (see An Applied Cultural Anthropologist at Work, Chapter 11, p. 261; see also Seal, Bloom, and Somlai 2000). To formulate as thorough an understanding of his research population as possible, Bloom must relay his collaborators' stories accurately, yet such accuracy could compromise confidentiality. Ultimately, in the specific instance described earlier, Bloom decided to include a complete transcript of the interview in a version of his report that would be distributed only to key persons involved in the project. He also produced a summary of his findings and recommendations, which did not include the narrative data, for more general distribution. This solution "proved to be satisfactory to all" (F. Bloom, pers. comm.).

Some applied cultural anthropologists have found it very difficult to adhere to ethical guidelines, such as those mandated by the SfAA code of ethics (see below), regarding confidentiality. Applied anthropologist Steven McNabb, involved in research to assess the impact of the 1989 *Exxon Valdez* oil spill in Prince William Sound, Alaska, once faced a legal subpoena that would have forced him to break informant confidentiality by turning over to the court documents that would reveal his informants' identities (McNabb 1995). He was able to keep his promise of confidentiality to his research subjects only by destroying all relevant records prior to being subpoenaed (McNabb 1995:332). McNabb's experience serves as a warning to applied cultural anthropologists that "we ethically cannot claim that we will insure informants' anonymity if we do not have the means to do so" (McNabb 1995:333; see also "Proprietary Research," p. 92).

Informed Consent.   Western scientists are united in the conviction that it is unethical not only to put human research subjects at possible risk of harm but even to extract information from them without their express, enlightened agreement. This consensus originated in large part within the discipline of medicine, particularly as a response to the abhorrent medical experiments carried out in the name of science in Nazi Germany in the 1930s and 1940s. It was consolidated by the disclosure of a number of other morally questionable postwar researches undertaken in the United States. An example is the Tuskegee syphilis study, beginning in 1932, in which a group of several hundred poor, black, male syphilitics were monitored and studied by the U.S. Public Health Service. The research subjects were never either informed of their health status or treated—even after it was discovered that penicillin was effective against their disease (see Faden and Beauchamp 1986).

This and other similar episodes resulted in the idea of **informed consent,** which today extends well beyond biomedical research to include research in the social and behavioral sciences (Fluehr-Lobban 1994; 1998:184; see also Ervin 2000:30–31). Informed consent means explicit agreement, on the part of a research study participant, to participate in the research, the participant having been apprised of everything of actual or potential importance and interest about the study, including the risks and the uses to which the data collected will be put (see, for example, Sieber 1998:131). Inherent in the concept is the notion that consent should

⟡ *In the 1930s, the U.S. Public Health Service failed to inform participants in the Tuskegee syphilis study of their health status; nor was their condition treated. In 1997, then President Bill Clinton apologized to the study participants (including Herman Shaw, 94) on behalf of the nation.*

be not only informed but also completely voluntary; a participant should not be co-erced into participation in a project in any way (for example, by the promise of some later benefit).

In the usual informed consent procedure, a potential research project partici-pant is presented with an easily understandable, concise, written statement, termed a *consent statement,* which provides relevant details about the research: its objectives, methods, risks, and anticipated outcome. The consent statement also reveals the project's backers and funding sources and the uses to which the results of the re-search will or may be put. The individual is asked to read, sign, and date the state-ment; this action presumably indicates that he or she is then fully informed. Signed consent statements usually constitute legal proof of informed consent and are cus-tomarily required by the various bodies authorizing research on human subjects (see "Institutional Review Boards," p. 92). The only exception is the rare case in which signing a consent statement would somehow jeopardize a study participant.

Potential study participants who are functionally incapable of giving informed consent (children, for example, or the mentally retarded) are asked to give their "as-sent." Under these circumstances, a person who has the participant's best interests genuinely at heart is designated as a stand-in for the participant and signs the con-sent statement on his or her behalf (Sieber 1998:131).

Informed consent involves more than mere acquiescence. Truly informed con-sent requires the prior establishment of mutual respect, rapport, and trust (Sieber 1998:132–133). To the extent possible, it also requires neutralizing the researcher–subject asymmetry inherent in the idea of one individual "using" another for re-search purposes. (To facilitate this, it has been suggested that the term *informed per-mission* be substituted for *informed consent.*) And it requires open and ongoing com-munication and negotiation between researcher and study participant (see AAA 1998:III-A-4). This is because study participants may sign informed consent state-ments willingly at the beginning of a research project yet not fully comprehend what they are involved in until the research is well under way (Sieber 1998:130). Ethical research thus includes continuous communication between researchers and study participants.

In any field of endeavor, what actually happens sometimes diverges from the ideal scenario. Although the notion of informed consent is applicable to any and every kind of medical or social scientific research, obtaining informed consent is more complex in the social sciences than in most other disciplines (Gert 1995:31), and under some research circumstances, it may be either inappropriate to seek or impossible to obtain. In such cases, the researcher is left to wrestle with the question of whether or not to pursue the research without it.

Researcher Leslie Irvine, for example, studied Codependents Anonymous (CoDA), a twelve-step substance-abuse program modeled after Alcoholics Anony-mous (Irvine 1998:167 ff.). She found it impossible to obtain informed consent from members of this group because of CoDA's rule that all participants (including Irvine herself) maintain complete anonymity. There was no individual in charge who could give assent on behalf of the group, and when Irvine attempted to distribute flyers so members could contact her individually for voluntary interviews, she found that the rules of CoDA prohibit the distribution of any literature not directly related to the or-ganization's goals. After much soul-searching, Irvine's research went forward without informed consent, based on the rationalization that CoDA meetings are open to all participants, attending for any reason—including researchers (Irvine 1998:178).

Another major reason why informed consent may be impossible to obtain is the result of some study participants' lack of educational and other opportunities. Much applied cultural anthropology, for example, is undertaken in the context of development, defined as the attempt to address broad, deeply rooted social problems such as poverty, social inequality, illiteracy, and overpopulation (see Chapter 5). In these circumstances, research populations are sometimes illiterate, relatively unsophisticated, or reluctant, for cultural reasons, to sign forms of any kind, including consent forms (Hyder 2000). For instance, one development worker attempted to collect data from Hispanic farm-workers who were illegal immigrants in the United States. The purpose of the research was to help the local school district meet the needs of the migrants' children. The researcher was unable to obtain informed consent from the children's parents, who assumed that he would report them as illegal immigrants to the U.S. immigration authorities (Sieber 1998:128).

Clandestine Research. If research subjects are not informed of the source(s) of funding, purpose, expected outcome, and/or implications of a research effort, or if the results of the research are not made freely available to all interested stakeholders, the research is termed **clandestine research.** The several codes of ethics guiding the behavior of anthropologists are firmly in accord on the subject of clandestine research: it is invariably unethical, "even if the researcher believes that the end justifies the means, *i.e.,* that the deception practiced is justified by the gain in knowledge" (Fluehr-Lobban 1996:18; see also Fluehr-Lobban 1998:182). Some anthropological researchers feel that for the sake of total openness, interviewees should always be shown drafts of all material they generate or provide to their sponsors, in addition to final research reports (Stake 1998:102).

Again, the ideal is sometimes difficult or even impossible to achieve. Irvine's (1998) research with CoDA participants went forward not only without informed consent, but also clandestinely. To follow the standard ethical guidelines governing clandestine research, Irvine would have had to disclose her identity, motives, and any potential risks involved in participation, but such disclosure was precluded by CoDA regulations. In this case, the very act of participant observation ruled out Irvine's disclosing herself as a researcher.

Working with Large Target Groups. The kinds of ethical considerations that affect individual participants in applied research also hold true for whole groups of people targeted for beneficial change. Such groups are termed **target groups,** and they may consist of many thousands of people (particularly in development projects and/or projects involving policy research). In such cases, it is not possible to obtain informed consent from everyone who may be affected by a proposed project. However, an attempt to assess the potential effects of a large-scale project is often made beforehand in a formal, systematic way (van Willigen 1993:171; see also Kozaitis 2000:58).

Such appraisal, termed social impact assessment (SIA), was described in some detail in Chapter 2, where it was defined as a determination of the potential effects of a new policy or an intervention on the population intended to benefit from it. In some cases, social impact assessment is mandated by law, policy, or agency regulations.[5]

The Case of Business Anthropology.   The ethical responsibilities of a researcher to his or her research population are nowhere more complicated than in the case of the subfield of applied anthropology called business anthropology (see Chapter 9), in which the fundamental motivation behind the work of the applied anthropologist is profit for his or her employer rather than social benefit per se. Business anthropologist John W. Sherry (see An Applied Cultural Anthropologist at Work, Chapter 9, p. 214) acknowledges that doing ethical, responsible applied cultural anthropology in a corporate setting involves "constant tension."

> By better understanding the needs and desires of real people, a corporation cannot only better serve people's needs, but also make money. Hopefully this is an accurate view of what we do, but it is never quite that obvious. As ethnography becomes an increasingly popular tool among American corporations, it has become evident that ethnographic methods can just as easily become tools for understanding how to manipulate people—for instance, by arranging retail spaces so that shoppers "naturally" notice some products instead of others. Are we designing products to address the once unarticulated needs of real people, or are we simply finding more sophisticated ways to dupe people into buying the products we want them to buy? (Sherry 2000: pers. comm.)

In sum: to circumvent the possibility of harming members of their study or beneficiary populations, it is vitally important that applied cultural anthropologists adhere as closely as possible to the institutionalized research protocols their discipline has set out for them (see below). In the case of beneficiary populations, the ethics of social research demand the creation of "a mutually respectful, win–win relationship" between the researcher and the target community, in which beneficiaries feel they can participate comfortably and fully, useful data emerges, and the intended beneficiaries consider the work helpful (Sieber 1998:128; see also Garza 1991). In the case of individual research collaborators, their right to privacy must be protected, and (if possible) they must fully understand exactly how the information they provide will be used. As one social scientist has put it, "the value of the best research is not likely to outweigh injury to a person exposed" (Stake 1998:102–103).[6]

FOOD FOR THOUGHT   Suppose you have been hired by a large public school district, with students from many different ethnic groups and socioeconomic classes, to help improve poor standardized test scores and lower a high dropout rate. In your research on the effects of ethnicity and socioeconomic status on learning, you interview teachers, parents, and administrators. You also want to talk to as many students as possible, to learn what subjects, teachers, and teaching methods they like or dislike. Yet you are wary of the impact that your presence, and your attention to some students but not others, may have. How would you (1) assess the impact of your presence and research on the students, (2) protect students' privacy, and (3) establish "a mutually respectful, win–win relationship" with this particular target group?

Applied Cultural Anthropologists and Employers

Although their work is often supported by research foundations or other funding agencies, cultural anthropologists pursuing academic or "pure" research essentially work for themselves. Typically their fundamental intent (setting aside personal motivations such as self-satisfaction or securing academic tenure) is to contribute to anthropological knowledge, and while they are usually obliged to demonstrate to their financial supporters that they are able to do so (and later, if they want further funding, that they have), academic researchers generally set their own goals and devise their own research strategies.

Applied cultural anthropologists, in contrast, work not for themselves but for employers or, in the case of part-time or consulting work, **clients.** Employers or clients can be individuals but are much more likely to be organizations—private or public, national or international, profit-making or not-for-profit. It is understood by both parties that the applied anthropologist's job is to provide the employer or client with data, insights, and recommendations; employers and clients in turn might be said to "purchase" these "products." Under these circumstances, it is usually the employer or client, not the applied cultural anthropologist, who sets an applied project's goals, limits, budget, and duration, and sometimes even its overall research strategy as well—despite the fact that the employer or client may have little understanding of the ethical principles under which applied cultural anthropologists work (Gilbert et al. 1991:205). Perhaps most especially in cases in which cultural anthropologists are junior members of multidisciplinary research teams, they may have "little say over the design of a project or how the material will be used or disseminated" (Fluehr-Lobban 1991:176).

As either full-time employees or as temporary or part-time consultants, applied cultural anthropologists as employees must resolve a number of major ethical questions, to their own satisfaction, before beginning their research. Important among these questions are the following:

- What are the overall goals of the employer or client?
- What are the goals of the specific project(s) on which the applied cultural anthropologist is expected to work?
- What are the uses to which the applied anthropologist's employer or client will put the data, insights, and recommendations that emerge from the work?
- Is there any potential that any aspect of the project will cause harm to any individual or group?

These and similar ethical questions are magnified because of applied cultural anthropologists' high visibility. Their work for a wide variety of employers, from businesses to charitable foundations to development organizations to governments, "carries with [it] a responsibility to represent the discipline well to the larger world" (Gilbert et al. 1991:205).

Proprietary Research. When research in applied cultural anthropology is commissioned and paid for by an employer, a number of different agencies and individuals (such as editors or government officials) may exert control, to one degree or another, over the outcome (Wolcott 1999:111). For example, employers may feel that they, not an applied cultural anthropologist, have the right to publish the research findings, edit them, withhold them, or otherwise control the way in which they will be used. Research conducted under such assumptions is termed **proprietary research.** If no understanding regarding rights has been reached prior to the applied cultural anthropologist's employment, serious ethical problems may arise—for example, conflicts of interest between the anthropologist's employer and members of the research population (see Fluehr-Lobban 1998:179, 182).

In a case reminiscent of Steven McNabb's experience, described earlier in this chapter, applied anthropologist "Jerry Vaughn" (a pseudonym) was hired by a federal agency to conduct a social impact assessment to determine to what extent the environment surrounding a Native American community would be affected by government development plans (Jacobs 1987:22). During a period of participant observation among the Native Americans in question, Vaughn amassed copious field notes, which included sensitive personal information conveyed during frank and open interviews. In a lengthy report to his employer, Vaughn concluded that the culture of the aboriginal people involved would be irretrievably altered if the government's plans went forward.

At that point, the director of the federal agency, who was undoubtedly unhappy with this conclusion, asked Vaughn to turn over all of his field notes in order for the agency to solicit another opinion. Vaughn refused, citing his collaborators' right to confidentiality. Eventually, with legal help, he won his case, on the grounds that when a contract fails to make ownership of data clear, the anthropologist retains his traditional right to these data (Jacobs 1987:22–23). Cases like this one demonstrate the need for applied anthropologists to make clear to their employers, before research begins, that the ethical requirement to protect the research population supersedes the employer's right of ownership over any data the anthropologist believes might cause harm to the research population.

Development Organizations. Almost all of the major agencies and organizations devoted to development or with interests in development—including governments, international aid agencies, nongovernmental organizations, private foundations, private corporations, and charitable organizations—employ applied cultural anthropologists, either part- or full-time. The relationship between anthropologist and employer or client may be especially problematic in the case of applied work for these organizations (see Chapter 5).

At first glance, it might appear difficult to argue against the value of development, which was defined above as the attempt to address widespread and deeply rooted social problems. It may be similarly difficult to criticize the work of development organizations, which typically involves helping poor people to gain access to material commodities such as adequate food, water, and housing; basic services such as education and health care; and rights such as self-government and freedom of religious expression. Yet when the agendas of development organizations are translated into actions, ethical conflicts abound. Applied cultural anthropologists employed by these organizations often find that their employers' goals and practices are in conflict with those of other agencies, with anthropological notions of scholarly responsibility and integrity, or even with the actual needs and wishes of study populations or groups targeted for intervention. Thus, development efforts have been, and continue to be, sharply criticized, both within anthropology (see, e.g., Escobar 1995) and outside it, and the roles and responsibilities of applied cultural anthropologists to the development organizations for which they work continue to be discussed and clarified within the discipline. Chapter 5 addresses the ethics of development in detail.

Applied Cultural Anthropologists and Professional Colleagues

Much of the work of applied cultural anthropologists is undertaken not individually but in multidisciplinary teams, which may consist of professionals representing many disciplines in addition to anthropology. Behaving according to the ethical guidelines of cultural anthropology is thus only one of applied cultural anthropologists' ethical responsibilities. They must also educate their non-anthropologist colleagues to their discipline's ethical principles, ensuring to their own satisfaction that the behavior of their colleagues is in no way incompatible with these principles. Additionally, they must be open to and respectful of the principles of their colleagues' disciplines (Gilbert et al. 1991:208).

Ethical considerations vis-à-vis colleagues obviously make applied cultural anthropologists' work more complicated. Yet this work "offer(s) a unique opportunity to make clear and public the ethical perspectives of our profession to . . . other 'publics'" (Gilbert et al. 1991:209). The new ethical guidelines recently ratified by the American Anthropological Association (see below) offer specific instruction to applied cultural anthropologists on ways to interrelate with colleagues in mutually acceptable and satisfying ways.

ETHICAL GUIDELINES FOR APPLIED CULTURAL ANTHROPOLOGISTS

Legislation

In the United States, public knowledge of harmful research involving human subjects, such as the Nazi experiments and the Tuskegee study, resulted in the establishment, after World War II, of a federal-level investigative body to examine the ethics of research involving human subjects. Though mainly in response to morally unacceptable medical research, this commission's deliberations were of interest to researchers in any and all disciplines, including both academic and applied anthropology, in which human beings, as the objects of research, might be harmed, deceived, or even left uninformed. Within anthropology, interest in the work of the commission was heightened by a number of political developments either directly or peripherally involving applied cultural anthropologists. Notable among these were "Project Camelot" (see Chapter 3, p. 69; see also Fluehr-Lobban 2002:20), an effort on the part of the U.S. government to collect social-scientific information with which to assist friendly governments faced with political instability, and the U.S. military involvement in the conflict in Southeast Asia.

Eventually, in 1974, Congress passed the National Research Act, requiring that panels of appropriately qualified scientists and ethicists review all plans for federally funded research involving human subjects. The act required, among other terms and conditions, that project investigators secure informed consent from study participants (Wax 1987:7; see also Wulff 1979; Akeroyd 1984). This proviso, in particular, disturbed cultural anthropologists, who pointed out that the earlier fieldwork of some of the discipline's most important scholars, such as Bronislaw Malinowski, E. E. Evans-Pritchard, and Raymond Firth, could not have been undertaken had these fieldworkers felt constrained to abide by it (Wax 1987:7). Anthropologists were also concerned about the possibility that in some circumstances, informed consent might actually jeopardize research populations (Siebert 1998:129).

Nevertheless, the National Research Act (which has undergone limited revisions since 1974) continues broadly to guide human-subjects research in both the biomedical and social-scientific disciplines. Today, compliance with the provisions of the National Research Act is overseen by the Department of Health and Human Services (DHHS). Within DHHS, the Office of Protection from Research Risk maintains a website where the most current federal regulations governing research involving human subjects are posted (see *Anthropology Career Resources Handbook*). Other countries have similar federal-level regulations and oversight agencies.

Institutional Review Boards

A major tenet of the National Research Act was the establishment of **institutional review boards (IRBs),** panels of ethicists and scientists qualified to arbitrate ethical issues and guide the behavior of researchers accordingly. Today these panels exist in virtually all colleges, universities, and other research institutions with employees who are involved in human subjects research, whether federal funding is involved or not.

IRBs not only protect research subjects from unacceptable risk, but also protect researchers in the event of complaints or legal suits (Sieber 1998:129). They vary widely in terms of the strictness with which ethical guidelines are interpreted (Fluehr-Lobban 1998:183) but are usually flexible enough to be open to negotiation on the subject of how research in cultural anthropology differs from other kinds of human-subjects research (ibid.:184). Thus, for example, when evaluating anthropological research plans, IRBs may allow exceptions to the general guidelines governing informed consent (Siebert 1998:129; Gert 1995:31).

Despite the existence of IRBs in both America and Europe, a certain proportion of research involving human subjects escapes review, due to the lack of research review procedures in many countries in the developing world. In a survey of 210 developing country health researchers, one investigator (Hyder 2000) found that 22 percent of studies in which these researchers were involved—much of it development work funded by national foreign aid organizations (see Chapter 5)—had not been subjected to any ethical review in the countries where the research was implemented.

FOOD FOR THOUGHT   A nonprofit U.S. development organization, concerned about world over-population and dedicated to promoting contraception, hires a (male) applied cultural anthropologist, working as a freelance consultant, to research contraceptive techniques and family-size decisions in a West African country. In the field, the anthropologist discovers that local religious leaders, who had not been informed beforehand about the project, object strongly to the idea of the researcher's informants—particularly female informants—discussing such subjects with an outsider of the opposite sex because of possible negative consequences to their reputations. The project has been approved by the institutional review board of its sponsoring agency. What should the anthropologist do?

Anthropological Codes of Ethics

To guide both academic and applied anthropologists through the morass of ethical considerations they face, a number of statements urging or guiding ethical behavior, most of them drawn up as formal ethical codes, have been put forward within the discipline. The first of these statements appeared in a 1919 letter from Franz Boas to the periodical *The Nation*. In his letter, Boas complained that several American applied anthropologists, working for the U.S. government, were hiding behind the discipline of anthropology in order to spy on other governments (Fluehr-Lobban 2002: 20). Boas's harsh accusation earned him the official censure of the American Anthropological Association and expulsion from his position on its governing board.

Despite the ferment caused within anthropology by Boas's letter, however, and also despite the severity of the sanction imposed on him, the controversy subsided. The American Anthropological Association did not view the episode as calling for the establishment of a formal code of ethics, and cultural anthropologists, both academic and applied, continued working without one. In the ensuing decades (and especially during World War II), as an increasing number of cultural anthropologists took on applied work in government or the private sector, there was general intradisciplinary agreement about the appropriateness of this work (Moos 1995:34; see also Chapter 3).

The SfAA Code.   The first set of guidelines developed specifically to steer applied cultural anthropologists in their work was not established until after World War II. In 1949, the first membership organization of applied anthropologists, the Society for Applied Anthropology, or SfAA (see Chapter 3), drew up a list of principles to guide the professional behavior of applied anthropologists (Mead, Chapple, and Brown 1949). The SfAA code, "Professional and Ethical Responsibilities" (see Figure 4.1), was revised in 1963 and again in 1983 (SfAA 1983).

The AAA Code.   In the 1950s, the idea of foreign aid blossomed in Western countries, based on the premise that wealthier countries could simultaneously forge alliances with less well-off countries and extend both humanitarian and military aid to them (see Chapters 3 and 5). This was an area in which applied cultural

◇ **FIGURE 4.1**   **Professional and Ethical Responsibilities of the Society for Applied Anthropology (revised 1983)**

This statement is a guide to professional behavior for the members and fellows of the Society for Applied Anthropology. As members or fellows of the Society we shall act in ways that are consistent with the responsibilities stated below irrespective of the specific circumstances of our employment.

1. To the people we study we owe disclosure of our research goals, methods and sponsorship. The participation of people in our research activities shall only be on a voluntary and informed basis. We shall provide a means throughout our research activities and in subsequent publications to maintain the confidentiality of those we study. The people we study must be made aware of the likely limits of confidentiality and must not be promised a greater degree of confidentiality than can be realistically expected under current legal circumstances in our respective nations. We shall, within the limits of our knowledge, disclose any significant risk to those we study that may result from our activities.

2. To the communities ultimately affected by our actions we owe respect for their dignity, integrity and worth. We recognize that human survival is contingent upon the continued existence of a diversity of human communities, and guide our professional activities accordingly. We will avoid taking or recommending action on behalf of a sponsor which is harmful to the interests of a community.

3. To our social science colleagues we have the responsibility not to engage in actions that impedes their reasonable professional activities. Among other things this means that, while respecting the needs, responsibilities, and legitimate proprietary interests of our sponsors we should not impede the flow of information about research outcomes and professional practice techniques. We shall accurately report the contributions of colleagues to our work. We shall not condone falsification or distortion by others. We should not prejudice communities or agencies against a colleague for reasons of personal gain.

4. To our students, interns or trainees we owe non-discriminatory access to our training services. We shall provide training which is informed, accurate and relevant to the needs of the larger society. We recognize the need for continuing education so as to maintain our skill and knowledge at a high level. Our training should inform students as to their ethical responsibilities. Student contributions to our professional activities, including both research and publication, should be adequately recognized.

5. To our employers and other sponsors we owe accurate reporting of our qualifications and competent, efficient and timely performance of the work we undertake for them. We shall establish a clear understanding with each employer or other sponsor as to the nature of our professional responsibilities. We shall report our research and other activities accurately. We have the obligation to attempt to prevent distortion or suppression of research results or policy recommendations by concerned agencies.

6. To society as a whole we owe the benefit of our special knowledge and skills in interpreting socio-cultural systems. We should communicate our understanding of human life to the society at large.

Source: Fluehr-Lobban 1991:263–264.

anthropologists were soon to become heavily involved, through their work for multilateral and bilateral aid organizations, private charitable institutions, and NGOs. Inevitably, the involvement of cultural anthropologists in foreign affairs prompted some soul-searching—and also some self-criticism—within the discipline, regarding its ethical implications (Davies 1999:45). The issue came to a head in cultural anthropology in the 1960s (see Chapter 3), thanks in large part to "Project Camelot" and the Vietnam War. At last, in 1969, twenty years after the publication of the SfAA code of ethics, the American Anthropological Association established its Committee on Research Problems and Ethics. Urged on by articles appearing in professional journals (for example, Jorgenson 1971), this committee produced the AAA's first official code of ethics, entitled "Principles of Professional Responsibility," in 1971 (American Anthropological Association 1991, orig. 1971).

The NAPA Code.　As the number of applied cultural anthropologists grew in the early 1980s, some of them, already members of the AAA, formed the National Association for the Practice of Anthropology (NAPA) (see Chapter 1, pp. 2, 4). Dedicated to addressing the specific needs of applied anthropologists, this new section became an official branch of the AAA in 1983. The establishment of NAPA was significant because it signaled the AAA's official recognition of the recent growth and new importance of applied anthropology, as well as the differences between theoretical and applied anthropology (see Chapter 3).

　　The applied anthropologists who formed the membership of NAPA in the 1980s were unhappy with the existing AAA code of ethics. A major cause for concern was their feeling that it was not always possible for applied cultural anthropologists to live up to the stricture in the AAA code that the anthropologist's primary responsibility must be to the people studied, since applied anthropologists also owed allegiance to their employers (Fluehr-Lobban 1998:177). After an unsuccessful attempt, in 1984, to revise the AAA code along lines more compatible with applied work, members of NAPA drew up their own code of ethics, entitled "Ethical Guidelines for Practitioners," in 1988 (see Figure 4.2). This code was much better suited to the kinds of endeavors most apt to be undertaken by applied anthropologists: consulting work and proprietary research (Fluehr-Lobban 1998:177).

The Revised AAA Code.　In 1994, the American Anthropological Association decided to review and revise its code and formed a committee of anthropologists, consisting of representatives of each of the major subfields, to draft the revision. Between March 1995 and January 1997, committee members worked on a revised code, which included a special section devoted to applied anthropology. The draft was discussed in open sessions at the 1995 and 1996 annual meetings of the AAA. Among the issues with which the committee wrestled that were of particular import to applied cultural anthropologists were responsibilities to research populations, the difference between clandestine and proprietary research, and the notion of justifiable deception in research (Fluehr-Lobban 1996:17).

　　NAPA, while supporting the draft AAA code in general terms, suggested several changes (Jordan 1996:17). First, the NAPA committee felt that the draft code's mandate to "disseminate the results of . . . research publicly within a reasonable time" was not always possible for applied anthropologists (Jordan 1996:17) because

◇ **FIGURE 4.2   Ethical Guidelines for Practitioners, National Association of Practicing Anthropologists (1988)**

These guidelines have been developed by the National Association for the Practice of Anthropology as a guide to the professional and ethical responsibilities that practicing anthropologists should uphold. A practicing anthropologist is a professionally-trained anthropologist who is employed or retained to apply his or her specialized knowledge to problem solving related to human welfare and human activities. The designation "practicing anthropologist" includes full-time practitioners who work for clients such as social-service organizations, government agencies and business and industrial firms. This term also includes part-time practitioners, usually academically-based anthropologists, who accept occasional assignments with such clients. The substantive work of practicing anthropologists may include applied research, program design and implementation, client advocacy and advisory roles and activities related to the communication of anthropological perspectives. These guidelines are provided with the recognition that practicing anthropologists are involved in many types of policy-related research, frequently affecting individuals and groups with diverse and sometimes conflicting interests. No code or set of guidelines can anticipate unique circumstances or direct practitioner actions in specific situations. The individual practitioner must be willing to make carefully considered ethical choices and be prepared to make clear the assumptions, facts and issues on which those choices are based. These guidelines therefore address *general* contexts, priorities and relationships which should be considered in ethical decision making in anthropological practice.

1. Our primary responsibility is to respect and consider the welfare and human rights of all categories of people affected by decisions, programs or research in which we take part. However, we recognize that many research and practice settings involve conflicts between benefits accruing to different parties affected by our research. It is our ethical responsibility, to the extent feasible, to bring to bear on decision making, our own or that of others, information concerning the actual or potential impacts of such activities on all whom they might affect. It is also our responsibility to assure, to the extent possible, that the views of groups so affected are made clear and given full and serious consideration by decision makers and planners, in order to preserve options and choices for affected groups.

2. To our resource persons or research subjects we owe full and timely disclosure of the objectives, methods and sponsorship of our activities. We should recognize the rights of resource persons, whether individuals or groups, to receive recognition for their contributions or to remain anonymous if they so desire or to decline participation altogether. These persons should be informed of our commitment to the principle of confidentiality and of the steps we will take to insure confidentiality. We should be sensitive to issues related to confidentiality throughout the design of research or other activities involving resource persons and should thoroughly investigate and understand all of the limitations on our claims of confidentiality and disclosure.

3. To our employers we owe competent, efficient, fully professional skills and techniques, timely performance of our work and communication of our findings and recommendations in understandable, non-jargonistic language.

    As practicing anthropologists, we are frequently involved with employers or clients in legally contracted arrangements. It is our responsibility to carefully review contracts prior to signing and be willing to execute the terms and conditions stipulated in the contract once it has been signed.

    At the *outset* of a relationship or contract with an employer or client, we have an obligation to determine whether or not the work we are requested to perform is consistent with our commitment to deal fairly with the rights and welfare of persons affected by our work, recognizing that

Source: Fluehr-Lobban 1991:270–273.

different constituencies may be affected in different ways. At this time, we should also discuss with our employer or client the intended use of the data or materials to be generated by our work and clarify the extent to which information developed during our activities can be made available to the public. Issues surrounding the protection of subject confidentiality and disclosure of information or findings should be thoroughly reviewed with the potential employer or client. We will not undertake activities which compromise our ethical responsibilities.

We will carry out our work in such a manner that the employer fully understands our ethical priorities, commitments and responsibilities. When, at any time during the course of work performance, the demands of the employer require or appear to require us to violate the ethical standards of our profession, we have the responsibility to clarify the nature of the conflict between the request and our standards and to propose alternatives that are consistent with our standards. If such a conflict cannot be resolved, we should terminate the relationship.

4. In our relations with students and trainees, we will be candid, fair, nonexploitative, nondiscriminatory, and committed to the students' or trainees' welfare. We recognize that such mentoring does involve an exchange in which practitioners share their knowledge and experience in return for the significant effort and contribution of the students/trainees. We should be honest and thorough in our presentation of material and should strive to improve our teaching and training techniques and our methods of evaluating the effectiveness of our instruction.

As practicing anthropologists we are frequently called upon to instruct, train or teach individuals, anthropologists and others in nonacademic settings (workshop participants, in-service trainees, continuation or certification program trainees and research teams). To such persons, we owe training that is informed, timely and relevant to their needs.

Our instruction should inform both students and trainees of the ethical responsibilities involved in the collection and use of data. To our students and trainees we owe respect for and openness to nonanthropological methods and perspectives. Student and trainee contributions to our work, including publications, should be accurately and completely attributed.

5. To our colleagues, anthropologists and others, we have a responsibility to conduct our work in a manner that facilitates their activities or that does not unjustly compromise their ability to carry out professional work.

The cross-disciplinary nature of the work of practicing anthropology requires us to be informed and respectful of the disciplinary and professional perspectives, methodologies and ethical requirements on nonanthropological colleagues with whom we work.

We will accurately report the contribution of our colleagues to our research, practice-related activities and publications.

6. To the discipline of anthropology we have a responsibility to act in a manner that presents the discipline to the public and to other professional colleagues in a favorable light. We will point out the value of anthropological contributions to the understanding of human problems and humankind. Where appropriate in the context of our work, we will encourage the use of anthropological approaches and recommend the participation of other anthropologists.

We will contribute to the growth of our discipline through communicating and publishing scientific and practical information about the work in which we are engaged, including as appropriate, theory, processes, outcomes and professional techniques and methods.

of the problem of proprietary research. The final version of the code was therefore amended to read: "Applied anthropologists must intend and expect to utilize the results of their work appropriately (*i.e.*, publication, teaching, program and policy development) within a reasonable time" (American Anthropological Association 1998: Section V-1). NAPA'S request that the qualification "when possible" be added was not approved.

Second, NAPA felt the draft code's injunction to "do no harm" was "too simplistic" (Jordan 1996:17) and requested that a qualifier be added: "understanding that the applied anthropological researcher may be involved in many types of policy-related research, frequently affecting individuals and groups with diverse and sometimes conflicting interests. The individual practitioner must be willing to make carefully considered ethical choices and be prepared to make clear the assumptions, facts and issues on which those choices are based" (Jordan 1996:18). This qualifier was approved with only minor changes.

Finally, the NAPA committee felt that the AAA should reinstate the section regarding the responsibility of AAA to adjudicate claims of unethical professional conflict (Jordan 1996:18). However, in the final version of the 1998 code, the AAA specifically declines to adjudicate ethical claims (Section I).

FOOD FOR THOUGHT Based on what you know so far about applied cultural anthropology, can you think of a hypothetical situation in which, by obtaining informed consent prior to research or intervention, an applied cultural anthropologist might actually cause harm to members of a research population?

The final draft of the AAA code, based on comments received from NAPA members and other anthropologists, was drawn up in 1997 and ratified by the membership in 1998 (American Anthropological Association 1998; see also Fluehr-Lobban 2002:20). Under this new code, all anthropological work is subject to the same ethical guidelines (American Anthropological Association 1998, Section V [1]). Significantly, the revised code eliminates distinctions between pure and applied research. "Quite simply, research is research, and standards of ethical conduct in research are the same" (Fluehr-Lobban 1998:178–179).

Other Ethical Codes

Although the newly revised AAA code attempts to cover ethical issues encountered by both academic and applied cultural anthropologists, some anthropologists doubt that a single code of ethics can be appropriate for both academic and applied purposes (Frankel and Trend 1991:179). As if to acknowledge the fact that it is not the *ne plus ultra* of ethical statements, the 1998 AAA code includes a final section (Section VIII) listing other codes deemed "relevant" for anthropologists, although it does not mandate adherence to any of them. Most of the codes listed apply to anthropologists working in subfields other than cultural anthropology, but three United Nations documents—the 1948 "Universal Declaration of Human Rights," the 1983 "Convention on the Elimination of All Forms of Discrimination Against Women,"

◇ *The American Anthropological Association's code of ethics specifies that the U.N.'s 1948 Universal Declaration of Human Rights is "relevant" for anthropologists. In 1958, former First Lady and human rights advocate Eleanor Roosevelt celebrated the tenth anniversary of the U.N. Declaration with U.N. officials.*

and the 1987 "Convention on the Rights of the Child" do have a direct bearing on applied cultural anthropology.

Oddly, Section VIII of the AAA code does not mention several other codes that are also relevant to applied anthropology: those established by the AAA's sister organizations in other countries. For example, the Society of Applied Anthropology in Canada has published a code entitled "Ethical Guidelines" (1983). In Britain, anthropological research is governed by a code of ethics, "Ethical Guidelines for Good Research Practice," formulated by the Association of Social Anthropologists of the Commonwealth and approved by the Royal Anthropological Institute.

CONCLUSION

It is important for prospective applied cultural anthropologists to understand that the attempt to help promote beneficial social change of any kind, in any venue, always carries with it serious, complex, and in some cases intractable ethical problems. These problems are still very much under discussion, both within applied cultural anthropology and within its parent discipline.

Today, opinions on the subject of applied research, and interventions based on that research, represent a continuum between two extremes. At one extreme is the opinion that applied research in cultural anthropology constitutes "a prostitution of valuable professional talents for monies and prestige . . . [and] a betrayal of the peoples whose welfare anthropology . . . claimed to cherish" (Wax 1987:5). At the other extreme is the view that what would be truly unethical would be cultural anthropologists' *failure* to intervene in the lives of others, whenever and wherever human beings are disenfranchised (Scheper-Hughes 1995). These opposing views will be revisited repeatedly throughout this book.

◇　◇　◇

KEY TERMS

clandestine research   research about which all information is not made freely available to interested stakeholders

client   an applied cultural anthropologist's employer; an individual or organization contracting with an applied cultural anthropologist to "purchase" data, insights, and recommendations from the anthropologist

informed consent   the formal agreement, on the part of a research study participant, to participate in the research after having been fully advised of all relevant details, including the risks

institutional review board (IRB)   a panel of ethicists and scientists qualified to arbitrate ethical issues and guide research involving human subjects

proprietary research   research undertaken by an applied anthropologist but commissioned and funded by the anthropologist's employer or client, to which the employer or client feels entitled

social impact assessment (SIA)   a determination of the impact of an applied project on the population intended to benefit from it

stakeholder   anyone with any interests in a specific applied project

target group   a group of people intended to benefit from an applied project. The use of this term has been criticized by some who feel it is disparaging, but it is nevertheless very commonly employed. It is used in this book without pejorative intent.

NOTES

1. Although both were written almost a generation ago, George N. Appel's (1978) *Ethical Dilemmas in Anthropological Inquiry: A Case Book,* and Joan Cassell and Murray Wax's (1980) article "Ethical Problems of Fieldwork" each contain useful and interesting discussions of such considerations.
2. Some specific examples of unsuccessful interventions on the part of applied cultural anthropologists were mentioned in Chapters 2 (*e.g.*, the Philippines example) and 3 (*e.g.*, the "Project Camelot" example).
3. Other "universal rights" are enumerated and discussed in Chapter 5, in the context of development anthropology. Other "universal values" include the avoidance of death, disability, loss of freedom, and loss of pleasure (Gert 1995:30–31).
4. The American Anthropological Association's ethical code also includes responsibilities toward society at large, animal species, human material remains, and the environment. The full text of this code can be found in *Anthropology Newsletter* 39 (6):19–20 and in Bernard 1998:195–202.
5. For fuller discussions of SIA, see Finsterbusch et al. 1983, Derman and Whiteford 1985, van Willigen 1993:171–187, and Ervin 2000:98–111.
6. On the ethical considerations raised by anthropologists' engaging in romantic or sexual relations in the field, see Gearing 1995.

REFERENCES

Ackroyd, Anne
   1984. "Ethics in Relation to Informants: The Profession and Governments." In *Ethnographic Research: A Guide to General Conduct*, edited by Roy F. Ellen, 133–154. London: Academic Press.

American Anthropological Association
   1991 (orig. 1971). "Principles of Professional Responsibility." In *Ethics and the Profession of Anthropology: Dialogue for a New Era*, edited by Carolyn Fluehr-Lobban, Appendix C, 247–252. Philadelphia: University of Pennsylvania Press.

1998. "Code of Ethics of the American Anthropological Association." *Anthropology Newsletter* 39 (6): 19–20.

Appell, George N.
1978. *Ethical Dilemmas in Anthropological Inquiry: A Case Book.* Waltham, MA: Crossroads Press.

Bernard, H. Russell (ed.)
1998. *Handbook of Methods in Cultural Anthropology.* Walnut Creek, CA: Altamira Press.

Cassell, Joan, and Sue-Ellen Jacobs (eds.)
1987. *Handbook on Ethical Issues in Anthropology* (AAA Special Publications no. 23). Washington, DC: American Anthropological Association.

Cassell, Joan, and Murrray L. Wax (eds.)
1980. "Ethical Problems of Fieldwork." *Social Problems* 27:259–378.

Davies, Charlotte Aull
1999. *Reflexive Ethnography.* London: Routledge.

D'Andrade, Roy
1995. "Moral Models in Anthropology." *Current Anthropology* 36 (3):399–408.

Derman, William, and Scott Whiteford (eds.)
1985. *Social Impact Analysis and Development Planning in the Third World.* Boulder, CO: Westview Press.

Downe, Pamela J.
1999. "Participant Advocacy and Research with Prostitutes in Costa Rica." *Practicing Anthropology* 21 (3):21–24.

Ervin, Alexander M.
2000. *Applied Anthropology: Tools and Perspectives for Contemporary Practice.* Boston: Allyn and Bacon.

Escobar, Arturo
1995. *Encountering Development: The Making and Unmaking of the Third World.* Princeton, NJ: Princeton University Press.

Faden, R. R., and T. L. Beauchamp
1986. *A History and Theory of Informed Consent.* New York: Oxford University Press.

Finsterbusch, Kurt, L. G. Llewellyn, and C. P. Wolf (eds.)
1983. *Social Impact Assessment Methods.* Beverly Hills, CA: Sage Publications.

Fluehr-Lobban, Carolyn (ed.)
1991. *Ethics and the Profession of Anthropology: Dialogue for a New Era.* Philadelphia: University of Pennsylvania Press.

1994. "Informed Consent in Anthropological Research: We Are Not Exempt." *Human Organization* 53 (1):1–9.

1996. "Developing the New AAA Code of Ethics." *Anthropology Newsletter* 37 (4):17–18.

1998. "Ethics." In *Handbook of Methods in Cultural Anthropology*, edited by H. Russell Bernard, 173–202. Walnut Creek, CA: Altamira Press.

2002. "A Century of Ethics and Professional Anthropology." *Anthropology News* 43 (3):20.

Frankel, Barbara, and M. G. Trend
1991. "Principles, Pressures, and Paychecks: The Anthropologist as Employee." In *Ethics and the Profession of Anthropology*, edited by Carolyn Fluehr-Lobban, 177–197. Philadelphia: University of Pennsylvania Press.

Garza, Christina E.
1991. "Studying the Natives on the Shop Floor." *Business Week*, Sept. 30, 1991: 74–78.

Gearing, Jean
1995. "Fear and Loving in the West Indies." In *Taboo: Sex, Identity, and Erotic Subjectivity in Anthropological Fieldwork*, edited by Don Kulick and Margaret Willson, 186–218. London: Routledge.

Gert, Bernard
1995. "Universal Values and Professional Codes of Ethics." *Anthropology Newsletter* 36 (7):30–31.

Gilbert, M. Jean, Nathaniel Tashima, and Claudia C. Fishman
1991. "Ethics and Practicing Anthropologists' Dialogue with the Larger World: Considerations for the Formulation of Ethical Guidelines for Practicing Anthropologists." In *Ethics and the Profession of Anthropology*, edited by Carolyn Fluehr-Lobban, 200–210. Philadelphia: University of Pennsylvania Press.

Handwerker, W. Penn
1997. "Universal Human Rights and the Problem of Unbounded Cultural Meanings." *American Anthropologist* 99 (4):799–809.

Hill, Carole E.
2000. "Strategic Issues for Rebuilding a Theory and Practice Synthesis." In *The Unity of Theory and Practice in Anthropology: Rebuilding a Fractured Synthesis* (NAPA Bulletin 18), edited by Carole E. Hill and Marietta L. Baba, 1–16. Washington, DC: NAPA.

Hyder, Adnan A.
2000. "International Research Ethics: Perspectives from Developing Country Researchers." Paper presented at 27th annual meeting of the Global Health Council, Washington, DC, June 6–9, 2000.

Irvine, Leslie
1998. "Organizational Ethics and Fieldwork Realities: Negotiating Ethical Boundaries in Codependents Anonymous." In *Doing Ethnographic Research*, edited by Scott Grills, 167–183. Thousand Oaks, CA: Sage Publications.

Jacobs, Sue-Ellen
1987. "Cases and Solutions." In *Handbook on Ethical Issues in Anthropology* (AAA Special Publications No. 23), edited by Joan Cassell and Sue-Ellen Jacobs, 20–36. Washington, DC: American Anthropological Association.

Jordan, Ann
1996. "Review of the AAA Code of Ethics." *Anthropology Newsletter* 37 (4):17–18 (April 1996).

Jorgenson, Joseph G.
1971. "On Ethics and Anthropology." *Current Anthropology* 12:321–334.

Kozaitis, Kathryn A.
2000. "The Rise of Anthropological Praxis." In *The Unity of Theory and Practice in Anthropology: Rebuilding a Fractured Synthesis* (NAPA Bulletin 18), edited by Carole E. Hill and Marietta L. Baba, 45–66. Washington, DC: NAPA.

Kutsche, Paul
1998. *Field Ethnography: A Manual for Doing Cultural Anthropology.* Upper Saddle River, NJ: Prentice Hall.

McNabb, Steven
1995. "Social Research and Litigation: Good Intentions Versus Good Ethics." *Human Organization* 54: 331–335.

Mead, Margaret, Elliot D. Chapple, and G. Gordon Brown
1949. "Report of the Committee on Ethics." *Human Organization* 8 (2):20–21.

Moos, Felix
1995. "Anthropological Ethics and the Military." *Anthropology Newsletter* 36 (9):34.

Perez, Carlos A.
1997. "Participatory Research: Implications for Applied Anthropology." *Practicing Anthropology* 19 (3): 2–7.

Preister, Kevin
1987. "Issue-Centered Social Impact Assessment." In *Anthropological Praxis: Translating Knowledge into Action*, edited by Robert M. Wulff and Shirley J. Fiske, 39–55. Boulder, CO: Westview Press.

Ringberg, Torsten
1995. "Is Academic Anthropology Unethical?" *Anthropology Newsletter* 36 (1):48.

Salmon, Merrilee H.
2001 (orig. 1997). "Ethical Considerations in Anthropology and Archaeology, or Relativism and Justice for All." In *Taking Sides: Clashing Views on Controversial Issues in Anthropology*, edited by Kirk M. Endicott and Robert Welsch, 362–370. Guilford, CT: McGraw-Hill/Dushkin.

Scheper-Hughes, Nancy
1995. "The Primacy of the Ethical: Propositions for a Militant Anthropology." *Current Anthropology* 36 (3):409–420.

Seal, David Wyatt, Frederick R. Bloom, and Anton M. Somlai
2000. "Dilemmas in Conducting Qualitative Sex Research in Applied Field Settings." *Health Education and Behavior* 27 (1):10–23.

Sieber, Joan E.
1998. "Planning Ethically Responsible Research." In *Handbook of Applied Social Research Methods*, edited by Leonard Bickman, and Debra J. Rog, 127–156. Thousand Oaks, CA: Sage Publications.

Smith, Jennie M.
2001. *When the Hands Are Many: Community Organization and Social Change in Rural Haiti.* Ithaca, NY: Cornell University Press.

Society for Applied Anthropology
1983. "Professional and Ethical Responsibilities." In *Ethics and the Profession of Anthropology: Dialogue for a New Era*, edited by Carolyn Fluehr-Lobban, Appendix F, 263–264. Philadelphia: University of Pennsylvania Press.

Stake, Robert E.
1998. "Case Studies." In *Strategies of Qualitative Inquiry*, edited by Norman K. Denzin and Yvonna S. Lincoln, 86–109. Thousand Oaks, CA: Sage Publications.

van Willigen, John
1993. *Applied Anthropology: An Introduction* (rev. ed.). Westport, CT: Bergin and Garvey.

Wax, Murray L.
1987. "Some Issues and Sources on Ethics in Anthropology." In *Handbook on Ethical Issues in Anthropology* (AAA Special Publications No. 23), edited by Joan Cassell and Sue-Ellen Jacobs, 4–10. Washington, DC: American Anthropological Association.

Wolcott, Harry F.
1999. *Ethnography: A Way of Seeing.* Walnut Creek, CA: Altamira Press.

Wolf, C. P.
1983. "A Methodological Overview." In *Social Impact Assessment Methods*, edited by Kurt Finsterbusch, L.G. Llewellyn, and C.P. Wolf, 15–35. Beverly Hills, CA: Sage Publications.

Wulff, Keith M. (ed.)
1979. *Regulation of Scientific Inquiry: Societal Concerns with Research* (AAAS Symposium No. 37). Boulder, CO: Westview Press.

CHAPTER 5

DEVELOPMENT ANTHROPOLOGY

INTRODUCTION

THE ANTHROPOLOGY–DEVELOPMENT
CONNECTION
  Development Anthropology
  Anthropological Contributions to
  Development Projects
  Development Anthropologists and
  Multidisciplinary Teams

INTERNATIONAL DEVELOPMENT
  The "Developing" World

DEVELOPMENT THEORIES AND PRINCIPLES
  Some Previous Models
  Contemporary Ideas

DEVELOPMENT ORGANIZATIONS

WOMEN IN DEVELOPMENT (WID)
  Why WID?
  Gender and Development (GAD)

THE DOWNSIDE OF DEVELOPMENT
AND DEVELOPMENT ANTHROPOLOGY'S
RESPONSE
  Moral Legitimacy
  Political Agendas
  Unequal Power Relations
  Effectiveness

CONCLUSION

INTRODUCTION

In Nepal, the average annual income per person is the equivalent of about U.S. $200 (World Health Organization [WHO] 1998:182). In Brazil, the mortality rate for children under 5 years is 116 per 1,000 children among the poorest fifth of the population, but among the richest fifth, it is only 11 per 1,000 (World Bank 2000:5). Among married women in Zaire, only 3 percent know about and use modern, safe, reliable contraceptive methods (Population References Bureau [PRB] 1997). In Afghanistan, fewer than one third of all adults can read and write (WHO 1998:226). The life expectancy of a male born today in Sierra Leone is only 33 years (PRB 1997). In Papua New Guinea, most one-year-olds have not been immunized against measles (WHO 1998:231). Less than half the population of Uganda has regular access to basic medicines such as aspirin (WHO 1998:159). Even in the affluent, industrialized nations of the world, including the United States, poverty, illiteracy, unemployment, substandard living conditions, human rights abuses, and preventable health problems affect millions.

105

Some of the problems reflected in these statistics are life-and-death concerns; others are quality-of-life matters. The majority of them reflect long-lived, deeply rooted social issues rather than conditions for which quick technological solutions are available. Although their extent and gravity vary from country to country and from culture to culture, these problems share several important characteristics. They affect communities and whole nations, not just individuals; they defy quantification, both in terms of their scope and the efficacy of any solutions imposed; and they have proven immensely difficult to solve or even to alleviate.

Broadly speaking, the attempt to assist in the identification and implementation of solutions to such problems, whether at the local, national, or international level, is termed **development.** It may be initiated and carried out at the local level, with or without professional assistance (this is termed **grass-roots development**). More commonly, however, development work is undertaken, on a larger scale, by professionals representing many different fields, including cultural anthropology. These professionals may be indigenous to the country or region where development is taking place or they may be foreigners; they may be paid employees or volunteers; they may be religious or secular in their personal beliefs and motivations (Dudley 1993:9). What categorizes them as a group is their conviction that by learning from local people, and then working with them toward the achievement of specific, locally identified goals, they can help alleviate the kinds of social problems that afflict human groups all over the world so profoundly, and so enduringly, that they are often referred to as "global" problems.

Inherent in the term *development* today are three fundamental ideas. The first is that beneficial social transformation *can* be achieved by making intentional, directed

◇ *Development is the attempt to alleviate interrelated social problems such as poverty, illiteracy, ill health, and substandard living conditions. Such problems afflict millions world-wide, including this impoverished slum dweller in Bombay (Mambai), India.*

changes—changes designed to secure essential goods and services, raise living standards, increase economic productivity, elevate health status indicators and educational levels, improve infrastructure, protect environmental resources, guarantee human and civil rights, or heighten political awareness and participation. Second, such intervention is morally justified, even if the grounds for its justification vary. Third, the solution—or at least the amelioration—of global social problems depends, to a greater or lesser degree (depending on individual development workers' personal philosophies), on economic growth and material prosperity.

While neither development problems nor development efforts are unique to the less industrialized countries of the world (see Devereux and Hoddinott 1993, especially pages 164ff.), both publicly-provided social services and private charitable efforts tend to be better funded and more comprehensive in more affluent, Westernized countries. Thus, poverty, social inequality, illiteracy, and a lack of access to adequate medical care—though devastating to those affected in these countries—tend to be less widespread. This chapter therefore stresses applied cultural anthropologists' contributions to **international development,** a career area in which international funding and expertise are used to address long-standing social problems in the less developed countries of the world.

THE ANTHROPOLOGY–DEVELOPMENT CONNECTION

Development Anthropology

Distinctions are sometimes drawn among different types of development work. The term *economic development* refers to specific efforts to stimulate economic growth, redistribute income more equitably, and reduce poverty, while the term *agricultural development* refers to attempts to increase the quantity and dependability of the food supply by introducing modern agricultural technologies that will, for example, improve crop yields or the nutritional content of plant foods. *Community development* involves efforts to strengthen communities of local people and raise their living standards by lessening economic and social disparities, fostering empowerment, and encouraging the establishment of community-based self-help organizations for mutual economic support and political advocacy. *Human development* refers to attempts to foster purposeful change for the better in areas such as education or civil rights. *International development*, as the term is used in this chapter, refers to any of these—so long as international funding and international participants are involved.

When cultural anthropologists—as opposed to economists or educators or medical doctors or agricultural experts—participate in development efforts, their work is referred to as **development anthropology** (see Green 1986; Ferguson 1997:164ff.; Nolan 2002), defined as the use of anthropological ideas and methods in development work. Widespread anthropological involvement in development efforts dates to the 1980s, when development specialists representing other areas of expertise began to attribute earlier development failures, in part, to a lack of understanding about culture (Dudley 1993:13). The goal of development anthropologists is the same as the goal of applied cultural anthropologists working in other contexts—to help find workable solutions to specific problems affecting specific groups of people.

Anthropological Contributions to Development Projects

The importance of applied cultural anthropology to development efforts is twofold. First, development requires understanding and addressing social issues, the central concern of cultural anthropologists (Skar 1985:2). Who, for example, should benefit from development? Who should decide which groups should benefit from development and which should not? What kinds of knowledge or action will result in beneficial change? What kinds might be harmful? What constitutes positive intervention, and what constitutes mere interference? Of the many different kinds of development specialists, cultural anthropologists are best equipped to handle such questions. Second, successful development universally requires not only generalized knowledge of human social behaviors and systems but also concrete, specific knowledge of the customs, traditions, values, and perceived needs that prevail in specific development settings.

A development project that took place in Zaire provides an example of the importance of including the anthropological viewpoint. Development specialists intent on improving the agricultural yields of poor Zairean farmers noted that crops were being grown in weedy, eroding fields. They assumed, erroneously as it turned out, that farmers' failure to weed their crops or plant trees to prevent erosion was due to ignorance. Development anthropologist James Fairhead was able to provide the project with an emic perspective. What at first glance looked like hopelessly overgrown and untended agricultural fields actually reflected local people's knowledge that weeds in drought-susceptible fields collect moisture from dew (Fairhead 1993:188). What initially appeared to be local farmers' ignorance about the causes of erosion was explicable in terms of their land tenure system (landlords do not allow tenants to plant trees) and local symbolic associations of trees (trees can be grown only by men) (Fairhead 1993:196). These insights contributed greatly to the eventual success of the project.

FOOD FOR THOUGHT

An applied cultural anthropologist said recently, "The objective of all [development] aid is to bring about change, whether in terms of how a seed is sown or to whose benefit political power is used. Unlike academic anthropological studies, aid demands an understanding of the contradictions involved in the benevolent exercise of power" (Dudley 1993:1). What might these "contradictions" be?

Development Anthropologists and Multidisciplinary Teams

Development work is by definition multidisciplinary, calling on the expertise not only of applied cultural anthropologists but also agronomists, communications specialists, economists, educators, engineers, environmentalists, health care professionals, marketing experts, sociologists, and many others. Thus, an applied cultural anthropologist contributing to a development project typically works with specialists from several or many other disciplines. Ideally, team members cooperate closely to achieve a project's goals. Occasionally, however, *multidisciplinarity* is just a "paper term which screens the reality of a disparate set of individuals working . . . in isolated professional pigeon-holes" (Dudley 1993:10).

INTERNATIONAL DEVELOPMENT

Most applied cultural anthropologists professionally involved in development efforts do their work internationally. A large part of the reason is that cultural anthropology has historically been viewed as "the science of 'less developed' peoples" (Ferguson 1997:152), so the involvement of cultural anthropologists in the poorer and less developed countries of the world seems entirely fitting.

Cultural anthropology's initial interest and participation in the international development arena was born out of the idea of foreign assistance in the aftermath of World War II (see Chapter 3; see also Escobar 1995:6); most of the earliest development anthropologists were hired to provide information about foreign cultures to international aid agencies. Today's development anthropologists have moved well beyond that role. With local people increasingly identifying and implementing their own projects, development anthropologists are now more likely to serve potential project beneficiaries as facilitators than as actual implementers (Dudley 1993:13).

The "Developing" World

Development Indicators.   To suggest the level of development in a particular country, the United Nations has established what it calls **development indicators**—statistics believed to be broadly reflective of the quality of life worldwide. Examples of development indicators, for any given country, include the country's **gross domestic product** (GDP, the total value of all goods and services produced in a country over a given time period), the average life expectancy of its citizens at birth, its infant mortality rate, the percentage of its children who have been immunized against five preventable illnesses, and its adult literacy rate. Based on these indicators, countries are categorized as *developed* (for example, the United States and Japan), *transitional* (for example, central and eastern European countries), or *developing* (for example, China and India). Much of what international development workers—including development anthropologists—do is directed at helping people in the developing and transitional countries of the world to achieve improvements in their countries' development indicators.

Certain economic, social, and health-related criteria characterize developing and transitional countries (collectively termed the *Third World;* see Chapter 3, note 2, p. 76). First, these countries tend to be poorer than others, in terms of economic indicators such as per capita (per person) income, gross domestic product (GDP), or various measures of the standard of living such as educational levels or health status indicators.

Second, the economies of developing countries, while often the products of Western colonialism, mercantilism, and capitalism, do not conform to the standard Western model. Typically less money circulates, industrial production is accomplished with less technological sophistication than in the industrialized world, and international trade is less well established.

And third, in developing countries the number of people in the workforce, compared to the number of people who are too young or too old to work, is small, again relative to other countries. (Demographers typically deem people under the age of fifteen as too young to work and those over sixty-four as too old to work.) The ratio of the first of these groups to the second is termed the **dependency ratio.** The main reason for the relatively small proportion of working-age people in developing countries is not that there is a large proportion of elderly people, but rather that the birth rate is relatively high and the rate of population growth therefore relatively rapid. Such growth (see Figure 5.1) means that there is a large number of young people compared with older people. This is not generally true of the industrialized countries.

The developing countries are occasionally referred to as "undeveloped" or "underdeveloped" countries. Such terms seem to imply that these countries are somehow inferior, while other countries—the "developed" countries (Western

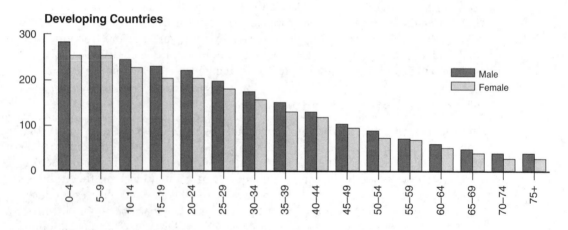

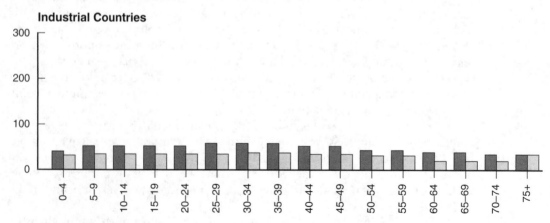

◇ **FIGURE 5.1   Age Distribution of the Populations of Developing and Industrialized Countries**

Source: Population Matters Issue Paper: "Family Planning in Developing Countries: An Unfinished Success Story," by Julie Da Vauzo and David M. Adamson, 1998. Santa Monica, CA: RAND.

countries, or countries that have successfully engaged in Western-style economic development) are superior, having completed (or at least progressed further in) the development process. Most development anthropologists therefore prefer to avoid terms like *less developed* as unnecessarily pejorative. The terms *nonindustrialized* or *newly industrializing* are sometimes used, but these terms hardly seem less pejorative than *less developed*. In this book, the term *developing country* is used for lack of a better term. Bear in mind, however, that every country is in a sense a "developing" country, since not even the most technologically advanced country can be said to be completely "developed."

"Less Developed" Countries (LDCs).   The poorest of the developing countries are often referred to as **less developed** (or **least developed**) **countries (LDCs).**[1] While almost all countries have problems in the areas of poverty, lack of access to health care, undereducation, lack of infrastructure, environmental degradation, and so on, LDCs are the countries with the most serious problems in these areas. Unfortunately and perhaps surprisingly, the number of these countries around the globe is increasing rather than decreasing. In 1975, according to the United Nations, there were twenty-seven such countries; today, there are forty-eight (WHO 1998:117). The infant mortality rate in LDCs—the number of children who die in infancy, compared with those who survive—has risen over the past fifty years, and average life expectancy in LDCs is twenty-one years less than in the developed world—an average of fifty-three years versus seventy-four (WHO 1998: 232). On average, the per capita gross national product (GNP) of these countries, classified as "low income" by the World Bank, is the equivalent of U.S. $520 per year (World Bank 2000:12).

The reasons why some countries are LDCs while others are not are many and complicated (see Diamond 1997). No single cause, nor even any set of circumstances resulting in relatively high numbers of relatively serious and pervasive development problems, can be identified. Two commonalities shared among many LDCs, however, are (1) that they were colonies of some Western nation in the past, and (2) that they were home to small-scale cultures introduced very rapidly to modern technology and brought very rapidly into the modern global economy. Most of today's LDCs were both.

FOOD FOR THOUGHT   List as many reasons as you can that might explain why countries that were colonized in the past, or countries in which indigenous populations became "modernized" very quickly, tend to be "less developed" countries today.

Other Developing Countries.   The second category of countries in which much international development work has taken place, those the United Nations refers to as transitional countries, are those whose economies are in transition from developing to industrialized. In economic terms, these are mostly middle-income countries. GNP per capita in these countries is about $2,990 per year, compared with $520 per year for the low-income countries and $25,480 for high-income (First World, or "developed") countries (World Bank 2000:12).

DEVELOPMENT THEORIES AND PRINCIPLES

Some Previous Models

Earlier it was pointed out that the idea of large-scale, institutionalized development assistance began after World War II. Attempts to heal the ravages of the war in Europe—for example, through financial aid programs instituted by the International Bank for Reconstruction and Development and the United States' Marshall Plan—were so successful that in 1949, the United Nations expanded the idea of development assistance to include sixteen nonindustrialized countries. International development, as the concept is understood today, had begun. In the 1950s, foreign aid agencies and development NGOs became increasingly common in the industrialized nations of the world, and new international lending institutions were created.

From the beginning, it was apparent that development was a highly complex effort. Chapter 3 mentioned that the motivations of the first development assistance organizations, all of them in industrialized, so-called Northern countries,[2] were at once economic, political, and humanitarian (as are those of today's aid agencies). Nor was implementation a straightforward matter. Should aid take the form of cash, materials, or expertise? Should it consist of outright donations or loans? Should it most resemble fatherly beneficence, neighborly support, or economic partnership? Through the years since World War II, the answers to these questions, and consequently the philosophies guiding foreign aid organizations, have evolved and changed considerably. Three of the many ideas influencing donors between the 1950s and about 1980 were modernization theory, dependency theory, and the notion of basic human needs.

Modernization Theory.   In the 1950s and 1960s, international development was heavily influenced by **modernization theory,** an idea initially put forward by academic political scientists researching social change. More specifically, these researchers were interested in how societies and economies make the transition from traditional to modern forms (see Escobar 1995; Gardner and Lewis 1996; Arce and Long 2000). Indeed, these theorists *defined* development as the change process by which societies make the transition from traditional to modern. Their theory postulated that development would inevitably take place as societies gradually abandoned traditional cultural features, such as patriarchy, nonliteracy, and subsistence farming, and became increasingly urban and industrialized. Western, industrial society, characterized by features such as capitalism, a high level of technological expertise, and democratic political systems, was envisioned as an exemplary model of modernization.

Thus, throughout this early period, development agencies in wealthy *Northern* countries provided financial and material support to so-called *Southern* countries to help develop their economies and infrastructures according to the modernization model. Since underdevelopment was in large part attributed to a lack of money and technology, expensive technological solutions were thought to be the cure, and large-scale economic development projects were implemented in many countries in the developing world. Most of these projects were top-down attempts at problem solving (see Chapter 2), imposed on their intended beneficiaries by well-meaning

donors from the outside, and most were undertaken without benefit of anthropological expertise. Huge new dams blocked rivers to generate electricity; schools and
hospitals were built; airports and highways were carved out of deserts and rain
forests to encourage commerce; natural resources were exploited to create jobs and
generate income.

Many of these first international development projects, the majority of which
were undertaken by the various agencies of the United Nations, stirred controversy
because they infringed on the rights of local people or damaged the environment.
Some actually worsened the living standards of their intended beneficiaries (see especially Johnston 1994). A giant dam, for example, might provide electricity for a
developing country but at the same time flood river-valley croplands, thus destroying the livelihoods of hundreds or thousands of local farmers. In 1961, in the hope
that more careful centralized planning of these large-scale infrastructure development projects would help prevent further failures and ensure that the beneficial effects of development would "trickle down" to the neediest, the United Nations
crafted a ten-year plan, the UN Development Decade Resolution. A second "development decade" was launched ten years later, in 1971, and a third in 1981.

Yet after many attempts and the expenditure of billions of dollars, development agencies were forced to acknowledge that large-scale technological solutions,
organized and run by centralized agencies, often failed to produce the intended results. Some international development efforts produced only short-term benefits;
others actually exacerbated existing problems (the agricultural development project
described in Chapter 2, undertaken in the 1980s in the Philippines, provides a good
example). World poverty and inequality persisted. The concept of development embodied in modernization theory is now considered "seriously flawed" (Arce and
Long 2000:5), mainly because its basic assumptions—that all impoverished and underdeveloped countries are on the same trajectory, and that economic growth and
political reform, like a rising tide, would raise all boats—did not prove true. Vestiges
of this theory continue to influence development thinking; the World Bank, for example, still strenuously promotes economic expansion as the antidote to underdevelopment (Gardner and Lewis 1996:12). However, top-down approaches to development are today generally acknowledged to be ineffectual.

Dependency Theory.   On the opposite side of the coin from modernization theory was **dependency theory,** an idea first put forward in the late 1940s and strongly
influenced by Marxism. Dependency theorists attributed underdevelopment in the
poor ("peripheral") countries of the world as a product of their dependency upon
rich, Northern ("core") countries (see, for example, Worsley 1990). This dependency
was envisioned as mainly economic; poor countries were dependent on rich ones as
markets for their exports. Capitalism was viewed as exploitative; "while rich nations
get richer, the rest inevitably get poorer" (Gardner and Lewis 1996:16). Dependency
could occur within countries as well as between them, with urban elites, often the primary beneficiaries of development aid, exploiting the rural masses.

Dependency theorists believed that the top-down remedies to underdevelopment suggested by modernization theory were inevitably doomed to failure. The best
solution was radical structural reform—for example, through state socialism à la
China or Cuba (ibid.: 17). Proponents of this solution—liberal political philosophers,

some NGOs, and the leaders of a number of Third World countries—were largely un-successful, except to the extent that political blocs such as the Cold War–era "Non-Aligned Movement" (Third World countries that collectively rejected allying them-selves with either the First or Second worlds) resulted in some degree of Southern empowerment.

Like modernization theory, traces of this idea continue to influence develop-ment thinking (Gardner and Lewis 1996:12). Numerous indigenous NGOs, for ex-ample, "reject aid as a form of neo-imperialism, and argue that positive change can come only from within Southern societies" (Gardner and Lewis 1996:19–20). Today, however, neither dependency theory nor modernization theory is believed to supply a comprehensive explanation for underdevelopment or to suggest viable solutions.

Basic Needs.   Starting about the middle of the 1970s, a major shift in develop-ment philosophy began to make itself felt. This shift was precipitated by a number of factors. At the macro level, the fact of previous development failures was com-pounded by new realities: price fluctuations in the commodities exported by Third World countries escalated Third World debt, and demands from international lend-ing institutions for debt repayment were followed by a deepening economic reces-sion in the early 1980s. At the micro level, there was a perceived lack of awareness—even a perceived indifference—on the part of development's intended beneficiaries.

Development organizations such as the World Bank and USAID, forced to ac-knowledge that their development efforts over a span of thirty years had not, on the whole, achieved their goals, began to pay increasing attention to the importance of social-scientific expertise (Ferguson 1997:164). Some explicitly attributed earlier development failures, at least in part, to a lack of understanding about culture (Dud-ley 1993:13). With the 1970s hiring boom in academic anthropology now defunct (see Chapter 3), an increasing number of cultural anthropologists was thus drawn into the development arena. By the mid-1980s, anthropological contributions to in-stitutionalized development efforts had become commonplace.

An important idea emerging from this period was based on the belief that all human beings are entitled to certain social, economic, and political benefits and rights. On the social side, all people are entitled to expect that their community (today, this usually means their government or the larger world community) will support them in two ways. First, it will satisfy their **basic needs** (the bare subsis-tence necessities required for a satisfactory quality of life, such as nourishing food in sufficient quantity, clean water, safe and comfortable housing, and protection from harm). Second, it will provide them with certain **basic services** (the fundamental social services needed for a satisfactory quality of life, such as a primary-level educa-tion and basic preventive and curative health services). (Two important correlates to these ideas are that economically, all people have the right to work and to reap the rewards of their labor; and politically, people everywhere have the right to congre-gate, to speak freely, to govern themselves, and to express their religious and other beliefs as they choose.)

These notions are embodied in the Universal Declaration of Human Rights adopted by the United Nations in 1948 (UNIFO 1983) and also in numerous docu-ments agreed to, since then, by the member states of the United Nations. However, they were not thought of as basic philosophical underpinnings of development, nor as justification for it, until it had become apparent that the top-down foreign assistance model would not, in fact, produce worldwide economic growth that would result in a trickle-down effect that would ultimately benefit the poor (Gardner and Lewis 1997:7).

In time, a succession of new development strategies, with designations such as "basic human needs," "putting people first," "farmer first," "development by people," and "participatory action research" replaced the top-down economic development model (see, for example, Chambers 1983; Cernea 1985; Perez 1997). No longer were expensive, large-scale, paternalistic solutions believed to be the most effective antidote for development problems. Development agencies, sometimes employing applied cultural anthropologists as project consultants, began to take social, cultural, and environmental factors into account in planning and implementing development projects. Thanks in part to anthropological insights, solutions imposed from the outside gave way to a new insistence on community involvement and local self-help.

In spite of the new needs orientation and insistence on local self-reliance, however, many development projects still fell short of their goals, and controversy and criticism continued to be their constant accompaniment. It became ever clearer that just as underdevelopment has varied and complicated causes, identifying these causes and implementing solutions to them are extraordinarily complex undertakings.

Contemporary Ideas

Ideally, international development efforts should have the following attributes:

- They should occur at the invitation of the local people.
- They should truly enhance the quality of life of the intended beneficiaries.
- They should not be detrimental to the quality of life of others.
- They should address the perceived needs of the people they are intended to benefit rather than those of outsiders.
- They should decrease rather than exacerbate existing economic and social inequalities.
- They should produce long-lasting changes for the better rather than changes that evaporate when development assistance ends.

Based on lessons learned in the past, several basic principles for responsible development have been established. Two of them, community participation and sustainability, were described in Chapter 2 as fundamental to applied cultural anthropology in general; they are especially strongly associated with international development.

Community Participation. The idea of community participation was defined in Chapter 2 as the active involvement of the intended beneficiaries of directed change. This approach, sometimes referred to as bottom-up to contrast it with the top-down approach, is basic to most international development efforts today (Dudley 1993:7). Project implementers rarely donate money, equipment, or expertise without taking into account the opinions, needs, traditions, and lifestyles of their intended beneficiaries. This being the case, the importance of including cultural anthropologists in development work is obvious: it is they who are responsible for providing the emic perspective (see Appendix 2) by unearthing, understanding, and communicating local people's values and preferences, and then ensuring that these are incorporated into development projects.

As Chapter 2 (pp. 30–31) pointed out, community participation is by no means a perfect solution to all development problems (Keare 2001); there is "danger in creating the illusion that participatory research is all there is to ideologically sound aid" (Dudley 1993:163). For example, community participation inevitably raises the question of differences in power and authority among groups of participants stratified by sex, age, ethnicity, class, and so on. When local people identify their own needs, the opinions of the more powerful among them often win out. The power differential between donor and beneficiary can also be problematic (see Chapter 4). The success of community participation therefore depends on how sensitive aid workers are not only to the needs and abilities of their intended beneficiaries (Keare 2001:163) but also to the social and cultural dynamics of local situations. Thus, although community participation is considered a *sine qua non* of development today, beneficial social change must be both "encouraged from the top and . . . demanded from below" (Keare 2001:163). Increasingly, appropriate community participation is viewed as consisting of a blend of the two approaches (ibid.).

Sustainability.   Similarly, **sustainability,** the idea that the effects of beneficial change projects should be able to be sustained by their beneficiaries after outside assistance has ended, remains a vitally important premise of modern international development (see Chapter 2, pp. 32–33). Although it had surfaced previously, the idea is most closely associated with a 1987 United Nations report on the relationship between economic development and environmental stability (see Harries-Jones 1992: 158; Rich 1994:196; Escobar 1995:192ff.).[3] The commission issuing the report defined *sustainability* as "meet[ing] the needs of the present without compromising the ability of future generations to meet their own needs" (World Commission on Environment and Development 1987:43). The report proposed, as solutions to problems of environmental degradation resulting from economic growth, both conservation of energy and natural resources, and the involvement of local people in the development process. Implementing these remedies is, of course, more easily said than done.

Today, as it is used in an international context, the term *sustainability* has expanded to include several core notions. First, the answer to world poverty reduction is long-term economic development. Second, development and the environment are inextricably linked. Third, with appropriate management, development can reduce world poverty without harming the environment, thus allowing the beneficial results of development to continue to accumulate into the indefinite future.

These notions sound like "mother-and-apple-pie formulation[s] that everyone can agree on" (Rich 1994:196). However, like the notion of community participation, sustainability incorporates a number of problems. The most obvious is that despite conservation efforts, economic growth is still a major cause of environmental degradation (Rich 1994:197). In Uganda, for example, poor farmers living near the vast Bwindi Forest, notable for its extraordinary diversity of flora and fauna and as the home of endangered mountain gorillas, traditionally exploited the forest and its resources for their livelihood (Mukolwe et al. 1995). Because (like rural subsistence farmers elsewhere) they valued large families, their numbers grew, necessitating more and more tree cutting for homes, firewood, and agricultural fields. A few years ago, alarmed at the rate at which the forest was shrinking, the Ugandan government declared Bwindi a protected area and forbade further tree cutting (ibid.:139). The local farmers understood the value of environmental preservation, but their families' subsistence needs were paramount, so they continued—now illegally—to use the forest land and its resources as they always had. Solving problems such as this will require "profound structural changes . . . in the societies and economies of all countries" (Rich 1994:197).

FOOD FOR THOUGHT Some see the idea of sustainability as fundamentally "masculinist and colonialist . . . [it is] assumed that the benevolent [white] hand of the West will save the Earth" (Escobar 1995:193). Based on the discussion in Chapter 2 of the social, technological, and environmental goals of sustainable development, do you think sustainable development, appropriately implemented with these goals in mind, can be considered either "masculinist" or "colonialist"? If not, why not? If so, how can these problems be avoided?

Though devised with the best of intentions, sustainable development has yet to realize its promise. As a result, a number of refinements have been proposed. One of these, Primary Environmental Care (PEC), has shown great potential for achieving success.[4] Intended for implementation at the local level, PEC promotes sustainable development by integrating three crucial elements: a basic needs approach that ensures the satisfaction of people's basic lifestyle and health requirements, local empowerment, and the conservation of local natural resources (Bajracharya 1994: 154). The principles on which the concept is based are outlined in Figure 5.2.

Part of the problem of achieving sustainable development, of course, is that the populations of Western and Westernized nations have so far proven unwilling to practice what their representatives at UNCED (the 1992 United Nations Conference on Environment and Development in Rio de Janeiro, also known as the Earth Summit) and elsewhere have preached. The sobering truth of the matter is that our own Western lifestyle is inherently unsustainable. The most significant contribution Westerners can make is to "live and be seen to live the way of life which we recommend to our poorer neighbours" (Dudley 1993:169).

The Value of Technical Assistance. Over the years, ideas about how best to encourage community participation, promote sustainability, and achieve development have changed as donor organizations gained practical experience. In the top-down years following World War II (see Chapter 3), donations of cash sometimes disappeared; buildings sometimes failed to meet recipients' needs or crumbled into disrepair; equipment sometimes broke down or was stolen or used for other than its intended purposes. It gradually became clear that aid recipients benefited more, and over a longer period of time, when the aid took the form not of money or material things but of expertise, which could be permanently transferred to recipients. Today, therefore, much development aid is in the form of **technical assistance** (also called technology transfer), which emphasizes the transfer of ideas and skills rather than money or material goods from donor to recipient.

◇ **FIGURE 5.2** **Principles of the Primary Environmental Care Approach to Sustainable Development**

Local People and Communities

- must have the opportunity to identify, organize, and participate in their own development based on their own self-identified needs
- must have the necessary tenure rights, information, and financial resources to be able to use natural resources in more creative ways
- must be encouraged to apply their indigenous knowledge in the development of appropriate technologies

Government Institutions and Local Officials

- must provide the political support and necessary services needed to promote the principles above

Development Agencies

- must facilitate human resources development over the long term by engaging local people in dialogue, being adaptive and flexible, and continuing their support over longer periods of time

Source: Adapted from Bajracharya 1995:154–155.

At first glance, technical assistance may seem incompatible with true community participation, since ideas and skills are obviously being given and received (Dudley 1993). However, technical assistance actually complements the potent ideas of both community participation and sustainable development. To transfer ideas and skills from donors to recipients, the participation of members of the beneficiary community is obviously necessary. And because ideas and skills cannot be stolen or worn out but can be passed along to others, development based on technical assistance has the potential to be socially—if not always technologically or environmentally—sustainable.

Today, the field of international development is changing rapidly. Major players include the United States, the European community, and, within the last decade or so, Japan. A burgeoning number of NGOs in the developing world is enjoying increasing impact.[5] Improvements to the development process continue to be made.[6] For example, international development specialists now realize the importance of involving, in their work, not just any indigenes (today often called **partners** or **host country counterparts**), but indigenous people representing all levels of the socioeconomic and educational spectrum. These partners may be well-educated professionals such as doctors, teachers, engineers, or even cultural anthropologists. In researching the role of women in Indonesian rice agriculture, for example, applied anthropologist Margaret Casey, mentioned in Chapter 2, partnered with an Indonesian sociologist (Casey 1993:125). Or they may be grass-roots-level people, impoverished and lacking in formal education. The latter are as important as the former: "the individual villager [and] shanty town dweller . . . are the true engines and instruments of social and technological change" (Dudley 1993:xi).

DEVELOPMENT ORGANIZATIONS

Three different types of development organizations together account for most international development work: multilateral organizations, bilateral organizations, and nongovernmental organizations. Many hundreds if not thousands of applied cultural anthropologists are employed by these organizations, whose motivations for rendering assistance vary from the highly political to the unconditionally charitable.

Chapter 3 defined multilateral ("many-sided") organizations as aid organizations made up of a number of member countries. The United Nations, consisting of almost all the countries in the world, is by far the largest. This umbrella organization is divided into numerous branches, many of which address aspects of development. The United Nations Children's Fund (UNICEF), for example, is concerned with the problems of the world's children; the World Health Organization (WHO) is responsible for identifying and addressing global public health issues; UNIFEM is responsible for women's issues; and the Food and Agricultural Organization (FAO) focuses on agricultural issues worldwide. (All of the development efforts of the United Nations are coordinated by the United Nations Development Program, or UNDP, which was established in 1966.) Multilateral organizations offer "multilateral aid," development assistance given by a group of countries acting in concert. Because representatives of many nations make the decisions about what these organizations do, multilateral aid is somewhat less apt than other kinds of aid to come with a political price tag attached.

Chapter 3 noted that bilateral ("two-sided") organizations are the foreign assistance agencies of individual governments. Examples include the U.S. Agency for International Development (USAID), Britain's Overseas Development Administration (ODA), the Danish International Development Authority (DANIDA), the Canadian International Development Agency (CIDA), the Japanese International Cooperation Agency (JICA), and the German Agency for Technical Cooperation (GTZ). Since decisions regarding bilateral aid—what to give, to whom to give it, and for what purpose—are made by a donor nation's government, this kind of aid is apt to be given for political as well as humanitarian purposes. Between 1986 and 1996, for example, over one third of the total U.S. foreign assistance budget went to just two countries, Egypt and Israel, largely in support of U.S. political interest in stability in the Middle East. Similarly, USAID has recently withdrawn a major proportion of its assistance to the small island nations of the Caribbean, considered by the United States to be of strategic importance until the disintegration of the Soviet Union and the end of the Cold War.

Finally, nongovernmental organizations (NGOs), sometimes known as **private voluntary organizations (PVOs),** are heavily involved in international development. NGOs were defined in Chapter 1 as private, nonprofit aid organizations of many different kinds and sizes. Some are secular charitable organizations, such as the International Red Cross; some are religious charities, such as Catholic Relief Services; some are private foundations, such as the Rockefeller Foundation; and some are local (or grass-roots) organizations. Most have limited budgets, so the projects they sponsor are smaller in scale than projects sponsored by multilaterals or bilaterals. And since most NGOs do not have political axes to grind (although they may have ideological ones), the aid they give is more apt to be for humanitarian than political purposes.

Perhaps because of their emphasis on charity, development projects sponsored and implemented by NGOs are often more successful than others, despite the fact that they are apt to be much smaller in scale. Over the past half-century's history of international development assistance, expensive, large-scale projects implemented by big, centralized, bureaucratic organizations have often proven less successful, and less sustainable, than less ambitious projects implemented by NGOs.

WOMEN IN DEVELOPMENT

The term *women in development* sounds as if it might refer to the professional activities of females in the international development arena. A high proportion of international development workers are indeed female, in part because women tend to work best with women in development contexts, particularly in traditional cultures in which males are prohibited from involvement in the women's domain. But the term **women in development (WID)** refers not to this but rather to the idea of explicitly incorporating local women in development projects.

Why WID?

Why should there be a special branch of international development focusing specifically on women, especially when no logical counterpart—Men in Development—exists? The reason is that for many years, development workers tended to view women in developing countries mainly as stay-at-home caretakers of others, rather than as participants—actual or potential—in the economic or political lives of their countries (see Young 1993; Jiggins 1994; Jahan 1995). This view was appropriate for some cultural settings; in Muslim societies, for example, women were traditionally excluded from the public (or "extra-domestic") sphere, and in some of them, even now, the idea of female participation in the workforce or in public life is only slowly gaining acceptance. In certain other societies—Eastern Caribbean countries, for example— there is a long-standing tradition of female participation in the public domain (see, for example, Senior 1991). But just a few years ago, even in countries and cultures in which women's involvement in the workforce or in public life was common, women's economic contributions tended to be overlooked by development workers.

There are two reasons for this. First, due to historical and traditional sexual inequalities all over the world, males are still the dominant actors in the workforce in all cultures, in terms of the amount of income they earn, the level of the positions they occupy, and their influence in economic and political decision making. Second, much of the work women do in the public domain, worldwide, is in the **informal sector**—the economic sector in which employment is unskilled, often part-time, and often not reported to the government for tax purposes. Examples of such work include "cottage" (at-home) crafts production, unskilled factory work (called piece work, since workers are paid by the number of items, from garments to small electric appliances, they produce), seasonal agricultural work, in-home child care, street-corner peddling, and domestic work in private homes, hotels, and restaurants. Such jobs tend to be relatively poorly paid, low in status, and much more likely than "male" jobs to be seasonal, part-time, or "off the books."

 In the "informal" economic sector, employment is typically unskilled, part-time, and "off the books." In Castries, the capital of St. Lucia, female participants in the country's informal economy sell brooms and other home-made items on the sidewalk.

FOOD FOR THOUGHT In most countries, citizens are required to pay taxes on their income, based on information supplied by their employers to the government. Most "informal" workers, however, are either self-employed or are paid in cash, so their earnings frequently go unreported. Devise an argument for either the fairness or unfairness of the existence of the informal economy with regard to a country's tax-paying citizens.

Behind the increasing participation of women in the labor force worldwide lies a universal reality: as societies develop, people produce fewer and fewer of their own subsistence necessities, relying increasingly on their local or national economies for everything from food to fuel to health care. To purchase the things they need but no longer produce for themselves, people need cash. But males—the traditional wage earners in money-based economies around the globe—are finding it increasingly difficult to earn enough to purchase the necessities of life for their households, let alone the ever-widening array of desirable modern goods available in today's marketplace. Thus it has fallen to their female partners to earn the needed extra cash. No doubt because of this history, employers in developing countries commonly consider female employees' income to be supplemental to household finances—one reason sometimes cited for the fact that females earn less than males. In truth, a woman's earnings are often crucial to her family's well-being.

Informal or not, however, the work of females in most developing countries has been increasingly difficult to overlook in the past twenty years or so, since it represents an ever-increasing proportion of household budgets and GDP. Whatever their past cultural traditions, more and more women are entering the public domain (while continuing, in most cases, to fulfill their traditional caregiving role in the domestic domain). Development anthropologists, some with academic roots in feminist anthropology, have been instrumental in this important social transformation, contributing their view of women's crucial role in society and the socially constructed nature of the roles and relationships of males and females in societies around the globe (Nussbaum 2000; see also Crewe and Harrison 1998:51).

The work of development anthropologist Margaret Casey on a project intended to benefit Indonesian rice farmers, described in Chapter 2, provides an example. Project implementers dug wells and installed irrigation systems in order to increase agricultural output. But local farmers had little experience with irrigation, so extension services were set up in local villages to help them manage their new water-supply system. On the assumption that Indonesian rice farmers were male, these extension programs targeted men. In reality, however, local women were heavily involved in both agricultural production and decision making. Joining the project several years after its inception, anthropologist Casey was able to make recommendations for opening and adapting the extension services to women, in ways compatible with the cultural constraints facing women in Indonesian society.

Today, in response to the worldwide trend toward greater and greater incorporation of women in economic life (and despite the charge of a minority of development specialists who claim that emphasizing women is divisive), most development projects take women's needs, roles, and economic contributions very explicitly into account (see Gardner and Lewis 1996:66). The major international development agencies, both bilaterals and multilaterals, have established women's offices (USAID, for example, now has an Office of Women in Development, founded in 1974; the United Nations established UNIFEM in 1985) and have developed guidelines for incorporating women into development projects. In addition, almost three quarters of all national governments have developed plans to enhance and protect women's rights, and many have also created government agencies specifically devoted to women's interests. Many of these agencies are underbudgeted and are subsumed within other government organizations, so they do not, in general, have a great deal of political clout, but they are gaining in influence. And new grass-roots organizations, run by women to benefit women, have emerged in many countries. An example is the Kenya Water for Health Organization (KWAHO), described in Chapter 2, p. 37. A coalition of small women's groups sponsored by the Kenya National Council of Women, KWAHO is responsible for making clean, safe, fresh water available to a million (mostly rural) Kenyan households (Mwangola 1995).

The United Nations gave the development community's growing awareness of women's contributions a considerable boost when it declared the years 1975–1985 as the International Women's Decade, launching this recognition with a world conference in Mexico. Between then and 1995, when the Fourth World Conference on Women was held in Beijing, China, conferences were held every five years and effectively raised people's consciousness, all over the world, about issues such as job training and property rights for women, domestic violence prevention, and women's health.

Gender and Development (GAD)

Recently, another idea, called **gender and development (GAD),** grew out of the WID concept and has begun to be routinely incorporated in development projects (Razavi and Miller 1995; United Nations 1999). According to this idea, the roles of both males and females, especially as they complement one another, should be explicitly considered in the design and implementation of development projects. Today, most international development projects—often with input from applied cultural anthropologists—have a clear-cut WID/GAD emphasis. Applied cultural anthropologists are also sometimes called upon to provide gender-related training to participants in international development projects (Gardner and Lewis 1996:66).

The link between WID/GAD and the older ideas of community participation and sustainability seems obvious; if projects are to be successful, they must include the participation of all community members, and ultimately no project will be socially sustainable if female community members have been overlooked—or, for that matter, if their role has been overemphasized. Like most innovations in the development field, the WID/GAD approach has been challenged on the grounds that it has not actually resulted in eliminating the "detrimental effects of development on

AN APPLIED CULTURAL ANTHROPOLOGIST AT WORK

SOHEIR EL SUKKARY-STOLBA

When Soheir Stolba was an undergraduate, her interests ranged from linguistics (she was a native Arabic speaker) to sociology to education to English literature (Sukkary-Stolba 1998:47). In graduate school, however, she chose to focus on cultural anthropology, receiving her Ph.D. from the University of California–Davis in 1978, with a knowledge of culture plus considerable linguistic expertise and a specialty in community development. After graduation, her education continued as she gained skills in project design, implementation, monitoring, and evaluation through on-the-job training as a development anthropologist.

Twenty years into a career as both a teacher and an applied development anthropologist, Stolba has worked, thus far, in nineteen different countries in Africa, Asia, and especially the Middle East. Her ability to speak more than one Arabic dialect and to write for publication in both English and Arabic have made her especially valuable as a consultant to Middle Eastern projects.

Many of the projects in which Stolba has participated have involved women and children. In Egypt, for example, she helped poor rural women, especially widows and single mothers, to increase their income and economic security by starting up small income-producing projects. In Yemen, she helped design family-planning training sessions for midwives and interviewed rural women about their use of water and their problems in procuring it. In Morocco, she was part of a research team investigating acute respiratory diseases among infants and children.

Dr. Stolba has some useful advice for students who may be considering careers in development anthropology. She has observed that many of the skills needed, including community outreach, community mobilization, training, evaluation, project design, and advocacy, are often not traditionally taught in anthropology graduate schools. Students interested in careers in development anthropology should therefore plan ahead by taking classes in women's studies, communications, management, teaching, evaluation, political science, and economics. In addition, possessing certain personality traits is helpful, among them resourcefulness, creativity, loyalty, flexibility, an enjoyment of travel and of meeting people from other cultures, a sincere desire to help others, and the ability to adjust to the sometimes harsh realities of the field.

women" (Gardner and Lewis 1996:66). Nevertheless, most well-planned development projects now include both women and men from the very beginning (and, moreover, women and men of different ages, educational levels, and occupations) and assume that women and men are entitled to the same benefits—for example, access to land, credit, training, or health care.

THE DOWNSIDE OF DEVELOPMENT AND DEVELOPMENT ANTHROPOLOGY'S RESPONSE

Development has proven to be a peculiarly problematic endeavor, with vociferous detractors as well as ardent defenders.[7] This chapter would be incomplete and inaccurate without mention of development's critics and their arguments. Presently, the most serious concerns center on four areas: development's moral legitimacy, its underlying political agenda, questions of power and paternalism, and questions of effectiveness. It is particularly important for students contemplating careers in development anthropology to understand why some people (including many U.S. taxpayers) have reservations about the idea of rich nations helping poor ones to develop economically, socially, and politically.

Moral Legitimacy

A number of critics have censured development efforts on ethical grounds, arguing that outsiders have no moral justification for meddling in other people's lives or other nations' economies, however noble their intentions (see "The Question of Interference" in Chapter 4, p. 81). Development anthropologists and other social scientists typically counter such criticisms with reference to the well-established ideology of community participation, which incorporates the notion that beneficiaries should identify their own problems, request assistance in identifying solutions to them, and participate fully in implementing solutions. Community participation of course reflects an ideal, not always a real, scenario; development projects do sometimes attempt to impose solutions from the top down or even to solve problems that their intended beneficiaries are unaware they have (Dudley 1993:155). As Chapters 4 and 6 explain, however, at least some—perhaps most—applied cultural anthropologists believe that what would be truly unethical would be to sit by and do nothing in the face of global problems such as poverty and social inequality (see also Scheper-Hughes 1995).

FOOD FOR THOUGHT   Not all development projects have been undertaken at the request of their intended beneficiaries. In some cases, beneficiaries have been unaware that they needed change or have even resisted it. Proponents of this kind of development defend their work with the argument that because a person "cannot diagnose a disease does not mean they are not suffering from it" (Dudley 1993:156). Take a stand for the moral rightness or wrongness of this argument, and explain the reasons for your position.

Political Agendas

A frequently heard criticism of international development is that it often serves the political or economic goals of donor nations as much as or more than the needs of its intended beneficiaries. As was mentioned above, this is most apt to be true of development efforts sponsored by one country's foreign aid agency for the benefit of people in another country.

In response to this criticism, most anthropologists involved in development efforts would readily admit that, ideally, foreign aid should be provided, on a strictly humanitarian basis, to all needy countries. However, the large number of countries in which hunger, poor health, economic underdevelopment, and social disenfranchisement exist makes that impossible. Many development anthropologists feel that if countries like the United States can serve their own geopolitical interests while simultaneously assisting at least some of the world's needy people, the effort is well worthwhile. Others defuse this criticism by restricting their activities to the provision of technical assistance at the community level, which is usually regarded as "more innocuous" than other kinds of development activities (Dudley 1993:141).

Unequal Power Relations

Ferguson (1990) and Escobar (1995), in particular, have challenged the morality of development efforts based on the power differential inherent in the relationship between outside implementers of development assistance and the recipients of that assistance. Certainly "aid is predicated on the existence of outsiders with resources" (Dudley 1993:8), and when the outsiders are mainly rich Westerners and the beneficiaries are mainly poor non-Westerners, the argument takes on added force. Development efforts can be viewed as paternalistic or even racist, perpetuating "the hegemonic idea of the West's superiority" (Escobar 1995:8) or contributing to what has been called a "dependency mentality" on the part of beneficiaries.

There is truth in these allegations. Some recipients of development assistance are manifestly "controlled by development," to a greater or lesser degree, and "can only manoeuvre within the limits set by it" (Gardner and Lewis 1996:72). Indeed, some international development advocates acknowledge that aid is inescapably paternalistic, if benevolently so: "we believe that we are enlightened, and that we have truths to pass on to . . . the unenlightened" (Dudley 1993:155).

Development anthropologists have rebutted such criticisms, insofar as is possible, by pointing to the primacy and self-regulation of local groups involved in development projects. They have, for example, cited cross-cultural differences in ways of knowing (Gardner and Lewis 1996:73). Scientific and local knowledge are quite different. Thus the beneficiaries of development projects "do not passively receive knowledge . . . from the outside, but dynamically interact with it" (Gardner and Lewis 1996:74). Other development anthropologists have argued that the implementers of development projects fully understand that their intended beneficiaries possess intelligence and managerial capability; what they lack is "access to and control over resources," and development workers are there not to dictate solutions but to help with "the removal of constraints" (Pottier 1993:1). And, as mentioned above, development workers have questioned the moral rectitude of doing nothing in the face of hardship on the part of "the other." In the view of many applied cultural anthropologists involved in development work, the moral imperative to assist the needy not only justifies development, it "requires" it (Evans and Adler 1979:3).

Effectiveness

Finally, there are those who claim that, all too often, international development efforts—especially those undertaken by multilateral and bilateral agencies as opposed to NGOs—fail (see especially Escobar 1995). It is demonstrably true that "much [development] aid does no good and some does harm" (Dudley 1993:9); examples of development projects in which money, time, and effort were ultimately wasted were presented in Chapter 2. Other examples, some of them much larger in scale, are plentiful (see Ferguson 1990, 1997; Johnston 1994; Rich 1994; Escobar 1995; Crewe and Harrison 1998). Although such failures occurred more often in the past than they do now, it is sometimes suggested that because of them, development efforts should cease.

To this criticism, development professionals respond that they have learned a great deal, over the past two decades or so, about how to do things right. They point as well to the worldwide effects of recent major development successes. In 1996, for instance, the world's output of goods and services grew by 5.6 percent, the highest rate in twenty years. Thanks to improved medical care, better nutrition, and improved living standards, average life expectancy around the world has increased more in the past forty years than in the previous four thousand. Almost two out of three countries now choose their leaders democratically (Wolfensohn 1997:4–5).

Other criticisms are occasionally heard: that development anthropologists allow the agendas of development organizations to become their real masters (see, for example, Escobar 1991); that they have only minimal influence on policy formulation within these organizations (see, for example, Ferguson 1997:165); and most important, that they fail to plumb thoroughly the "larger theoretical and historical issues that development issues raise" (Ferguson 1997:166). It is obvious that as a philosophy, a movement, and a career area, international development is still an imperfect endeavor, and it will take a great deal more than the realization that top-down assistance is highly likely to fail, or the conscious consideration of cultural and environmental issues, to create a development philosophy and practice that obviate critics' concerns. Collectively, however, development is demonstrably inching toward the goal of helping to bring about beneficial changes in needy people's economic, social, political, educational, and health status.

FOOD FOR THOUGHT   One cultural anthropologist, concerned that "'science' has become a bad word in anthropology" (D'Andrade 1995:408), believes that "any moral authority anthropology may hold depends on an objective understanding of the world" (D'Andrade 1995:399). Another cultural anthropologist disagrees, arguing instead for an "active, politically committed, morally engaged" (and, obviously, non-objective) anthropology (Scheper-Hughes 1995:415). In light of the information in this chapter on development, which anthropologist do you think is right? Why?

CONCLUSION

According to James D. Wolfensohn, current president of the World Bank, international development should strive for "inclusion"—"bringing people into society who have never been part of it before" (Wolfensohn 1997:3). "The people of developing countries must be in the driver's seat," says Wolfensohn, perhaps reflecting more wishful thinking than reality.

If Westerners are going to be successful in implementing international development projects that put people in developing countries "in the driver's seat," the expertise of applied cultural anthropologists will be vital. One reason is that local factors never precisely fit the current development paradigm, whatever it may be. Instead, the lifestyle-related activities of local people—their health practices, farming practices, educational aspirations, and so on—are always embedded in local systems of knowledge and belief. Indeed, concepts such as development, progress, and quality-of-life improvement are themselves culturally constructed. Of the various kinds of social scientists who contribute to global development efforts, cultural anthropologists alone are trained (and should, in the future, be better trained; see Nolan 2002:2262) to tailor local requirements and values both to broad development concepts and specific development models.

Another reason why cultural anthropology will continue to be vitally important for successful development is that no single or static development philosophy or methodology has ever been agreed upon; the model has always been flexible. Applied cultural anthropologists alone have been willing to "constructively query the value of maintaining the assumptions, institutions, imagery, and methods of inquiry to which [other] development workers are, or become, attached" (Pottier 1993:8). Perhaps the most important contributions of cultural anthropology to development have been, and will continue to be, a willingness to learn from the intended beneficiaries of development and a continually critical, continually reflexive vision of the field.

K E Y   T E R M S

basic needs   the bare subsistence necessities for a satisfactory quality of life, including food, water, housing, and protection from harm

basic services   the fundamental social services needed for a satisfactory quality of life, including a primary-level education and basic preventive and curative health services

dependency ratio   in a developing country, the ratio of the number of people in the workforce to the number of people who are too young or too old to work

dependency theory   the idea that underdevelopment in the poorer countries of the world is a product of their dependency upon exploitative, rich countries

development   the attempt to help identify and implement solutions to the social and technological problems of poor communities and nations

development anthropology   the use of anthropological ideas and methods in development work

development indicators   statistics believed to broadly reflect the quality of life worldwide

gender and development (GAD) the idea that the roles of both males and females should be considered in the design and implementation of development projects

grass-roots development development efforts initiated at the local level, with or without outside assistance

gross domestic product (GDP) the total value of all goods and services produced in a country over a certain period of time

host country counterparts (partners) those who are intended to benefit from an international development project; now often used in preference to *targets* or *recipients*

informal sector the economic sector in which employment is unskilled, often part-time, and often not reported to the government for tax purposes

international development the attempt, involving international funding and expertise, to identify and implement solutions to long-standing social problems in the less developed countries of the world

less (or least) developed country (LDC) one of the poorest countries

modernization theory the idea, prevalent in the 1950s and 1960s, that development would inevitably take place as societies abandoned traditional cultural features and became more Westernized

partners see *host country counterparts*

private voluntary organization (PVO) an alternative term for a nongovernmental organization (NGO)

sustainability in a development context, the idea that economic development as an enduring solution to world poverty must be accompanied by environmental conservation

technical assistance a form of development assistance that emphasizes the transfer of ideas and skills rather than money or material goods from donor to recipient

women in development (WID) the idea of explicitly incorporating local women in development projects

NOTES

1. For a critique of these terms as "tropes" of the development industry, see Escobar 1995:47.
2. The industrialized countries are sometimes referred to collectively as "the North," although not all of them are in the Northern Hemisphere (for example, Australia). Likewise, the less developed countries are sometimes referred to collectively as "the South," although not all of them are in the Southern Hemisphere (for example, Mongolia).
3. The commission that produced this report was headed by the then prime minister of Norway, Gro Brundtland (now head of the World Health Organization), and the report, entitled *Our Common Future*, is hence frequently referred to as "the Brundtland Commission report." See World Commission on Environment and Development 1987.
4. The idea of Primary Environmental Care, based on the earlier-established concept of primary health care (see Chapter 12), was conceived in 1990 by the Development Assistance Committee of the Organization for Economic Cooperation and Development (OECD).
5. For a comprehensive analysis of the impact of private humanitarian aid organizations in the international development arena, see Luce 1990.
6. For a critical analysis of development successes and failures, see Crewe and Harrison 1998, especially Chapter 1.
7. Arturo Escobar, James Ferguson, and Bruce Rich are perhaps the best known of development's critics.

REFERENCES

Arce, Alberto, and Norman Long (eds.)
2000. *Anthropology, Development, and Modernities.* London: Routledge.

Bajracharya, Deepak
1995. "Primary Environmental Care: An Approach to Sustainable Livelihood." In *Down to Earth: Community Perspectives on Health, Development, and the Environment,* edited by Bonnie Bradford and Margaret A. Gwynne, 153–163. West Hartford, CT: Kumarian Press.

Casey, Margaret
1993. Development in Madura: An Anthropological Approach. In *Practising Development: Social Science Perspectives,* edited by Johan Potter, 110–137. London: Routledge.

Cernea, Michael (ed.)
1985. *Putting People First: Sociological Variables in Rural Development.* New York: Oxford University Press.

Chambers, Robert
1983. *Rural Development: Putting the Last First.* New York: Longman.

Clatts, Michael
1991. *Order and Change in a Southeast Asian Community: An Ethnographic Perspective on Development Initiatives.* Ph.D. Dissertation, Department of Anthropology, State University of New York at Stony Brook.

Crewe, Emma, and Elizabeth Harrison
1998. *Whose Development? An Ethnography of Aid.* London: Zed Books.

D'Andrade, Roy
1995. "Moral Models in Anthropology." *Current Anthropology* 36 (3):399–408.

Devereux, Stephen, and John Hoddinott, (eds.)
1993. *Fieldwork in Developing Countries.* Boulder, CO: Lynne Reinner Publishers.

Diamond, Jared
1997. *Guns, Germs, and Steel: The Fates of Human Societies.* New York: Norton.

Dudley, Eric
1993. *The Critical Villager: Beyond Community Participation.* London: Routledge.

Escobar, Arturo
1991. "Anthropology and the Development Encounter: The Making and Marketing of Development Anthropology." *American Ethnologist* 18 (4):16–40.
1995. *Encountering Development: The Making and Unmaking of the Third World.* Princeton: Princeton University Press.

Evans, Donald D., and Laurie Nogg Adler
1979. *Appropriate Technology for Development: A Discussion and Case Histories.* Boulder, CO: Westview Press.

Fairhead, James
1993. "Representing Knowledge: The 'New Farmer' in Research Fashions." In *Practising Development: Social Science Perspectives,* edited by Johan Pottier, 187–204. London: Routledge.

Ferguson, James
1990. *The Anti-Politics Machine: "Development," Depoliticization, and Bureaucratic Power in Lesotho.* Cambridge, UK: Cambridge University Press.
1997. "Anthropology and its Evil Twin: 'Development' in the Constitution of a Discipline." In *International Development and the Social Sciences,* edited by Frederick Cooper and Randall Packard, 150–175. Berkeley: University of California Press.

Gardner, Katy, and David Lewis
1996. *Anthropology, Development, and the Post-Modern Challenge.* London: Pluto Press.

Green, Edward C. (ed.)
1986. *Practicing Development Anthropology.* Boulder, CO: Westview.

Harries-Jones, Peter
1992. "Sustainable Anthropology: Ecology and Anthropology in the Future." In *Contemporary Futures: Perspectives from Social Anthropology,* edited by Sandra Wallman, 157–171. London: Routledge.

Jahan, Rounaq
1995. *The Elusive Agenda: Mainstreaming Women in Development.* London: Zed Books.

Jiggins, Janice
1994. *Changing the Boundaries: Women-Centered Perspectives on Population and the Environment.* Washington, DC: Island Press.

Johnston, Barbara Rose
1994. *Who Pays the Price?* Washington, DC: Island Press.

Keare, Douglas H.
2001. "Learning to Clap: Reflections on Top-Down vs. Bottom-Up Development." *Human Organization* 60 (2):159–165.

Luce, Randall C.
1990. "Anthropologists and Private, Humanitarian Aid Agencies." In *Social Change and Applied Anthropology: Essays in Honor of David W. Brokensha,* edited by Miriam S. Chaiken, and Anne K. Fleuret, 32–42. Boulder, CO: Westview Press.

Mwangola, Margaret
1995. "Bringing Clean Water to Kenyan Households." In *Down to Earth: Community Perspectives on Health, Development and the Environment*, edited by Bonnie Bradford and Margaret A. Gwynne, 85–91. West Hartford, CT: Kumarian Press.

Mukolwe, Jennifer, Therese McGinn, and Cynthia L. Carlson
1995. "Linking Population and Environmental Conservation Activities in Southwestern Uganda." In *Down to Earth: Community Perspectives on Health, Development, and the Environment*, edited by Bonnie Bradford and Margaret A. Gwynne, 134–142. West Hartford, CT: Kumarian Press.

Nolan, Riall
2002. *Development Anthropology: Encounters in the Real World*. Boulder, CO: Westview Press.

Nussbaum, Martha C.
2000. *Women and Human Development: The Capabilities Approach*. Cambridge, UK: Cambridge University Press.

Ocasio, Raymond, Theresa A. Kilbane, and Judith A. Hermanson
1995. "An Urban Environmental Sanitation Loan Program in Honduras." In *Down to Earth: Community Perspectives on Health, Development, and the Environment*, edited by Bonnie Bradford and Margaret A. Gwynne, 23–34. West Hartford, CT: Kumarian Press.

Perez, Carlos A.
1997. "Participatory Research: Implications for Applied Anthropology." *Practicing Anthropology* 19 (3):2–7.

Population Reference Bureau (PRB)
1997. *1997 World Population Data Sheet*. Washington, DC: PRB.

Pottier, Johan (ed.)
1993. *Practising Development: Social Science Perspectives*. London: Routledge.

Razavi, S., and C. Miller
1995. *From WID to GAD: Conceptual Shifts in the Women and Development Discourse* (UNDP and UNRISD Occasional Paper No. 1). Geneva, Switzerland: UNRISD.

Rich, Bruce
1994. *Mortgaging the Earth: The World Bank, Environmental Impoverishment, and the Crisis of Development*. Boston: Beacon Press.

Scheper-Hughes, Nancy
1995. "The Primacy of the Ethical: Propositions for a Militant Anthropology." *Current Anthropology* 36 (3):409–420.

Senior, Olive
1991. *Working Miracles: Women's Lives in the English-Speaking Caribbean*. London: James Currey.

Skar, Harald O.
1985. *Anthropological Contributions to Planned Change and Development*. Goteborg, Sweden: Acta Universitatis Gothoburgensis.

Sukkary-Stolba, Soheir
1998. "Development Anthropology: A Rewarding Career for Middle East Anthropologists." *Anthropology Newsletter*, April 1998:47.

UNIFO
1983. *International Human Rights Instruments of the United Nations, 1948–1982*. Pleasantville, NY: UNIFO Publishers.

United Nations
1999. *World Survey on the Role of Women in Development*. New York: United Nations.

Wolfensohn, James D.
1997. *Address to the Board of Governors of the World Bank, Sept. 23, 1997*. Washington, DC: World Bank.

World Bank
2000. *World Development Indicators, 2000*. Washington, DC: The World Bank.

World Commission on Environment and Development
1987. *Our Common Future*. Oxford, UK: Oxford University Press.

World Health Organization (WHO)
1998. *The World Health Report 1998: Life in the 21st Century: A Vision for All*. Geneva, Switzerland: World Health Organization.

Worsley, Peter
1990. "Models of the Modern World-System." In *Global Culture, Nationalism, Globalization, and Modernity*, edited by M. Featherstone, 83–96. London: Sage.

Young, Kate
1993. *Planning Development with Women: Making a World of Difference*. New York: St. Martin's Press.

CHAPTER

6 ADVOCACY ANTHROPOLOGY

INTRODUCTION

Development anthropology, described in Chapter 5, involves helping to find sustainable solutions to lifestyle-related problems encountered by the members of needy groups, both at home and abroad. A core principle of contemporary development work is community participation, the notion that needy people should identify their own problems, request assistance, and subsequently take part in every step of the process of implementing beneficial social change.

Some needy people, however, lack sufficient information, resources, or influence to be able to identify their most serious problems accurately, seek assistance single-handedly, or promote their interests effectively. This is most likely to occur among people existing at the margins of mainstream society: the homeless, for example, or members of certain ethnic minorities, or people who live in relatively isolated, small-scale societies. **Advocacy anthropology** is the branch of development anthropology that proactively represents, defends, and supports the members of disempowered or disenfranchised groups, helping them identify their collective needs, seek assistance with problems they cannot rectify alone, and work together to achieve their goals. Advocacy anthropology is specifically concerned with "identifying, critiquing, and addressing imbalances in the allocation of power, economic resources, social status, material goods, and other desired social or economic elements in a community, society, or globally" (Trotter and Schensul 1998:693). This kind of applied anthropology can be undertaken at home or abroad, on a short-term or long-term basis, and it can involve research, various kinds of direct action, and policy formulation.

By this broad definition, any cultural anthropologist, theoretical or applied, who serves the cause of a disempowered group at its request—whether within their community or outside of it or through the provision of research data, training, consciousness raising, lobbying, networking, or even more direct action—could be considered an advocacy anthropologist. Some cultural anthropologists would disagree with this definition, preferring a more restricted view in which anthropological advocacy functions primarily as research undertaken in support of community-defined goals (see, for example, van Willigen 1993:109: "the anthropologist serves not as a direct change agent, but as an auxiliary to community leaders"). In this view, actively helping to implement specific solutions to the perceived problems of others is inappropriate; the advocate's role should be to help educate the people concerned so they can make informed decisions and then to stand back while they make their own choices. There is no universal consensus among those anthropologists who think of themselves as advocates on which role is preferable, but the majority play the more active role.

Advocacy may be a particularly good fit with both applied and theoretical anthropological research, for several reasons. First, despite what some see as a long-term trend in cultural anthropology toward less rather than more engagement with research populations (for example, Nader 1999), many cultural anthropologists today believe that it is not enough to participate in, observe, record, and analyze the cultures of their study populations; they should give something back to the communities they study, if the members of these communities so desire. Second, cultural anthropologists typically develop both affection and concern for the people among whom they do their research. Many come to identify closely with them. And third, cultural anthropologists are particularly well placed, by virtue of their relatively high level of education and their socioeconomic status within the context of Western culture, to provide the members of disenfranchised groups with useful information from research, to help them give voice to their needs and wishes, to establish contacts with agencies that can provide help, to facilitate access to needed resources, and to lobby for specific benefits or policies.

Ethnographer Inge Bolin, who did fieldwork in Chichubamba, a peasant village in the mountainous highlands of Peru, provides an example of how classic theoretical fieldwork can lead to advocacy. Over generations, Chichubamba's inhabitants had become increasingly impoverished as each family divided its farmland among its children (Bolin 1992). Residents realized that education was their children's most promising route out of poverty, but they had neither a school nor funds with which to build one. They did, however, have strong backs, willing hands, and a plot of land. They turned to anthropologist Bolin, who was doing ethnographic fieldwork in the area, for assistance. She was able to provide what the villagers lacked: information about organizations that might consider funding a school construction project and expertise in writing grant proposals. With her help, the villagers drew up a persuasive proposal, including a budget and a description of the historical and socioeconomic context behind the community's request, and submitted it to a funding organization. The request was approved, and Chichubamba soon had its school.

Advocacy is by no means appropriate in all or even most contexts in which cultural anthropologists work. A study population may not seek it. Moreover, advocacy is "value-explicit," in van Willigen's (1993) terms, and there is great variety among cultural anthropologists in the extent to which they feel comfortable with the degree and depth of personal involvement and commitment required. A few researchers may be disinclined to become involved with their research populations' problems in any way. Others, who may or may not define themselves as advocates, seek actively to help with local problems, "adopting the view that their research implies wider responsibilities for bringing about change" (Gardner and Lewis 1996:48). Those who do identify themselves as advocacy anthropologists go even further, working expressly on behalf of the disenfranchised. Some legal anthropologists (Chapter 8), for example, serve as legal advocates, representing needy communities or individuals in courts of law or working to win them legal protections. In its purest form, advocacy is undertaken not as an adjunct to other research, either applied or theoretical, but for its own sake.

FOOD FOR THOUGHT   An applied cultural anthropologist who specialized in the health of Caribbean women was employed as a consultant by a private charitable foundation to research the health needs of women in the region. If urgent need existed, the foundation would provide assistance. The anthropologist had long ago encountered great need in the region and very much wished to encourage assistance. She therefore decided that her most effective role would be to document this need, through research and interviews with local health officials, and then translate it into terms that would encourage the foundation board to approve funding. Ultimately, an assistance program was established. Based on the definition provided above, can this anthropologist be considered an anthropological advocate?

One common pattern is for a cultural anthropologist to become involved in advocacy slowly, over a period of years, on behalf of a group of people among whom he or she has done theoretical research in the past. An example is David Maybury-Lewis, who in the 1960s worked among the Shavante, small-scale horticulturalists and part-time hunters living in the Brazilian rainforest (Maybury-Lewis 1967). At the time, Maybury-Lewis realized that the culture of the Shavante would inevitably deteriorate and, in the long run, probably die out, since ranchers, loggers, and oil prospectors were already much interested in the possibility of commercial exploitation of Shavante lands.[1] At the request of Shavante leaders, he agreed to lobby external agencies on their behalf, with the goal of protecting the group's culture.

Eventually he persuaded the government of Brazil to protect the land the Shavante occupied—theirs by history and tradition if not by deed—from commercial exploitation by outsiders.

Later, in 1972, Maybury-Lewis founded Cultural Survival, a nonprofit organization dedicated to supporting and defending small-scale cultures against exploitation from the outside—including exploitation by anthropologists. Today this organization works with indigenes in many parts of the world, in arenas including legal representation, public policy initiatives, human rights advocacy, environmental conservation, land tenure, education, and economic development. Cultural Survival is by no means unique; many other anthropological advocacy organizations have been established in the past three decades, both in the West and in the developing world.[2] Through them, advocates attempt to raise public awareness about the plight of disenfranchised peoples, solicit assistance on their behalf, and sometimes raise money by selling various items such as native-made products.

To the extent that overlapping concepts can be differentiated, this chapter distinguishes between two main kinds of advocacy anthropology. The first, referred to here as **community advocacy,** is concerned with specific initiatives, such as promotion of economic development, education, health care, or similar benefits, requested by the residents of local communities, in both industrialized and developing countries. Inge Bolin's assistance to the people of Chichubamba is an example. The second, **cultural advocacy,** broader in scope than community advocacy, is concerned, over the long term, with the whole range of problems faced by minority populations or small-scale indigenous societies, whose cultures, languages, traditions, lands, and/or rights are threatened by Westernization. David Maybury-Lewis's work is an example. (A third kind of advocacy, **cultural brokerage,** which involves promoting mutually beneficial relationships among the various stakeholders in development projects, is common to both community advocacy and cultural advocacy; see below.)

ADVOCACY AND DEVELOPMENT ANTHROPOLOGY: A COMPARISON

At first glance, advocacy anthropology may seem little different from its parent, development anthropology (see Chapter 5). Both are applied subdisciplines of cultural anthropology, devoted to helping the disenfranchised find solutions to their problems through the use of anthropological expertise. Both are simultaneously research-based, action-oriented, and policy-relevant. Both can be undertaken from inside or outside of academia. Both address practical goals, instead of pursuing scientific enlightenment for its own sake. Both can be emotionally engaging and ethically challenging.

The main differences between the two kinds of applied cultural anthropology are differences of degree rather than kind. They lie in four areas: the depth of personal commitment required of the cultural anthropologist; the amount of time allotted to the achievement of specific goals; the nature of the relationship between anthropologist and intended beneficiary; and the funding circumstances under which projects are carried out.

Personal Commitment

Advocacy anthropology can be viewed as taking the subjective involvement required of development work a step further. Indeed, one kind of advocacy, cultural advocacy, is sometimes referred to as "committed anthropology" because of the deep personal investment it requires (Gardner and Lewis 1996:47). Advocacy anthropologists tend to be more explicitly altruistic than development anthropologists; to have more ambitious philanthropic goals; to be more deeply committed, over longer periods of time, to particular peoples or causes; and to be more personally involved in their work. They "tak[e] sides and mak[e] commitments" (Nolan 2002:82). Even in the policy arena, they go well beyond "informed but neutral inputs" (Winthrop 1997: 41). Often, they identify closely with their intended beneficiaries.

Advocacy anthropologist Rhoda Halperin, for example, is an ardent defender of her study population, members of a working-class community situated at the fringes (both geographically and socially) of Cincinnati, Ohio (Halperin 1998). The ethnically mixed residents of the "East End," historically united by mutual obligations and social relationships revolving around kinship, religion, and economics, now find their community (in the sense of both physical territory and social cohesiveness) threatened by external developers. Halperin identifies passionately with the East Enders, viewing them as representatives of oppressed working-class people everywhere who are trying to resist the powerful forces of urbanism and capitalism that are threatening to obliterate their culture. She believes it is her responsibility as an ethnographer to educate outside urban planners about the true nature of the East End community, whose residents may lose their jobs, homes, and way of life if development proceeds. For Halperin, advocacy is not a choice, but rather a deeply personal obligation.

FOOD FOR THOUGHT Are there potential disadvantages to community members when their ethnographer becomes personally involved in their problems and commits herself to advocacy on their behalf? If so, what are these disadvantages? What about possible disadvantages to the ethnographer? Explain your responses.

Time Frame

The work of development anthropologists is typically organized and accomplished through projects or programs that address specific development problems and are limited in time (see Chapter 5). Examples might include designing a program to improve elementary education in a particular developing country, implementing an irrigation project, or analyzing the effectiveness or efficiency of a national public health system. When the specific agenda is completed and/or the funding runs out, the project or program ends. Advocacy anthropologists, in contrast, are more likely to work without time limits, in general support of communities or even whole cultures, rather than to address specific, time-critical problems. Some, like David Maybury-Lewis, devote much of a lifetime to advocacy on behalf of a particular community or culture.

The Anthropologist–Beneficiary Relationship

Most advocacy anthropologists spend much of their time working directly with local counterparts in host communities or countries. The relationship is apt to be a close one. A cultural anthropologist in the field (often for some specific purpose other than advocacy) observes a problem that she can help to rectify, discusses it with members of the study population, is invited to contribute to a solution, and creates for herself the particular advocacy role—such as representative, facilitator, or educator—that is most appropriate to the circumstances. Inge Bolin and David Maybury-Lewis provide examples of how advocates craft advocacy roles for themselves in response to local situations and then work closely with members of their study populations to help them realize specific benefits.

A somewhat different but equally close relationship developed between medical anthropologist Pamela J. Downe and a group of street prostitutes with whom she worked in Costa Rica, where prostitution is legal (Downe 1999). Downe's research was intended to investigate how the women perceived biomedical concepts, such as contagion and risk, and how they then used these ideas to cope with the constant threat of illness inherent in commercial sex work.

"Much of the advocacy associated with anthropological fieldwork is reasonably formal, well-planned, and focused," Downe observes, but her advocacy work with the prostitutes was spontaneous and informal (Downe 1999:21). Even more significant, her role as advocate was crafted not by Downe herself but by the prostitutes. At the time of their mutual collaboration on Downe's health research project, the prostitutes were threatened with the possibility that they would be forced to submit to mandatory health testing and would have to carry government-issued health cards. They felt this would place them at risk for potential abuses such as unjustifiable detainment by the police (Downe 1999:22). Realizing that Downe was in a good position to present to the authorities an alternative to the "infected whore" stereotype that informed government policy, the prostitutes crafted an advocacy role for her, turning her research into a resource for their cause.

Downe calls the relationship that ensued "participant advocacy." The role of participant advocate emerges when "community members themselves construct an advocacy position for the researcher, who then responds to the community's work and research initiatives" (Downe 1999:23). "Your work and your name [are] useful to us," the prostitutes told Downe, "because we can use them to generate the attention that we need" (ibid.). The prostitutes did exactly that, and eventually the government decided to postpone the introduction of health cards. Downe states that she never intended to become a participant advocate, but found it to be "among the richest aspects of [her] work" (Downe 1999:24).

It should be noted that close contact between advocacy anthropologists and beneficiary populations is not a universal pattern. Some advocacy anthropologists spend much of their time working from outside the groups they assist, to elicit the interest and support of people who—like the anthropologists themselves—are outsiders but who are unfamiliar with the group and its problems. These advocates write newspaper, magazine, and Internet articles about their groups, network with other interested individuals and groups, give TV and newspaper interviews and lectures, raise funds, and perhaps lobby national governments or international organizations for legal changes that would protect their groups' human and civil rights. Thus, although a direct relationship with community members is the more common pattern, in some cases advocacy work is actually less hands-on than development work. Many advocates, of course, play both roles.

Funding

Chapter 5 pointed out that development work is typically project-based. The development anthropologist usually works for an aid agency, on specific projects designed to achieve agency-defined and agency-funded goals. Advocacy anthropology, in contrast, is much less apt to be project-based (Gardner and Lewis 1996:46). Advocacy anthropologists, working in concert with others, develop mutually acceptable agendas, usually without the need to conform to agency-driven objectives. Funding is typically provided by one or more of the many hundreds of NGOs and PVOs that have been established, specifically to address and fund advocacy agendas, in the past half-century or so. Some of these are dedicated to a particular cause (for example, women's reproductive health), some to a particular group (for example, the Maasai of Africa). Many of them have become well known to the public, since they seek support through direct-mail campaigns and advertising in the media. Many are based in the United States, although they exist worldwide. In Kenya alone, eight organizations do advocacy work on behalf of just one group of people, the Maasai, at the local, national, and international levels.

Despite differences of commitment, time frame, anthropologist–beneficiary relationships, and funding arrangements, the line dividing development anthropology

✧ *Funding for advocacy work is often provided by NGOs or PVOs dedicated to specific causes or agendas, such as women's reproductive health. At a women's health clinic in Jakarta, Indonesia, women and children learn how to protect their health.*

from advocacy anthropology is blurry. One applied cultural anthropologist, Lily Kak, who is profiled in Chapter 12, pp. 288–289, worked for many years for a Washington-based NGO with a long history of undertaking USAID-funding projects in the area of family planning and women's reproductive health. Although Dr. Kak describes herself as an international health specialist, she so passionately believes in the right of all women to have access to reliable family planning, and has devoted so many years of her life to helping poor women around the world to gain this access, that she could justifiably be considered an advocacy anthropologist.

THE GROWTH OF ADVOCACY ANTHROPOLOGY

Advocacy has a long tradition in applied anthropology (Gardner and Lewis 1996:47). A few examples will suffice to illustrate how the idea of using principles of cultural anthropology to promote the best interests of disenfranchised groups of people occurred to some of the earliest cultural anthropologists, and how this idea has changed, both in implementation and scope, through the ensuing years.

As early as 1835, in England, a group of wealthy philanthropists with anthropological interests grew concerned about the displacement, exploitation, and genocide of the indigenous people of England's colony in Australia. Aboriginal Australians, for example, were deemed incompetent to give evidence in court under oath, which meant that they were virtually unable to defend themselves (Molony 1987:99). Forming the Aborigines Protection Society, these philanthropists dedicated themselves to learning about the Aborigines and promoting their welfare, mainly by providing funding. Although they undoubtedly did not realize it at the time, the members of this society were among the earliest anthropological advocates.

This and most other early examples of advocacy were based on what would later be called a top-down approach to assistance (see Chapter 5). In retrospect, this kind of advocacy, which assumed that advocates could "represent the special interests of another group of people better than . . . the members of that group," seems paternalistic, but in the nineteenth century there still existed numerous disenfranchised groups whose members had little knowledge of, or experience with, the social and political realities of the dominant society around them (Chambers 1989:26).

During the early years of the twentieth century, American anthropologists' interest in, and admiration for, Native Americans was often tinged with empathy for their plight, and individual anthropologists occasionally played what would now be called advocacy roles in support of their research populations. An example is Frank Speck, an academic anthropologist whose interest in a theoretical problem—defining the land tenure system that had existed in native North America before contact by Western Europeans (Speck 1915)—was accompanied by a deep sympathy for the plight of Native Americans in his own time. Disturbed by the fact that these indigenes had been unfairly deprived of what was rightfully theirs by tradition, Speck attempted to raise public awareness of this wrong in a series of publications and lectures extending throughout his lifetime. This nonparticipatory advocacy strategy seems out of date today, but it "was appropriate to a time when the university still wore the mantle of authority" (La Rusic 1990:23).

In the early 1940s, Brazilian anthropologist Claudio Villas Boas joined a government expedition to explore Brazil's vast tropical rain forest to assess its potential for economic development (*New York Times* 1998:45). By this time, the advocate's role had changed somewhat. Dismayed at the devastating effect that development projects such as logging and road building would inevitably have on the cultures of the small, isolated, previously uncontacted groups of native peoples he encountered, Villas Boas became an activist on their behalf. He spent the next twenty years working with isolated Amazonian groups to help them save their threatened cultures from obliteration, mainly in a lobbying and networking role (ibid.:45). Villas Boas failed to persuade the Brazilian government to abandon its commercial interests in the indigenes' land, but he did manage to convince it to establish a national foundation devoted to protecting the indigenes' rights and to carve out a 10,000-square-mile national park where some eighteen indigenous groups were able to find refuge from the developers. He also helped establish a new Brazilian organization, the National Indian Foundation, to protect the indigenes' rights. By today's standards, this work still seems top-down and somewhat paternalistic—the indigenes played a relatively limited role in the establishment of the national park and foundation—but it was more socially and politically engaged than earlier advocacy efforts.

FOOD FOR THOUGHT In 1947, anthropologists Walter Goldschmidt and Theodore Haas were commissioned by the U.S. government to write a report on traditional land tenure and land use among Native American groups on the Northwest Coast (Goldschmidt and Haas 1998). Today, Native Americans seeking to regain title to their traditional lands, or pressing for the right to use and regulate the natural resources on their lands, still use this report to bolster their legal claims. Where does the work of Goldschmidt and Haas fit into the categories listed on Table 6.1 (p. 140)?

The 1950s witnessed Allan Holmberg's advocacy on behalf of the peasants of Vicos (see Chapter 3), and the start of Sol Tax's work with the Fox, a Native American group (see Chapter 2, p. 30 and Chapter 3, p. 68). Both Holmberg and Tax grounded their work in the idea of indigenous participation. Tax, for example, strongly encouraged the Fox to identify their own problems and to participate in every aspect of solving them. This stance differed considerably from the lobbying activities and top-down donations of material goods and money of earlier advocates.

In the 1960s, after "resettlement anthropologist" Thayer Scudder had studied an African group that had been relocated because of the construction of a dam on the Zambezi River, he put his research data to use by lobbying for more humane treatment of involuntary refugees and other displaced people. Later, Scudder's work informed the World Bank's guidelines on involuntary resettlement resulting from bank-financed projects (Scudder 1981; Scudder and Colson 1982; Gardner and Lewis 1996:47). Scudder thus took anthropological advocacy a step further: his field research played a significant role in policy formulation.

As early as the 1950s, the term *cultural brokerage*, referring loosely to mediation or negotiation between stakeholders in development projects (for example, between

◇ **TABLE 6.1   Styles of Advocacy**

Style	Advocate's Role	Attributes of Style	Examples in Chapter
Representative	Philanthropist, champion, lecturer, proxy, financier	Top down, paternalistic	Aborigines Protection Society, Frank Speck
Facilitator	Lobbyist , activist, networker, implementer	Less top down, still paternalistic	Villas Boas
Informant	Collaborator, conduit, resource person, mediator	More participatory, less paternalistic	Tax, Holmberg
Analyst	Data analyst, planner, policy expert	Policy-oriented, forward-looking	Scudder
Mediator	Compromiser, middleman, facilitator	Participatory, educational, advocacy *with* rather than *for*	Maybury-Lewis, Bolin
Community advocate	Ideological compatriot, close collaborator	Personal, highly participatory	Schensul, Downe

Source: Chambers 1985:26–33; Schensul 1973, 1974.

community members and representatives of outside agencies), was sometimes used in the context of advocacy work. Today cultural brokerage is considered an important aspect of development. The many roles of an applied cultural anthropologist serving as a cultural broker include "promoting collaboration and coordination, trading information, sharing resources, engaging in joint planning and action, and reacting quickly to address problems as they arise" (Nolan 2002:80).

Noting that over the years the term *cultural broker* has embodied various shades of meaning, Chambers (1989:28–33) distinguished several different "styles" of cultural brokerage. His useful list can serve as a basis for a rough chronology of trends in anthropological advocacy (see Table 6.1). In the representative role, the anthropologist acts as a stand-in for a group of people who cannot, for some reason, speak for themselves. As a facilitator, an advocate enables representatives of two groups to come to terms with each other. The advocate as informant provides information about one group for the benefit of another. The analyst role involves long-range data analysis leading to policy development while an anthropologist playing the mediator role searches for compromises between opposing groups, in lieu of legal action. The first three of these styles of advocacy are much less in evidence now than in the past, as disenfranchised people become increasingly well educated and empowered. The next two "represent a maturation of the ways in which anthropologists have responded to opportunities to participate in decision-making activities" (Chambers 1989:33).

In the 1970s, applied anthropologist Stephen Schensul, working at the time for a mental health program in a heavily Latino neighborhood in Chicago, added a sixth style of advocacy. Schensul was charged with providing research data to the directors of the program. Observing that the directors were committed to their own model of services provision and generally resistant to new ideas, Schensul began to identify more strongly with the local people the program was intended to serve than with the service providers. Eventually, he forged a close working relationship with community leaders, helping them undertake research and write grant proposals. Schensul called this very personally involved advocacy style "community advocacy anthropology" (Schensul 1973, 1974; van Willigen 1993:109–110).

Thus, by the 1970s, a number of different approaches to advocacy work had been developed (van Willigen 1993:28ff.). By the early 1980s, the subject was important enough for interested cultural anthropologists to join together in a workshop to discuss both the theoretical and practical aspects of this issue (Paine 1990). The general consensus of those present at the workshop was that advocacy should be an inherent aspect of cultural anthropology: "an anthropologist without concern is no anthropologist at all" (Anthony P. Cohen, quoted in Paine 1990). At the same time, however, workshop participants wondered whether or not this view was representative of the discipline of anthropology in general (Paine 1990:249).

Since then, it has become quite clear that many cultural anthropologists, although certainly not all, agree with Cohen that advocacy at some level on behalf of a study population—if the population requests it and is involved in it—is an appropriate role for cultural anthropologists. Their increasing interest and involvement in advocacy parallels the noticeable trend, beginning in the nineteenth century, from doing advocacy "for" a group to doing advocacy "with" a group (Downe 1999:23). Thus advocacy has become a "relatively well established tradition within anthropology, at least within the US," where anthropologists now undertake a number of different roles, including direct activism and lobbying, on behalf of disenfranchised groups (Gardner and Lewis 1996:47).

TWO FUNDAMENTAL PRINCIPLES

Basic Human Rights

An unalterable principle that advocacy anthropologists take as axiomatic is that all people have certain social, economic, and political rights, regardless of ethnicity, socioeconomic status, gender, or other personal attributes (see Johnston 1994, 2000; Magnarella 2000). Among these are the right to adequate shelter, to nutritious food in sufficient quantity, to clean water, to a safe and healthy environment, to educational and employment opportunities, and to freedom of religious and political expression. Despite this general agreement, however, and also despite the best efforts of international organizations such as the International Red Cross and the United Nations,[3] rights abuses continue to occur in many countries around the world, including industrialized countries. A major overall goal of advocacy anthropology is to work with minority or indigenous groups as they struggle to realize their basic rights as human beings.

Environmental rights provide a good example. Around the world, communities that can be differentiated from others on the basis of ethnicity, small size, or inferior socioeconomic status are more likely than other communities to find themselves on the receiving end of environmental problems, such as toxic waste dumping and pollution from industrial production. In developing countries, indigenous groups, dependent on their local environment for making their living, often suffer very direct economic and lifestyle consequences as a result of logging, mining, or road building in the name of "progress." In industrialized countries, members of ethnic minorities may find that mines or waste treatment facilities have turned up virtually in their back yards (Bullard 1992.) In the United States, for example, uranium- and coal-mining operations on the Navajo reservation pollute the local environment but do not provide the expected energy benefits: these mines supply New Mexico with thirty-two times the energy it needs, yet 85 percent of Navajo households lack electric power (Butler and LaDuke 1995:117).

Most small-scale and minority groups lack the funds, the numbers, or in some cases the education or political influence necessary to defend themselves against environmental injustice. Some advocacy anthropologists thus contribute to the **environmental justice movement,** working to support indigenous or minority groups in their struggle to attain their basic right to a safe, healthy environment (Bryant 1995).

Self-Determination

A second principle at the heart of anthropological advocacy is the crucial notion that the right to determine the future belongs to the people whose future is in question, not to any other individual or group, including anthropologists. It has become clear that it is not outside professionals but rather disenfranchised people themselves who are best qualified to identify their specific problems, develop workable solutions, and mobilize their communities to implement these solutions. An important corollary of this premise, perhaps counterintuitive at first glance, is that the members of disenfranchised groups should make their own choices even if advocates believe these choices are the wrong ones. Thus, for example, if a group of indigenous people collectively wishes to become more Westernized; if they want to leave their rural villages and traditional lands in favor of wage labor in factories owned by members of a different culture; if they want to own cars and video cameras, televisions and cell phones, jeans and baseball caps; if they want to smoke cigarettes and drink beer; even if they choose *not* to fight for the continued existence of their culture or subculture as a distinct entity, the advocacy anthropologist supports their choice.

To illustrate this point, David Maybury-Lewis describes what happened recently when lumber companies offered an indigenous Brazilian group a great deal of money for timbering rights to its land (Maybury-Lewis 1990:144). Advocacy anthropologists tried to persuade the group to decline the offer, fearing that the loss of a portion of the forest on which the indigenes depended for their livelihood would mean that subsequent generations would have to find another kind of subsistence adaptation. But ultimately the indigenes, to whom the warnings of the anthropologists about ecological devastation apparently seemed overblown, decided to accept the offer. At that point, the anthropologists stopped objecting, and the project went forward. As Maybury-Lewis points out, it would have been "the worst sort of paternalism" if the anthropologists had forced their opinion on the indigenes (ibid.). They were committed to letting the local people make their own decision.

Advocacy anthropologists encourage indigenous peoples to choose how extensively and how rapidly to embrace modernization. In the Australian desert, Aborigine boys use a laptop computer

To anthropological advocates, self-determination may be the most problematic aspect of advocacy, not only because it can be painful to witness but also because it is sometimes at odds with other development principles. Like any other kind of development effort, for example, advocacy anthropology strives to achieve beneficial results that are sustainable (see Chapters 2, 5). Yet certain economic activities, such as logging and slash-and-burn farming, are inherently unsustainable: forests, once felled, regrow only after many generations, if ever; farmland, planted repeatedly, loses soil nutrients. This means that any short-term economic solutions an indigenous group may choose—even those that may produce a financial windfall for them—are, from the point of view of advocacy anthropologists, much less desirable than long-term, sustainable ones. However, self-determination is an inviolable principle of anthropological advocacy, so important that it must override all other considerations.

ETHICAL CONSIDERATIONS

From the beginning, advocacy anthropology has posed ethical problems more formidable than those with which most other applied cultural anthropologists—even development anthropologists—must wrestle (see Chapter 4). Letters and seminar notes written during the 1950s Fox project, for example, include "tortured considerations and reconsiderations of the University of Chicago anthropology students who were trying to determine the ethics of intervening in the lives of the Fox Indians" (La Rusic 1990:22). Every cultural advocate must ask himself or herself a fundamental question: should I be doing this? What makes the ethics of advocacy anthropology particularly challenging is that advocacy involves not just a dispassionate search for sustainable solutions to certain human problems, and not just well-intended intervention in the lives of amenable others, but deep, personal, often long-term commitment.

The questions responsible advocacy anthropologists must ask themselves—questions to which this book cannot supply definitive answers—include the following:

- *Does advocacy anthropology contradict the canons of academic anthropology?* (Paine 1990:xiii). Other kinds of applied anthropologists must resolve the disparity between what they were taught in graduate school—that their role in the field is to observe and report, not to try to change, the status quo—and applied anthropology's explicit commitment to change. Yet they can, if they wish, maintain some semblance of objectivity. Advocates, however, must not only resolve that disparity but also bridge the intellectual gap between the ideal of academic objectivity and unabashed subjectivity.

AN APPLIED CULTURAL ANTHROPOLOGIST AT WORK

MITZI GOHEEN

Off and on over the course of many years, cultural anthropologist Mitzi Goheen has lived and worked in the Nso' Chiefdom, located in the grassfields of western Cameroon. She is by now so much a part of this community that she has a house, a car, a dog, and a retinue of housemates there, and considers Nso' her second home. The local people have returned her affection and respect for them by bestowing a traditional title upon "their" anthropologist. The title carries with it both honor and responsibility.

When not living and working in Nso', Dr. Goheen is professor of anthropology at Amherst College in Massachusetts. Well known as a specialist in the peoples and cultures of West Africa, she has a particular interest in political economy. This subject is the focus of her recent book *Men Own the Fields, Women Own the Crops*, an examination of the effects on state formation of the different kinds and amounts of power and authority exercised by men and women in West Africa. Male–female relationships, she says, are a "critical locus of negotiations over power and meaning in late-twentieth-century Africa."

As a scholar and an academic, Dr. Goheen does not think of herself as an applied cultural anthropologist, much less an anthropological advocate. Like many other cultural anthropologists, however, she often puts her topical and geographical expertise to practical use in serving the people among whom she lives and works. As a titled leader, for example, Dr. Goheen has certain obligations to her Cameroonian friends, which she fulfills by taking care of them in direct, practical ways. She is godmother to a Cameroonian child, helps young men of the community negotiate bridewealth payments, and maintains a fund at the local Baptist mission hospital to pay her friends' medical bills (mission hospitals provide the majority of health care in rural areas of Cameroon). She also helps villagers make hospital care decisions—and often transports them to the hospital as well. She will soon be teaching a course in a management training program developed for hospital administrators.

In addition, Dr. Goheen serves on the board of directors of a local lending organization called KWIHEED. Part of the larger, international Grameen Bank, KWIHEED exists to extend small loans ("microenterprise" loans) to local women. Even though the amounts of money involved are very small (often as little as $25 and never more than $100), these loans enable their recipients to become players in the local economy—for example, by purchas-

- *If applied anthropology is intended to benefit the whole public, is it unethical, as an advocacy anthropologist, to help only marginalized people?* (Anciaux 2000:47).
- *Does advocacy contribute to a "dependency mentality" on the part of those it is intended to benefit?* This is a question that both advocates and beneficiaries must ask. In Haiti, for example, an "army" of donors and aid workers arrived in the 1990s; by 1997, foreign aid accounted for nearly 80 percent of the country's national budget. That aid, however, only exacerbated the country's poverty. Even Haitians are now asking whether outside help merely breeds dependency and undermines grass-roots efforts (Smith 2001:27–31).
- *Does advocacy in any way "reinforce the global privilege of North over South and West over non-West"?* (Downe 1999:23). Like development, advocacy has occasionally been criticized as inherently paternalistic, or even racist. Even committed

ing seeds with which to grow cash crops. Engaging in professional activities such as gardening is a source of self-esteem and empowerment for the women, and the income they earn means that their families are better off. Dr. Goheen and the other KWIHEED board members oversee the allocation of microenterprise funds in two local villages. Periodically they travel to these villages to solicit verbal proposals from women applying for loans. Applicants must make a good case for why they need a loan, what they plan to do with it, and how soon they will be able to pay it off.

Dr. Goheen's intimate familiarity with the local culture helps her carry out her responsibilities to KWIHEED. "Understanding—from the local level—who really needs these loans, what kinds of enterprises can succeed locally, which enterprises will really benefit from a small infusion of capital, what is the best way to get women to organize to help each other, and what it means to local women to succeed economically—this is cultural knowledge," she says.

Dr. Goheen's activities on behalf of Cameroonians exemplify some of the many ways in which academic anthropologists can put their "cultural knowledge" to work. One need not hold the title of applied anthropolo-

gist to put anthropological theory, method, and expertise to good use, nor the title advocacy anthropologist to provide support for the members of small-scale communities.

Dr. Mitzi Goheen (center) has lived and worked in the NSO' Chiefdom in Cameroon for many years. In 1993, wearing traditional Cameroonian garb, she visited with two Wanto' friends, Koaju and Dede.

advocates, working in genuine partnership with their intended beneficiaries, sometimes find it difficult to reconcile the need of obviously less fortunate others with a view of themselves as more powerful and perhaps in some sense even superior for possessing the means to alleviate that misfortune.

■ *Exactly whom is the advocacy anthropologist representing?* (Paine 1990:xv; Maybury-Lewis 1990:143). Every group is fragmented, every community factionalized to some extent. When some members of a group need and have requested one kind of assistance, but other members want another, an advocate may be forced to choose sides. Alternatively, the advocate's research findings may be accepted as valid by some stakeholders but not by others (Anciaux 2000:47).

■ *What responsibilities do advocacy anthropologists have to ensure that their data and methods are not appropriated by their collaborators for other, less worthy, purposes?* (Downe 1999:23).

■ *Should applied cultural anthropologists who work for advocacy organizations, which are apt to have very definite agendas, values, and policies, interject their personal values or opinions into their work if these are not entirely congruent with the values or policies of their employers?* (Anciaux 200:480).

■ *What should the advocacy anthropologist do when collective rights are at odds with individual rights?* If the rights of certain societies to pursue long-standing traditions are acknowledged and protected, for example, this may "justify illiberal practices such as infanticide, female circumcision, widow burning, and other threats to individual liberty" (Thompson 1997:788–789).

There are critics on both sides of the advocacy issue: some say advocacy goes too far (for example, Hastrup and Elass 1990), others that it does not go far enough (for example, Singer, Huertas, and Scott 2000). The former see advocacy anthropology as paternalistic, biased, and incompatible with the principle of cultural relativism (Hastrup and Elass 1990). The latter believe that cultural anthropologists should aid and defend "vulnerable populations" more habitually and more assiduously than they do at present (Singer, Huertas, and Scott 2000:398; see also Scheper-Hughes 1995). These pro-advocacy anthropologists have raised the question of whether all anthropologists working with marginalized, low-income, or at-risk populations should be required to take "aggressive" action on their behalf (ibid.:397): "should we be focused on building a morally engaged approach to research that is guided by an ethic of care and responsibility?" (ibid.:398). There is no simple answer, only a challenge to responsible researchers to confront the issue.

FOOD FOR THOUGHT   Anthropologist Pamela Downe (see p. 136), not originally intending to serve her study population as an advocate, was confronted with a fieldwork situation in which an advocacy role was created for her. As a cultural anthropologist in the field, what would you do in Downe's situation? Why?

The most recent version of the Code of Ethics of the American Anthropological Association (see Chapter 4, p. 97) leaves the ethical questions surrounding advocacy unanswered. According to the code, "Anthropologists may choose to move beyond disseminating research results to a position of advocacy. This is an individual decision, but not an ethical responsibility" (AAA 1998:III-C-2).

CULTURAL ADVOCACY

The term *cultural advocacy* was defined earlier as advocacy on behalf of small-scale, indigenous societies or minority groups whose cultures, languages, traditions, lands, and/or rights are threatened by other, usually more Westernized, people (Thompson 1997). This kind of advocacy anthropology tends to be associated with resistance to outside interference—for example, "supporting opposition from local communities to the building of a dam or the preservation of local culture in the face of change and repression" (Gardner and Lewis 1996:47).

Indigenous and minority groups tend to be relatively poor economically; relatively unversed in the intricacies of the culture of those who may be seeking to dominate, exploit, or incorporate them; and relatively weak in the context of more dominant political organizations—all of which may make it difficult for them to either preserve or change their culture, as they may wish, without advocacy. On the other hand, the members of indigenous and minority groups are highly intelligent, and capable of deciding which changes to their culture are potentially valuable and which ones potentially dangerous. Moreover, they have the unquestionable right to choose both the extent to which they want their culture to change and the direction that change will take. Thus cultural advocates typically frame their work in terms of the *empowerment* of indigenous or minority groups; the term means helping the members of these groups to assert themselves economically, socially, and politically, without making decisions for them.

Cultural advocacy is quite different from **cultural preservation,** the attempt to preserve the cultural status quo. Both efforts are valuable under the appropriate circumstances. The members of some cultures seek beneficial change, while the members of others strive to retain some of their traditional lifeways, or—if certain traditional aspects of their cultures are already lost—to return to them. Recent efforts to revive and preserve the Welsh language provide a good example. Politically, Wales is part of Britain, and by the 1970s, the ancient Welsh language had all but died out; it was spoken only by a few old-timers in the rural, northern part of the country. Over the past three decades, however, the Welsh have made very concerted efforts to reinstate their language. They exerted enough pressure on the British government that today highway signs in Wales are in both English and Welsh, and schoolchildren are learning to speak their traditional tongue.

Change and preservation are not necessarily mutually exclusive; it is quite possible for indigenes to enjoy improved health, better education, and higher living standards, and to preserve much of their traditional culture at the same time. Thus cultural advocates often help indigenous people learn about modern ideas and technologies; gain access to mainstream health care, welfare, and educational opportunities; develop sustainable income-producing projects and markets for products manufactured from local resources; manage their natural resources; train for and find jobs; or become involved in the mainstream political process through voting and other forms of political participation. The point of cultural advocacy is not necessarily to preserve past traditions or keep indigenous people from changing, but instead to facilitate their adaptation to their present situation, whatever that situation may be, while at the same time helping them retain as much of their traditional culture as they desire.

Historically, the problems with which indigenous and minority groups have most often requested anthropological help are loss of **cultural identity** (all those aspects of a culture that define it and distinguish it from other cultures), loss of land and/or natural resources, poor health and nutrition, and political disenfranchisement. The last of these is often accompanied by human rights abuses.

Loss of Cultural Identity

The advocacy role in which cultural anthropologists can perhaps contribute the most is helping indigenous and minority groups preserve their cultural identity. The travel writer Alex Shoumatoff describes the loss of cultural identity, due to the impact of culture contact, of a group of Brazilian indigenes, the Kaxuiana (Shoumatoff 1986:103):

> *Bernardinho showed me . . . a wooden club with a vulture's head, carved in masterly fashion. . . . "We used to kill people with this fifty years ago," he said. A cotton hammock, intricately woven . . . hung in one corner. Bernardinho said that it had taken his mother a month to make. . . . The knowledge of how to make such things had apparently not been passed on to his generation; nor, apparently, had the ability to tell any of the Kaxuiana myths. . . . It looked as if the next generation would be absorbed into the larger population. . . . The Kaxuiana population here had probably fallen below replacement level. Being Indian had no prestige in the [outside] world . . . but the members of this small group still had tribal solidarity, perhaps heightened by the knowledge that they were the last of their kind.*

The negative effects of the loss of cultural identity suffered by the Kaxuiana are mirrored by the experiences of other small-scale groups. Native American Inuit (Eskimo) people, formerly gatherers and hunters, today suffer high rates of poverty and alcoholism in sedentary villages (Kawagley 1995). Small, rural Eastern Caribbean communities are being transformed as a result of an influx of North American goods, tourists, and TV shows (Gmelch and Gmelch 1997). Cultural losses such as these are indisputably distressing, and what makes them perhaps even more so is that in most cases, indigenous people in the process of losing their cultural identity are aware, like Bernardinho, of what is happening, but believe they are powerless to stop the process. Most cultural advocacy is devoted to the victims of unanticipated and unwanted culture change.

Helping a group preserve its cultural identity is much more difficult than it may appear at first glance. Indigenous and minority groups are often faced with wrenching decisions that cause internal conflict. Some members of a group may want to reap the many benefits of Westernization, while others want to preserve the group's cultural identity. Many are caught in the middle, torn between these two poles. Perhaps the most important role of cultural advocates is to assist the members of minority or indigenous groups to make difficult choices between preserving various aspects of their cultural identity and taking advantage of opportunities presented by modernization or commercialization. A number of advocacy groups exist through which cultural advocates may work (see the *Anthropology Career Resources Handbook*).

Loss of Land and/or Natural Resources

Since the beginning of the Age of Exploration, members of dominant large-scale cultures have deprived indigenes of their traditionally held lands, usually for purposes of colonization or exploitation of natural resources. Over the centuries, much of the most productive land around the world has been appropriated by conquerors. Occasionally, however, colonizers passed up such land, not out of kindness, respect for nature, or a desire to protect an indigenous group's heritage or lifestyle, but because they were unaware of the presence or value of its oil, timber, or minerals. Today, representatives of commercial interests, with the advantage of modern exploration and extraction technologies, are not so naive.

A number of anthropological advocates now work with indigenes to help them choose among various options for land and resource preservation, conservation, or use. Indigenous people are viewed as crucial components of modern conservation efforts. They may be poor and undereducated, but they are also intelligent and far-sighted. Moreover, from a human rights point of view, indigenous people themselves, not outsiders, should be responsible for land and resources. A new environmental conservation paradigm, **community-based conservation (CBC),** embodies this philosophy. CBC is a way of encouraging the full participation of local people in environmental decision making and management. A relatively new role for anthropological advocates is to help implement CBC. For instance, advocacy anthropologists are exploring with indigenes what alternative subsistence activities will be compatible with environmental conservation and still provide the indigenes with a living.

Poor Health and Nutrition

Largely due to culture contact, members of indigenous groups are exposed to an increasing array of health threats. In some cases, they suffer from avoidable and/or curable infectious diseases, such as measles or tuberculosis, because of a lack of understanding about prevention or treatment, a lack of access to modern health care facilities, or national health budgets that are too overburdened to offer modern health care to remote, isolated groups. Today AIDS—preventable with education and behavior modification—is perhaps the most visible of these threats, but common childhood diseases also take a heavy toll of lives in the developing world (see Chapter 12). In addition, small-scale populations are increasingly suffering from the so-called diseases of affluence: degenerative diseases, such as cancer and heart disease, associated with a modern lifestyle.

In many cases, no direct or immediate association can be drawn between ac-
culturation and a specific disease; the effects are long-term. A typical pattern is for a
small-scale group—once isolated from injurious substances such as mass-produced
alcohol and tobacco products, and well-nourished by a traditional diet rich in home-
grown cereal grains and legumes—to succumb to alcohol or nicotine dependency
and to reject locally produced foods in favor of less healthy, more costly, higher-
status imported foods (Foster 1992).

This kind of lifestyle and dietary shift is compounded in countries in which, for
economic reasons, people stop growing fruits, vegetables, and grains for their own
consumption in favor of growing nonnourishing but cash-producing export crops,
such as coffee or sisal. All over the developing world, large-scale commercial agricultural production for export has resulted in a constantly dwindling number of privately held small farms and the consequent loss of food security (Stonich 1994:110).
Cultural advocates believe their appropriate role in health and nutrition is not to
discourage either traditional health practices, which are often efficacious, or traditional culinary choices, which are usually highly nutritious. Instead, many work to
widen indigenes' choices by helping them gain access to nutrition education and a
minimum level of modern biomedical health care (see Chapter 12).

Political Disenfranchisement and Human Rights Abuses

A major overall goal of cultural advocacy is to help indigenous and minority groups
obtain economic, political, and social justice (see "Basic Human Rights," p. 141).
Much of the work of cultural advocates around the world is devoted to such problems, sometimes through personal activism but more often through institutions
such as various arms of the United Nations, international organizations such as
Amnesty International, national rights organizations, and NGOs. Cultural advocates
working in the human rights arena are more likely to work for large, highly visible
cultural advocacy organizations than for small NGOs or independently.

News-making human rights abuses, such as the genocide that has taken place
recently in Rwanda, Bosnia, and other countries, will be familiar to most readers.
One aspect of the contemporary human rights debate that is less well known than
civil rights issues is the notion of **intellectual property rights (IPR)** (Greaves
1994; Riley 2001). As the term is most commonly used today, *intellectual property*
usually refers to salable "products of the mind" such as information technologies,
but in this case it refers to bodies of knowledge that members of indigenous or minority groups have developed over many generations and that form an important
part of their culture. In some cases, outsiders may attempt to exploit intellectual
property unfairly or without payment; for example, a pharmaceuticals company
might press an indigenous group to reveal what it knows about the medicinal properties of local plants and then synthesize or reproduce beneficial plant products for
commercial sale. Other examples of intellectual property are artistic traditions and
techniques, religious rituals, and myths. Within the field of cultural advocacy, IPR is
growing rapidly.

FOOD FOR THOUGHT

Of the several different roles for advocacy anthropologists described in this chapter, which would you be most comfortable playing, and why? Devise a fictional scenario in which you are an advocacy anthropologist playing this role.

COMMUNITY ADVOCACY

Community advocacy, as the term is used here, involves advocacy on behalf of members of a specific, usually small-scale community, such as a neighborhood or village, in either an industrialized or developing country. Bolin's advocacy in Chichubamba was cited earlier as an example; Downe's in Costa Rica is another. There is a specific goal, and although a specific time-frame for achieving this goal may be lacking, it is assumed on both sides that the advocacy will end when the goal is achieved. The size of the community, the specificity of the goal, and the impermanence of the relationship distinguish community advocacy from cultural advocacy. However, the depth of the cultural anthropologist's personal interest in the community and the intensity of his or her commitment to helping its members achieve their goals are often the same.

The community advocate may work "direct[ly] and "intimate[ly]" with members of the community—typically its leaders—rather than with or through an outside organization (van Willigen 1993:109). Alternatively, he or she may work for an outside agency, such as a religious organization, woman's group, or advocacy organization, at the request of—or at least with the knowledge and permission of—members of the community. In either case, the advocate provides research data, training, organizational assistance, access to networks, and empathy, with the express purpose of facilitating the community members' efforts to improve their lives somehow.

The work of advocacy anthropologist Tina Quiroz in "Breverton" (a pseudonym), a northwestern U.S. city in which she undertook ethnographic research, provides an example of community advocacy. A recent, rapid influx of Spanish-speaking immigrants had created a substantial Latino youth subculture in Breverton (Quiroz 1998). Unfortunately, city officials, most of them long-time residents of the city, had a negative and stereotypical view of Latino culture and thus found it easy to believe that certain cultural traits associated with young people—for example, their use of certain Spanish words and their style of dress—were suggestive of gang membership. For many young people, "simply being a Latino [had] come to be interpreted as involvement in criminal activity, and more specifically, youth gangs" (Quiroz 1998:11).

Quiroz learned, to her dismay, that the city had commissioned a committee to prepare a "gang manual" to facilitate the identification of lawbreakers. A draft of this manual contained so much cultural misinformation that Quiroz felt strongly it should never be published. She therefore arranged to meet with the committee to explain that its knee-jerk association of certain cultural traits with criminal activity was inaccurate and unfair. Eventually, plans to publish the manual were dropped. Quiroz believes her testimony was instrumental in this decision (Quiroz 1998:15).

In her words, "the application of anthropological methodology, advocacy, and community activism served as a catalyst for positive social change in the community" (Quiroz 1998:15).

CONCLUSION

At the beginning of this book, applied cultural anthropology was contrasted with theoretical anthropology. The two kinds of anthropology may seem like opposites: applied cultural anthropologists' express goal is to change people's lives for the better, while theoreticians' goal is to contribute to human knowledge. However, applied and theoretical cultural anthropology share an important common element: the concept of cultural relativism, the idea that every culture should be evaluated in terms of its own shared precepts and values, not those of any other culture (see Appendix 2 and Chapter 4, p. 83). This concept is as fundamental to anthropological advocacy as it is to theoretical cultural anthropology.

Advocacy involves "subordination of one's own goals to those of the group, working . . . *in terms of standards and procedures as defined by the group*" (Nolan 2002:82; emphasis added). It "requires the ability to suspend judgment" (Maybury-Lewis 1990:147). It is not imposed on a group from the outside; members of the group must collectively ask for it. Policy decisions affecting the group are not taken by the advocates; they are taken by the people themselves. What eventually happens does not reflect either the judgment or the will of advocates; it reflects those of the people themselves. From the point of view of the applied anthropologists involved, this is true cultural relativism.

◇   ◇   ◇

KEY   TERMS

advocacy anthropology   the branch of development anthropology that proactively represents, defends, and supports the disenfranchised

community advocacy   anthropological advocacy concerned with specific initiatives requested by the residents of local communities, in both industrialized and developing countries

community-based conservation   a way of encouraging the full participation of local people in environmental decision making and management

cultural advocacy   anthropological advocacy concerned, over the long term, with the problems faced by minority groups and small-scale, indigenous societies, whose cultures, languages, traditions, lands, and/or rights are threatened by Westernization

cultural brokerage   a kind of cultural advocacy involving the promotion of mutually beneficial relationships among the various stakeholders in development projects

cultural identity   all those aspects of a culture that define it and distinguish it from other cultures

cultural preservation   the attempt to preserve the cultural status quo

environmental justice movement   advocacy to raise the environmental consciousness of indigenous or minority groups and support them in their struggle for environmental self-determination

intellectual property rights   in the context of cultural advocacy, the right of indigenous people to control bodies of knowledge that they have developed over many generations and that form part of their culture

NOTES

1. Shavante culture includes an unusual and interesting political system. They recognize no elected
or appointed leaders; instead, political power and
social control are exerted by a number of constantly vying political factions, each headed by a
charismatic leader whose authority is achieved by
group consensus.
2. Other well-known examples include Survival International and The International Work Group for
Indigenous Affairs (IWGIA); see the *Anthropology
Career Resources Handbook* for information on these
and other similar groups.
3. The United Nations has declared 1995–2004 the
International Decade of the World's Indigenous
Peoples. Its Human Rights Committee is in the
process of drafting a Declaration on the Rights of
Indigenous Peoples.

REFERENCES

American Anthropological Association (AAA)
1998. "Code of Ethics of the American Anthropological Association." *Anthropology Newsletter* 39 (6):
19–20.

Anciaux, Alain
2000. "International Voices: Are We Learning from
History?" *Practicing Anthropology* 22 (4):47–48.

Bolin, Inge
1992. "Achieving Reciprocity: Anthropological Research and Development Assistance." *Practicing Anthropology* 14 (4):12–15.

Bryant, Bunyan (ed.)
1995. *Environmental Justice: Issues, Policies, and Strug-
gles*. Washington, DC: Island Press.

Bullard, Robert D.
1992. *Confronting Environmental Racism: Voices from
the Grassroots*. Boston: South End Press.

Butler, Nilak, and Winona LaDuke
1995. "Economic Development and Destruction of
Indigenous Lands." In *Down to Earth: Community Perspectives on Health, Development, and the Environment*,
edited by Bonnie Bradford and Margaret A.
Gwynne, 113–122. West Hartford, CT: Kumarian
Press.

Chambers, Erve
1989 (orig. 1985). *Applied Anthropology: A Practical
Guide*. Prospect Heights, IL: Waveland Press.

Downe, Pamela J.
1999. "Participant Advocacy and Research with
Prostitutes in Costa Rica." *Practicing Anthropology* 21
(3):21–24.

Foster, Phillips
1992. *The World Food Problem: Tackling the Causes of
Undernutrition in the Third World*. Boulder, CO:
Lynne Rienner Publishers.

Gardner, Katy, and David Lewis
1996. *Anthropology, Development, and the Post-Modern
Challenge*. London: Pluto Press.

Gmelch, George, and Sharon Bohn Gmelch
1997. *The Parish Behind God's Back: The Changing Culture of Rural Barbados*. Ann Arbor: University of
Michigan Press.

Goldschmidt, Walter R., and Theodore H. Haas
1998. *Haa Aani, Our Land: Tlingit and Haida Land
Rights and Use*, edited and with an introduction by
Thomas F. Thornton. Seattle: University of Washington Press.

Greaves, Tom (ed.)
1994. *Intellectual Property Rights for Indigenous Peoples: A Source Book*. Oklahoma City, OK: Society for
Applied Anthropology.

Halperin, Rhoda H.
1998. *Practicing Community: Class, Culture, and Power
in an Urban Neighborhood*. Austin: University of
Texas Press.

Hastrup, Kirsten, and Peter Elass
1990. "Anthropological Advocacy: A Contradiction
in Terms." *Current Anthropology* 31 (3): 301–311.

Johnston, Barbara Rose (ed.)
1994. *Who Pays the Price? The Sociocultural Context of
Environmental Crisis*. Washington, DC: Island Press.

2000. "Practicing Anthropology in the Human
Rights Arena." In *Careers in Anthropology: Profiles of
Practitioner Anthropologists* (NAPA Bulletin No. 20),
edited by Paula L. W. Sabloff, 39–44. Washington,
DC: American Anthropological Association.

Kawagley, A. Oscar
1995. *A Yupiaq Worldview*. Prospect Heights, IL:
Waveland Press.

La Rusic, Ignatius
1990 (orig. 1985). "Reinventing the Advocacy Wheel?" In *Advocacy and Anthropology: First Encounters,* edited by Robert Paine, 22–27. St. John's, Newfoundland: Memorial University of Newfoundland.

Magnarella, Paul J.
2000. "Human Rights of Indigenous Peoples in International Law." *Anthropology News* 41 (4):35–36.

Maybury-Lewis, David H. P.
1967. *Akwe-Shavante Society.* Oxford, UK: Clarendon Press.

1990. "A Special Sort of Pleading: Anthropology at the Service of Ethnic Groups." In *Advocacy and Anthropology: First Encounters,* edited by Robert Paine, 130–148. St. John's, Newfoundland: Memorial University of Newfoundland.

Molony, John
1987. *The Penguin History of Australia.* Ringwood, Victoria, Australia: Penguin Books Australia, Ltd.

Nader, Laura
1999. "Thinking Public Interest Anthropology, 1890s–1990s." *General Anthropology* 5 (2):1–9.

New York Times
1998. "C. Villas Boas, 82, a Defender of Brazil's Indians." *The New York Times,* March 8, 1998: 45.

Nolan, Riall
2002. *Development Anthropology: Encounters in the Real World.* Boulder, CO: Westview Press.

Paine, Robert (ed.)
1990 (orig. 1985). *Advocacy and Anthropology: First Encounters.* St. John's, Newfoundland: Memorial University of Newfoundland.

Quiroz, Tina Kabarec
1998. "Latino Youth, Gangs, and Community Activism: A Case of Advocacy Anthropology." *Practicing Anthropology* 20 (4):11–15.

Riley, Mary
2001. "T.I.G. (Topical Interest Group) for Intellectual Property Rights." *SfAA Newsletter* 12 (2):13–14.

Schensul, Stephen L.
1973. "Action Research: The Applied Anthropologist in a Community Mental Health Program." In *Anthropology Beyond the University* (Southern Anthropological Society Proceedings, No 7), edited by A. Redfield, pp. 106–119. Athens, GA: University of Georgia Press.

1974. "Skills Needed in Action Anthropology: Lessons from El Centro de la Causa." *Human Organization* 33:203–209.

Scheper-Hughes, Nancy
1995. "The Primacy of the Ethical: Propositions for a Militant Anthropology." *Current Anthropology* 36 (3):409–420.

Scudder, Thayer
1981. "What It Means to Be Dammed: The Anthropology of Large-Scale Development Projects in the Tropics and Subtropics." *Engineering and Science* 54: 9–15.

Scudder, Thayer, and Elizabeth Colson
1982. "From Welfare to Development: A Conceptual Framework for the Analysis of Dislocated People." In *Involuntary Migration and Resettlement: The Problems and Responses of Dislocated People,* edited by Art Hansen and Anthony Oliver-Smith, 267–287. Boulder, CO: Westview Press.

Shoumatoff, Alex
1986. "A Reporter at Large (Amazons)." *The New Yorker,* March 24, 1986: 85–107.

Singer, Merrill, Elsa Huertas, and Glenn Scott
2000. "Am I My Brother's Keeper? A Case Study of the Responsibilities of Research." *Human Organization* 59 (4):389–398.

Smith, Jennie M.
2001. *When the Hands Are Many: Community Organization and Social Change in Rural Haiti.* Ithaca: Cornell University Press.

Speck, Frank G.
1915. "The Family Hunting Band as the Basis of Algonkian Social Organization." *American Anthropologist* 13:289–305.

Stonich, Susan C.
1994. "Producing Food for Export: Environmental Quality and Social Justice Implications of Shrimp Mariculture in Honduras." In *Who Pays the Price?,* edited by Barbara R. Johnston, 110–120. Washington, DC: Island Press.

Thompson, Richard H.
1997. "Ethnic Minorities and the Case for Collective Rights." *American Anthropologist* 99 (4):786–798.

Trotter, Robert T., II, and Jean J. Schensul
1998. "Methods in Applied Anthropology." In *Handbook of Methods in Cultural Anthropology,* edited by Bernard H. Russell, 691–735. Walnut Creek, CA: Altamira Press.

van Willigen, John
1993. *Applied Anthropology: An Introduction.* Westport, CT: Bergin and Garvey.

Winthrop, Robert
1997. "The Real World: Advocates, Experts, and the Art of Being Useful." *Practicing Anthropology* 19 (3): 41–42.

CHAPTER

7 SOCIAL WORK

INTRODUCTION

In American colleges and universities, social work and cultural anthropology are taught in separate departments, and studying these subjects, at either the undergraduate or the graduate level, leads to different degrees. Although the two disciplines have a great deal in common, one can get a degree in social work without ever having studied anthropology, and vice versa. Perhaps for this reason, few anthropology students—including majors—are aware that anthropology (along with its sister social science, sociology) provides excellent preparation for a future career in social work (Ginsberg 1998:40–41).

If the relationship between an undergraduate major in anthropology and an eventual career in social work is not made explicit in anthropology courses, this does not lessen the relevance of cultural anthropology for social work. It does mean, however, that anthropologists are apt to choose social work as a career area more on the basis of their personal inclinations and experiences than their undergraduate course of study. Most anthropologists headed for a career in social work find their own way to this career.

The experience of one former anthropology student, now a social worker, is typical. As a high school senior in the early 1990s, Carol L. traveled with her civics class from the small Midwestern city where she lived to Washington, DC. The object of the trip was to give the students a firsthand look at how the federal government worked. Through their local congressional representative, they were able to attend a session of Congress, during which an important bill was debated. Carol had been well prepared by her civics teacher for this experience and found her glimpse into the democratic process in action both interesting and instructive. She had not, however, been prepared for an experience she found even more compelling: the sight of the hundreds of homeless men and women who seemed to inhabit nearly every doorway and park bench in Washington. It was the number of women, particularly, that surprised and dismayed her. Reacting more from emotion than careful consideration, Carol decided that her future career, whatever it might be, would have to involve working with—and trying to help—homeless women.

Carol later attended her state university, which lacked a department of social work, and chose to major in psychology, hoping this focus would help clarify her career goals and steer her in an appropriate direction professionally. She found time, however, for several courses in cultural anthropology—courses that she took out of personal interest rather than any clear idea of anthropology's relevance to a future career working on behalf of homeless women.

One upper-division anthropology course Carol particularly enjoyed, on gender theory, explored the many anthropological ideas that help explain the roles and relative status of males and females in cultures all over the world—including modern, industrialized Western culture. Toward the end of the semester, she looked over a list of suggested readings provided by her applied cultural anthropology professor.

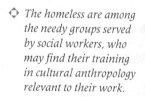

◇ *The homeless are among the needy groups served by social workers, who may find their training in cultural anthropology relevant to their work.*

On the list was a short book entitled *The Unequal Homeless: Men on the Streets, Women in Their Place* (Passaro 1996). Happy to have stumbled across something that personally interested her, she checked the book out of the university library and read it in a single evening. Written by a cultural anthropologist who had conducted research among homeless people in New York City, it described how American beliefs and values regarding gender are reflected in the behavior and self-image of the urban homeless. It also contained specific information on how anthropological training had facilitated the author's work with the homeless, enabling her, for example, to consider the multiple perspectives required for this kind of work (Passaro 1996:4).

For the first time, Carol saw a clear link between cultural anthropology and her career goals. She switched her undergraduate major to anthropology and at the end of her senior year was accepted into a two-year graduate program leading to the Master of Social Work degree. Today she is the coordinator of an outpatient program, headquartered at a hospital in a southeastern city, whose mission is to address the basic health care needs of the city's substantial homeless population.[1]

Social work is a group of related professional activities—some clinical, some administrative, and some research-oriented—that falls into a broad, challenging, and personally rewarding professional area known as human services.[2] These activities vary widely; over the course of a career, a social worker might counsel dysfunctional families, administer a drug treatment program, and study the linkages between old age and depression. They are united, however, by a single, broad goal: to help people who have social problems, meaning problems with society or with other people.

To one degree or another, people with social problems are poorly integrated into the social institutions that specifically affect them—for example, the family, community, or business. Often they have difficulty in accepting and adhering to the norms and values of these institutions. Thus, according to the **National Association of Social Workers (NASW),** an umbrella organization of which all accredited social workers in the United States are members, the primary goal of social work is to "promote or restore a mutually beneficial interaction between individuals and society" (NASW 1981). This goal is frequently viewed in terms of "normalizing" or "optimizing" the well-being of both individuals and societies (Russell and Edgar 1998:1). However, because the needs and problems of people who are "poorly integrated into the social institutions that affect them" are so diverse, there is no single way of extending help to them. This makes the field of social work both complex and heterogeneous. As one social worker put it, "[we] don't exactly teach; we don't usually direct other people; we don't exactly lead; we don't exactly counsel; but we do a little of all of that in the course of our work" (Ginsburg 1998:ix).

FOOD FOR THOUGHT Because social problems are most apt to erupt at the point at which individuals intersect or interact with the surrounding social environment, it is in the "transactions between the person and the parts of that person's world that the quality of life can be enhanced or damaged" (Morales and Sheafor 1992:15–16). Give examples of these "transactions."

Social workers work either with individuals or with groups; the latter may be defined by kinship (such as families), age (such as juvenile delinquents), disability (such as the blind), social status (such as pregnant, unmarried teenagers), economic status (such as the unemployed), sexual orientation (such as gay and lesbian individuals), or past experience (such as veterans suffering from post-traumatic stress syndrome). They do not address every type of human problem (Garvin and Tropman 1992:107); purely individual or idiosyncratic problems, such as neurosis or psychosis, are more likely to be dealt with by psychologists or psychiatrists than by social workers. Most specialize in a specific type of social problem—for example, homelessness, juvenile delinquency, or living with HIV/AIDS.

The importance of cultural anthropology for social work lies in the underlying conditions that precipitate social problems. Poverty, social isolation, family strife, and substance abuse—to name just a few of the most common root causes of social maladaptation—are all *cultural* matters, and problems stemming from any of them result not just from the idiosyncratic experiences, behaviors, and beliefs of troubled individuals but also from their roles and positions within the cultures and subcultures to which they belong. Such problems also tend to be interrelated, making their resolution amenable to cultural anthropology's holistic approach.

Social workers dealing with abused children, for example, have come to recognize a group of features associated with this problem, such as low parental self-esteem and substance abuse, that constitute elements of what might be called a "child-abusing culture" (Lecca et al. 1998:143). Abused children and their caretakers come to social workers "not as blank slates, but steeped thoroughly in their culture" (ibid.: 143–144). A fundamental understanding of the complex linkages between culture and behavior would have obvious implications for addressing child abuse.

THE DEVELOPMENT OF SOCIAL WORK

Providing support for those with social problems is hardly a new field of endeavor; because certain members of every society are especially solicitous of the disenfranchised, some form of individual or group charitable service on behalf of the less fortunate has characterized many if not most past societies. Since their inception, the major world religions have all recognized and encouraged the obligation of the socially advantaged to provide help to the needy. At an institutional level, poorhouses or "almshouses" for the indigent, orphanages for parentless or abandoned children, shelters for unmarried mothers, and charity hospitals for those too poor to afford medical care—all typically organized and run by volunteers and frequently sponsored by religious institutions—have existed since at least the Middle Ages. However, social work, as a formalized, institutionalized model for assisting the disadvantaged and as an area of professional endeavor, did not emerge until the middle of the nineteenth century, in the then newly industrializing countries of the world.

The emergence of social work in these venues and at this particular time was a direct response to the rapidly growing, increasingly heterogeneous, and decreasingly family-oriented populations of the industrializing countries. Together, industrialization, urbanism, and population growth—and, in the United States, the Civil

War—produced increasing numbers of people experiencing social problems (Morales and Sheafor 1992:10; Ginsberg 1998:11). The first paid social work professionals in the United States (many of them women, working outside their homes for the first time) were the employees of the government's Special Relief Department, charged with helping Union soldiers and members of their families to deal with social and health problems caused by the Civil War (Morales and Sheafor 1992:41).

As early as 1869, a Charity Organization Society was chartered in London, and other cities soon followed suit (Garvin and Tropman 1992:112). Shortly thereafter, in the United States, Massachusetts established the first state social services agency, the Board of Charities, to oversee and coordinate the voluntary social service efforts of various charitable organizations. Later, in the 1870s, this board became a model for the professional oversight of charitable efforts in other states and eventually for modern, state-run social services agencies. By the time of World War I, social work had become an acknowledged profession, although it does not appear that any commonalities, much less linkages, with cultural anthropology were yet recognized.

Since then, social work has continued to grow as a discrete profession, attracting practitioners, instituting educational programs, developing professional standards, establishing a code of ethics, forming professional organizations, and continually adding new areas of specialization: homelessness, unemployment, physical disability, drug abuse, old age. In the United States and other countries, numerous national and state or provincial legislative measures (such as the U.S. Social Security Act of 1935) ensured the continued expansion of this field.

Today social workers are employed in both the public and private sectors. Employers include agencies of government at various levels; businesses (see "Corporate Social Work," p. 172); and private for-profit and charitable organizations. While most social workers are agency-based, a significant and growing minority are in private practice, either as individuals or as members of private group practices. One reason for the recent growth of private practice has been a new willingness on the part of medical insurers to cover social work as an alternative to more expensive psychotherapy. Another reason may be a growing willingness on the part of middle-class people to seek help from social workers, based on their awareness of the effectiveness of social work among the disenfranchised poor.

CORE CONCEPTS OF CONTEMPORARY SOCIAL WORK

Social Betterment

Perhaps the most fundamental idea underlying social work is the concept of **social betterment.** This is the notion that the lives of disenfranchised, handicapped, socially alienated, or otherwise troubled individuals *can* be improved, through the use of specific social change strategies, including direct intervention and the creation and maintenance of social service institutions. The acceptance of this idea was crucial in the evolution of social services from private, charitable provision to public provision. The idea has two corollaries: individuals trained in social work have the expertise to implement beneficial social change strategies, and they have the moral obligation to do so.

Social Intervention

A comprehensive term for what social workers do, **social intervention** includes a number of different activities, undertaken on behalf of many different constituencies: individuals; couples; families; other, often larger, social groups (such as communities); social services provider systems; and policy-making organizations. Direct one-on-one therapy is perhaps the most visible aspect of social intervention, but the term also incorporates three other ideas. First, social intervention assumes the willing and active participation of troubled individuals in finding resolutions to their social problems. Second, intervention in this sense does not imply interference, intrusion, or infringement on individual or group rights. Social workers use the term "parsimonious intervention" to suggest that the "strategy of choice is the one requiring the least disruptive intervention" (Loewenberg 1983:7). Finally, social intervention is time-limited. It ends when the problem that required it has been resolved or when the amount of time contracted between the parties involved has elapsed. The provision of ongoing social services—for example, an unemployed person's continuing monthly receipt of an income-maintenance check—is not considered social intervention, although counseling to help that individual to rejoin the labor force would be (Loewenberg 1983:8).

Socialization

Also fundamental to social work is the notion of **socialization,** the process through which an individual learns to play an appropriate role in his or her society. The concept is a familiar one to cultural anthropologists. In every culture, individuals are expected to play out the social roles appropriate to the positions they occupy in the social structures of the groups to which they belong. Most people become socialized unconsciously and without great difficulty, through experience, formal education, and role model imitation (Garvin and Tropman 1992:107). Some, however, for reasons as diverse as physical or mental disability, the effects of living in poverty, or immigration into an unfamiliar social setting, encounter socialization problems severe enough to affect their interactions with others and, ultimately, their quality of life. Such individuals may be unable to define an appropriate role for themselves in society, to enjoy mutually beneficial relationships with family members, to find or hold a job, to move easily among their peers, or to resist substance addiction. Social workers are trained to recognize insufficient or defective socialization and are committed to improving the quality of life for inadequately socialized individuals by helping them engage in behaviors that result in beneficial social change (Morales and Sheafor 1992:5).

Social Functioning

The definition of social work espoused by the National Association of Social Workers states that "social work is the professional activity of helping individuals, groups, or communities enhance or restore their capacity for social functioning" (NASW 1973: 4). **Social functioning** (or, alternatively, *social living*) is the generic problem area social workers are trained to address: to improve people's "person-in-environment fit" (Williams-Gray 2001:55).

A given individual's level of social functioning depends on how well he or she deals with the sum total of all transactions with his or her surrounding social environment (made up of other individuals and groups at various distances from, and standing in various relationships to, that individual). Inadequate social functioning, which results in social maladaptation in many different forms, has numerous and complex causes and can afflict individuals of any age. The work of social workers—generically termed *social intervention,* defined above—might alternatively be defined as efforts to bring about improved social functioning.

The Building Blocks of Social Work: Clients, Cases, and Files

Clients.   This term was defined in Chapter 4 as it is generally used in applied cultural anthropology: an applied cultural anthropologist's employer, typically an individual or organization who contracts with an applied cultural anthropologist to "purchase" anthropological data, insights, and recommendations. The term **client** is used in a different sense in social work, to mean a troubled individual with whom a social worker interacts professionally. (Some social workers now prefer to use the term *consumer* in place of *client*). A social worker's clients are distinguished and defined in two ways: in terms of a specific problem (for example, unemployment or drug abuse) and in terms of age group (for example, the elderly). Many social workers specialize in serving members of one or two specific client groups, defined by both problem and age, such as homeless Vietnam War veterans, young unmarried mothers, or adolescent truants.

In each case, the social worker views the individual client in holistic rather than specific terms, taking into consideration not only the problem or pathology that brought the client to treatment but also his or her overall social and economic circumstances and psychological state. The social worker makes a concerted effort to empower the client by encouraging full commitment to, and participation in, the therapeutic process and then allowing him or her as much control over the process as possible. The help offered may include psychological counseling, vocational guidance, administrative support (such as arranging foster home placement for children), family counseling, or various kinds of rehabilitation. If a social worker is unable to provide direct help, he or she assumes responsibility for steering a client to others who can provide whatever services are needed.

FOOD FOR THOUGHT   One social worker has commented that the "nitty-gritty of . . . [social] work entails rolling up one's sleeves and talking with all sorts of people in their own language" (Meyerson 1988:5–6, quoted in Trice 1993:49). Think about the examples of the kinds of people who might become social workers' clients that were noted in this section. What might it mean to communicate with these various clients "in their own language"?

Cases.   Collectively, all the information a social worker accumulates about a client and his or her social problem (or problems; many clients have more than one) is called a **case.** A case is developed based on **casework,** the interaction between a social worker and a client. A typical case includes detailed information not only about a client's immediate problem, circumstances, and needs, but also about relevant background topics such as his or her family, personal history, current lifestyle and relationships, education, work experiences, attitudes, values, and so on. A social worker who accumulates case information and uses it to investigate problems and render assistance directly to a client is sometimes referred to as a **caseworker.**

Files.   A caseworker's (or sometimes several caseworkers') written account of a case, together with any supporting documents (names, addresses, phone numbers, legal documents, interview notes, test results, referrals, and so on), constitutes a client's **file.** Collectively, the data that make up a file present the facts of the case and an account of the social worker's actions. But a file is more than just a physical collection of papers or computer disks containing the facts needed for managing a case and a list of activities undertaken. Because assembling a file forces a social worker to summarize and reflect on a case, the file also contains the formal and informal observations, insights, judgment, and therapeutic recommendations of the caseworker(s) who assembled it. In some respects, a file is similar to an ethnography of a single individual.

A single file thus has multiple purposes. Manifestly, it is a compilation of data about a particular individual and his or her social situation, a record of work performed by a social worker or an agency in response to that situation, a professional summary of options and recommendations developed to improve the situation, and a body of data necessary for the future evaluation of the case. Just as important, however, a file is a creative tool: "[it] brings together records that may be combined into hybrid assessments and novel understandings. The words on the pages allow for a fusion of new interpretations, understandings, and strategies for intervention" (de Montigny 1995:173).

CULTURAL ANTHROPOLOGY AND SOCIAL WORK: THE CULTURE CONCEPT AND OTHER CONGRUITIES

In addition to being the most fundamental and most useful idea in cultural anthropology, the culture concept (see Appendices 1 and 2) is undoubtedly anthropology's most significant contribution to social work (Garvin and Tropman 1992:51). In working with clients representing many different cultural and subcultural groups, defined in terms of ethnicity, demography, age, and many other factors, an understanding of the powerful influence of culture on behavior is crucial because social problems can be resolved only within the context of clients' own culture-bound attitudes, values, and beliefs (Garvin and Tropman 1992:51). Recently this recognition has spawned a voluminous literature on the applicability of the culture concept to social work (for example, Pederson and Ivey 1993; Lago and Thompson 1996; Pederson 1997; Lecca et al. 1998; Palmer and Laungani 1999).

Clients who are members of ethnic minorities provide the most obvious example of the importance of the culture concept to social work. Minority populations are increasing in size in most of the industrialized countries of the world; today, over one third of all people in the United States define themselves as members of some ethnic minority (Sue and Sue 1999:8). Members of minority groups are more likely than others to have certain problems—such as poverty, immigrant status, or discrimination—that social work can help alleviate (ibid.:11). This means that social workers and social welfare agencies must be prepared to meet the needs of individuals whose beliefs, values, and behaviors may be very different from their own (Lecca et al. 1998:3; Sue and Sue 1999:53ff.).

As an example, Loewenberg (1983:175–176) relates the experience of a social worker who encountered a recent immigrant from Japan. The social worker noticed that this client "smiled constantly, no matter what the topic of discussion" and speculated that either the client was extremely happy about living in the United States or else was somewhat out of touch with reality. Neither conjecture proved to be correct. In Japanese culture, the social worker learned, "it is considered proper to smile in the presence of an authority person. As far as this client was concerned, the social worker was an authority figure who deserved to be recognized with the traditional symbols of respect" (ibid.).

It is imperative that social workers understand that certain social conditions, objectively defined, are viewed very differently in different cultures. Poverty, for example, is "sanctified in one culture, considered an individual misfortune in another, an indicator of personal failure in a third, and the result of societal errors in a fourth" (Loewenberg 1983:16). Different values surrounding marriage and motherhood

◇ *Social workers' effectiveness in assisting clients from various cultural backgrounds is termed their "cultural competence." As an example, social workers direct clients who are members of minority ethnic or language groups to culturally and linguistically appropriate social services.*

produce radically different views of premarital pregnancy in different societies. Behaviors considered aberrant in one context—for example, self-aggrandizement, or personal aggression—may be tolerated or even encouraged in another context, sometimes even within a single society.

FOOD FOR THOUGHT In postmodern Western society, personal aggression is deplored in some contexts, such as the grade-school classroom, and encouraged in others, such as the professional sports arena. Can the concept of culture, defined in Appendix 1 as including behaviors and ideas that help to make life meaningful to the members of human groups, logically incorporate inconsistencies such as this one?

Social workers, like cultural anthropologists interacting with informants in the field, bring culture-bound ideas to their client encounters. Thus the social worker's own culture may play a significant role, for better or for worse, in his or her encounters with clients. A propensity toward cultural bias, for example, could seriously distort the social worker's observations (Loewenberg 1983:227). "Social workers have a tendency to observe those client characteristics which are important in their own culture, even when these items are of little significance for the client. And they will interpret their observations in terms of the value system with which they are the most familiar—their own value system" (ibid.).

The recognition, on the part of social work professionals, of the potential problems involved in working with clients from different cultural backgrounds has led to the concept, within the profession, of **cultural competence** (McPhatter 1997:261; Lecca et al. 1998:53; Williams-Gray 2001:58), alternatively termed **therapy competence** (Sue and Sue 1999). Cultural competence, which owes much to the anthropological concept of cultural relativism (see Appendix 2 and Chapter 4, p. 83), is the ability, on the part of both social workers and social welfare agencies, to provide members of minority groups with effective assistance, based on a series of specific guidelines. A social worker's cultural competence involves an acceptance of cultural differences, respect for those differences, an ongoing self-assessment of one's own and one's agency's policies regarding culture, and continuous learning about cultural difference standards (see Figure 7.1). On the part of agencies, cultural competence requires, in addition, including minority staff members; and adapting service delivery models to meet the needs of minority clients (Lecca et al. 1998:53).

The different groups represented among the population served by social workers are, of course, defined not only in terms of culture and ethnicity but also in terms of occupation, gender, age, socioeconomic stratum, and so on. Whatever their ethnic background, for example, people living in poverty have been viewed as having a distinct culture (Lewis 1966). So have American adolescents (Malekoff 1997), drug addicts (Bourgois 1989), the members of various occupational groups (Trice 1993), and the mentally retarded (Green 1998). Indeed, the world of social workers itself has been described as culturally distinct from all others (de Montigny 1995:45–46).

Urban drug addicts provide an example of a distinct cultural subgroup. The world of addicts, separate from that of nonaddicts, embodies—like any other—

◇ **FIGURE 7.1   Cultural Competence Guidelines**

1. Be familiar with your own culture-bound values.
2. Approach clients as individuals first; then seek to understand their heritage.
3. To preserve confidentiality, do not use individuals who are related to the client as translators.
4. Admit your ignorance of the client's culture, and ask questions about it.
5. Do not assume that a specific appearance correlates with specific beliefs, values, or practices.
6. Recognize that all minority groups are bicultural.
7. Try to distinguish between individual family practices and broader cultural traditions.
8. Behave so as to gain and retain the client's trust.

Source: Adapted from Lecca et al. 1998:214 and Williams-Gray 2001:80.

specific culturally approved behaviors (such as intimidation and violence), specific ideologies (such as resistance to the norms of mainstream society), and specific values (such as toughness and personal autonomy) (Bourgois 1989:7ff.).[3] Like the members of any culture, drug addicts play specific roles in a hierarchical social structure (Bourgois 1989:8). A social worker with an understanding of both the implications of the culture concept in general, and of the culture of drug addicts in particular, is well prepared to understand, empathize with, and offer help to a drug addict referred to him or her for counsel and care.

Likewise, to work with the mentally retarded "one has to become . . . a cultural interpreter of [two] different cultures" (Green 1998:24). Today mentally retarded adults, once incarcerated in state institutions together with the mentally ill, often live together in supervised, privately run group homes, where they benefit collectively from various publicly and privately funded programs intended to enrich their lives. Many of these programs are community-based and encourage visits by retarded people to local parks, restaurants, museums, and workplaces. Applied cultural anthropologist Jonathan Green worked with groups of mentally retarded adults in a community-based therapeutic program to introduce the clients in his care to the arts and music (Green 1998:21). According to Green, "my own training and talents in anthropology supported these areas . . . specifically, my anthropological skills in participating in and observing the community of the retarded with which I worked allowed me to gain new insights in how to foster their growth and achievement" (Green 1998:23).

FOOD FOR THOUGHT   It is axiomatic in social work that "a good understanding of culture . . . is essential for a good therapeutic outcome" (Lecca et al. 1998:144), but culture in this sense refers not just to ethnic background but to many other factors as well. This being the case, what points might be added to Figure 7.1 to make it more relevant to social work with subcultural groups such as drug addicts or the mentally retarded?

Apart from the culture concept, there are a number of other correspondences, both theoretical and methodological, between cultural anthropology and social work. This chapter began with a vignette describing one anthropology student's discovery of the applicability of gender theory, as interpreted by cultural anthropologists, to social work with the homeless. Understanding the differences in roles and status between males and females in Western society illuminates important differences between homeless men and women (Passaro 1996). Homeless women more easily benefit from traditional gender ideologies than homeless men do; they play out their expected gender roles by appearing dependent and needy. Since a "dependent, needy woman . . . is no challenge to dominant beliefs," women are rather quickly placed in temporary shelters and then apartments (ibid.:2). Homeless men, in contrast, occupy a "culturally contradictory" position, "super-manly" due to their independence, but at the same time "unmanly" because they are dependent and unable to support themselves (Passaro 1996:1–2). Viewed as unworthy of help, homeless men tend to be "treated far worse by the welfare system than women are" (Passaro 1996:2).

Cultural relativism was mentioned earlier as having contributed to the notion of cultural competence. According to Jonathan Green (see p. 165), the concept of cultural relativism helped him to place equal value on two vastly different cultures, his own and that of the mentally retarded adults with whom he worked, a population "historically . . . cast aside as untouchable and worthless" (Green 1998:23). Another helpful anthropological concept for Green was the emic, or "insider," viewpoint (see Appendix 2). "One has to learn to understand the emic cultural view of the retarded in order to be able to communicate with them," he writes. "I was forced to see and value things from a very different perspective" (Green 1998:24). Other social workers have drawn on their anthropological expertise in areas such as kinship, political organization, religion, or even general systems theory.

There are methodological similarities, too, between social work and cultural anthropology. For example, social workers address people's problems by collecting information from them in interviews, a technique similar to the informant interviewing undertaken by ethnographers in the field. In both cases, the interviewer attempts to learn from the interviewee as a representative of a particular group, whether that group is defined in terms of a specific culture or a specific social problem. The main difference is that the social worker is explicitly interventionist. He or she has an additional goal: to glean information about each specific interviewee's personal problems, as a first step in helping to alleviate them.

FOOD FOR THOUGHT It was pointed out earlier in this chapter that a client's file is similar to an ethnography of that individual. Based on the familiar principles of informant interviewing by cultural anthropologists, enumerate and explain the methodological similarities between a client interview and an ethnographic interview. Your might include, for example, the interviewer's "outsider" status and holistic viewpoint.

Social network analysis, a way of gathering and organizing information about social structure by focusing on individuals or small groups and their relationships with others (see Appendix 2), provides another example of the methodological congruence between anthropology and social work (see also Davies 1998). Social workers frequently employ network analysis to explore clients' job relationships, family support systems, landlord–tenant relationships, and so on. In Memphis, for example, social workers were tasked with identifying and rectifying gaps in understanding and communication between public service agencies and the groups of people they were intended to serve (Hyland et al. 1987:109). When the local power company—one of the agencies examined—developed a public assistance program to help low-income customers reduce their energy costs by weatherizing their homes, the intended beneficiaries of this energy conservation program—already angry at the company because of rising utility bills and the difficulties of dealing with a big, impersonal bureaucracy—at first refused to participate. Thanks to their anthropological training in how social network systems function, the social workers understood that "neighborhood level networks and groups had deep-seated beliefs about government agencies and the utility company" (ibid.: 115). The insights provided by the social workers helped make the assistance program a success.

ROLES FOR SOCIAL WORKERS

Most social workers address the needs of people with social problems in one of three ways: (1) through casework, (2) through the management of programs intended to assist socially troubled people; or (3) through research. The first of these activities, which involves direct interaction between social worker and clients (either as individuals or in groups), is the most prevalent; over two thirds of all social workers are engaged in direct client service. About 20 percent of social workers are involved in the second of these activities, program administration; a much smaller number are involved in various kinds of social research (Garvin and Tropman 1992:473).

Casework

Because their efforts account for the bulk of all social work, the two thirds of all social workers who serve as caseworkers represent the "front line" of the profession (de Montigny 1995). They may work either in the public sector (for example, for family service agencies, prisons, schools, hospitals, or substance-abuse clinics) or in the private sector (for example, for religious organizations, private adoption agencies, businesses, or NGOs). Funding for both public and private services is provided by federal and state agencies (including at the federal level the U.S. Department of Health and Human Services, the U.S. Department of Labor, or the Veterans Administration); additionally, some private charitable organizations fund social welfare programs.

In either context, private or public, the caseworker's job necessitates one-on-one involvement with troubled individuals or—often—couples, families, or groups. Casework has been described as "a primarily psychotherapeutic method, consisting of interviews dealing with the client's problems, as defined by the client, in the context of the worker–client relationship" (Morales and Sheafor 1992:613). The caseworker identifies the nature and source of a social problem or problems and helps the client or clients accomplish whatever is necessary to overcome or deal with the situation.

AN APPLIED CULTURAL ANTHROPOLOGIST AT WORK

LESLIE RANERI

Social worker Leslie Raneri, an employee of Texas Children's Hospital in Houston, Texas, works with HIV-infected children and their families. Most of the children, who range in age from newborn to nineteen years old, were infected at birth by their HIV-positive mothers, but a few of them are sexual abuse victims, hemophiliacs who contracted the HIV virus through blood transfusions, or adolescents infected through unsafe sex. Some of Raneri's young clients live with their biological families, where typically the mother is also HIV-infected. Others, whose parents have died or whose parents' lifestyle is incompatible with the care of an HIV-infected child, are cared for by a grandparent, aunt, or other relative. A few live with foster families or adoptive families. Most of the families are poor, but even among the few who are middle-class, having an HIV-infected family member has caused financial hardship.

Raneri works with ninety to one hundred clients at any one time. She sees most of them about once a month—those who are doing very well, less often. This heavy workload means not only that she spends many hours a week in direct client contact; in addition, much of her time is spent in talking with others on behalf of her clients and taking care of administrative matters. "Paperwork," she says, "is a big factor in social work."

As an undergraduate, Raneri studied both anthropology and sociology at Rice University, graduating in 1992. Both subjects helped her prepare for the career in social work she had been anticipating since high school. Immediately after receiving her B.A. degree, Raneri entered graduate school at the University of Texas at Austin, and two years later, in 1994, she was awarded the degree of Master of Social Work (MSW). She has been working as a social worker with children and women with HIV ever since.

As a social worker, Raneri's most important job is to identify and address her clients' multi-

ple needs and problems. In most cases, HIV is only one of many problems confronting a given client; "often," she says, "it's not even at the top of the list." The types of problems she helps to solve tend to be of two different kinds. First, there are concrete matters involving, for example, helping clients apply for government programs, gain access to available community resources such as food pantries, or secure financial, housing, or transportation assistance from other agencies, both public and private. Second, most of her clients have deep-seated personal problems. To identify these, Raneri talks to her clients and their families at length, usually during clinic visits, asking them what is going on in their lives, how they are coping with their prescribed medicines, and how they are getting along both at school and at home.

Recently, in addition to her hands-on work with her Texas clients, Raneri has taken on another role, this one international in scope: she is contributing a social work perspective to a broad-based, privately-funded program of HIV/AIDS research and education currently being implemented in Romania and several southern African countries. This new aspect of her work involves learning how the issues relating to HIV/AIDS vary in different parts of the world and, more specifically, helping Romanian and southern African health care professionals address these issues in culturally specific ways.

The anthropological concept of culture figures prominently in Raneri's work. "Cultural awareness is a big part of being a social worker," she observes. "If you don't understand a client's culture, then you can't give effective help, because you and the client are talking two different languages." Much of her client-centered work involves brokerage between representatives of two different cultures. For example, she is often called upon to "translate what the family is saying to the medical people, and then interpret what the medical folks are saying to the patient and the family. It requires some understanding of both worlds." It helps to have an understanding of the specific differences in the cultural backgrounds of her clients, who are mainly African American, Hispanic, and Caucasian. She cautions, however, that "culture is more than just ethnicity." A client's ethnic group affiliation, for example, "says very little about socioeconomic status and very little about a family's understanding of what this disease [HIV/AIDS] is and what the implications are for their lives."

Apart from her broad appreciation of cultural differences, Raneri has been able to put the concept of cultural relativism to use. "As a social worker," she says, "one of the things the ethnographic method taught me was that I need to be aware of where my own biases fit into how I interpret what the client is doing and saying. [Cultural anthropology] taught me to be more self-aware, to listen to what clients are saying, and to understand what my own background is. I utilize [the concept of cultural relativism] to see the client better."

Raneri feels she has benefited most specifically from her undergraduate classes in anthropological linguistics and gender theory. Some of her clients speak only Spanish. She is able to communicate with them in this language and understands how being a Spanish speaker affects one's worldview. Her study of gender theory has helped her understand "how gender roles can be culturally constructed and how people enact gender differently." Raneri also feels she has benefited from studying anthropological methods—especially ethnographic interviewing—because of the obvious overlap with a social worker's interview technique. "Developing a case," she observes, "is really an ethnographic approach."

Studying cultural anthropology as an undergraduate helped social worker Leslie Raneri prepare for a career that focuses on HIV-infected children, their families, and their caregivers. In Rumania, Raneri helps Rumanian nurses who work with HIV-infected children to cope with job stress.

Caseworkers who specialize in working with groups of people who share a common problem, rather than with individuals, are called **group workers** (see, for example, Malekoff 1997). Their aim, like that of all caseworkers, is to help people to make beneficial social changes, but in the case of group workers the group itself functions as an element of treatment. A group might consist, for example, of several rebellious adolescent girls, each of whom has had a previous brush with the law. By discussing the meanings and motivations behind their propensity for getting into trouble in the context of a group of sympathetic peers, the group members are better able to learn to moderate their behavior, revise their values, and identify and accomplish personal goals (Morales and Sheafor 1992:197).

Broadly speaking, most caseworkers perform the same four types of activities that typify the work of other applied cultural anthropologists (see Chapter 1). They help their clients identify specific, correctable problems; they develop plans for solving those problems, in concert with their clients; together with their clients, they take action (or "intervene") to address those problems; and finally, they evaluate the results of their efforts, in order to assess whether or not a given problem has been solved in the best possible way (see Figure 7.2).

Most of the typical caseworker's daily effort involves the second of these four activities, intervention. Sometimes intervention can be very abrupt and direct, as when a caseworker must intervene immediately to halt child abuse (de Montigny 1995: 155 ff.). Much more often, however, an intervention takes place over a significant period of time—weeks, months, or even years—during which a caseworker and client interact on a regularly scheduled basis.

The intervention process is often described in terms of stages—for instance, an initial familiarization stage in which client and caseworker meet and begin to explore the client's problem; a middle stage during which the client and caseworker carry out specific activities aimed at helping the client attain specific goals; and a final stage in which the caseworker–client interaction ends and its success is evaluated (Garvin and Tropman 1992:117–126). For present purposes, however, it will be more relevant to provide examples of three specific ways in which caseworkers assist their clients: through advocacy, brokerage, and protection.

◇ **FIGURE 7.2   Typical Steps in the Social Work Process**

1. Assessment of client's problem(s) and needs
2. Diagnosis of problem(s)
3. Development and consideration of possible options for solution
4. Selection of most promising option
5. Development of plan of specific action
6. Implementation of plan
7. Ongoing evaluation of activities involved in the plan
8. If necessary, modification of the needs assessment, diagnosis, and plan of action

Source: Adapted from Garvin and Tropman 1992:237.

Advocacy.   Many clients, due to poverty, lack of education, or lack of empowerment, are unable to represent themselves and their interests adequately to outsiders. Thus, one of the most important aspects of a caseworker's involvement with
clients, either individually or in groups, is to serve as his or her clients' "supporter,
advisor, champion, and, if need be, representative" as they interact with others
(Morales and Sheafor 1992:571). The role is similar in many ways to that of an anthropological advocate, especially a community advocate (see Chapter 6), except
that social workers may serve as advocates for individuals in addition to groups. A
caseworker might, for example, help a client navigate the public assistance bureaucracy in order to secure needed unemployment compensation or housing or medical treatment.

An important element of advocacy is education. Caseworkers often serve as
teachers, guiding their clients to sources of needed information about available social services, medical care, financial help, or employment. Since clients requiring advocacy tend to view their advocates as authority figures, a particular challenge for
social workers in the advocacy role may be to avoid relationships that are unbalanced in terms of power and authority. An imbalance of this kind may inhibit the
long-term effectiveness of the social worker–client interaction.

FOOD FOR THOUGHT   In the social sciences, objectivity is considered a virtue: most social scientists
attempt to separate their own political views or religious beliefs from their
work. Chapter 6 pointed out, however, that anthropological advocates—
involved, for example, in cultural advocacy—must address a professional
discrepancy between the ideal of academic objectivity and the subjectivity
inherent in fostering directed change. What correspondences and differences
exist between the work of anthropological advocates and that of social
workers acting as client advocates? Do you see anything unethical about
a social worker adopting a partisan stance?

Brokerage.   A second activity in which caseworkers spend a great deal of their
time is brokerage—serving as go-betweens, or mediators, between their clients and
other individuals or groups (Morales and Sheafor 1992:572). A social worker might,
for example, serve as an intermediary between a youthful client and his or her parents, helping each "side" to present its concerns to the other, helping interpret the
behavior of the parents for the client and vice versa, resolving misunderstandings,
and arriving at a compromise by which all involved could attain their most important goals. If two people or parties with opposing views can understand each other's
viewpoint, they have the potential to resolve their differences.

Protection.   A significant proportion of any social worker's clients are people who
have been, or are being, abused or neglected by others. Many of the children a typical
social worker sees, for example, will have been abused physically, emotionally, or
even sexually by some adult (Morales and Sheafor 1992:128). On the other side of
the coin, some of the clients with whom a caseworker interacts will pose a threat to
other individuals or to society. A third important role for caseworkers, therefore, is

protection: the caseworker acts as a protector or guardian, safeguarding the welfare of the client and, if needed, other members of society as well. This role can be quite dramatic, as when a caseworker must secure immediate protective custody for the client. More often, however, it is less exciting, involving activities such as facilitating a talented but destructive graffiti vandal's admission into an art program.

Administration

Some social workers—often after having spent some period of time as caseworkers—choose jobs in which their work benefits troubled people indirectly, serving as the managers, administrators, or supervisors of social assistance programs. This subfield of social work is termed **social administration.** Some social workers in this subfield administer a single program; others coordinate the programs of several or many different social service agencies. Social workers with the Violence Prevention Coalition of Greater Los Angeles, for example, coordinate the efforts of social workers, teachers, school administrators, law enforcement officers, state and local legislators, representatives of the judicial system, academics, volunteers—even members of urban youth gangs—in an effort to bring the epidemic of teen violence in Los Angeles to a halt (Evans and Weiss 1995; see also Malekoff 1997:215ff.). In a sense, social administration is the most important aspect of social work, since social assistance cannot be delivered without proficient program organization and administration (Ginsberg 1998:139).

Research

To be effective, social assistance programs must be based on facts and ideas emerging from scientific research into the underlying social and economic problems affecting society. A number of cultural anthropologists who elect to become social workers therefore choose **social research** careers, specializing in examining and understanding social problems and designing solutions to them. Some social researchers study specific social problems, such as alcohol abuse or poverty, in order to determine the underlying causes and demographic distribution of these problems. Others specialize in helping develop **social welfare policy**—governmental strategies, whether in the form of laws or simply guidelines, for dealing with social welfare problems. For example, cultural anthropologists are currently studying social assistance policies in the United States, which in recent years have trended away from entitlement programs and toward welfare-to-work programs; they will be contributing an anthropological perspective to the upcoming congressional debate on welfare reform (Morgan 2001). Still other social researchers analyze social statistics or teach social research in colleges or universities.

CORPORATE SOCIAL WORK

In the final decades of the twentieth century, for-profit businesses, many of which were once neglectful or even exploitative of their rank-and-file employees, became increasingly aware of the relationship between corporate profits and employees' general well-being. This association led to the emergence of **corporate** (or **occupational**) **social work.** Corporate social workers serve clients in their workplaces, providing services underwritten by corporate employers.[4] This is now the most rapidly growing kind of social work (Morales and Sheafor 1992:154).

Corporate social work emerged in the 1970s, a decade during which Americans became increasingly concerned about the preservation of human rights, especially civil and women's rights, and increasingly tolerant about matters such as sexual orientation, ethnicity, and physical disability. At the same time, Americans began to be more open about discussing certain social problems, such as alcoholism, domestic violence, or child abuse—problems which had previously been deemed inappropriate for public airing. These new attitudes had a direct effect on the business world. Many of the biggest U.S. corporations, eager to dispel the image that they were patriarchal, insensitive, intolerant, or exploitative of workers, began to address issues such as job stress, affirmative action, the employment of the disabled, sexual harassment in the workplace, occupational safety—even smokers' rights. Corporations also became more diverse in terms of their employees' sex, age, ethnicity, physical abilities, and sexual orientation, and more willing to retain and work with employees whose specific characteristics were viewed, by the employees themselves or by their coworkers, as problematic.

FOOD FOR THOUGHT While most corporate social workers provide direct services to a corporation's employees (the "employee service" model of corporate social work), some are hired specifically to help a corporation make a favorable impact on its local community (the "corporate social responsibility" model) (Morales and Sheafor 1992:140). Among other responsibilities, these social workers arrange for corporate charitable contributions and lobby for legislative changes that management wishes to support. What possible ethical problems might be inherent in this second model?

Today it is estimated that some three thousand U.S. companies employ social workers. They counsel troubled employees, of course, often referring those with problems such as drug addiction or marital difficulties to the appropriate community services (most corporations do not provide such services in-house). But they also administer company health insurance plans, oversee environmental safety programs, run benefits orientation sessions, and manage pension plans and retirees' organizations.

CONCLUSION

A career in social work, as in any professional field, incorporates both advantages and disadvantages, but the disadvantages of a career in social work seem to be more widely known than those inherent in other career fields. Many anthropology students actively considering this career area receive negative reactions about social work from their families, peers, and the media. They are told that social work pays poorly, compared to many other career fields (Garvin and Tropman 1992:470); that in recent years, federal government cutbacks have reduced funding for social service programs below what social service providers consider necessary (Lecca et al. 1998: 271); that social work is a "women's job" (about three quarters of the members of the National Association of Social Workers are female); that social work requires extraordinary personal dedication and often long hours as well; that because most social workers are employed by public sector agencies, they cannot escape the endless meetings and paperwork that characterize public bureaucracies; and that social workers suffer high rates of burnout, compared with other kinds of professionals (de Montigny 1995:15). Why, then, are there some 150,000 social workers practicing today in the United States alone?

Social work has several distinct advantages over other careers for which the study of anthropology is relevant. An important consideration for some students is that—depending on the level at which one wishes to work—this career requires less formal education than many others; some social work professionals have only Bachelor of Social Work (B.S.W.) degrees, although most have master's (M.S.W.) degrees and some go on to receive doctorates in social work (see Council on Social Work Education 1996). Another consideration is that demand for social workers is high and is likely to remain high, driven by legislation such as the Older Americans Act and the Americans with Disabilities Act.

By far the most important advantage of a career in social work, however, is the satisfaction its practitioners derive. For anthropology students who embody the idealistic view that dedicated individuals can help troubled, needy people change their lives for the better, providing this kind of help yields great personal rewards. As one social worker put it, "Few would want to be social workers if they did not believe they were helping others. After all, that is the essence of what we are about" (Ginsberg 1998:ix).

KEY TERMS

case all the relevant information about a client and his or her problem(s)

casework the interaction between a social worker and a client

caseworker a social worker who accumulates case information and uses it to investigate problems and render assistance

client as used in social work, any troubled individual with whom a social worker interacts professionally

corporate social work social work conducted in clients' workplaces

cultural competence the ability, on the part of both social workers and agencies, to provide members of minority groups with effective assistance, based on a series of specific standards such as an acceptance of and respect for cultural differences

file a social worker's written account of a case, together with any supporting documents

group worker a social worker who specializes in working with groups of people rather than individuals

National Association of Social Workers (NASW)   an umbrella organization of which all accredited social workers in the United States are members

occupational social work   for present purposes, a synonym for corporate social work

social administration   the planning, management, administration, or supervision of social assistance programs

social betterment   the idea that the lives of disenfranchised, handicapped, or otherwise troubled individuals can be improved through the use of specific social change strategies

social functioning   the generic problem area that social workers are trained to address

social intervention   a comprehensive term for what social workers do on behalf of individuals, couples, families, other social groups, social services provider systems, and policy-making organizations

social research   the examination and understanding of social problems, and the development of solutions to them

social welfare policy   governmental strategies for dealing with social welfare problems

social work   a group of related professional activities intended to help people who have social problems

socialization   the process through which an individual learns to play appropriate roles in his or her society

therapy competence   a synonym for cultural competence

NOTES

1. In Britain, social workers with anthropological training are sometimes referred to as welfare anthropologists (Russell and Edgar 1998:3). The term is not used in the United States, where the same individuals would be referred to as social workers.
2. Other careers in this area, sometimes referred to as the helping professions, include teaching, psychiatry, religious ministry, nursing, marriage counseling, and clinically applied medical anthropology (see Chapter 11). Social work can and often does overlap with these careers.
3. Interestingly, some of the values of the urban drug culture—toughness and personal autonomy are both examples—are also mainstream American values (Bourgois 1989).
4. Corporate social work overlaps considerably with certain aspects of business anthropology (see Chapter 9).

REFERENCES

Bourgois, Phillippe
   1989. "Crack in Spanish Harlem: Culture and Economy in the Inner City." *Anthropology Today* 5 (4):6–11.

Council on Social Work Education
   1996. *Directory of Colleges and Universities with Accredited Social Work Degree Programs*. Alexandria, VA: Council on Social Work Education, Inc.

de Montigny, Gerald A. J.
   1995. *Social Working: An Ethnography of Front-Line Practice*. Toronto: University of Toronto Press.

Davies, Charlotte A.
   1998. "Caring Communities or Effective Networks?" In *The Anthropology of Welfare*, edited by Iain R. Edgar and Andrew Russell, 121–136. London: Routledge.

Evans, Caswell A., and Billie Phyllis Weiss
   1995. "Developing a Violence Prevention Coalition in Los Angeles." In *Down to Earth: Community Perspectives on Health, Development, and the Environment*, edited by Bonnie Bradford and Margaret A. Gwynne, 35–42. West Hartford, CT: Kumarian Press.

Garvin, Charles D., and John E. Tropman
1992. *Social Work in Contemporary Society*. Englewood Cliffs, NJ: Prentice Hall.

Ginsberg, Leon H.
1998. *Careers in Social Work*. Boston: Allyn and Bacon.

Green, Jonathan S.
1998. "Anthropology and Goodenough: Cognitive and Cooperative Approaches to Educating the Adult Mentally Retarded." *Practicing Anthropology* 20 (4):21–24.

Hyland, Stanley, Bridget Ciaramitaro, Charles Williams, and Rosalind Cottrell
1987. "Redesigning Social Service Delivery Policy: The Anthropologist as Mediator." In *Anthropological Praxis: Translating Knowledge into Action*, edited by Robert M. Wulff and Shirley J. Fiske, 109–117. Boulder, CO: Westview Press.

Lago, C., and J. Thompson
1996. *Race, Culture, and Counselling*. Buckingham, U.K.: Open University Press.

Lecca, Pedro J., I. Quervalu, J. V. Nunes, and H. F. Gonzales
1998. *Cultural Competency in Health, Social, and Human Services: Directions for the Twenty-First Century*. New York: Garland Publishing, Inc.

Lewis, Oscar
1966. "The Culture of Poverty." *Scientific American* 215 (4):19–25.

Loewenberg, F. M.
1983. *Fundamentals of Social Intervention* (2nd ed.). New York: Columbia University Press.

Malekoff, Andrew
1997. *Group Work with Adolescents: Principles and Practice*. New York: The Guilford Press.

McPhatter, A.
1997. "Cultural Competence in Child Welfare." *Journal of Policy, Practice, and Program* 86 (1):255–278.

Meyerson, Debra
1988. *On Studying Ambiguities in Cultures*. Paper presented at annual meeting of the Academy of Management, Aug. 13–15, Anaheim, CA.

Morales, Armando T., and Bradford W. Sheafor
1992. *Social Work: A Profession of Many Faces* (6th ed). Boston: Allyn and Bacon.

Morgan, Sandra
2001. "Anthropological Perspectives on Welfare Reform." *Anthropology News* 42 (8):24.

National Association of Social Workers (NASW)
1973. *Standards for Social Service Manpower*. Washington, DC: NASW.
1981. "Working Statement on the Purpose of Social Work." *Social Work* 26 (1):1–6.

Palmer, Stephen, and Pittu Laungani (eds.)
1999. *Counselling in a Multicultural Society*. Thousand Oaks, CA: Sage Publications.

Passaro, Joanne
1996. *The Unequal Homeless: Men on the Streets, Women in Their Place*. New York: Routledge.

Pederson, Paul B.
1997. *Culture-Centered Counseling Interventions*. Thousand Oaks, CA: Sage Publications.

Pederson, Paul B., and Allen Ivey
1993. *Culture-Centered Counseling and Interviewing Skills: A Practical Guide*. Westport, CT: Praeger.

Russell, Andrew, and Iain R. Edgar
1998. "Research and Practice in the Anthropology of Welfare." In *The Anthropology of Welfare*, edited by Iain R. Edgar and Andrew Russell, 1–15. London: Routledge.

Sue, Derald Wing, and David Sue
1999. *Counseling the Culturally Different: Theory and Practice* (3rd ed.). New York: John Wiley and Sons, Inc.

Trice, Harrison M.
1993. *Occupational Subcultures in the Workplace*. Ithaca, NY: ILR Press.

Williams-Gray, Brenda
2001. "A Framework for Culturally Responsive Practice." In *Culturally Diverse Parent-Child and Family Relationships*, edited by Nancy Boyd Webb, 55–83. New York: Columbia University Press.

CHAPTER

8 THE LAW AND LAW ENFORCEMENT

INTRODUCTION

Seattle, April 7—Amidst a din of drumbeats on one side and hoots from a flag-waving crowd on the other, the Senate Indian Affairs Committee today held its only hearing in the West on a bill that would sharply alter the power of the nation's 554 America Indian tribes.

—*New York Times*, April 7, 1998

Native American groups in the United States have long enjoyed "tribal sovereign immunity," which allows them a measure of self-government (Egan 1998). It also protects them from civil lawsuits, which is particularly important to Native American groups because many of them are so poor that they could easily be bankrupted by a suit. Recently, however, under pressure from (mostly white) property rights groups who feel Native Americans enjoy an unfair legal advantage, a bill to abolish this policy was proposed in the U.S. Senate. Its supporters argued that sovereign immunity permits the existence of "governments under the American flag that [are] entirely irresponsible for their actions" (Egan 1998:A12). To illustrate the point, the bill's supporters pointed to an amphitheater being built on a Native American reservation in Washington State. They charged that the building project had not been subject to the usual environmental review, yet—because of the immunity policy—environmentalists were unable to sue to stop the potentially environmentally damaging construction.

Underlying the discussions on the proposed new bill were some challenging legal questions. How should *Native American* be defined, for legal purposes? How should a group's claim to be Native American be proven? Should there be laws in the United States that pertain only to Native American groups? If so, what should those laws be? Who should decide on such laws? Who should be responsible for enforcing them, and for penalizing any infractions?

To find equitable answers to legal questions like these, it would obviously be helpful to be able to call on the objective expertise of specialists in both the law and the culture of the people involved. The same would be true if the matter at hand were how best to respond to a series of break-ins in a poor urban neighborhood, defend a member of an ethnic minority who had been accused of a crime, or decide upon the right of a nonmainstream religious organization to include hallucinogens in its worship services. Wherever legal problems involve the rights and behavior of members of subgroups or subcultures, cultural anthropologists specializing in the cross-cultural study and analysis of legal systems, termed **legal anthropology** (alternatively, the **anthropology of law**), can help (see Rouland 1993).[1] The work of legal anthropologists in applied contexts is termed **applied legal anthropology.**

LEGAL SYSTEMS AND OTHER SYSTEMS OF SOCIAL CONTROL

Maintaining Social Order

Every society, if it is to remain in existence, must have in place a system by which social order is maintained. The system must be understood throughout the society and consistently enforced, and it must include rules of conduct to which individuals in the society are expected to conform, procedures according to which rule breaking can be ascertained, and methods of deterrence or punishment to help ensure adherence to the rules and prevent repeated rule breaking. A society with no such system would soon collapse into anarchy. Without rules governing the ownership of property, for instance, any individual might feel free to seize property from another; without rules governing personal injury, any individual might feel free to inflict injury on another.

It is difficult even to imagine such a chaotic scenario. It is also unnecessary, since all societies, from the smallest in scale and technologically simplest to the largest, most complex, and most "modern," have some means of maintaining **social control.** The term refers to all the ways in which a society restricts the behavior of individuals and groups to activities that the society's rulers or a majority of its members (depending on the society's political system) deem permissible.

The means for achieving social control vary, depending on whether a society is ancient or modern, small-scale or large-scale, nonliterate or literate, oligarchic or democratic. Yet such means exist universally, covering not only what individuals are permitted to do, but—in some societies—what they are permitted to say, think, read, hear, and even wear. In societies with written laws, the responsibility for maintaining social control and the authority to do so are delegated to professionals, and the ways in which social control is maintained add up to the society's legal system. In small-scale, traditional societies without written laws, neither formal legal systems nor full-time legal professionals exist, yet these societies do have informal systems of social control (see Table 8.1).

◇ **TABLE 8.1   Types of Societies and Associated Social Control Systems**

Type of Political Organization	Size and Complexity	Major Subsistence Strategy	Social Structure	Social Control System
Band	Smallest, least complex; 25 to 50 people	Gathering and hunting	Generally egalitarian	Noncentralized; no offices; temporary leaders; political decisions made informally, by consensus; few rights to personal property
Tribe	Larger, more complex than bands; few hundred to several thousand members	Horticulture; pastoralism	Personal inequality; weakly developed social classes	Noncentralized; offices rare; leadership attained informally; factions possible; warfare common
Chiefdom	Larger, more complex than tribes; population may number in the thousands	Nonmechanized agriculture	Distinct social classes	Centralized authority; chief is officeholder; political decisions made formally
State	Largest, most complex political organization; tens of thousands to millions of members	Large-scale technologically complex agriculture; industrial production	Highly stratified	Centralized government; authority based on law; rights of citizenship; complex bureaucracies

Source: Hicks and Gwynne 1996:302.

Establishing Norms and Laws

The two major means by which social control is maintained in human societies are through the establishment and enforcement of norms and laws. **Norms** are a society's informal rules, to which people generally conform due not to coercion but rather to tradition and peer pressure. In modern societies, norms generally govern only those behaviors that pose no threat either to individuals or groups. The behaviors collectively referred to as table manners in modern, Western societies provide an example. **Laws,** in contrast, are a society's formal, written, binding, enforceable rules. They are established either by precedent or by proclamation on the part of some individual or group with the authority, or the power, to do so. A society's members generally conform to its laws because to violate them would be to risk punishment. The compendium of formal, written, binding, enforceable rules in a given society is termed **the law.**

Unlike norms, laws are enforced by various agencies deriving coercive and punitive authority from whatever individual or group dominates the society politically. In the United States (and in all other modern nations as well), this agency is a complex political structure termed *the government,* which exists at many levels—local, county, state, and/or federal. Like the members of most other societies, U.S. citizens recognize the government as having both the authority and the power to devise laws, change them, and enforce them, and to spell out what punishments are appropriate for individuals who break them.

Nonliterate Societies.   In nonliterate societies—those whose members neither read nor write—there are, of course, no written laws; instead, a compendium of norms to ensure social control is held in memory and passed orally from one generation to the next.[2] Often these are transmitted in the form of myths; people say, for example, "We must behave this way because our founding ancestor instructed us to do so." The enforcement of norms in nonliterate societies typically takes the form of **sanctions,** which are social reactions to approved or disapproved behavior. Society's reactions to approved behaviors are termed **positive sanctions;** a round of applause is an example. Society's reactions to disapproved behaviors are termed **negative sanctions;** social ostracism is an example.

Applied legal anthropologists are much interested in systems of social control in nonliterate societies because these systems often work exceedingly well, both in terms of maintaining social harmony and restoring it when necessary (see, for example, Gibbs 1963; Nader 1989). Indeed, some applied legal anthropologists today, concerned about the many problems inherent in the legal systems of industrialized societies, are looking to nonliterate societies to provide new models, more efficient and more humane than current Western models, for social control and conflict resolution—models that may be adaptable to industrialized settings.

Modern Industrial Societies.   Norms exist in modern industrial societies just as they do in nonliterate ones, and they are enforced via the same kinds of sanctions. Whereas norms are applied universally in nonliterate societies, however, in industrial societies they vary widely from subculture to subculture and group to group. Consider table manners again. Standards of decorum while dining differ with the occasion, setting, and individuals involved; eating behavior that is considered acceptable at a backyard barbecue would be negatively sanctioned at a fancy restaurant.

Laws, in contrast to norms, apply universally and are a matter for formal control rather than informal sanction. They are found only in state-level societies, ancient or modern; indeed, the existence of a code of laws is a defining characteristic of states. Laws are implemented by four distinct kinds of agencies: (1) legislative bodies (which create or enact laws), (2) law enforcement agencies (which ensure obedience to laws), (3) dispute resolution agencies, such as courts or alternative dispute resolution organizations (which determine whether laws have been broken and if so what, if any, penalties should be applied), and (4) correctional institutions (which incarcerate and attempt to rehabilitate those who have broken laws).

FOOD FOR THOUGHT The table manners example, above, suggests that norms may vary within a society—at least within a complex society, such as modern Western industrialized society. What other norms vary by occasion, setting, or personal preference in this kind of society? Does the fact that norms are differentially applied render them less effective as a means of social control than laws?

PREPARATION FOR ROLES IN APPLIED LEGAL ANTHROPOLOGY

Of the four kinds of agencies charged with the responsibility for maintaining social control in modern industrial societies—legislative, enforcement, dispute resolution, and corrections agencies—most applied legal anthropologists work in only two: law enforcement and dispute resolution agencies. In addition, a relatively small number of applied cultural anthropologists are involved in the corrections aspect of modern legal systems: for example, as advocates for prisoners or as parole officers. Cultural anthropologists' roles in these three areas are described in detail below. The fourth aspect of Western social control systems, lawmaking at various levels, undoubtedly also reflects expertise in legal anthropology; certainly the research of legal anthropologists has sometimes helped to inform the work of policy makers. However, the number of actual legislators who may have been trained in legal anthropology, if any, is unknown.

Applied legal anthropologists' ability to make important contributions to various aspects of the legal system is derived in part from the specific research skills in which they are trained, such as interviewing (Heinrich 1993:2), and in part from their formal cross-cultural study and analysis of the legal systems of different cultures. Indeed, legal anthropologist Steven Heinrich argues that the Western legal system is itself a discrete culture. "Anthropological training teaches one how to gather and classify primary data from another culture," he writes. "In addition, anthropology teaches one how to abstract basic cultural principles from those data, [and] . . . to use this information to interact effectively with, and interpret the behavior of, individuals who operate according to the grammar of this other culture"

(Heinrich 1993:2). Thus, Heinrich's anthropological training has had a direct impact on his ability to understand what he terms "legal culture" (ibid.). A parole officer with a master's degree in anthropology makes the same point in more immediate terms: "We all behave according to some prevailing culture, and if I can understand that, then it obviously facilitates my work" (Stephens 2002:67). He credits his study of anthropology with illuminating not only the criminal subculture but also "the structure and relationships of the criminal justice system" (ibid.).

However, there is another, equally important, element in preparing cultural anthropologists for roles in applied legal anthropology. Much of what applied anthropologists do involves advocacy (see Chapter 6). Applied anthropologists working as law enforcement officials may not only protect but also work to promote the best interests of members of specific minority groups, particularly marginalized groups. Applied anthropologists directly involved in legal proceedings may not only defend but also serve as legal advocates for communities or individuals, working to secure their human and civil rights. Both careers thus overlap with, and incorporate principles of, advocacy anthropology (Chapter 6). An applied cultural anthropologist practicing in either area must not only hold an academic degree in anthropology; he or she must also embody a strong conviction that anthropological observation and analysis of disenfranchised groups must be supplemented by proactive assistance, as well as a strong measure of affection and concern for the members of these groups.

In addition to the cross-cultural study of systems of law, study in other subfields of cultural anthropology, at both the undergraduate and graduate levels, can help prepare applied anthropologists for careers in law enforcement, dispute resolution, or corrections. An example of a relevant subfield is race relations in the context of multiethnic societies, a matter of considerable legal significance in the United States since the enactment of Title 6 of the Civil Rights Act of 1972 (this provision prohibits discrimination by employers on the basis of race). Other examples include the various theories of human behavior espoused, for example, by cognitive anthropologists, cultural materialists, and so on; gender theory (Title 6 also prohibits discrimination on the basis of sex); the anthropology of work (applied legal anthropologists with expertise in dispute resolution may be called upon to assist in labor negotiations, for example); linguistic anthropology (especially nonverbal means of communication); and political anthropology (especially comparative political systems).

APPLIED LEGAL ANTHROPOLOGY AND LAW ENFORCEMENT

Policing

The main responsibilities of those charged with law enforcement in modern industrialized societies are maintaining public order, protecting the public from harm, and enforcing the code of laws. These basic responsibilities have not changed over the years, but the specific ways in which they are carried out have been greatly transformed. In the process, cultural anthropology has become increasingly relevant to police work.

The Development of "Modern Policing."   Today's diverse American law enforcement system began with the first colonists; the town of Boston instituted a citizen-staffed "night watch" as early as 1631 (Vila and Morris 1999:6; see also Emsley 2000). Throughout the seventeenth and eighteenth centuries, ordinary citizens, poorly paid and untrained, were charged with enforcing local rules, collecting taxes, and apprehending criminals. In the nineteenth century, however, rapid population growth and social upheaval necessitated a switch to a different model. Cities commissioned standing police forces; sparsely populated areas were policed by federal marshals and local county and town sheriffs. In general, those charged with upholding the law were local citizens with a thorough understanding of the culture of their constituents, but as such, not a few succumbed to political favoritism and corruption (Vila and Morris 1999:xxv–xxviii).

By the early twentieth century, reformers were diligently attempting to improve both the efficiency and integrity with which the law was enforced. New policies, standards, and goals, collectively termed *modern policing*, were developed, and police departments began to work toward more effective, more efficient services provided by officers who were more honest and better trained than their forbears. In an effort to reduce opportunities for corruption, for example, police departments instituted rotating assignments. This lessened the amount of contact between individual officers and local communities and hence reduced the opportunity for corrupt relationships to develop.

Into the middle of the twentieth century, police forces were more reactive than proactive; they viewed, as their major responsibilities, responding quickly to citizens' requests for assistance after they got into trouble, investigating crimes that had already taken place, and apprehending people after they had broken the law. In some parts of the law enforcement community, however, ideas for two additional, more proactive, responsibilities for police officers were occasionally aired: problem anticipation and problem prevention, both of which would require officers to have some degree of understanding of the backgrounds and day-to-day lives of their constituents. As early as 1965, a report published by the International Association of Police Professors (now the Academy of Criminal Justice Sciences) observed that "social problems . . . require an increasing knowledge of the social sciences" (Stinchcomb 1990:4).

The late 1960s and 1970s were a time of social turbulence in the United States, much of it surrounding the civil rights and women's rights movements, the widening of illegal drug use, and the Vietnam War. Police departments, especially urban ones, encountered numerous problems in dealing with this unrest—problems that were exacerbated by departments' "over-reliance on technologies such as the patrol car and the two-way radio, which . . . effectively isolated many officers from the communities they served" (Sealock 2002: pers. comm.). Widespread civilian criticism of the rough tactics with which police officers often responded to demonstrators, rioters, and law-breakers during these two decades encouraged discussion, throughout the law enforcement community, of better, less reactive, less confrontational ways of maintaining social control (Dempsey 1994:16).

By the 1980s, a transformation in policing was taking place. The "grossly underpaid, uneducated, untrained, bribe-taking white 1920s cop, walking a beat and supervised by political cronies, had been replaced by highly trained, and generally

◇ *Under the "community policing" philosophy, law enforcement officials interact closely with (and often among) the people they serve. Because of its community orientation, community policing is apt to be more culturally sensitive than earlier law enforcement models.*

honest, officers who earned decent wages" (Vila and Morris 1999:xxviii). Yet crime rates remained high throughout the 1980s. This suggested that, despite significant administrative and technological improvements, further reform was needed to meet the challenge of policing rapidly-growing and increasingly urbanized populations, in the context of the many late-twentieth-century social and technological changes that were at the same time increasing the opportunities for crime (ibid.:xxviii).

Community Policing.   To address this problem, a new idea, termed **community policing** (alternatively **community-oriented policing [COP]** or **public accountability**) emerged in the early 1990s. The offspring of earlier discussions about the possibility of forging a less reactive, more prevention-oriented system of social control, community policing is both a philosophy of law enforcement and a set of methods for improving the quality of the relationships between law enforcement officials and citizens (see Trojanowicz and Bucqueroux 1990). It rests on the notion that "police should play a major role in helping communities solve problems, especially problems related to crime" (Vila and Morris 1999:xxix). Instead of merely responding to crime, police officers should join together with community members to identify and attempt to eliminate its underlying causes (ibid.). In some cases, this would require officers to live in the communities they serve (Dickerson 2000), a notion not unlike anthropologists' community participation strategy.

The new philosophy was by no means embraced universally, nor did it escape controversy. Some denigrated community policing as "a cheap solution . . . based on stereotypes" (Dickerson 2000:67); some felt it made police officers into "social workers" (Sealock 2002: pers. comm). Others, however, applauded both the drop in crime in cities in which community policing was implemented (Dickerson 2000:6; see also Rohe et al. 1996) and citizens' increased expressions of confidence in law enforcement officials. More community-oriented, and, hence, more culturally sensitive and inclusive, community policing became increasingly commonplace.

Although traditional, reactive policing continues to prevail in many police departments, today's law enforcement officers are no longer universally male and armed with guns; they are both male and female, and—although licensed to carry weapons—sometimes unarmed. Depending on the specific police force, they may no longer spend most of their time behind the wheel of a patrol car; instead, they may "walk the beat," which gives them much greater visibility in communities and offers more opportunities for personal contact. Rather than being assigned responsibility for a geographical area that is arbitrarily defined by the number of blocks or square miles it contains, and rather than rotating on a daily or weekly basis from one area to another, officers may be assigned, on a long-term basis, to a particular neighborhood (a residential unit much studied by cultural anthropologists)—often a neighborhood whose residents share an officer's own ethnic and socioeconomic background and whose culture and language the officer thus understands well. Rather than enforcing the law remotely, many law enforcement officers are now part of the community they police, actively encouraging those for whom they are responsible to help maintain social order.

In many of the U.S. jurisdictions where it has been implemented, community policing has paid off for citizens and law enforcement officials alike. Neighborhood residents have the opportunity to recognize, become familiar with, and learn to trust "their" police officer, certain that he or she understands and shares their values and concerns. For their part, law enforcement officers feel more comfortable in familiar surroundings and receive more support and help from citizens than they do in areas in which they are complete strangers. Statistics collected by local police forces consistently show that the greater the rapport between law enforcement officers and their constituents, the less local lawbreaking.

Problem-Solving Policing.   In addition to community policing, a second law-enforcement strategy, related to community policing, has emerged within the past decade or so to improve the effectiveness of those charged with upholding the law. Once again, as in the case of community policing, the strategy is informed by certain anthropological precepts. **Problem-solving policing** is a philosophy of law enforcement based on a conscious recognition that the fundamental causes of lawbreaking are social problems, including poverty, racial and religious intolerance, and illegal drug use (Dempsey 1994:163).

The central idea behind problem-solving policing is that rather than simply responding to incident after incident, or even implementing the helpful precepts of community policing, it is preferable for law enforcement officials to work in concert with the citizens of the neighborhoods and communities they police, to attempt to identify and alleviate the underlying social problems that cause the incidents in the first place (Dempsey 1994:168). The strategy can be broken down into four separate actions or activities: scanning, analysis, response, and assessment (Dempsey 1994:168–169). First, law enforcement officials attempt to shift their focus away from individual incidents of crime or public disorder in order to "scan" groups of similar crimes (such as robberies) for any underlying patterns. Second, once a pattern has been discerned, law enforcement officials analyze it, with the help of community residents and nonpolice agencies, both public and private, to determine its essential nature, causes, and possible solutions. Third, they deal with each problem identified as socially patterned by constructing a plan of action. Finally, they assess the effectiveness of their response by comparing present results with those of the past.

Cooperative Policing.   Recently, law enforcement officials have begun to realize that despite the local effectiveness of community policing and problem-solving policing, these strategies do not take into account the fact that communities are also greatly affected by economic and social trends that transcend local boundaries (Erickson 2000:173). This means that even those law enforcement officials who have successfully implemented community policing and problem-solving policing locally may be "hard pressed . . . to address problems that are pushed into their communities by outside forces"—problems such as drug trafficking, gambling, or gang-related activities (ibid.:174). Thus, even if citizens are well served by public safety services delivered at the community level, they must still rely heavily on services delivered from the county, state, and federal levels.

Cooperative policing is a broad strategy, implemented on a statewide basis, for encouraging cooperation among law enforcement officials at every level, from local police forces to state police to district attorneys to state attorneys general (Erickson 2000:173). This broad-based, inclusive approach enables law enforcement, public safety, and criminal justice agencies to forge partnerships, enhance interagency communication, and combine their resources for maximum effectiveness, thereby providing more comprehensive services that better cover community needs (ibid.:174–175).

Collectively, community policing, problem-solving policing, and cooperative policing—while still undergoing growth and refinement (see Table 8.2)—have often proven highly effective. Today's many law enforcement officials—policewomen and policemen, constables, sheriffs, state troopers, or special agents, depending on the level (municipal, county, state, or federal) at which they work—no longer merely react after the law has been broken; they proactively work to head off lawbreaking by attempting to understand people's values, feelings, motivations, behaviors, and the social contexts in which these occur, and by helping people to understand and obey the laws under which they are obliged to live. To guide them in their new roles and responsibilities, they are now bound by the Law Enforcement Code of Ethics (see Dempsey 1994:326) and the Police Code of Conduct (ibid.: 327–328). It seems likely that in the future, the relationships between law enforcement officials and the communities of people they serve will grow closer. As this happens, the relevance of a cultural anthropology background to police work will only increase.

◇ **TABLE 8.2** Law Enforcement Officials' Activities under Three Philosophies of Policing

Community Policing

- Work with community members to identify and eliminate causes of crime
- "Walk the beat" on long-term assignments in specific neighborhoods
- Reside locally in neighborhoods in which residents share officer's ethnicity, socioeconomic background, and language
- Become part of the community served

Problem-Solving Policing

- Recognize that social problems (such as poverty, racial and religious intolerance, illegal drug use) are a fundamental cause of lawbreaking
- Work with community members and public and private nonpolice agencies to identify crimes that are socially patterned
- Develop action plans for dealing with crimes identified as socially patterned
- Assess the effectiveness of action plans by comparing past and present results

Cooperative Policing

- Forge partnerships among law enforcement officials at every level: local, county, state
- Enhance communication among officials at different levels
- Combine resources with officials at different levels
- Provide more comprehensive services that better answer community needs

FOOD FOR THOUGHT

"If providing formal social control is a fundamental problem of living in large, productive social groups, so too is controlling the police" (Vila and Morris 1999:xxciv), as episodes such as the infamous 1991 beating of Rodney King at the hands of Los Angeles police officers, as well as several incidents in the late 1990s involving New York City police officers, demonstrate. What are some of the ways in which police officers might be "controlled"? Can codes of ethics (see p. 186) help? Would a background in cultural anthropology help to prevent police brutality? Explain your answers.

Other Opportunities in Law Enforcement

There are a number of other ways in which one might combine an interest in cultural anthropology with law enforcement. The U.S. Bureau of Indian Affairs (BIA), for example, is responsible for law enforcement on Native American reservations. The U.S. government views reservations as semi-sovereign entities and allows them a large measure of self-governance by tribal law. But when a federal crime is committed on Native American land, the U.S. government becomes involved, and it is officers of the BIA who undertake the necessary investigation, make arrests, and help prosecute the lawbreaker. Another branch of the federal government, the U.S. Immigration and Naturalization Service (INS), is responsible for enforcing laws regarding the immigration and naturalization of non–U.S. citizens. The Border Patrol, an agency of the INS, guards the 8,000-mile-long borders of the United States, mainly to deter illegal immigration and smuggling. Training in cultural anthropology would be useful in any of these areas of law enforcement.

The Relevance of Cultural Anthropology for Law Enforcement

In the past, careers in law enforcement typically did not require a college education, much less training in cultural anthropology, and even today, many police departments—especially those making concerted attempts to increase cultural diversity—do not require a college degree because this requirement tends to discourage minority applications. In recent years, however, law enforcement has become much more complex and technical, requiring more and different kinds of skills. Many of these (for example, computer skills or interpersonal communications skills) can best be acquired through higher education. The requirements for law enforcement jobs are changing accordingly. In New York City, for example, all police recruits must now have two years of either college or military service, and all captains must have a four-year college education (Flynn 1999:B6). About one fifth of the approximately 40,000 members of the NYPD now hold college degrees. Another 535 have advanced degrees, such as doctorates or law degrees (ibid.). In the future, the proportion of degree holders is expected to rise sharply.[3]

The modern policing strategies discussed above illustrate the point that because today's law enforcement officers deal directly with the social problems of individual citizens and groups of citizens, college-level preparation in cultural anthropology is increasingly relevant. In addition to their specific policing skills, law enforcement officers must be perceptive students of human behavior, constantly aware of the multiple and intersecting effects of social status, ethnicity, religion, educational level, socioeconomic level, political empowerment, and sex on human behavior. What impact does a person's status in a given social group have upon his or her interactions with others? What are the implications for social behavior of a person's religious belief, or the lack of it? In the context of a particular group, what impact does youth, or poverty, or political powerlessness have on a person's behavior toward others? A sensitive and informed understanding of such anthropological matters is highly relevant to effective law enforcement.

The many aspects of police work for which anthropological training are relevant have been ably described by thirty-three-year police-force veteran (and cultural anthropologist) Malcolm Young (Young 1993). Some of Young's observations about the similarities between policing and cultural anthropology are quite general, such as his experience of culture shock when beginning a job in a new community, or the distinctions he draws between rural and urban "cop cultures." More specifically,

Young finds numerous correspondences between the police force of which he was a member and the tribally organized societies studied by cultural anthropologists. For example, he notes that an "us/them" worldview is characteristic of members of both police forces and tribally organized groups, an observation that enabled him to better understand his own behavior and that of his fellow police officers. Young is one of very few law enforcement officers to have written about the many specific correspondences between police work and cultural anthropology, but any law enforcement officer with anthropological training has no doubt made similar observations.

FOOD FOR THOUGHT Like members of other occupations, police share a unique set of beliefs, behaviors, and traditions that add up to what is called the "police subculture." Aspects of this subculture are said to include "clannishness, secrecy, and isolation from those not in the group" (Dempsey 1994:108). What might account for these attributes? Is there a basic "police personality," or are these attributes related to elements of a law enforcement officer's lifestyle, such as stress or unusual working hours? In the aggregate, is the famous "Blue Wall of Silence" positive or negative for law enforcement officers and society at large?

APPLIED LEGAL ANTHROPOLOGY AND DISPUTE RESOLUTION

In non-Western cultures, disputes are resolved in a number of different ways, some of which (such as divination or feuding) are unfamiliar to Westerners (see Wolfe and Yang 1996:144). In the United States, however, disputes must be resolved in one of only two ways, according to U.S. law. One way is by a **court,** a governmental agency with the authority to carry out the law and resolve legal disputes. Going to court is the only option in criminal cases—those in which a misdemeanor or, more seriously, a felony (either of which constitutes a threat to society under the law) may have been committed. Both require a trial and **adjudication**—a decision by a judge and sometimes also a jury. Either process typically results in a severe penalty, such as a fine, imprisonment, or even death, for a finding of guilt.

Unless they also happen to be either judges or jury members, applied legal anthropologists do not adjudicate. Rendering judgment regarding the law is done only by individuals who have legal authority to do so.

The other way disputes are resolved in Western societies is out of court (see Coughlin 1993). Typically, disputes resolved out of court are civil cases, legally defined as disagreements between "persons in their private capacity, whether individuals, partnerships, or corporations."[4] Out-of-court dispute resolution is a professional arena currently dominated by professionals with degrees in disciplines other than anthropology (Magistro 1997:9), but one in which applied legal anthropologists are finding an increasingly important role. The disputes in which they are typically in-volved are resolved in one of two ways, by arbitration or by mediation, depending on the nature of the dispute.

Arbitration

Under the dispute resolution method termed **arbitration,** the parties to a dispute present their complaints to a neutral third party, called an **arbitrator,**[5] agreeing be-forehand to accept this person's decision. Because of the disputing parties' prior agreement to accept the arbitrator's judgment, this kind of dispute resolution is sometimes called "binding arbitration." The decision of the arbitrator is equal in force to a court verdict (Coughlin 1993:358).

Although training in cultural anthropology is not required for this kind of work, a number of applied legal anthropologists work as professional arbitrators. For some, arbitration is a full-time occupation; some labor unions, for example, have full-time arbitrators on staff, since labor negotiations are often conducted through arbitration rather than in courts of law. Insurance companies also hire arbi-trators for negotiating insurance claims involving, for example, uninsured or hit-and-run drivers (Coughlin 1993:358); in fact, automobile insurance policies often contain an "uninsured motorist clause" specifying that in case of disagreement be-tween an insurance company and an insured driver over the amount of damage caused to the insured person or his/her property by an uninsured driver, the amount of the damage is subject to arbitration (Coughlin 1993:358). Aside from these full-time roles, however, most applied legal anthropologists who specialize in arbitration serve as consultants who are hired by businesses or unions on a tempo-rary basis, as the need arises.

Mediation

The second means of conflict resolution in which applied legal anthropologists are frequently involved is **mediation,** the use of a neutral third party (or sometimes a panel consisting of several neutral individuals) to help settle a dispute. There is a par-ticularly good "fit" between mediation and legal anthropology because in small-scale, non-Western societies, disputes are often resolved in just this way.[6] Mediation differs from arbitration in that the mediator simply facilitates negotiation between the op-posing parties; he or she does not make any decision, much less a legally binding one—the disputants themselves do. The mediation process is both voluntary and in-formal, although the results, if agreed to in writing by both parties, are legally binding.

Disputes for which mediated resolutions are appropriate are likely to be rela-tively minor ones (from the point of view of the law, although not necessarily that of the disputants), such as borrowed-lawnmower or loud-noise arguments between neighbors, landlord–tenant disputes, cases involving accidental and reparable dam-age to personal property, or lifestyle quarrels between parents and teenage children. Some divorces are now mediated to reduce both expense and acrimony. The media-tor calls the opposing parties together, and maintains order while each side states its grievances. The mediator then helps steer the disputants through an amicable discussion of their differences, suggesting various possibilities for resolution. Typically no time limit is placed on this process; the discussion continues until the disputants have found a mutually acceptable compromise and—if one of the parties has suffered a material loss at the hands of the other—have agreed on some form of compensation. After a resolution has been achieved, both parties to the dispute sign an agreement, which, once signed, carries the force of a legally binding document.

Resorting to mediation as opposed to going to court is becoming more and more popular in the United States and other Western countries. Many communities in the United States now maintain "mediation centers" (alternatively, "neighborhood justice centers" or "dispute resolution centers") as an alternative to courts of law. Court officials are apt to promote mediation because it helps prevent an already overloaded judiciary system from becoming even more clogged with minor cases. Disputants like it because it tends to be much less expensive, less time consuming, and less anxiety producing than going to court.

Applied anthropologists skilled in dispute resolution may find roles abroad as well as at home. Anthropologist John Magistro (1997) has written compellingly of the need for anthropologists to contribute their conflict management and dispute resolution skills to interethnic problems in international settings. While a member of an interdisciplinary team documenting the social, economic, political, and ecological effects on local herders, farmers, and fishermen of damming a river in Senegal, West Africa, Magistro witnessed a violent confrontation between members of two riverside groups. The underlying political issue was the deportation of minorities from both Mauritania and Senegal. The conflict widened, eventually resulting in numerous deaths, much property destruction, and an enormous refugee problem in both countries (Magistro 1997:6). The experience caused Magistro to rethink his role as a "detached outside observer" and to realize how much institutions involved in social mediation—federal, local, and nongovernmental—could benefit from greater anthropological input (Magistro 1997:9).

Anthropologists are uniquely situated, given their emphases on participant observation and field-based studies of social organization at multiple levels of analysis (individual, household, intra- and inter-community) to integrate more effectively their analytic and pedagogic skills with the growing field of conflict management and dispute resolution. (Magistro 1997:6)

FOOD FOR THOUGHT

Burton (1996) draws a distinction between two types of adversarial situations: those in which disputants are able to change their views or behavior to achieve compromise, and those—more difficult to resolve—in which disputants' views or behavior are "nonmalleable." The first type is amenable to what Burton terms "dispute settlement," facilitated by a mediator, but the second type requires "conflict resolution," involving a thorough analysis of the deeply rooted, often institutional, causes of the dispute. Do you see a distinction between these two types of disputes? Would the study of cultural anthropology be any less relevant to the first type than the second? Why or why not?

AN APPLIED CULTURAL ANTHROPOLOGIST AT WORK

VIVIAN J. ROHRL

Vivian J. Rohrl, Professor Emerita of Anthropology at San Diego State University and a professional mediator, became interested in the practical applications of cultural anthropology while a graduate student at the University of Chicago. One of her professors was Sol Tax, who coined the term *action anthropology* (later *participatory action research*), for indigenous involvement in development (Rohrl 2000:33; see also Chapter 3, p. 68). Students in Dr. Tax's course conducted applied field projects among Midwestern Native American groups. Later, Rohrl went on to do anthropological fieldwork among Ojibwa Indians, earning her Ph.D. from the University of Minnesota.

While still an undergraduate at Chicago, Rohrl attended a lecture given by legal scholar Karl Llewellyn, who was co-author, with anthropologist E. Adamson Hoebel, of *The Cheyenne Way*. The lecture sparked her interest in the law; Dr. Hoebel, who wrote *The Law of Primitive Man* and was credited with founding the field of legal anthropology, eventually became her thesis adviser at Minnesota. Her Ph.D. dissertation, later published (Rohrl 1981), included a detailed description of an Ojibwa "trouble-case" in which a dispute was settled without the use of a formal court.

A few years later, Rohrl was asked to join a team of lawyers and social scientists at American University Law School in Washington, D.C., tasked with exploring alternatives to the conventional court system. The specific goal of the project, which was funded under a grant from the National Institute of Justice, was to identify ways in which at least some disputes might be resolved without lengthy and costly court trials. As the project anthropologist, Rohrl conducted cross-cultural research on dispute resolution and discovered that in cultures that lacked courts, mediation and other methods of dispute processing worked well. She suggested applying these methods, in modified form, to disputes in Westernized societies.

Shortly thereafter, as a member of the Anthropology Department at San Diego State University, Rohrl introduced into the curriculum a new course on the anthropology of law and dispute resolution, and pursued her new interest in mediation by attending an orientation meeting at the San Diego Mediation Center. Anthropology, she realized, can be seen as a kind of mediation between cultures, in that—by means of enhanced communication—it bridges cultural differences between peoples who view the world very differently from one another. She soon became a trained volunteer mediator, specializing in mediations involving communication between people with different ethnic backgrounds.

One of her cases was initiated by a Caribbean woman who took her former neighbor to small claims court, allegedly for being noisy and disruptive, using the complainant's parking space, and damaging her furniture. The San Diego Small Claims Court gives the opposing parties the option of trying to mediate before being heard in the court. As the mediator in this case, Rohrl first asked each disputant to tell her story from her own point of view. She then asked each disputant to repeat her opponent's story, to show that both had listened. After summarizing each position, Rohrl then initiated a discussion between the two women about a time in the past when they had been friends. When she felt both women were ready, Rohrl asked them to supply possible solutions to resolve their disagreement. It became clear during the mediation session that the "offender" had not meant any harm; she was under stress, she said, caused by people with whom she was living. The "offender" tearfully apologized; the complainant hugged the accused and advised her to stay away from "those bad people," and friendship was restored.

Rohrl observes that the skills involved in mediation, including empathy as well as linguistic and general communications skills, overlap with those required of a good participant observer. She thus advises students interested in becoming mediators to take courses in anthropological field research methods in addition to applied anthropology and legal anthropology. Related courses offered in other departments—for example, courses in political

science, communications, or public administration—may also be helpful. Schools of education sometimes offer courses in which mediation skills are taught, since there is an increasing emphasis on dispute resolution among peers in the school system.

Over the years, as her teaching and research responsibilities have permitted, Vivian Rohrl has mediated a total of some eighty legal cases—an average of several cases per year. She is currently analyzing her data on mediation with a view to identifying new legal areas in which mediation can be used. She is also assessing how mediation techniques can be fine-tuned to make them even more applicable for use in Westernized contexts.

Anthropologist Vivian J. Rohrl (center) engaged in a mock mediation with colleagues Gerald Monk and Lei Guang. Since most actual mediations are considered confidential, mock mediations are used as teaching devices.

The Expert Witness

Yet another role for a cultural anthropologist with expertise in legal systems is serving as an **expert witness** in legal cases (La Rusic 1985; Dobyns 1987; Joans 1997; Trigger and Blowes 2001). An expert witness is a professional, representing any of a number of different fields, who has specialized knowledge or training in some subject that has a bearing on the ability of a court to uphold and discharge the law. In a murder trial, for instance, an expert witness familiar with DNA analysis might be called upon to testify that blood found on the clothing of the accused matched that of the victim.

Most expert witnesses are drawn from the biological and physical (or "hard") sciences (medical doctors and engineers, for example), and the testimony they provide typically elucidates highly technical matters for the sake of a judge and/or jury who may lack expertise in these matters (Coughlin 1993:39). Physical anthropologists often testify in legal cases involving the identification of human remains (see Appendix 4). Psychologists are also routinely called upon as expert witnesses, either in cases in which a defendant's state of mind may be exculpatory or in which the outcome is likely to have psychological ramifications, such as child custody cases.

More rarely, cultural anthropologists are asked to serve as expert witnesses. A cultural anthropologist with expertise in human social organization may be asked, for example, to offer anthropological insights into family organization in a child custody case (see, for example, Joans 1997); an anthropologist specializing in human ecology may be asked to shed light on the social and cultural impact of proposed development efforts when the legality of these is challenged in court.[7] Most commonly, however, cultural anthropologists serve as experts on the beliefs, values, and behaviors characterizing particular cultures or subcultures, and hence on the motivations and behaviors of individuals with particular cultural backgrounds who have been charged with wrongdoing. A cultural anthropologist as expert witness may argue, for example, that an accused drunk driver's alcoholism is culture-bound.

In most instances in which an expert witness—whether anthropologist or not—is called upon, the witness has no direct knowledge of the case. So that the witness will not be put in a position of being asked to testify about particulars of which he or she has no specific information, the lawyers for the defense and the prosecution usually frame questions that are either general in nature ("Is it true that individuals in the defendant's home community routinely use verbal death threats metaphorically in the context of arguments?") or hypothetical ("If the defendant were to have threatened the victim verbally, would that necessarily indicate intent to murder, given the defendant's cultural background?"). Hypothetical questions are often based on testimony about a point that the jury has already heard; the expert witness is "asked to base his opinion on the assumption that the testimony in the question is true" (Coughlin 1993:39).

Invoking culture as an explanation for the behavior of an individual involved in a legal matter is termed the **culture defense.** The concept is controversial and has never been adequately defined for legal purposes, with the result that "jurists . . . operate with no clear idea of what is required to prove the plea 'my culture made me do it'" (Torry 2000:59). Nevertheless, the culture defense is often used when a defendant belongs to an identifiable cultural group—for example, a member of a youth gang, a new immigrant who retains traditional views and behaviors, or a member of a religious cult (ibid.:68).

The culture defense is based on the notion that an individual's culture can compel specific behaviors, an idea termed **cultural dictation** (Torry 2000). This idea raises an interesting question: for purposes of the law, how much of individuals' behavior is attributable to choice (or what is commonly called free will), and how much to culture? The issue is important for legal cases because in the Western legal tradition, the measure of blame is reduced when individuals commit wrongs under the force of some compulsion (ibid.:69). In keeping with this common dictate, the legal system recognizes cultural dictates as "possible excusatory elements" (ibid.:69).

FOOD FOR THOUGHT

Few if any cultural anthropologists would claim that all culturally motivated behavior is compelled, but many would agree that individuals' behavior is in some degree shaped by their culture (Torry 2000:68). To what extent do you think a person's cultural background affects his or her behavior? Does this vary from culture to culture? from behavior to behavior? As a juror in a court of law, would you "buy" the culture defense? Explain your answer.

A recent court case for which the testimony of an expert witness trained in cultural anthropology was sought involved an immigrant from an Asian country who was living in the United States. During an argument at a restaurant, this individual believed he had been insulted, and in his anger he struck his adversary with a wine bottle, injuring him slightly. Assault charges were pressed. The lawyer for the accused hoped to establish before the jury that verbal insults are taken much more seriously in certain Asian cultures than in the United States, and that therefore the defendant's limited physical response was, for him, culturally appropriate. To establish this, the lawyer turned for help to a cultural anthropologist with special expertise in Asian culture, who agreed to serve as an expert witness. Unfortunately for the defendant in this particular case, the jury dismissed the anthropologist's cultural explanation for the assault, and the assailant was convicted.

Cultural anthropologists serving as expert witnesses occasionally encounter reluctance, on the part of courts, to accept their testimony, probably because anthropology is less well known, to non-anthropologists, than some other professional disciplines. Anthropologist Barbara Joans, for example, was asked to testify on behalf of a father in a child custody dispute. The father was prepared to raise the child in the context of an extended family, while the mother—thrice divorced and about to marry for the fourth time—would provide a "traditional" nuclear family. Joans was prepared to testify that in the United States, extended families are "every bit as normal . . . as nuclear ones, in fact a bit more common" (Joans 1997:11) and that the father and his large, close-knit extended family would provide a warmer, healthier, more nurturing environment for the child than a household consisting only of the mother and her new husband. To Joans's dismay, the judge refused to allow her anthropological brief to be submitted. "Anthropology still has a long way to go before courts view our field with the same kind of respect given to psychologists," Joans says (ibid.:13).

◇ *Lawyers sometimes defend their clients by calling on the controversial "culture defense," in which the culture of a defendant is seen as an explanation for his or her behavior.*

Legal anthropologist William Torry (2000) has recently called for increased participation in, and increased input into, legal matters on the part of cultural anthropologists. To back up this participation, Torry further suggests that anthropologists, long-time commentators on the rights of social groups (see Chapter 6), should undertake research into the question of individual responsibilities, especially in light of the culture defense. We need "standardized benchmarks" to validate a "culture made me do it" presumption, according to Torry (Torry 2000:69).

Serving as an expert witness is a role that cultural anthropologists usually undertake on a part-time, consulting basis, but it is one that more and more cultural anthropologists are expected to play in the future, due not only to the increasing heterogeneity of the American population but also to the trend in America for more and more litigation (Dobyns 1987:366). A cultural anthropologist in the role of expert witness may face a more difficult challenge, however, than a "hard" scientist in a similar position, since cultural anthropology is so subjective a discipline. It may even happen that the subjective opinions of one cultural anthropologist are pitted in court against those of another (La Rusic 1985:168).

FOOD FOR THOUGHT

Anthropologist Michael Robinson did fieldwork in Australia among an aboriginal group that applied, in the Australian Federal Court, for a land title (Trigger and Blowes 2001). Because he had genealogical and other information supporting the group's title claim, Robinson was called upon as an expert witness in the case. During the trial, the State subpoenaed Robinson's field notes. Robinson argued that in anthropology, field notes are considered confidential so as to protect informants' anonymity, but the court ruled against him. Does this case suggest that—in some instances, at least—cultural anthropologists should refuse to serve as expert witnesses? How might cultural anthropologists preserve their informant's confidentiality if asked to testify in court?

APPLIED LEGAL ANTHROPOLOGY
AND THE CORRECTIONAL SYSTEM

The system of social control found in Western societies has traditionally involved re-moving those found guilty of serious offenses from society for some period of time, for two reasons: to punish miscreants for their crimes and to prevent them from committing additional crimes. Today, however, penal systems have two additional goals: to preserve prisoners' human rights by treating them in a humane and equi-table way and to rehabilitate them so they will be able to rejoin society as produc-tive, law-abiding citizens when their prison terms have been served. In addition, modern penal systems incorporate the idea of parole, in which a corrections agency monitors the activities of a lawbreaker who is permitted to live outside a corrections facility. Human rights preservation and rehabilitation are as important a part of the treatment of parolees as of inmates (see Stephens 2002:64–68).

The goals of modern penal systems are difficult to achieve, since prisoners vary widely by sex, age, educational level, socioeconomic status, religion, ethnicity, and so on, but modern correctional institutions have made major strides to meet them. When a prisoner enters the correctional system, data intended to help corrections officials design effective and humane prison policies and programs are now rou-tinely collected. Prisoners are questioned, for example, about whether they are ad-dicted to alcohol or drugs, information that helps prison officials plan and carry out treatment programs geared to prisoners' specific dependency problems and exten-sive enough to serve all prisoners who need them. The importance of collecting this kind of information would be hard to overestimate, because without treatment pro-grams developed on the basis of reliable data, the likelihood of prisoner rehabilita-tion is slim, and without rehabilitation, most freed inmates will eventually be incar-cerated again (Grobsmith 1992:7, 1994:183). Armed with adequate data, prison authorities can justify requests to the state or federal government for additional re-sources to develop more and better treatment programs.

The goal of providing sensitive, humane treatment to all prisoners has proven even more difficult to achieve than the goal of providing effective rehabilitative services. To meet this goal, corrections officials must have as thorough as possible an understanding of the different cultures and subcultures represented by the prisoners in their care. Unfortunately, however, cultural data are only occasionally collected from prisoners in a systematic way. Despite their enlightened approach to rehabili-tation, too often prison officials make little attempt to understand the beliefs, values, and cultural practices of incoming prisoners; indeed, most prison officials are igno-rant of the subcultures from which their charges are drawn.

Recently, some prison officials have begun to call on the expertise of applied cultural anthropologists at the time prisoners first enter the penal system, in order to upgrade the quality of the data authorities collect about them. Elizabeth Grobsmith, a professor of anthropology at the University of Nebraska, for example, has served for over twenty years as a consultant to the Nebraska Department of Correctional Services. In this role, she helps prison officials to better understand the culture of the state's Native American prisoners, who represent close to 4 percent of the Ne-braska prison population (see Grobsmith 1992, 1994).

Grobsmith's work with Native American prisoners began in 1975, when the U.S. District Court in Nebraska decreed that Native Americans must be allowed to maintain their traditional culture, including their religious practices, while in prison. These practices incorporated what seemed to prison officials to be unusual and therefore suspicious activities. One religious ritual, for example, involved unwrapping a sacred pipe and other religious articles according to traditional procedures, an activity incompatible with the long-standing prison protocol mandating careful inspection of all items prisoners are allowed to use. Healing ceremonies carried out by Native American ritual specialists from outside the prison sometimes required a totally darkened room and the use of scalpels or blades. Guards confused the sage, cedar, and sweetgrass burned during religious rituals and private prayers with marijuana. Prisoners, for their part, were offended by their jailers' suspicions and accusations, and behaved accordingly. Rather than submitting to drug tests they found humiliating, for example, they refused to be tested, thus appearing guilty.

Grobsmith discovered that the problem of cross-cultural communication between Native American prisoners and jailers was multidimensional: most prison officials and guards had no education in Native American culture, and Native American inmates found it difficult to articulate, for authorities, the beliefs underlying their practices. As a specialist in Native American culture, Grobsmith was able to interpret the meaning of Native American customs for prison authorities and convince them of the traditional legitimacy of such customs.

An important aspect of Grobsmith's work focuses on Native Americans' drug and alcohol dependency problems, which often play a part in their lawbreaking. On the basis of a nationwide survey of Native American prisoners, many of whom had alcohol and drug problems, she was able to make policy recommendations to assist in the development of treatment programs that take the Native Americans' culture into account (Grobsmith 1994:183ff.).

Native Americans are only one of many subcultural groups within the prison population that could benefit from the application of anthropological methods, techniques, and data (Grobsmith 1992:5). Insights from cultural anthropology may enable corrections officers to provide more humane treatment and more effective rehabilitative services to populations such as female prisoners, elderly prisoners, gang members, or parolees, in addition to incarcerated members of particular ethnic groups.

CONCLUSION

Cross-culturally, there is great variety both in systems of social control and methods of conflict resolution, and the subdiscipline of legal anthropology developed, and exists today, mainly to document, analyze, and compare these systems and methods. Most of the legal anthropologists working in this domain are academics and theoreticians not primarily engaged in applied work.

However, the expertise of professionals with training in legal anthropology is increasingly sought outside of academia, and new ideas for maintaining social control and achieving conflict resolution are in growing demand all over the world (Wolfe and Yang 1996:144). A major reason is that population numbers are increasing in most industrialized countries, especially in some urban areas, and certain social problems are worsening. The traffic in illegal drugs, for example, is higher than in the past. Legal anthropologists, with a cross-cultural understanding of how social control is achieved and maintained in different kinds of societies, are in a position to make major contributions to the search for solutions to practical problems of social control.

Legal anthropologist Honggang Yang studies the potential contribution of legal anthropology to the American legal system (Yang 1993). One specific step Yang recommends is to educate Westerners about effective non-Western systems of social control, especially the successful social control strategies used in peaceful non-Western societies. Another recommendation is to train those charged with upholding the law in the kinds of social control and conflict resolution skills that have proven useful in non-Western settings (Wolfe and Yang 1996:144–145). If followed, these sensible recommendations will require increased involvement on the part of applied legal anthropologists in theory building and policy formulation in the areas of law enforcement, dispute resolution, and corrections.

KEY TERMS

adjudication   a decision by a judge and sometimes also a jury, which usually results in a penalty if guilt is found

anthropology of law   an alternative term for *legal anthropology*

applied legal anthropology   the work of legal anthropologists in applied contexts involving the legal rights and behavior of members of subgroups or subcultures

arbitration   a form of dispute resolution in which the parties to the dispute present their complaints to a neutral third party called an arbitrator, agreeing beforehand to accept this person's decision

arbitrator (or **arbiter**)   in arbitration, a neutral third party to whom two disputing parties present their complaints, and whose decision is final

community-oriented policing (COP)   a synonym for *community policing*

community policing   a philosophy of law enforcement and a set of methods for improving relationships between law enforcement officials and citizens; its fundamental principle is mutual familiarity and understanding

cooperative policing   a philosophy of law enforcement, implemented on a statewide basis, in which cooperation among law enforcement officials at every level is encouraged

court   a governmental agency with the authority to carry out the law and resolve legal disputes

culture defense   invoking culture to explain the behavior of an individual involved in a legal matter

cultural dictation   the idea that an individual's culture can compel specific behavior

expert witness   a person with specialized knowledge or training in some subject that has a bearing on the ability of a court to decide on the guilt or innocence of an accused person

laws   a society's formal, written, binding, enforceable rules, to which people generally conform because they have to, or risk punishment by some individual or group with punitive authority

legal anthropology   the cross-cultural study and analysis of legal systems

mediation   the use of a neutral third party (or sometimes a panel consisting of several individuals) to help settle a dispute

negative sanctions   society's reactions to disapproved behaviors

norms   a society's informal rules, to which people generally conform not because they are forced to but because they have been taught to

positive sanctions   society's reactions to approved behaviors

problem-solving policing   a philosophy of law enforcement based on the recognition that social problems are a fundamental cause of lawbreaking; its fundamental principle is that law enforcement officials and citizens should work together to identify and alleviate the underlying social problems that result in lawbreaking

public accountability   a synonym for *community policing*

sanctions   society's reactions to approved or disapproved behavior

social control   the ways in which a society restricts the behavior of individuals and groups to activities that the society's rulers or members (depending on the society's political system) deem permissible

the law   the compendium of formal, written, binding, enforceable rules in a given society

NOTES

1. Some of anthropology's most influential theorists in the area of legal anthropology are J. M. H. Beattie, Paul Bohannan, Max Gluckman, E. Adamson Hoebel, and Laura Nader.

2. Today, of course, all societies are literate in the sense that all are subsumed within some literate state, and are bound by that state's laws.

3. Most states now participate in the Police Corps Program, funded by the U.S. Department of Justice. The program helps states to increase their number of college-educated police officers by reimbursing some of the costs of a four-year degree, in return for graduates' commitment to serve in a specific police department for a fixed period of time, usually four years. In some cases, the officer specifically agrees to embrace community policing.

4. Civil law encompasses all legal matters that fall outside criminal law. Examples include negligence, contract, estate, and family issues. Civil cases may be resolved either in or out of court, but out-of-court resolution is common.

5. Or *arbiter;* the two terms are synonymous.

6. A good example of mediation in small-scale, non-Western societies is the informal "moot" court, or "house palaver," of the Kpelle of Liberia (see Gibbs 1963).

7. The involvement of cultural anthropologists in litigation over impact issues is increasing due to federal and state legislation requiring the assessment of the social and cultural as well as the environmental impact of government-funded projects.

REFERENCES

Burton, John W.
1996. *Conflict Resolution: Its Languages and Processes.* Landham, MD: Scarecrow Press.

Coughlin, George Gordon, Jr.
1993. *Your Handbook of Everyday Law* (5th ed.). New York: HarperCollins Publishers.

Dempsey, John S.
1994. *Policing: An Introduction to Law Enforcement.* Minneapolis/St. Paul, MN: West Publishing Co.

Dickerson, Debra
2000. "Cops in the 'Hood.'" In *Police in Society*, edited by Terence J. Fitzgerald, 63–67. New York: H. W. Wilson Co.

Dobyns, Henry F.
1987. "Taking the Witness Stand." In *Applied Anthropology in America* (2nd ed.), edited by Elizabeth M. Eddy and William L. Partridge, 366–380. New York: Columbia University Press.

Egan, Timothy
1998. "Debate About Tribal Rights Turns Rancorous." *New York Times*, April 7, 1998:A12.

Emsley, Clive
2000. "The Origins of the Modern Police." In *Police in Society*, edited by Terence J. Fitzgerald, 9–17. New York: H. W. Wilson Co.

Erickson, Lee C.
2000. "Cooperative Policing: Bridging the Gap of Community Policing." In *Police in Society*, edited by Terence J. Fitzgerald, 173–182. New York: H. W. Wilson Co.

Fitzgerald, Terence J. (ed.)
2000. *Police in Society*. New York: H. W. Wilson Co.

Flynn, Kevin
1999. "Ivy Leaguers with a Ph.D." *New York Times*, Jan. 27, 1999: B1–B6.

Gibbs, James L.
1963. "The Kpelle Moot." In *Applying Anthropology* (3rd ed.), edited by Aaron Podolefsky and Peter J. Brown, 265–272 [reprinted from *Africa* 33 (1)]. Mountain View, CA: Mayfield Publishing Co.

Grobsmith, Elizabeth S.
1992. "Applying Anthropology to Amerian Indian Correctional Concerns." *Practicing Anthropology* 14 (3):5–8.

1994. *Indians in Prison: Incarcerated Native Americans in Nebraska.* Lincoln: University of Nebraska Press.

Heinrich, Steven A.
1993. "Commentary: Law and the Value of Anthropology." *Practicing Anthropology* 15 (1):2, 33.

Hicks, David, and Margaret A. Gwynne
1996. *Cultural Anthropology.* New York: HarperCollins College Publishers.

Joans, Barbara
1997. "Infighting in San Francisco: Anthropology in Family Court." *Practicing Anthropology* 19 (4):10–13.

La Rusic, Ignatius
1995. "Expert Witness?" In *Advocacy and Anthropology,* edited by Robert Paine, 165–169. St. John's, Newfoundland: Institute of Social and Economic Research.

Magistro, John
1997. "An Emerging Role for Applied Anthropology: Conflict Management and Dispute Resolution." *Practicing Anthropology* 19 (1):5–9.

Nader, Laura
1989. "The Crown, the Colonists, and the Course of Zapotec Village Law." In *History and Power in the Study of Law: New Directions in Legal Anthropology,* edited by June Starr and Jane F. Collier, 320–344. Ithaca: Cornell University Press.

Rohe, Willliam M., R. E. Adams, Thomas A. Arcury, John Memory, and James Klopovic
1996. *Community-Oriented Policing: The North Carolina Experience.* Chapel Hill, NC: University of North Carolina Center for Urban and Regional Studies.

Rohrl, Vivian J.
1981. *Change for Continuity.* Lanham, MD: University Press of America.

2000. "Yes, In Our Backyard." *Practicing Anthropology* 22 (2):33–37.

Rouland, Norbert
1993. *Legal Anthropology.* Stanford: Stanford University Press.

Stephens, W. Richard
2002. *Careers in Anthropology.* Boston: Allyn and Bacon.

Stinchcomb, James D.
1990. *Opportunities in Law Enforcement and Criminal Justice Careers.* Lincolnwood, IL: VGM Career Horizons.

Torry, William I.
2000. "Culture and Individual Responsibility: Touchstones of the Culture Defense." *Human Organization* 59 (1):58–69.

Trigger, David, and Robert Blowes
2001. "Anthropologists, Lawyers, and Issues for Expert Witnesses: Native Title Claims in Australia." *Practicing Anthropology* 23 (1):15–20.

Trojanowicz, Robert C., and Bonnie Bucqueroux
1990. *Community Policing: A Contemporary Perspective.* Cincinnati: Anderson.

Vila, Bryan, and Cynthia Morris
1999. *The Role of Police in American Society.* Westport, CT: Greenwood Press.

Wolfe, Alvin W., and Honggang Yang (eds.)
1996. *Anthropological Contributions to Conflict Resolution.* Athens, GA: University of Georgia Press.

Yang, Honggang
1993. *The Practical Use of Ethnographic Knowledge: Face-Saving Devices in Conflict Resolution.* Portland, OR: Paper presented at the 1993 National Conference on Peacemaking and Conflict Resolution.

Young, Malcolm
1993. *In the Sticks: Cultural Identity in a Rural Police Force.* Oxford, UK: Clarendon Press.

CHAPTER

9 BUSINESS ANTHROPOLOGY

INTRODUCTION

Matthew D. graduated from a small liberal arts college in the Northeastern United States, with a major in cultural anthropology. He chose this major not with a future career in mind, since he had long planned to go into his family's business, but rather because he enjoyed learning about people, especially people whose way of life was very different from his own.

Matthew had worked for his family's business, an aircraft-parts manufacturing company located on the outskirts of Boston, every summer since high school, so he was familiar with the manufacturing process, the resulting products, and company finances. But since he had not worked in all of the company's departments, his father, who was the CEO, decided to rotate him through each department so he could gain experience and an accurate overall picture of the business. Right after graduation, therefore, Matthew was assigned to the supplies and equipment department and given the impressive-sounding title of assistant manager. While the department's head manager handled the scheduling and financing of purchases of supplies and equipment, Matthew's major responsibility was to oversee the work of six employees who did the actual purchasing of all the materials—from sheet metal to paper clips—that the company needed.

Most of the employees in the S&E department had been with the company for many years, and when Matthew arrived they were doing things pretty much as they always had. Purchase orders, for example, were filled out by hand, in triplicate. Matthew soon persuaded his father that for the sake of efficiency, the purchasing system should be computerized. Computers were ordered, and the staff was notified of the upcoming change. But this created a problem that neither Matthew nor his father had anticipated: the employees, comfortable with the way things had always been done, were very reluctant to switch to a new system—and they said so. Matthew realized he was facing a potentially serious personnel problem, involving not only efficiency but also employee morale.

In mulling over this problem, Matthew realized that his position in the S&E department was similar to that of leaders in the type of sociopolitical organization that cultural anthropologists term a "tribe."[1] They may have authority, usually by virtue of descent and tradition, but they often lack real power to enforce their will. Similarly, Matthew had authority, conveyed by the title of assistant manager, but no enforcement power. It occurred to him that he might put his anthropological understanding of the nature of power and authority in tribal society to use. He knew that tribal leaders win their constituents' cooperation by being amicable and charismatic, by understanding and supporting people's interests and values, and by building social networks.[2]

So Matthew turned on the charm. He was friendly, he networked, he asked questions about the buyers' concerns, he offered them support in matters not related to computerizing the purchasing system. All the while, he extolled the advantages of using computers. It took weeks of patience and hard work, but eventually he was able to win the buyers' interest and cooperation—despite their initial resistance to change, and also despite some resistance to him personally as the "new kid on the block." When the computers arrived, the transition to the new procurement system went smoothly.

Cultural anthropology has much to contribute to the problems and challenges, both organizational and operational, faced by for-profit businesses, because "most business problems are people problems" (Hamada 1999b:4).[3] The use of anthropological ideas and methods to achieve practical goals primarily in the private, for-profit sector is termed **business anthropology** or, alternatively, **corporate anthropology.** (A related term, **industrial anthropology,** refers specifically to anthropological research focusing on industry, defined in terms of its large scale, capital investment, and other criteria; see Baba 1986:1.) Business anthropologists—to cite only a few examples—help corporations develop culturally appropriate ways of doing business with suppliers, business partners, or customers; promote smooth working relationships among employees who are more and more likely, thanks to recent equal opportunity employment legislation, to represent different age groups, ethnic groups, and both sexes (Ferraro 1998:6); and facilitate organizational restructuring for greater economy and efficiency.

THE RECENT GROWTH OF BUSINESS ANTHROPOLOGY

Business anthropology is now the most rapidly growing subfield of applied cultural anthropology. In 1998 (the latest year for which accurate figures on the relative proportion of business anthropologists to other kinds of applied anthropologists are available), about 40 percent of all applied cultural anthropologists worked in the business world (Baba 1998). Some of these anthropologists are independent consultants who work for a number of different businesses; others are basically academics who undertake some consulting work in addition to their academic responsibilities. A somewhat smaller number of business anthropologists are full-time employees of corporations—mainly large U.S.-based, transnational companies. Hallmark Cards has an anthropologist. So does General Motors (collectively, the U.S. automotive industry employs at least a dozen anthropologists). So does Anderson Consulting (Hafner 1999:G1). In the past decade, Apple Computers, Motorola, Quaker Oats, Xerox, Nissan, Intel, Liberty Mutual, Coca-Cola, Procter and Gamble, Sears, and Nynex have all employed anthropologists (Garza 1991:74; Corcoran 1993; Sherry 1995:480; Aguilera 1996:741; Hafner 1999:G1).

The rapid growth that led to the numerical prominence of business anthropologists among their peers is nothing short of astonishing. Only a generation ago, during the Vietnam era, nonacademic anthropology in general was out of favor, and business anthropology in particular accounted for only a very small proportion of anthropological work (see Chapter 3). As one business anthropologist describes it, in the 1970s "culture as a business buzzword was still over a decade away, anthropologists were still hazily associated with King Tut's treasure or old bones, and a Ph.D. indicated a significant lack of pragmatism" (Aguilera 1996:735).

This general disparagement of business anthropology is perhaps all the more surprising given that anthropological involvement in this arena dates as far back as the 1930s, when a number of academic anthropologists who considered themselves experts in human relations became interested in the structure, work environment, and management of Western industrial organizations (see Chapter 3, p. 60). After World War II, however, the field eroded, in part due to the ready availability of academic jobs. In the 1950s, McCarthyism propelled a few cultural anthropologists out of academics and into employment with private sector organizations. But by the 1960s and 1970s, in part because of ethical concerns about nonacademic anthropology in general, most cultural anthropologists seemed to feel there was something crass and undignified about working for a profit-making organization. Some went further, asserting that "one simply [could] not be in business or industry and be on the side of what is fair and good" (Chambers 1989:128). Those anthropologists who were interested in businesses as social organizations were mainly academics who focused more on the theoretical than the practical aspects of businesses.

That attitude began to change in the mid-1970s. In 1975, business anthropology earned a vote of support from a well-respected academic, Conrad Arensberg, an endorsement that encouraged nonacademic endeavor in this arena. One of the first of the big corporations to hire a business anthropologist was Xerox, which in 1975 called on anthropological expertise to help computer scientists understand how information on paper "flowed" in offices (Corcoran 1993:H1). (Xerox now employs half a dozen cultural anthropologists.)

Arensberg was not, of course, single-handedly responsible for the shift in attitude. Some of the change was no doubt due to a decrease in demand for academic anthropologists and an increase in applied cultural anthropology in general (Burkhalter 1986:114). But two other trends affecting businesses may also have played a role. First, American businesses were paying ever greater attention to ways in which

they could become more streamlined for greater efficiency and hence greater profits. Since satisfied workers perform better than unhappy ones, companies began to
focus on how their organizations could better fulfill employees' needs and expectations. Many businesses established new departments of human relations, an area
ripe for cultural anthropological input. And second, American society was becoming
increasingly litigious, and workers' perceptions of discrimination or environmental
hazards in the workplace sometimes resulted in lawsuits. For some big companies,
calling on a business anthropologist to help prevent employee dissatisfaction was a
sensible precautionary measure. In the 1980s, with businesses increasingly manufacturing and selling their products internationally (and with academic jobs for anthropologists still in short supply), more and more corporations followed suit. Business anthropology has continued to increase in scope and numbers of practitioners
ever since.

Today, business anthropology is not only taught in graduate programs in
anthropology (see *Anthropology Career Resources Handbook*); it is also included in the
curricula of a number of American universities offering the M.B.A. (Master's in
Business Administration) degree. It is perhaps surprising, therefore, that the old association of business anthropology with "a lack of concern for human welfare"
(Chambers 1989:128) still persists today among some academic anthropologists. As
business anthropologist Marietta Baba puts it, "business [still] . . . doesn't sit well
with most anthropologists" (quoted in Corcoran 1993:H6). This attitude may reflect
a lack of understanding and appreciation, on the part of academic anthropologists,
of the skills and contributions of business anthropologists. If so, it is sure to continue
to weaken with time. However, to the extent that this attitude reflects a more widespread phenomenon—some academics' general disparagement of any kind of intellectual output other than the theoretical—it may never entirely disappear.

FOOD FOR THOUGHT   Apart from the possibilities mentioned above, why might some academic
anthropologists belittle the efforts of their colleagues in business anthropology—particularly at a time when applied anthropology in general is
becoming increasingly prevalent and increasingly accepted as a distinct
field of anthropology that is making significant theoretical contributions
to the discipline?

APPLIED CULTURAL ANTHROPOLOGISTS' ROLES IN BUSINESS

Most business anthropologists play one of two very different roles in the companies
for which they work. Some focus on the products that businesses produce (for example, by helping businesses to develop attractive, salable products and to market
these products successfully), while others focus on business organizations themselves (for example, by helping businesses to improve the efficiency with which
they are run).

No matter what their topical focus or employment status, however, business anthropologists rely on the same methods other kinds of applied cultural anthropologists use, especially participant observation, informant interviewing, focus groups, various survey methods, and network analysis (see Aguilera 1996:736). They also research and analyze many of the same cultural variables as other anthropologists, such as beliefs and values, social structure, and gender-related behavior differences. In general, their work includes the same steps that characterize other kinds of applied cultural anthropology (see Chapter 2, p. 27).

There is, however, a major methodological difference between business anthropology and other kinds of applied cultural anthropology. Because in most cases the ultimate goal of private sector economic activity is to sell products in order to make a profit, businesses are highly competitive. (This statement must be qualified by "in most cases" because in one part of the private sector, the private nonprofit sector, private citizens run businesses, charitable foundations, NGOs, PVOs, or religious institutions not to make a profit but for humanitarian purposes.) The profit motive usually means that the "product cycle" of any given item produced by a business—the amount of time between the development and introduction of a product and its decline—tends to be relatively short. For this reason, research undertaken by business anthropologists is usually of much shorter duration and involves far fewer informants than academic research does (Hafner 1999:G1).

Focus: The Organization

Corporate Cultures.   Perhaps the most important contribution of cultural anthropology to the world of business is the understanding that businesses are not only economic organizations, existing primarily to make a profit, but also groups of people, similar in many respects to the other kinds of human groups more traditionally studied by cultural anthropologists. A business, like a small-scale society or subculture, exists under a set of institutionalized rules and policies. It consists of many individuals, of both sexes and a wide range of ages and educational levels, who have different skills and levels of ability. It may include members of different ethnic groups and representatives of different socioeconomic strata. Each of these individuals plays a particular role in the institutional structure of the business, and this role conveys, on each, a particular status in the corporate hierarchy.

Words such as *hierarchy, role, structure,* and *status* suggest why the precepts of cultural anthropology are so relevant to businesses. Just like the other kinds of organizations cultural anthropologists study—ethnic groups, age groups, descent groups, common-interest groups, residential groups, and so on—every private sector enterprise has its own unique culture: its own social structure, its founding myth, its history, its customs and traditions, its documents and artifacts, its current gossip and in-jokes, its own particular work ethic and dress code, a particular way in which employees interact, a particular slot in an overall structure that includes governments, unions, and other private sector enterprises, and so on. In the case of a business, these add up to what is called the organization's **corporate** (or **organizational**) **culture** (see Godley and Westall 1996; Jordan 1997). The older the company, the richer and more complex its corporate culture.

◇ *Employees of a business share a "corporate culture" consisting of elements such as a particular social structure, work ethic, and dress code. Not infrequently, this shared culture leads to non-business relationships among co-workers.*

An important contribution of business anthropologists to business organizations is their systematic understanding of corporate or organizational culture (Kotter 1992; Reeves-Ellington 1999). They have the ability to "penetrate" corporate cultures (Garza 1991:74) and to elicit not only formal but also informal knowledge from them. (The ethical considerations surrounding this kind of research are discussed below.) Business anthropologist Eleanor Wynn, who has worked for a number of high-tech companies on a consulting basis, compares the work she did for one of them, the Xerox Corporation, to "going to deepest, darkest New Guinea. . . . What goes on in an R&D [research and development] computer lab . . . was one of the strangest things I'd ever seen" (quoted in Corcoran 1993:H6). Which individuals in the community are the leaders, and which the followers? What common beliefs, values, and attitudes do members of the group hold? What does the existing political hierarchy, according to which power and authority are wielded and responsibility is delegated, look like? How is information passed among group members? How do group members relate to and communicate with each other? What causes disputes among group members, and how are these resolved?

It is sometimes difficult to convey to business managers that probing the answers to these and other anthropological questions can lead to corporate policy recommendations that can help a business function more smoothly, and thus more profitably. Anthropological theory is hard to "sell" to the average businessperson (Aguilera 1996:737). Moreover, the task—once managers have accepted that business anthropology has merit—is often quite complex and theoretical, since a business anthropologist's analysis of the culture of a business organization can be approached in different ways. Any cultural anthropologist, attempting to unravel and make explicable the culture of a small-scale society, has a number of different models from which to choose: examples include Malinowski's functionalism, Levi-Strauss's structuralism, Geertz's symbolic approach, and Marcus's postmodern approach. Each of these models (and there are many others as well) provides a different means of conceiving of, and investigating, the culture of a group of people. Any of them can be used as a conceptual tool for investigating the culture of a business organization.

No matter what the model, a business anthropologist views a business as a bounded community of people to be studied, analyzed, and understood in the same terms as other such communities. Applied anthropologist Judith Benson, for example, worked for Kaiser Permanente, a health care management firm, where her responsibilities ranged from conducting focus groups, to setting up a computerized system for processing clients' complaints, to managing a local call center (Benson 2000). When Kaiser decided to embark on a "re-engineering" project intended to implement significant organizational changes within the company, Benson "smoothed the way for process change by providing guidance to team members on how to identify the cultural context within which the change would take place" (ibid.:26). One of her concerns was to ensure that any changes made to the corporate culture would be sustainable for affected employees, a task she addressed by developing a series of strategies that promoted communication, idea sharing, and collaboration among employees:

> I worked closely with individuals whom I recognized as potential roadblocks to the process change. . . . I spent time with these major stakeholders to understand their points of view. At the same time, I worked with team members so that they could develop the process change in a way that blended with rather than confronted the existing cultural context. (ibid.)

Occupational Cultures.   Just as businesses can be viewed as cultures, so, too, can occupational groups. In a big automobile manufacturing corporation, for example, the two largest of these groups, labor and management, can be viewed as two different subcultures, the members of which must communicate effectively and work harmoniously together if the business is to make a profit (Trice 1993:160ff.). To continue the example, an automobile manufacturing corporation also employs other, smaller groups of people—automotive designers, engineers, assembly workers, managers, secretaries, maintenance staff, and many others—each of which can be approached as a distinct subculture of the business. Workers in each group share a particular **occupational culture,** which makes them similar, in many respects, to the members of any other cultural grouping. The members of an occupational culture will almost certainly share "occupation-based myths, ceremonies, symbols, languages and gestures, physical artifacts, sagas and legends, rituals, taboos, and rites," and present themselves to the outside world in specific ways. They may spend leisure time together or even marry one another (Trice 1993:21, 33–34).

Its occupational culture provides a group of employees with "rules of the road," guiding members in how to get along with one another and achieve collective goals. For example, a typical group may "embrace ethnocentrism, a 'we-ness' that mobilizes members to be loyal insiders" (Trice 1993:20). They may view themselves as having a particular relationship to other occupational groups within the corporation, to similar occupational groups in other corporations, or to society at large. The business anthropologist, a specialist in the social meanings behind group identity, may be uniquely placed to facilitate positive relationships between different occupational groups working side by side in the same business (ibid.).

What are the advantages and disadvantages of social relationships among employees, both to businesses and to their employees? As a business manager, would you encourage or discourage after-hours social gatherings for employees? What about employee sports teams? political organizations? religious groups? Explain your answers.

Tacit Knowledge Management.   All workers gradually develop **tacit knowledge,** an informal body of knowledge gained in the course of doing a particular job (Baba 1998:B4). This kind of knowledge contrasts with formal knowledge in that it is not made explicit. For example, a factory worker may have an "informal mental map" of the way raw materials actually flow through a manufacturing process, a map that may reflect what really happens on the shop floor more accurately than what is shown on an idealized schematic drawing of the manufacturing process (ibid.). An important part of what business anthropologists do is to tease out tacit knowledge that would otherwise remain hidden.

Business executives who understand workers' various bodies of tacit knowledge can use these to improve the efficiency with which a business is run—which ultimately, of course, helps increase profits. This skill is called **tacit knowledge management.** The tacit knowledge of a group of experienced, long-term employees, for example, can sometimes be "captured" and taught to incoming employees (Baba 1998:B4). This may be accomplished formally, by means of orientation lectures or written guidelines for new employees, but is more often done quite informally, by having long-term employees talk to newcomers about a corporation's history and traditions (Laabs 1992:27).

Cultural Audits.   Sometimes businesses fail to reach their production or sales goals, despite reasonable investments in capital and labor. Sometimes they experience strikes or other disputes. In such cases, a business anthropologist may be hired to carry out a **cultural audit,** a detailed study of the company undertaken in order to pinpoint discrepancies between the company's goals and what is really going on (Weber 1986:43). A cultural audit can be conducted by a permanent employee of the company but is more apt to be done by an outside consultant. In either case, the results of a cultural audit are considered highly confidential, since companies—particularly publicly traded ones—usually prefer not to air their problems publicly.

To perform a cultural audit, a business anthropologist interviews employees at all levels of the business, from night watchmen to assembly workers to the managers on "mahogany row." The cultural auditor is interested not only in employees' opinions (both positive and negative) and their suggestions for improvement, but also in their values, feelings, attitudes, and expectations about the company and their place within it.

Interviewees are asked a wide range of questions. What are the company's goals, and what strategies are employed to reach these goals? What happens when these goals are not met? How can the workplace atmosphere best be characterized? What positions do the interviewees occupy in the company, and what do they feel they are contributing to the company's success? How they are expected to behave and to communicate with others? Do these expectations reflect reality? What mechanisms exist through which employees can make their opinions, ideas, or grievances heard? Are performance incentives offered, and, if so, to whom and under what circumstances? Do they work? Why or why not? These questions are merely examples of the types of questions asked by cultural auditors; the range is virtually limitless.

Sometimes a cultural auditor goes outside the immediate company to interview members of its board of directors or even its stockholders. The information collected is put together in the form of a report containing specific recommendations (or "options"), on the basis of which the company's managers or directors can take specific corrective actions.

A cultural audit undertaken at General Motors (GM), for many years one of the giants of the American automobile manufacturing industry, provides an example. A few years ago, management observed that some of the employees who had worked long-term in any one of GM's overseas branches seemed discontented and less than fully productive on their return to the United States (Briody and Baba 1991). Many returnees, for their part, felt their overseas work had not been sufficiently appreciated and that their status in the company had suffered because of their overseas service. Business anthropologist Elizabeth Briody, a full-time employee of GM, undertook a cultural audit of the company to help its managers solve the problem.

Briody conducted a series of interviews with GM employees at all levels of the company. The results were interesting. It turned out that some of GM's domestic operations were administratively linked, or "coupled," with overseas operations, while others were not (Briody and Baba 1991). Employees of "de-coupled" domestic operations saw themselves as GM's "elite" (Garza 1991:78). Their managers had little understanding of—or appreciation for—the importance of overseas work, and they sometimes shunted employees returning from overseas assignments into less promising career paths.

On the basis of her cultural audit, Briody was able to recommend some specific ways in which GM could improve returning employees' productivity and job satisfaction. In addition to coupling operations, she recommended, for example, the establishment of an exchange program in which American and foreign workers would trade places for a few years and then return to their original jobs without having sidetracked their careers (Garza 1991:78).

Organizational Change.   Businesses, like cultures, are dynamic rather than static. Big transnational corporations, in particular, are in a constant state of flux, expanding to take advantage of economies of scale, contracting or restructuring for greater efficiency, constantly implementing innovations to encourage greater productivity. One innovation that has become very popular in the past fifteen years is a change from a department-based structure to a team-based structure. An aerospace company in which all the engineers were formerly assigned to the engineering department, for example, has created new "integrated product teams" (IPTs) in which all the workers involved in producing one type of aircraft, from managers to engineers to shop floor workers, are organized into a single team. Another popular innovation is "self-directed work teams" (SDWTs), the members of which manage themselves (to a greater or lesser extent, depending on the company). Both kinds of teams have been shown to enhance productivity and to contribute to employees' sense that they are an integral and important part of a larger pattern (Jordan 1997, 1999). A major role for business anthropologists is to contribute to such organizational changes.

The team structure is particularly well suited to anthropological analysis. Applied anthropologist Judith Benson, for example, is employed by the Boeing Company, where integrated product teams have recently been incorporated into the structure of the business. Recently, Benson helped to improve Boeing's IPTs by interviewing shop floor mechanics. She was able to recommend specific changes in the way team leaders worked with their teams, which fostered Boeing's goal of involving its entire labor force in "determining the course of work" (Benson 2000:27).

Focus: The Product

A second major role for business anthropologists involves helping businesses to improve their products, develop new products, or improve the way their products are presented to consumers.

Product Development.   Some business anthropologists specialize in helping businesses design and develop products that will result in profits for the company. The key to success in this area is an understanding of **consumer demand**—consumers' level of desire and urgency to purchase a particular item or service—and how to stimulate it (see Sherry 1995, especially Part Four). What products are consumers likely to purchase? Which are they likely to avoid, and why? Which might be modified to enhance their appeal? Some product elements affecting consumer demand (such as price, ease of use, efficacy, and attractiveness) are obvious, but others, such as the unconscious meanings consumers may associate with particular products, are less so. To obtain information on consumer demand, business anthropologists conduct ethnographic research, interviewing and observing consumers in their "natural habitats" (Hafner 1999). The field methods they use include one-on-one interviews, focus groups, and even videotaping.

As an example, a business anthropologist recently undertook research on behalf of a corporation manufacturing surgical instruments, to assess medical doctors' demand for these instruments. The method used was to observe emergency-room doctors on the job, in order to gain insight into how the doctors actually used the instruments (Baba 1998:B4). In prior interviews, the doctors had reported that their main concern was that their instruments be highly accurate. However, the anthropologist discovered through direct observation that speed was actually more important than accuracy; the doctors preferred instruments that permitted them to work rapidly. This insight convinced the company to redesign its surgical instruments, and its market share increased (Baba 1998:B4).

The burgeoning high-technology field is particularly ripe for anthropological input into product development. Business anthropologists are increasingly called upon to help generate ideas for new technologies or new ways to use existing ones (Hafner 1999:G8) as well as to provide businesses with a clearer understanding of the effects of new technologies on consumers (Sherry 1999:19). In order to develop ideas for new products and services, for example, applied anthropologist Bonnie A. Nardi has studied the ways in which workers use technology at Apple Computers and AT&T (Hafner 1999:G1). Jean Canavan, a business anthropologist and manager of culture and technology initiatives at Motorola, has described how a 1996 study of pager use in rural China, where there is a scarcity of telephones, "prompted Motorola to start thinking seriously about two-way paging outside urban markets" (ibid.).

Marketing. Advertising is perhaps the most obvious of the marketing techniques employed by businesses, but there are many other steps in the successful marketing of consumer goods and services (see Sherry 1995:3–44). Business anthropologists involved in marketing use standard anthropological field methods (the same techniques are employed in social marketing; see "Social Marketing Methods," Chapter 10, p. 233). Their goals include helping private businesses identify the potential consumers of a product, raising consumers' awareness of the product, and creating demand for the product through, for example, appealing advertising, user-friendly websites, attractive packaging, appropriate product placement, and affordable pricing (ibid.). In the words of one applied anthropologist and marketing expert, "there is no better way to get closer to the consumer . . . than by using ethnography" (ibid.).

FOOD FOR THOUGHT

One business anthropologist, who as an undergraduate double-majored in anthropology and economics, is now a marketing communications specialist for a high-tech manufacturing company (Stephens 2002:39). One of her main responsibilities is producing content for the Web. She claims that studying anthropology gave her "a healthy respect for language" as well as an understanding of how people "present themselves" (ibid.). What other lessons or skills, derived from the study of cultural anthropology, might prepare one for a job in which the Internet was a major means of communication with a company's customers and potential customers? Would using the Net to communicate with the company's suppliers or financiers require the same or different skills? Explain your answer.

One area in which business anthropologists are playing a growing role is **market research,** defined as the "applications-oriented study of broad cultural patterns and trends, as well as subcultural or ethnic group variability, aimed at determining characteristics that affect consumer behavior" (Baba 1986:13). The market researcher attempts to determine the distinguishing features of various cultural contexts, and the factors that might motivate consumers, within those contexts to buy particular products. Related questions include identifying the places where consumers would expect to purchase particular products, what kind of packaging would encourage them to purchase these products, and how much money they would be willing to spend. The most common technique used by business anthropologists involved in market research is to conduct individual interviews or focus groups with potential purchasers of a product, in order to gain information on their needs, values, opinions, likes, and dislikes.

Since not all consumers are alike in any society, the market researcher usually differentiates among potential consumers by factors such as sex, generation, age, occupation, socioeconomic status, level of education, place of residence, ethnic group affiliation, and geographical context (see Burkhalter 1986:116–117). This aspect of market research is termed **market segmentation.** The business anthropologist attempts to understand, for example, what kinds of consumers, as distinguished by specific characteristics, would be likely to purchase a particular product, and how these consumers' expectations about the product (for performance or longevity, for example) might vary.

Business anthropologists involved in market research also analyze the constantly shifting symbolic meanings consumers attach to products. An important factor here is consumers' conscious or unconscious desire to create or enhance a particular image of themselves or their economic or social status. A number of corporations employ business anthropologists specifically to help them create image-enhancing products.

AN APPLIED CULTURAL ANTHROPOLOGIST AT WORK

JOHN W. SHERRY

I'm an anthropologist for Intel Corporation, the company that makes microprocessors. Most people think that sounds a little strange—an anthropologist working for a microprocessor manufacturer—but it's not as strange as you might think. Applied anthropology has a lengthy history in the business world, helping firms better understand their own internal organizations, and  today these firms are becoming increasingly interested in the use of ethnographic methods to gain a better understanding of their customers. This is particularly true in the high-tech industry, where the use of ethnographic methods is a fairly natural outgrowth of requirements gathering and participatory design. Some anthropologists have been doing this kind of work for a long time—two examples are Lucy Suchman (formerly of Xerox Palo Alto Research Center) and Bonnie Nardi, who has worked at Apple Computers and AT&T.

I feel very lucky to have a job like this. Sometimes anthropologists wind up in jobs they never even dreamed of. That wasn't true in my case—I'd been hoping that a technology company would be interested in getting a detailed understanding of how people actually use their products.

This possibility occurred to me while I was doing my Ph.D. dissertation research. I worked with a community-based environmental justice organization of the Navajo Nation, a group whose members were struggling to defend their land from mining, timber cutting, toxic waste dumping, and other abuses. They wanted to create an organization they felt was "truly Navajo," but at the same time, they needed to interact, via the medium of technology, with all kinds of outsiders—lawyers, grant makers, politicians, non-native activists, urban environmental groups. It's not hard to imagine the frustrations and challenges that both the outside groups and the technologies brought to the lives of these courageous Navajo activists. This kind of technology use, it seems, will only get more common as Western goods and services find their way into the most remote corners of the world.

Chevrolet, for example, eager to command a position at the top of the lucrative sport utility vehicle (SUV) market, hired business anthropologist Ilsa Schumacher to study how car buyers decide which vehicle to purchase (Shuldiner 1994). Focusing on the symbolic role played by automobiles and consumers' "intangible motivations" to purchase them, Schumacher conducted in-depth interviews with car buyers in order to discover what sort of image SUVs have in potential purchasers' minds. Some potential buyers, she found, were eager to overcome "gender identification." Women with children, in particular, liked the fact that SUVs, unlike station wagons, do not announce to the world "I'm a mother" (Shuldiner 1994:C6). Other consumers viewed SUVs as simultaneously safe and adventurous (ibid.:C3). Chevrolet's use of this kind of information has helped to make SUVs enormously popular. Indeed, says marketing expert Ilsa Schumacher, "if a marketer is skillful enough to equate his or her product with [its] deeper symbolism, they have the potential to turn it from just another good product into a cultural icon" (Shuldiner 1994:C3).

At Intel, in the Intel Architecture Labs, I work with a small group of social scientists in a group called People and Practices Research. Our collective goal is to identify new uses for computing power by understanding the needs of real people. We call it "design ethnography."

The process is pretty simple. We start by identifying a group of people that we know is not well served by current technology products—a minority group, for instance, or people over sixty years old, or small business owners. Once a specific group has been identified, we try to ascertain the activities, engaged in by its members, that technology—I should say, well-designed technology—might support or enhance or make more enjoyable, to the point that people might actually want it. Our fieldwork isn't all that different from academic anthropological fieldwork, except that it's usually shorter in duration and involves the liberal use of other resources (such as marketing or demographic research data—and, of course, any literature we can get our hands on).

Back in our offices, we use pictures, videos, transcripts of stories, and whatever other resources we can to give our engineering and design colleagues a rich sense of the concerns, the activities, and the lives of the people we worked with in the field. Sometimes we'll try to re-create the spaces they occupied—a family room or a small office, for example. Sometimes we'll show hundreds of pictures and tell accompanying stories to try to inspire new ways of thinking about how to deliver computing power to people in ways that fit with their lives and practices. Always the goal is to answer this question: what kinds of practices can we make better for people by adding technology? Half the battle is to understand where technology might be a disruption to people and to avoid the mistakes and frustrations that such disruptions cause.

It's a great job, and the good news is, there seems to be a growing market for applied cultural anthropologists in this field. A number of firms, including some of the "dot com" Internet firms, are actively looking for people with ethnographic research skills to help them better understand their customers, and thus create better products.

INTERNATIONAL BUSINESS ANTHROPOLOGY

Thus far, this chapter has addressed business anthropology as if businesses were self-contained social organizations, and the products and services they produce were intended to appeal only to North American consumers. Many of today's corporations, of course, are transnational: varying proportions of their operations and sales take place in foreign countries, and their products are intended to appeal to consumers worldwide. Most of the large, U.S.-based manufacturing corporations now have offices, and often manufacturing plants and sales outlets as well, in foreign countries, for reasons such as the availability of inexpensive labor, access to wider markets, or tax advantages.

Because transnational corporations aim to produce products in other countries and to market products to international consumers, **international business anthropology** accounts for an increasing proportion of all business anthropology. International business anthropologists help transnational corporations conduct business successfully in foreign countries, sell their products successfully to consumers in these countries, and manage employees who represent different cultures and traditions (see Serrie 1986; Ferraro 1998; Brannen and Fruin 1999). Their work centers on three main areas: international marketing, cross-cultural orientation, and cross-cultural translation. In all three areas, an understanding and appreciation of foreign countries, cultures, and peoples are fundamental.

International Marketing

When Henry Ford first began to manufacture automobiles in the United States, he sold them to U.S. buyers. An Englishman wishing to buy an automobile bought it in Britain, from a British manufacturer, not from the Ford Motor Company. Today, however, the market for Ford automobiles is worldwide.

Perhaps the most compelling reason behind this phenomenon is that new markets for Western-style consumer goods are constantly being created, especially in the developing world, thanks to continuing global economic development (see Chapter 5). In addition, the late-twentieth-century revolution in global communications has made certain widely advertised consumer products almost universally familiar, and innovations in transportation have helped ensure that products made in one country can be relatively quickly and inexpensively shipped to others. The globalization of industry (see Rhinesmith 1996) means that international corporations need employees with expertise in other cultures, and such corporations are increasingly hiring international business anthropologists who are familiar with the languages and the cultures of the foreign countries in which corporations wish to sell their products.

One of the main roles of international business anthropologists is marketing. Corporations wishing to market their products internationally must create advertising campaigns that portray their products in ways that appeal to people who live in different parts of the world and who have different values (see Table 9.1). They call upon business anthropologists to supply information, about countries targeted for foreign sales, on the values and customs of the country's population and on any cultural taboos that must be avoided.

⬦ **TABLE 9.1**   **Some Differences in Values and Characteristics
Between People of Different Cultures**

	Non-Western Cultures	Western or Westernized Cultures
Values	Collectivism; family achievement and reputation	Individualism; personal achievement and reputation
	Elderhood	Youthfulness
	Cooperation	Competition
	Symbolic associations derived from traditions other than Greco-Roman and Christian	Symbolic associations derived mainly from Greco-Roman and Christian traditions
Widespread Characteristics	Orientation toward the past	Orientation toward the future
	Formality in social relations	Informality in social relations
	Relative inequality of sexes	Relative equality of sexes
	Holistic worldview	Fragmented worldview
	Primacy of kinship affiliations	Primacy of affiliations other than kinship

Source: Adapted from Ferraro 1998:112.

FOOD FOR THOUGHT   In Eastern Caribbean countries, fresh fish, fruits, and vegetables—traditional diet staples—are inexpensive and readily available. However, for a decade or so, more expensive canned or frozen substitutes, imported from Canada and the United States, have been available in most grocery stores. Perhaps because these products are advertised whereas fresh local products generally are not, many people now prefer, and buy, imported foods. Are international companies, eager to expand sales into the less affluent countries of the world, justified in aggressively marketing items that are popular although higher-priced than their local equivalents? If not, why not? If so, should this activity be controlled or regulated? If so, by whom?

If company executives do not understand their target market from a cultural point of view, it can cost them dearly. Cultural anthropologist Dan Varisco, a specialist in Middle Eastern ethnography, tells of a U.S.-based company that was trying to sell sneakers in the Middle East. The company's product developers thought it would be a good idea to emboss a symbol representing Allah, the God of Islam, on the sole of each shoe. But stepping on a symbol of Allah is considered blasphemy by Muslims, so the company failed to sell many pairs of sneakers (D. Varisco: pers. comm.). Any anthropologist with a specialty in Middle Eastern ethnography could have foreseen this and warned the company against it.

Cross-Cultural Orientation

In the present era of increasing globalization, large companies are becoming more and more transnational, and hence more and more multicultural. Many corporations headquartered in North America or western Europe have established branch offices or manufacturing facilities in Latin American, Asian, African, and (more recently) eastern European countries. Other corporations, headquartered in other parts of the world (especially Japan), have established offices or facilities in the West. In these corporations, "peoples with very different values, experiences, and worldviews are brought together through the immediacy and convenience of modern transportation, telecommunications, and global information systems" (Hamada 1999b:3).

In most cases, the managers of these international corporations oversee workforces that are multicultural. From management's point of view, the workforce may be completely alien and unfamiliar. An example is provided by a paper-coating factory in the United States that was recently taken over by Japanese management (Brannen and Fruin 1999). In other cases, the employees of international corporations—particularly managers—are being sent abroad to work in overseas offices and plants. These employees are usually expected to remain abroad for several years, in order to amortize the considerable expense of moving them, their families, and their household goods to distant foreign locations. Because thousands of U.S.-based corporations now conduct business abroad, tens of thousands of workers and their families, termed *expatriates,* are sent overseas every year. It is estimated that on average, each North American employee who is sent abroad but fails to adjust to an overseas assignment, returning home before his or her assignment is completed, costs a company between three and five times the employee's base salary (Ferraro 1998:12).

These modern intercultural business relationships can result in cultural alienation: feelings, on the part of those working in multicultural work settings, of unhappiness, estrangement, stress, or irrelevance. Today such alienation is a common if unwelcome characteristic of transnational corporations, potentially highly detrimental in that it may diminish the effectiveness and efficiency with which employees carry out their jobs (Hamada 1999b:3). Alienated employees, immersed in an unfamiliar, polyethnic, corporate culture where those with whom they work (and among whom they may live) may not even speak their language, sometimes feel they are not fully integrated into the culture of the business, or that they are irrelevant in terms of decision making (Brannen and Fruin 1999:20).

To perform their jobs successfully, whether stationed in foreign countries or managing multicultural workforces, businesspeople must be able to interact smoothly with others whose culture is unfamiliar to them, not only on the job but off the job as well. Another of the responsibilities of international business anthropologists, therefore, is **cross-cultural orientation** (or **cross-cultural training**). The business anthropologist works closely with corporate employees, and sometimes family members as well, helping them to understand, appreciate, and adjust to working with (and sometimes living among) people whose culture is very different from their own (see Ferraro 1998:150ff.). A typical international business anthropologist specializing in cross-cultural orientation has particular expertise in one culture or one area of the world and is bilingual. He or she may provide language training for employees (and sometimes family members) as well as help them understand and appreciate the alien culture they are about to encounter.

Ultimately, for transnational businesses to succeed, they must "create their own cultures" (Brannen and Fruin 1999:25), cultures that must "blend, negotiate, and create new sets of values, beliefs and behavior that are not only organizationally appropriate in that they allow work to be done reliably, but are nationally and cross-nationally correct as well (ibid.:25). Business anthropologists specializing in cross-cultural orientation are increasingly being called upon to assist corporations in turning multiculturalism into a corporate asset.

Cross-Cultural Translation

Not every businessperson working with foreigners, at home or abroad, requires a lengthy orientation to their culture and language. A businessperson may travel to a foreign country for only a short time; a foreign corporation may send representatives to visit a Western one. Even short-term encounters, however, require specific information on the customs, beliefs, values, expectations, and behaviors of foreigners, in order for businesspeople to be able to cope gracefully with the cultural differences they encounter. A token of regard in one country, for example, might be interpreted as a bribe in another (Burkhalter 1987:20), and ignorance on either side could make or break a business deal. Nonverbal communication—facial expressions, gestures, posture, and so on—may be as important as words (Ferraro 1998:66–67).

When in-depth orientation to a foreign culture is not required, a corporation may hire a business anthropologist to provide **cross-cultural translation.** The term refers not to the translation of words from one language into another, but of appropriate conduct from one culture into another: specifically, the day-to-day etiquette of doing business abroad.

Thus an international businessperson traveling to China for a brief visit may not need an in-depth orientation to Chinese languages and culture but will certainly need to know, for example, that in China tipping is considered an insult. A traveler to Fiji will be more comfortable if he or she knows that punctuality is much less important in Fiji than it is in North America. Businesspeople traveling to Paraguay should know that two businessmen often embrace on meeting in that country. In Australia, the familiar American thumbs-up gesture is considered rude, and in Brazil, the OK sign, with the thumb and index finger forming a circle, is an obscene gesture. The familiar up-and-down and side-to-side motions of the head, signifying yes and no in the United States, have exactly the opposite meanings in Greece (Axtell 1985).

A corporation might also hire a consultant in cross-cultural translation to help prepare—or merely review—an advertising campaign targeting individuals in a foreign country. The failure to do this can be costly. The U.S. Dairy Association, for example, enjoyed great success domestically with its "Got Milk?" advertising campaign and decided to expand it to include Mexico. It was soon brought to the association's attention that the Spanish translation of "Got milk?" reads "Are you lactating?" (Anon. 1999:32).

◊ *Cross-cultural translation involves translating not words but appropriate behavior from one culture to another. International business people need to know, for instance, that the familiar American "thumbs up" gesture is considered rude elsewhere.*

THE ETHICS OF BUSINESS ANTHROPOLOGY

A fundamental principle of research in cultural anthropology (and the most important point in the American Anthropological Association's code of ethics) is that the anthropologist will never cause harm to his or her informants or collaborators (see Chapter 4). This principle applies to business anthropologists as rigorously as it does to other kinds of cultural anthropologists, applied or academic. Some of what business anthropologists do, however—especially in the area of organizational culture (such as eliciting informal or tacit knowledge from employees)—raises uncomfortable questions about how information collected by business anthropologists will be used (Baba 1998:B5).

FOOD FOR THOUGHT Suppose a business anthropologist, undertaking a cultural audit of a major company, interviewed several employees who independently claimed that the company's hiring practices were discriminatory. Responding to questions from the anthropologist, the employees making this claim admitted that they had not discussed it, either among themselves or with their supervisors, for fear of losing their jobs. Should the anthropologist include this serious allegation in her report to the company's management? Why or why not?

Ideally, the information business anthropologists provide to their corporate employers will benefit employees, by—for instance—enabling management to improve working conditions in a company. It is possible, however, that the results of anthropological research might also be used to employee's detriment—for example, to "streamline operations and eliminate jobs" or "make [individuals'] work more demanding or stressful" (Baba 1998:B5; see also Garza 1991:78). Business anthropologists are often faced with the need to fulfill their responsibilities to their employers while simultaneously protecting the interests of the employees on whose knowledge and trust the anthropologists rely for their livelihood (Baba 1998:B5).

Long-time business anthropologist Marietta Baba has recommended several steps business anthropologists can take to avoid behaving unethically. First, they should work only for employers "whose values are compatible with anthropological ethics" (Baba 1998:B5). Business anthropologists can discover this by briefing potential employers on cultural anthropology's—and their own—ethical principles before signing consulting contracts. Second, business anthropologists should understand how their findings might be used before they agree to work for a given business, most especially if the business is under pressure to improve the efficiency of its operations or increase productivity (ibid.). Finally, business anthropologists should ensure, before their research begins, that both managers and employees understand, and are satisfied with, the terms and conditions of the proposed research (ibid.).

CONCLUSION

Chapter 1 pointed out that applied cultural anthropology is often intentionally philanthropic; in most domains of application, a primary goal is to help to answer basic needs and provide basic services in order to improve needy people's quality of life. Indeed, the opportunity to work with and serve the interests of the less fortunate is what draws many applied cultural anthropologists into the field. Because government at various levels, and to a lesser extent not-for-profit organizations, shoulder the responsibility for answering people's basic needs and providing basic human services, a preponderance of applied cultural anthropologists—about 60 percent (Baba 1998: B4)—are employed either in the public or private nonprofit sectors.

Business anthropology differs conspicuously from other domains of applied anthropology in several respects: it is not mainly philanthropic in intent, but dedicated instead to helping businesses to become more profitable; it represents a minority (although a significant minority) of all applied cultural anthropology; and it is usually undertaken in the private, for-profit sector rather than the public or private nonprofit sectors. Applied cultural anthropology students, many of whom envision themselves in future careers in which they derive personal satisfaction from helping improve disenfranchised people's quality of life, sometimes express less interest in business anthropology than in other career areas because of one or a combination of these factors. Business anthropology deserves students' careful consideration, however, for three reasons.

First and most important, business anthropology is a service-oriented field like other domains of applied cultural anthropology. Business anthropologists may not deal with life-and-death issues—or even basic needs and services—but they indisputably help to improve people's quality of life. Those business anthropologists whose primary interest and unit of analysis is the business organization, and whose contributions to such organizations include researching and analyzing corporate and occupational cultures, undertaking cultural audits, eliciting and managing tacit knowledge, or developing and implementing cross-cultural orientation and translation programs, reap great personal rewards from contributing to the job satisfaction of working people around the world. Those whose primary unit of analysis is the product, and whose major responsibility is to help businesses develop salable products, elicit consumer demand for these products, and improve the way products are marketed, derive equally great satisfaction from helping provide people with products they need and want.

Second, while it is true that most business anthropologists work in the private sector, there are some public sector jobs available in this domain. Government agencies, at various levels, sometimes hire business anthropologists, for example, to assist members of minority groups to start up new businesses (see Burkhalter 1987) or to develop private–public partnerships. Occasionally, NGOs or other nonprofits employ business anthropologists to help with public relations, fund raising, or organizational restructuring.

Last but not least, the field of business anthropology is growing rapidly, meaning that jobs may be more readily available in this domain than in some others. Over the past twenty years, a steadily increasing proportion of all applied cultural anthropologists has embraced business anthropology as a career. At the same time, an increasing number of businesses—most of them large corporations—have come to realize and appreciate the value of business anthropologists' contributions. Not surprisingly, American business schools have begun to offer courses in business anthropology, books on the subject are being written, and professional papers are being published in anthropological journals. These developments all presage a continuing expansion of business anthropology.

Today, some 40 percent of all applied anthropologists work in the private, for-profit sector, most of them for large corporations or consulting companies, either full-time or as independent contractors (Baba 1998:B4). According to Larry Prusak of IBM, "there's going to be a huge flourishing of [business] anthropologists in the next twenty years. . . . we're in the infancy of this area" (Hafner 1999:G8).

KEY TERMS

business anthropology   the kind of applied cultural anthropology in which anthropological ideas and methods are used to achieve practical goals in the private sector

consumer demand   consumers' level of desire and urgency to purchase an item or service

corporate anthropology   a synonym for *business anthropology*

corporate culture   the culture of a business, including its social structure, history, myths, documents, artifacts, work ethic, and dress code; also termed *organizational culture*

cross-cultural orientation   an area of international business anthropology in which anthropologists help American workers, transferred to foreign countries, to adjust to their new living and working conditions

cross-cultural training   a synonym for *cross-cultural orientation*

cross-cultural translation   an area of international business anthropology concerned with the day-to-day etiquette of doing business abroad

cultural audit   in business anthropology, a study of the discrepancies between the ideal and actual conduct of business within a company

industrial anthropology   a near-synonym for *business anthropology,* which refers specifically to anthropological research focusing on large-scale industry

international business anthropology   business anthropology that involves helping transnational corporations conduct business successfully in foreign countries and sell their products successfully to consumers in these countries

market research   the study of the broad cultural patterns and trends, and variations on these by subculture or ethnic group, that affect consumer behavior

market segmentation   the process of breaking down groups of potential consumers by factors such as sex, generation, age, socioeconomic status, ethnic group affiliation, and geographical context

occupational culture   the culture of an occupational group in a business organization

organizational culture   see *corporate culture*

tacit knowledge   in business anthropology, an informal body of knowledge gained in the course of doing a particular job

tacit knowledge management   in business anthropology, the use of tacit knowledge to improve the efficiency with which a business is run

N O T E S

1. Some anthropologists object to the use of the term *tribe,* since it was widely used by European colonizers to label the groups of people they dominated and exploited. Others, however, find it useful, since it has long been employed in cultural anthropology to convey specific information about a group's political, economic, and social organization (see Winthrop 1999).

2. For a recent discussion based on a similar observation, see Fell 2000.
3. The issue of *Practicing Anthropology* (Vol. 21, No. 4, Fall 1999) in which this quote appears is a special issue devoted to business anthropology; see Hamada 1999a.

R E F E R E N C E S

Aguilera, Francisco E.
   1996. "Is Anthropology Good for the Company?" *American Anthropologist* 98 (4):735–742.

Anonymous
   1999. "Madison Avenue Relevance." *Anthropology Newsletter* 40 (4):32.

Axtell, Roger E. (ed.)
   1985. *Do's and Taboos Around the World: A Guide to International Behavior.* New York: John Wiley and Sons, Inc.

Baba, Marietta L.
   1986. *Business and Industrial Anthropology: An Overview* (NAPA Bulletin No. 2). Washington, DC: NAPA.

   1998. "Anthropologists in Corporate America: 'Knowledge Management' and Ethical Angst." *Chronicle of Higher Education,* May 8, 1998: B4–B5.

Benson, Judith
   2000. "Challenging a Paradigm in Two Directions: Anthropologists in Business and the Business of Practicing Anthropology." In *Careers in Anthropology: Profiles of Practitioner Anthropologists* (NAPA Bulletin No. 20), edited by Paula L. W. Sabloff, 23–27. Washington, DC: American Anthropological Association.

Brannen, Mary Yoko, and W. Mark Fruin
   1999. "Cultural Alienation in Today's Multinational Work Arenas: Behavioral Fallout from Globalization." *Practicing Anthropology* 21 (4):20–27.

Briody, Elizabeth K., and Marietta L. Baba
1991. "Explaining Differences in Repatriation Experiences: The Discovery of Coupled and Decoupled Systems." *American Anthropologist* 93 (2):322–344.

Burkhalter, S. Brian
1986. "The Anthropologist in Marketing." In *Anthropology and International Business,* edited by Hendrick Serrie, 113–124. Williamsburg, VA: Department of Anthropology, College of William and Mary.

1987. "If Only They Would Listen: The Anthropology of Business and the Business of Anthropology." *Practicing Anthropology* 7 (4):18–20.

Chambers, Erve
1989 (orig. 1985). *Applied Anthropology: A Practical Guide.* Prospect Heights, IL: Waveland Press.

Corcoran, Elizabeth
1993. "Anthropology, Inc." *The Washington Post,* Feb. 21, 1993:H1–H6.

Fell, Kath
2000. "Analyzing Organizational Chiefdoms." *Anthropology News* 41 (4):64–65.

Ferraro, Gary P.
1998. *Cultural Dimension of International Business* (3rd ed.). Upper Saddle River, NJ: Prentice Hall.

Garza, Christina E.
1991. "Studying the Natives on the Shop Floor." *Business Week,* Sept. 30, 1991: 74–78.

Godley, Andrew, and Oliver M. Westall (eds.)
1996. *Business History and Business Culture.* Manchester, NY: Manchester University Press.

Hafner, Katie
1999. "Coming of Age in Palo Alto." *New York Times,* June 10, 1999:G1–G8.

Hamada, Tomoko
1999a (ed.) *Anthropologists and Globalization of Business Organizations. Practicing Anthropology* 21 (4) (special issue).

1999b. "Practicing Anthropology in Business Organizations." *Practicing Anthropology* 21 (4):2–4.

Jordan, Ann T. (ed.)
1997. *Practicing Anthropology in Corporate America: Consulting on Organizational Culture* (NAPA Bulletin No. 14). Arlington, VA: American Anthropological Association.

1999. "An Anthropological Approach to the Study of Organizational Change: The Move to Self-Managed Work Teams." *Practicing Anthropology* 21 (4): 14–19.

Koerner, Brendan I.
1998. "Into the Wild Unknown of Workplace Culture: Anthropologists Revitalize Their Discipline." *U.S. News Online,* Aug. 10, 1998.

Kotter, John P.
1992. *Corporate Culture and Performance.* New York: Free Press.

Laabs, Jennifer
1992. "Corporate Anthropologists." *Personnel Journal* 7 (1):81–87.

Reeves-Ellington, Richard
1999. From Command to Demand Economies: Bulgarian Organizational Value Orientations." *Practicing Anthropology* 21 (4):5–13.

Rhinesmith, Stephen H.
1996. *A Manager's Guide to Globalization: Six Skills for Success in a Changing World.* Chicago: Irwin.

Serrie, Hendrick
1984. *Anthropology and International Business* (Vol. 28, Studies in Third World Societies). Williamsburg, VA: Department of Anthropology, College of William and Mary.

Sherry, John F., Jr. (ed.)
1995. *Contemporary Marketing and Consumer Behavior: An Anthropological Sourcebook.* Thousand Oaks, CA: Sage Publications.

Sherry, John W.
1999. "Real Work." *Anthropology Newsletter* 40 (3): 19–20.

Shuldiner, Herb
1994. "Auto Anthropology." *Newsday,* Dec. 9, 1994: C3–C6.

Stephens, W. Richard
2002. *Careers in Anthropology: What an Anthropology Degree Can Do For You.* Boston: Allyn and Bacon.

Trice, Harrison M.
1993. *Occupational Subcultures in the Workplace.* Ithaca, NY: ILR Press.

Weber, Anne
1986. "Anthropologists Look at the Office." *Business Monthly,* Dec. 1986:40–42.

Winthrop, Rob
1999. "The Real World: Words and Things." *Practicing Anthropology* 21 (4):42–43.

SOCIAL MARKETING

INTRODUCTION

In January 1989, several American newspapers ran a press release about a new anti-drunk-driving initiative spearheaded by the prestigious Harvard School of Public Health in Boston, Massachusetts. Harvard had teamed up with the film industry, the advertising industry, and the media to put together what was to become one of the most successful media campaigns in recent history (Kotler and Roberto 1989:3–4).

Harvard researchers had observed that people's attitudes toward driving after having consumed alcohol differed from culture to culture. Swedish party-goers, for example, would typically decline alcoholic drinks if they would be driving later. Swedish couples, out on a date, would discuss who would have the responsibility of driving home safely (Kotler and Roberto 1989:4). Americans, in contrast, seemed to assume that everyone at a party where alcohol was served would drink. The researchers found that by the time they reached the age of eighteen, most American teenagers reported having been a passenger in a car whose driver was drunk (ibid. 1989:4)

These observations gave birth to the idea of the designated driver. To publicize this idea and to encourage those Americans who used alcohol to accept and benefit from it, the Harvard consortium used methods and techniques devised by for-profit businesses for selling commercial products (see Chapter 9). In this case, however, the "product" being "sold" was a socially beneficial idea—designating a nondrinking driver to make sure drinking friends get home safely—rather than a commercial item.

A dozen years later, the impact of this effort on Americans' behavior and attitudes toward drinking and driving has been considerable. Few Americans can say they have never been exposed to its message. Many millions, for instance, have seen the image of popular blind musician Stevie Wonder saying, "Before I'll ride with a drunk, I'll drive myself." The idea of the designated driver has penetrated the American consciousness and is now a widely accepted element of American party-going culture.

The Stevie Wonder anti-drunk-driving image is an example of **social marketing,** the use of certain ideas and methods, whose origins lie mainly in economics and behavioral psychology, that are more commonly employed in commercial advertising to "sell" a socially beneficial product, activity, or service (see Andreason 1995). Other familiar examples of social marketing are the "Just Say No" campaign to discourage the use of illegal drugs (which included TV spots on the cartoon channels showing "cool" kids "just saying no" to drugs); the arresting fried-egg image

◇ *Social marketing draws on the concepts and techniques of commercial advertising to "sell" socially beneficial ideas or products. Here, a print ad conveys the idea that driving while drunk can be fatal.*

used in the "This Is Your Brain" antidrug campaign, the "crying Indian" environmental conservation campaign, and the "Stay in School" campaign.

Social marketing relies heavily for its effectiveness on a wide variety of ideas and techniques, well known to producers of consumer goods and services, which help persuade consumers to purchase commercial products and services. In addition to various kinds of advertising, these ideas and techniques include ways in which to identify people's need for a particular product or service; methods for identifying the market segment most likely to buy the product or service (see Chapter 9); ways in which to package products for maximum impact as they sit on the store shelf; techniques for the most advantageous physical placement of goods on the store shelf; and formulas for assigning a price to a product or service that will make a profit for its producer but not deter purchasers.

Besides advertising, another example of the many ideas that social marketing has drawn from commercial marketing is *exchange theory*, the economic principle that people will pay only as much as they think a product is worth. Just as commercial advertisers rely on exchange theory to assess the most appropriate pricing for a specific product, social marketing professionals use this theory to evaluate what a public service is worth to its potential beneficiaries, usually in non-monetary terms. The "price" to an individual for enrolling in a food stamp program may be a loss of self-esteem, and if that price is too high, an individual who could otherwise benefit from using food stamps will not enroll in the program. The price can be lowered, however, through a social marketing effort that convinces a poor mother that food stamps are one of many tools she can use to support her children responsibly (Brown 1997b).

SOCIAL MARKETING AS APPLIED CULTURAL ANTHROPOLOGY

As much as social marketing owes to commercial marketing and to the economic and psychological theories that underlie it, it is equally beholden to cultural anthropology. The underlying goal of all marketing, commercial or social, is to influence people's voluntary behavior, whether that behavior is "buying a Big Mac, flying United Airlines, practicing safe sex, or getting one's child immunized" (Andreason 1997:3), and all voluntary behavior takes place within a particular cultural context. Thus selling something successfully—whether a commercial product, a service, or a socially beneficial idea—rests on understanding the cultural milieu within which an individual's voluntary decision to buy will be made. To be successful, a would-be seller must target a specific group of people (called a **target audience**) with persuasive messages tailored to the group's specific lifestyle, beliefs, and values.

In short, all marketing messages must be culturally appropriate to be effective. The major difference between commercial and social marketing is that in a commercial context, the point of such messages is to persuade people to spend their money on a particular product or service, so that a business can make a profit. In social marketing, the point is to alleviate or solve some problem affecting society, or a segment of society, by encouraging people to change their unhealthy or otherwise nonfunctional behavior.

Social marketing is more difficult to accomplish successfully than commercial marketing. The main reason is that the beneficial changes that social marketers attempt to bring about often involve changing individuals' "cultural models" (Brown 1997b:27)—long-standing, deeply ingrained, shared ideas and values—rather than simply inducing them to buy a specific product. Western culture, for example, embodies a specific cultural model of physical beauty, which is associated with particular collective ideas and values (such as "youth is more beautiful than old age"). Social marketing professionals, in attempting to get people to change their behavior, must explicitly consider not only the overall cultural context, but also the (often deeply entrenched) cultural model. The reason why it is easier to persuade people to switch cigarette brands than to stop smoking is not only that smoking is physically addictive; in addition, the act of smoking embodies deeply ingrained cultural images and values.

FOOD FOR THOUGHT What components contribute to the Western cultural model of female physical beauty? How might these components influence Westerners' behavior? Is the behavior of males and females influenced differently by these components? Why or why not? Identify other cultural models prevalent in Western culture.

The primary role of cultural anthropology in social marketing is to identify cultural models, which differ among population subgroups by ethnicity, age, sex, religion, level of education, special interests, and many other factors. "The social marketer uses anthropology to identify the social and/or cultural factors that most influence behavior in different subgroups, and uses this information to design messages that will be most effective" (Brown 1997a:59). The cartoon figure of Joe Camel, which was enormously successful in encouraging pubescent children to smoke cigarettes, provides an example. The commercial advertising specialists who designed this particular advertising campaign fully understood the cultural models of self-esteem and social popularity among American youth. Thus, they knew how compelling the camel character—suave, self-confident, admired, and engaged in exciting activities such as flying jet planes—would be to adolescent males. Likewise, the designers of a recent social marketing campaign targeting cocaine users built on a widespread cultural model of what constitutes peace and security vis-à-vis jeopardy and insecurity. In this model, the presence of handguns is closely associated with insecurity, sudden danger, and fear. Thus they chose a stark black-and-white photograph of a young man with the barrel of a handgun inserted into one nostril, fully realizing its emotional impact among the group of young people at whom the campaign was directed.

These examples show that cultural models can be used to both negative and positive effect: for example, to *encourage* smoking or to *discourage* cocaine use. They also illustrate why social marketing, like commercial marketing (Chapter 9), is a natural fit for applied cultural anthropologists. The unique ability of cultural anthropology to identify and draw on people's knowledge, beliefs, and values means that applied cultural anthropologists are increasingly in demand to help design and implement effective social marketing messages. Specifically, cultural anthropologists contribute to social marketing efforts by

> *(1) helping to identify the likely "early adopters" of specific new behaviors; (2) learning how the behavior change can best be constructed to maximize adoption . . . ; (3) showing what words, phrases, and images are appropriate to describe the behavior change so that its benefits are clearly understood and the change advocated is as nonthreatening as possible; and (4) helping to select and train change agents who can be most empathetic and effective in a given "foreign" culture.* (Kottler and Andreason 1991:420–421, quoted in Brown 1997a:57–58)

THE USES OF SOCIAL MARKETING

Social marketing enjoys a wealth of applications, in the realms of both policy formulation and direct intervention, and in both international and domestic contexts. This breadth explains why international aid agencies, governments, and private social welfare organizations frequently make use of the social marketing approach in addressing social problems. If the problem is overpopulation, for example, social marketing might be used to promote contraceptives. If the problem is deaths due to infantile diarrhea, social marketing might be used to promote the use of oral rehydration salts. If the problem is the spread of HIV/AIDS, social marketing might be used to promote safer sex. There are literally hundreds of additional social problems that might be successfully addressed by social marketing, including illiteracy, poor nutrition, smoking, child abuse, ignorance of the value of breast-feeding, lack of prenatal care, domestic violence, undereducation, unsustainable agricultural practices, water pollution, alcohol and drug abuse, unsafe food-handling practices, automotive accidents, and vaccination noncompliance. No matter what the realm of application, however, social marketing efforts are intended to benefit not just individuals (as members of target audiences) but society as a whole.

Benefiting Individuals

Social marketing specialists have identified three principal circumstances under which individuals engage in behaviors that are ultimately harmful to themselves or to society. These are ignorance; negativity about or resistance toward a particular product, service, or alternative behavior; and what experts in the field call *benefit invisibility,* the inability of individuals to apprehend the advantages of a particular product, service, or alternative behavior (Andreason 1997:5–6).

Ignorance.   First, social marketing is helpful in situations in which people are ignorant of a beneficial product, activity, or service, or do not know enough about it to realize its potential benefits. The most common explanations for this kind of ignorance are youthful naiveté, poverty, and undereducation. An example is a young mother unaware of the nutritional, disease-protective, and contraceptive value of breast-feeding her infant, as opposed to bottle-feeding.

The term *background deficit* is sometimes used to denote this lack of essential information about the existence of a problem or a potential problem, while the term *big idea* is sometimes used for a "single, indivisible message"—in this case, the value of breast-feeding a baby—which, if understood and accepted, would presumably provide a solution to the problem (Dudley 1993:21). Social marketing campaigns have often realized major successes in situations in which people with specific problems either have a background deficit and/or do not understand (or have not been exposed to) the big idea.

Negativity.   Second, social marketing is frequently used in situations in which individuals are aware of a beneficial item, activity, or service but either have no interest in it or demonstrate *negative demand* for it—an actual resistance to the item, activity, or service. An example is the reluctance of some mothers to have their children immunized. Early childhood immunization is a free, government-provided service in many parts of the world, but mothers who are aware of this may nevertheless resist immunization—even where it is required by law—because of the possibility that a newly immunized child will suffer a day or two of pain and fever. The result of this negativity is that many children remain unvaccinated and hence at risk for a variety of illnesses, at least until they are barred, for noncompliance with government regulations, from enrolling in school at the age of five or six.

Benefit Invisibility.   Finally, social marketing is often effective in instances of benefit invisibility, of which there are two kinds. In some cases, the benefit derived from implementing some particular solution to a society wide problem cannot be observed: an example is an automobile accident that is avoided because the speed limit has been reduced from sixty-five to fifty-five miles per hour. In other cases of benefit invisibility, the beneficiary of the solution to a social problem is society as a whole, rather than any particular individual. For example, recyling old newspapers, which is simply a chore to individuals, does ultimately benefit whole communities in terms of overall environmental protection, but this benefit is difficult or impossible for any given individual to detect.

Benefiting Society

In the case of behaviors that harm not just the individuals who engage in them but also society as a whole—for example, drunk driving or polluting the air everyone breathes—individuals must obviously be discouraged from engaging in these behaviors for the good of society. Sober drivers and clean air are what economists call **public goods**: they benefit society as a whole. Public goods can be damaged through the behavior of individuals, yet access to them cannot be restricted to those who refrain from this damaging behavior, and users of public goods cannot be charged individually for the benefits they enjoy because of these goods. Clean air benefits all; a lack of clean air penalizes all; but there is no way in which individuals can be charged for, or pay for, the amount of clean air they breathe.

This being the case, free market economies cannot be relied upon to provide public goods: no commercial enterprise will make a profit if it attempts to charge people for the air they breathe. Public goods are thus very different from other, commercially viable, products or services. One way to solve the problem of who should provide public goods is for a government or nonprofit social welfare organization to ensure that the public has access to them. Social marketing is often used to preserve or promote public goods by raising public awareness and persuading people to behave responsibly toward themselves and their communities.

 FOOD FOR THOUGHT — Two examples of health-related social marketing campaigns are (1) Saturday morning TV cartoon "spots" to persuade children to wear bicycle helmets and (2) advertisements in women's magazines to encourage readers to perform breast self-exams. Explain why these two very sensible ideas do not have sufficient commercial value for private interests to pay for disseminating them.

PRINCIPLES OF SOCIAL MARKETING

Two Underlying Assumptions

Social marketing rests on two fundamental assumptions. The first is that there are behaviors that can be changed—and that are worth changing—for the sake of improving the quality of life of both individuals and society. The second basic assumption is that society as a whole, or its representatives, is responsible for helping individuals to make the choices that are in their own best interests and those of society (Smith 1997:22). Implicit in these two ideas is the notion that to be successful, social marketing must be undertaken professionally, by "educated, well-intentioned professionals"; they are best able to "effectively address a variety of societal problems and, in so doing, successfully improve the lives of specific communities within society, either domestically or abroad" (Goldberg et al. 1997:ix).

These basic assumptions illustrate why the most frequent (although not the only) users of social marketing techniques are public or private organizations responsible for protecting and enhancing the public welfare somehow. Multilateral aid organizations, governments (at various levels), and social welfare organizations—especially NGOs devoted to social betterment through the promotion of some specific agenda—rely heavily on social marketing campaigns to get socially beneficial messages across to the public, usually to specific population subgroups. A good example is the many NGOs, in the United States and elsewhere, dedicated to making birth control information and supplies available to poor, undereducated women.

Marketing and Countermarketing

Some social marketing efforts are intended to promote specific beneficial behaviors (such as observing the speed limit), while others are intended to deter specific harmful behaviors (such as smoking). The latter—social marketing efforts intended to discourage behaviors that pose a threat either to individuals or to society at large—are referred to as **countermarketing** or **demarketing** efforts.

The choice of positive promotion versus countermarketing depends on both the problem to be addressed and its context. In industrialized settings, such as the United States, most social marketing efforts have been aimed at deterring specific behaviors (countermarketing), while in the developing countries of the world, such efforts more typically promote specific behaviors. Health-related social marketing efforts provide a good example: in both industrialized and developing country settings, they focus on at-risk groups, but in the United States, the intent is usually to *stop* drunk driving, smoking, or unsafe sex, while in developing countries the intent is more frequently to *promote* early childhood immunization, prenatal care for expectant mothers, or condom use.

This difference is due not only to the fact that the industrialized and developing countries are beset by different kinds and degrees of social problems; it is also due to the different kinds of information available in these two contexts. For example, many residents of developing countries, because their health education has been either inadequate or nonexistent, literally do not possess the information about healthy behavior that Westerners know so well as to take for granted. Many Westerners, in contrast, are relatively cognizant of health issues, thanks to the media and the public education system, and do not feel they need a lot more edification, pro or con, about well-publicized and well-understood issues such as birth control, safer sex, or needle exchange.

FOOD FOR THOUGHT   In the United States, cigarette advertising has been banned from certain media, such as television, to which children are routinely exposed, in an effort to prevent them from smoking as teenagers or adults. Is restricting cigarette advertising more or less effective, over the long term, than the countermarketing of cigarettes? Construct a case, from an anthropological point of view, for one side of this argument or the other.

The Four *Ps*

Most readers of this book are familiar—at least subconsciously—with the techniques that the purveyors of commercial products and services use to persuade consumers to purchase their wares. Advertising, in any of its many forms, is the most obvious of these techniques, but there are many other steps in the marketing of consumer goods and services. These include (1) thinking of a product or service for which consumer demand either exists or can be created, and then developing and manufacturing the product or designing the service; (2) identifying the potential consumers of the product or service and the places where those consumers are likely to purchase it; (3) packaging the product or promoting the service so as to encourage purchase; and (4) setting the price so as not to deter consumers from purchasing the product or service.

In commercial marketing, these activities are often referred to as the **four *Ps*—** *product, promotion, price,* and *place* (see, for example, Stead and Hastings 1997:30; Bouvier and Bertrand 1999:104). The product is the item or service to be sold;

promotion refers to the advertising strategy used to encourage potential purchasers to buy the product or service; price is the amount of money to be charged; and place refers not only to the location where the product or service will be sold, but also to the various avenues its producers can use to reach their intended purchasers.

For cultural anthropologists, promotion may be the most immediately interesting of the four *P*s because promotion must be culturally appropriate if it is to succeed. Promotion plays an important part in most social marketing efforts, but advertising is only part of what is needed to get a socially beneficial message across (Stead and Hastings 1997:30). This point is important because relying on advertising "ignores the fundamental premise . . . that decision-making should be based on a clear understanding of consumer needs" (ibid.:31). That understanding is gained only by means of intensive social marketing research.

FOOD FOR THOUGHT Suppose that you are an advertising executive working for a manufacturing company. You are largely responsible for ensuring that your company's products are profitable. Select a product produced by your company and, using the four *P*s, describe how you would go about ensuring that this product sells well enough to recover all its research and development costs and make a handsome profit for the company as well.

SOCIAL MARKETING METHODS

No two social marketing projects are exactly alike: even as a consumer's decision-making process varies depending on the product or idea to be decided upon, so do the steps in a social marketing effort vary with the intended result. However, after identifying a social problem that may be amenable to social marketing techniques and assessing whether sufficient resources exist to address the problem, the series of stages followed in any social marketing effort is more or less fixed. It includes, at a minimum, (1) background research, (2) designing a solution that will reach a group of people who are negatively affected by the problem, (3) implementing the solution by raising awareness and creating demand, and (4) evaluating the success of the project. Each of these major stages in a social marketing effort incorporates a number of distinct steps (see Figure 10.1, p. 242).

Background Research

Research is at the heart of successful social marketing, since it is only by researching and understanding the relevant cultural model and the "specific characteristics of the social products that are being marketed" that social marketing can be successful (Kotler and Roberto 1989:62). Nutritionists, for example, are unlikely to be able to change people's eating habits for the better if they do not first gain a thorough understanding of the relevant cultural models associated with food: what foods people eat, why they choose to eat only some of the foods available in their environment and not others, what symbolic values they attach to various foods, and so forth (Terry 1994). Social marketing research makes use of a number of different techniques, including focus groups, participant observation, documentary research, informant interviews, and surveys (Brown 1997a:55). Of these, focus groups are probably the most commonly used and thus most important research method. To provide as clear an understanding as possible of both the audience and the product, social marketing research is as objective as possible. Indeed, objective research is what most strongly differentiates social marketing, as the term is used today, from earlier, more subjective, and often more coercive attempts on the part of governments and social welfare organizations to encourage groups of people to accept beneficial products, actions, or services. (The latter are sometimes referred to as attempts at *social engineering*.)

Using Focus Groups.   It would be difficult to overestimate the importance to social marketing professionals, as they attempt to discover which solutions will work in which situations, of focus groups. This research technique is described in Chapter 2, p. 40 (see also Bryant and Bailey 1991; Agar and MacDonald 1995; Morgan 1997; Morgan and Krueger 1997; Stewart and Shamdasani 1998; Krueger and Casey 2000). The technique is widely employed in commercial marketing as well as social marketing. In either instance, a focus group typically consists of a trained leader and six or eight lay people, brought together to discuss—and ideally to shed light on—a particular subject. The lay members of the group, not the leader, are considered the "experts" on the subject at hand. The subject of interest is usually not addressed directly; the spontaneous interaction of the participants with each other, and often with various props provided to them, are considered more revealing than their answers to direct questions.

Props—physical objects intended to be observed and manipulated by focus group members, for the purpose of stimulating thought and conversation—are a frequent component of focus group research for social marketing purposes. Prior to a recent social marketing campaign to promote breast-feeding, for example, planners realized they needed information on what sort of image breast-feeding might elicit among members of the target population. Focus group participants were therefore shown photographs of women, with and without babies, and were asked to sort them based on which pictured women would be likely to breast-feed and which to bottle-feed (Bryant and Bailey 1991:29). They were then asked questions to compare and contrast the characteristics of the two groups: What was each group of women like? How did they differ? What kind of mothers were they? What were they thinking and feeling at the time they were photographed (ibid.)?

Defining the Audience.   An important part of the background research preliminary to any social marketing effort is defining the specific group of people at which the effort will be directed. Only when this group has been pinpointed can relevant cultural models be identified. Although this group is generically referred to as the target audience, it actually consists of multiple audiences, termed the primary, secondary, and tertiary audiences.

A **primary target audience** is a group of people who are at risk due to a specific problem that may be solved or ameliorated by a social marketing effort. The primary target audience for an early childhood immunization campaign, for example, would be mothers of infants and preschool children. Social marketing campaign planners need to understand a great deal about their primary target audience, from the most general kind of information (such as the group's demographic and socioeconomic characteristics) to the specific (such as any preconceptions, misconceptions, or misgivings members of the group may have about the specific remedy to be suggested). If an ethnography has been written about this group, it may provide a "rich source of secondary data that helps to inform the social marketing process" (Brown 1997a:57).

The **secondary target audience** consists of people who may be in a position to influence members of the primary target audience. In the case of early childhood immunization, the secondary audience might include the spouses of primary target audience members, other family members, medical or religious practitioners, or friends.

The **tertiary target audience** consists of people in positions of leadership, authority, or high regard, whom members of the primary audience look to either for advice or as role models. These individuals might include government officials or entertainment, sports, or religious figures. If a social marketing campaign is to be successful, all three target groups—primary, secondary, and tertiary—must be exposed repeatedly to its message.

FOOD FOR THOUGHT   Do you see anything even slightly morally questionable about using influential people to help change the behavior of a primary target audience? Should members of secondary and tertiary target audiences be informed of their role as potential sources of influence? How would you explain this role to members of secondary and tertiary target audiences?

Targeting Diverse Audiences.   Social marketing efforts in both Westernized and developing countries must often target culturally and ethnically disparate groups of people of different sexes and perhaps different ages as well, which makes finding an acceptable solution to a social problem all the more difficult. A social marketing program designed to encourage young people to practice safer sex, whether they live in New York City or in Cameroon, must simultaneously appeal to individuals of both sexes and from many different ethnic backgrounds, who speak several different languages. Research conducted with the help of an appropriately diverse focus group can help social marketers identify widely acceptable solutions to social problems. Alternatively, social marketing professionals may divide their target audiences into **audience segments,** subgroups distinguished by ethnicity, language, age, socioeconomic status, or other factors, and develop multiple messages delivered through several different media, each culturally appropriate to its segment, to reach the members of different audience segments.

Background research in support of a social marketing effort was undertaken recently in the small West Indian island nation of St. Lucia, in the Eastern Caribbean (Gwynne, Roberts, and Compton 1994).[1] St. Lucia is a poor country, and the government does not collect enough money, in the form of taxes, to pay for all the social services it would like to provide to the population. Thus, although almost every St. Lucian citizen is eligible for free, government-provided health care, the government has experienced great difficulty in providing adequate public health services to its citizens. In order to bring more money into the health sector and to raise the quality and quantity of health services, the government decided to explore the possibility of instituting National Health Insurance (NHI). Every working person earning a regular paycheck would be required to contribute a small percentage of his or her salary to the plan and would henceforth be covered by health insurance.

Since working St. Lucians were already accustomed to free government-provided health care *without* having to contribute a small but compulsory amount for health insurance through a payroll deduction, a social marketing campaign was needed to "sell" the socially beneficial idea of national health insurance to those who would be paying for it. The first step was background research to determine under what circumstances NHI, if it were instituted, would be considered acceptable to those who would be obliged to pay for it. Research was also needed to determine the most appropriate target audience for any subsequent social marketing campaign, as well as the best way to reach that audience. Should all workers in the formal economic sector be targeted, or just government employees (who make up the bulk of the formal workforce in St. Lucia), or just private sector employees? Who would constitute the secondary and tertiary audiences? What advertising method would most efficiently convey the message about the benefits of NHI to the three target audiences?

This background research was undertaken by an American applied cultural anthropologist specializing in international health and Caribbean ethnography, working with two West Indian counterparts: a health economist and a specialist in **social advertising,** the design and use of advertising campaigns in the mass media for social marketing purposes. Together this small team spent several weeks conducting focus group sessions with representatives of the many St. Lucian stakeholders who would be affected by NHI, including public employees (such as firefighters and nurses), union members, and the employees of private firms. The anthropologist conducted numerous individual ethnographic interviews as well.

The results proved interesting. Taken together, the focus groups and individual interviews showed that most St. Lucians have a strong preference for private medical care over public care. The possibility that National Health Insurance might give them more affordable access to private doctors thus appealed to them. The focus group sessions also suggested that most St. Lucians employed in the formal sector would not balk at a small mandatory contribution of their income to NHI in exchange for a health insurance benefit—*if* that benefit could be used in the private sector. This background information gave St. Lucian health officials something to work with as they proceeded to develop a social marketing campaign to sell the idea of National Health Insurance.[2]

Designing a Solution

After having completed the background research and defined the primary, secondary, and tertiary target audiences, social marketing professionals use their research results to frame a solution to the problem—one that will reach the at-risk individuals in the primary target audience, as well as members of the secondary and tertiary audiences acting as conduits to the primary audience. Sometimes the solution is a concrete item to be used by members of the primary target audience to their benefit, such as a condom or a water purification tablet. When social marketing involves encouraging people to use a specific item, an important part of the effort (and one that may be of particular interest to cultural anthropologists) is designing an appealing product and then naming it and packaging it in a way that will make it attractive to its intended audience. Sometimes the solution is a specific activity that would benefit the primary target audience if it replaced an alternative behavior; breast-feeding as opposed to bottle-feeding a baby is an example. Sometimes the solution is a social service, such as higher education, from which members of the primary target audience would benefit if they could be persuaded to avail themselves of it.

In designing culturally appropriate solutions to specific problems, social marketing professionals rely heavily on theories drawn from behavioral psychology and commercial advertising. Theorists in these areas have discovered, for example, that decision making is a process, not an event. As a person decides to purchase something or to accept a new idea, he or she goes through a set series of steps, called a "hierarchy of effects" (Dudley 1993:124). The sequence varies depending on the decision to be made, and even the steps themselves vary. For example, one sequence, which reflects the decision to purchase a product, includes, as steps:

awareness → interest → desire → action

For a new idea (such as a change in behavior) to be accepted, the hierarchy of effects is somewhat different (ibid.):

awareness → interest → evaluation → trial stage → acceptance

FOOD FOR THOUGHT Suppose that at the campus bookstore, you see an attractive display of rugby shirts in your college's colors, bearing the college logo. You would like to have one, although you do not really need it. Enumerate as many steps as possible in your thought process as you decide whether or not to purchase a shirt.

In the process of designing a solution, social marketing professionals may feel that in order to avoid costly mistakes, they need to test the efficacy of their design prior to implementing their solution on a large scale. *Pilot projects*, limited in scope and in the expenditure of resources, are therefore sometimes undertaken as test cases. A pilot project is especially apt to be done for a proposed solution that will be implemented widely (Brown 1997a:56). The pilot project helps identify both the strengths and the weaknesses of the project design in time to make any needed changes.

Implementing the Solution

After identifying the appropriate target audiences for a social marketing effort and designing a solution likely to prove acceptable to the primary target audience, social marketing professionals must create a demand for the solution. Creating demand consists of two separate steps: first, raising the awareness of members of the target audience about both the problem and the proposed solution, and second, encouraging members of the target audience to want the solution, whether it be an object, action, or service.

Choosing a Channel.   To accomplish these two tasks, social marketers must determine the vehicle (or **channel**) that should be used to convey information about the solution to the target groups. Choosing the channel that will most effectively project the message about the availability and desirability of the solution depends, to a high degree, on the culture of the intended recipients of the message; it therefore represents a major part of the social marketing work of applied cultural anthropologists. If both the message and the channel are appealing and culturally appropriate, they will stimulate demand for the solution. In addition to the cultural inclinations of the intended audience, of course, the choice of channel must also be based on the audience's degree of literacy (see Dudley 1993:85). In many developing countries, people are illiterate or semiliterate, but they do have access to radios and television sets.

Types of Channels.   Most social marketing efforts make use of the public information media, in its many formats, as channels. This so-called **mass media approach** involves using TV commercials or shows, radio spots or programming, or magazine and newspaper advertisements to project social marketing messages. In the Eastern Caribbean, for example, listening to the radio is a popular pastime, and radio soap operas are a particular favorite of teenagers. A recent social marketing effort made use of this aspect of Caribbean cultural life to discourage early pregnancy. (Early and multiple pregnancies have contributed to overly rapid population growth, a serious problem in the region; the fertility rate is a relatively high 3.1 children per woman, and 80 percent of all births are to single mothers.) The channel used was a radio soap opera, *Apwe Plezi* (meaning, in the local patois, "after pleasure"—a phrase from the local saying "after the pleasure comes the pain"). The story line of this radio drama recounted the many tribulations of a teenage girl who had accidentally become pregnant. The message to Caribbean teenagers was unmistakable.

Depending on the cultural context, however, the mass media approach may not adequately reach the various target audiences. Another method, the **alternative media approach,** makes use of channels such as live performances by popular singers; posters or brochures displayed or distributed in locally popular meeting places; or giveaways such as T-shirts, pens, or baseball caps bearing social marketing messages or logos. As an example, another compelling social marketing effort in the Eastern Caribbean, intended to encourage children to consume more iron-rich foods, featured calypso, a unique and traditional West Indian kind of music that is

◈ *One frequently-used social marketing method, the point-of-purchase approach, is to display social marketing messages directly on products or packaging. Anti-smoking warnings on cigarette packs are an example.*

enormously popular in the region. A popular calypsonian appeared in public schools, performing an appealing song and dance routine about the benefits of an iron-rich diet.

Another widely used method is the **point-of-purchase approach,** in which a social marketing message is displayed on a product or its packaging. In this case, the product or packaging is considered a channel. Examples include the antismoking messages (such as "smoking shortens life expectancy") now required by law on cigarette packages in the United States and similar warnings on bottles containing alcoholic beverages.

No matter what type of channel is used, the goal is the same: to get the message across to as many members of the primary, secondary, and tertiary target audiences as possible, in a culturally appropriate way—a way the members of these audiences can understand and relate to. The cited examples of effective social marketing techniques employed in the Eastern Caribbean, for instance, employ African Americans (by far the largest ethnic group in the region) speaking with distinctively Caribbean accents.

In sum, there are no hard and fast rules about the channels used in social marketing efforts. Many rely on TV shows (Kotler and Roberto 1989:363) or radio spots (Currence 1997), while others use comic books (Dudley 1993:89–90), brochures or booklets (Kotler and Roberto 1989:71; Dudley 1993:86–87), or posters containing codes such as an *X* and a checkmark to suggest wrong and right (Dudley 1993:88). Even rap music has been used successfully in social marketing efforts. All these devices must be used with extreme care and a thorough understanding of the local cultural context. In Nepal, the conventional cartoon speech bubble used in a social marketing effort was interpreted by villagers as representing a large clove of garlic (ibid.:90)!

Evaluation

Most social marketing endeavors are monitored throughout the life of the program and formally evaluated, in some cases multiple times, with the same methodologies and measurements employed to evaluate other kinds of social change projects. Chapter 2, p. 48, describes different types of evaluations, the kinds of data collected, and the methods used.

SOCIAL MARKETING FOR HEALTH

In both westernized and developing contexts, the product, activity, or service being promoted in a social marketing campaign is very frequently health related (see Kernan and Domzal 1997). Interestingly, the use of social marketing principles in the public health arena came about in large part thanks to cultural anthropology's contribution of a cultural model orientation, even though the most frequently used social marketing research method, the focus group interview, was developed by other kinds of social scientists (Coreil 1990:8).

One health-related area in which social marketing has been heavily used to good effect, especially in developing countries, is family planning, especially the promotion of contraceptives (Sherris et al. 1985; Kotler and Roberto 1989:50–58; Harvey 1997). Contraceptive supplies and devices are frequently promoted through the same techniques used to advertise any commercial product, although in the case

AN APPLIED CULTURAL ANTHROPOLOGIST AT WORK

CHRISTOPHER A. BROWN

After earning his M.A. degree in applied anthropology from the University of South Florida at Tampa, Christopher Brown found a job as a research associate and project coordinator for a nonprofit social marketing firm in Tampa, Florida, called Best Start, Inc. The firm had a contract with a state agency in Texas, the Interagency Council on Early Childhood Intervention (ECI), tasked with administering a federally funded program to provide social services to families whose children are developmental delayed (Brown 1997b:27).

ECI staff realized they were reaching only a small proportion of the developmentally delayed children who were eligible for—and could benefit from—their services. Brown was given the challenging job of discovering what cultural models might explain why members of an ethnically diverse but universally low-income population would choose *not* to take advantage of a public health program that could benefit their children. This research

would include a number of different anthropological techniques, including participant observation, in-depth interviews, and "intercept interviews" (brief talks, usually lasting fifteen minutes or less, with individuals encountered at places where members of specific target audiences can be found). Next, Brown was to design a social marketing program that would help persuade the parents to change their behavior by enrolling their children in the program.

Brown suspected that at least some members of the target audience failed to enroll their developmentally delayed children in ECI because they did not routinely take their children to see a pediatrician—the primary source of referrals to the program. His research revealed that the children did see doctors from time to time but only for acute care; most parents did not schedule routine, preventive-care visits to the pediatrician. Unfortunately, children were not usually screened for developmental delays at acute care visits, so they were not being re-of contraceptives in developing countries, the promotion is usually commissioned and funded by a government or NGO (Bouvier and Bertrand 1999:104). Cultural anthropologists have contributed a great deal to such efforts. For example, the brand names given to contraceptives, and the way they are packaged, are crucial to their acceptance. In some countries, the name Pearl, which suggests "beauty and purity" (ibid.), has proven highly successful for an oral contraceptive pill, but there is no reason to believe this name would be appealing everywhere.

Not surprisingly, over the past fifteen years a number of very concerted social marketing efforts have beendirected at the prevention of HIV/AIDS (Fishbein et al. 1997:123–146). This disease is, of course, transmitted by a virus. However, transmission is dependent on very specific behaviors; one cannot become infected with HIV by breathing contaminated air or eating contaminated food, but only by direct contact with the virus by mechanisms such as having unprotected sex or injecting drugs with contaminated needles.

---

ferred to the ECI program. Compounding the problem was the cultural model for health care to which the parents subscribed: as children age, they need less preventive care. Based on this model, children were less and less apt to be screened as they grew older.

Brown reasoned that if he could identify the individuals whom parents considered experts on childhood development and developmental delays, he could use these experts to motivate parents to have their children screened. Through focus groups conducted in two low-income communities, he discovered that low-income parents considered physicians and parents of children with developmental delays to be experts on the subject. This research led to the recommendation to ECI that members of these two groups be used as a tertiary audience to validate an alternative cultural model—children of all ages need preventive care—and convey to parents the important message that all children need routine preventive care, including screening for developmental delays. "Anthropology helps public health practitioners to understand how sociocultural factors that shape environments affect the knowledge beliefs, attitudes, and values that determine how individuals behave," Brown says (1997b:29).

For Christopher Brown, a career in social marketing has been "a wonderful opportunity to practice anthropology" (Brown 1997a:60). Currently the vice president of state and community initiatives with the National Fatherhood Initiative (NFI), he uses his training in cultural anthropology to mobilize states and communities to promote responsible, committed, and involved fatherhood. This job involves training community-based organizations in how to create, manage, market, and evaluate programs and services for fathers. He has also carried social marketing into the fatherhood field through a two-day training program he designed, and which NFI offers, on social marketing for fatherhood programs. In addition, Brown speaks across the United States on the importance of fathers to the healthy development of children.

◇ **FIGURE 10.1   Steps in a Social Marketing Effort**

Identify a Problem

1. Determine whether the problem is amenable to social marketing.
2. Determine whether sufficient resources exist to address the problem.

Undertake Background Research

1. Select appropriate research methods, such as these:
   - Focus groups
   - Participant observation
   - Documentary research
   - Informant interviews
   - Surveys
2. Define potential target audiences:
   - Primary
   - Secondary
   - Tertiary
3. Identify relevant cultural models.
4. If necessary, identify audience segments.

Design a Solution

1. Select the solution most appropriate for primary target audience:
   - Concrete item
   - Activity
   - Social service
2. Test solution via pilot project.

Implement the Solution

1. Choose appropriate channel(s):
   - Mass media approach
   - Alternative media approach
   - Point-of-purchase approach
2. Use channels to raise awareness and create demand.

Evaluate the Results

HIV/AIDS prevention efforts are particularly well suited to social marketing because their main message is behavior change (refer to the case study in Chapter 1 entitled "A Short-Term Independent Consultancy," p. 17, for an example). The primary target audience is people who are at high risk for contracting the virus, and the solution is the acceptance, by members of the primary target audience, of any of a number of different products (such as condoms), actions (such as practicing safer sex), or services (such as needle exchange programs) that will help prevent transmission of the virus. Which of these solutions will be the most appropriate and acceptable depends on the at-risk individuals involved and their cultural context. Merely educating people about the many different behaviors that put them at risk for this disease, and suggesting specific products, actions, or, services, is insufficient; at-risk individuals' particular lifestyles, values, beliefs, and behaviors must be addressed directly, based on anthropological research.

A voluntary HIV counseling and testing (VCT) network in Zimbabwe, in southern Africa, provides an example of how social marketing can be used to prevent the spread of HIV/AIDS (Anonymous 1999:12–13). Zimbabwe has the highest AIDS prevalence in the world; one in four Zimbabwean adults is infected, and each week there are two thousand new infections and twelve hundred deaths. The VCT strategy targets at-risk individuals for personal counseling by health professionals, who help them create risk-reduction strategies tailored especially for them.

In 1998, Zimbabwe's Ministry of Health, aware of the success of VCT networks elsewhere, asked a local arm of an international NGO, funded by USAID, for help with developing VCT in Zimbabwe. The staff of the NGO designed a mix of services, including both HIV testing and confidential counseling, and targeted the groups of people who are at the highest risk for HIV/AIDS in Zimbabwe: young couples, adolescents, prostitutes (usually called *commercial sex workers* in the international health context), and transport industry workers. Many Zimbabweans are reluctant to let others know they are being counseled or tested for HIV/AIDS. To remove some of the stigma attached to visiting an HIV/AIDS facility, the planners arranged for VCT services to be offered in locations people commonly visit for other health services as well, such as clinics and hospitals.

Once they had designed what they believed would be the most effective and affordable program possible, the planners had to decide how to market the new services so that those who were the program's primary targets would learn about it and decide to use it. Social marketing was selected. Program implementers decided to use the mass media approach, so VCT was advertised on TV and radio and in various print media. They also decided to use the alternative media approach, embedding their message in plays acted by drama groups in each community where VCT services were offered.

According to VCT staff, "voluntary counseling, strengthened by social marketing, has an impact . . . on those motivated to seek out VCT services . . . as it works to destigmatize the idea of testing, and encourages people to communicate about HIV/AIDS" (Anonymous 1999:13). This program has proven to be both successful and cost effective, and by the end of 2002 it is expected to reach seventy-two thousand at-risk Zimbabwean clients. VCT staff envision even greater eventual impact, since "the social marketing model for VCT has prospects for replication in many settings" (ibid.).

CONCLUSION

Social marketing began to be used extensively in the 1980s, when multilateral organizations, governments, and social welfare organizations first realized that "marketing constitutes a proven and very powerful technology for bringing about socially desirable behaviors" (Andreason 1997:3). A social marketing movement arose, peopled not just by philanthropic individuals but by a growing number of organizations dedicated to the use of social marketing as a tool for promoting social welfare.[3]

Less than two decades old, social marketing is still in its infancy (Goldberg et al. 1997:ix). It is anticipated that further refinements in technique will be made, along with innovations and improvements in the channels through which social marketing messages are sent. Surely cultural anthropologists will continue to contribute significantly to the development of effective social marketing methodologies, even as applied cultural anthropologists will continue to use social marketing to implement beneficial social change. The variety of social problems addressed, the assortment of channels used, and the opportunity for creativity in using them make social marketing a particularly appealing career field for those trained in cultural anthropology whose interests also include mass communications, public opinion research, the arts (especially commercial art), business, or education.

For the moment, however, social marketing professionals, including applied anthropologists, are aware that social marketing does not exist in a vacuum. As a social change strategy, it is most likely to be effective when it accompanies other kinds of efforts—such as community development (Chapter 5) and anthropological advocacy (see Chapter 6)—that can also encourage beneficial social change.

K E Y   T E R M S

alternative media approach   in social marketing, the use of channels other than the mass media to send a message

audience segment   a portion of a target audience, distinguished from other segments on the basis of ethnicity, language, age, or other factors

channel   the specific medium or avenue through which a social marketing message is projected

countermarketing   a form of social marketing intended to deter behavior that poses a threat to individuals or society at large

demarketing   a synonym for *countermarketing*

four *Ps*   in commercial marketing, *product, promotion, price,* and *place*

mass media approach   in social marketing, the use of TV commercials, radio spots, or magazine and newspaper advertisements to send a message

point-of-purchase approach   in social marketing, displaying a social marketing message on a product or its packaging

primary target audience   a group of people who are at risk due to a specific problem that may be solved or ameliorated by a social marketing effort

public goods   goods (or services) that benefit society as a whole, yet do not respond to market forces

secondary target audience   a group of people who may be able to influence members of a primary target audience

social advertising   the design and use of advertising campaigns in the mass media for social marketing purposes

social marketing   the use of the ideas and methods more commonly used in commercial advertising to "sell" a socially beneficial product, activity, or service, for the benefit of both individuals and society

target audience   the entire group of people at which a social marketing effort is directed, including primary, secondary, and tertiary audiences

tertiary target audience   a group of people in positions of leadership or high regard whom members of a primary target audience look to for advice or as role models

NOTES

1. This project was funded by the U.S. Agency for International Development (USAID).
2. New government programs in any country take time to come to fruition, and today, several years later, it remains to be seen whether St. Lucia will implement the National Health Insurance plan.
3. In the United States, the Academy for Educational Development in Washington, D.C., is broadly devoted to development communications and is probably the best known of these organizations.

REFERENCES

Agar, Michael, and James MacDonald
1995. "Focus Groups and Ethnography." *Human Organization* 54 (1):78–87.

Andreason, A. R.
1995. *Marketing Social Change: Changing Behavior to Promote Health, Social Development, and the Environment.* San Francisco: Jossey Bass.

1997. "Challenges for the Science and Practice of Social Marketing." In *Social Marketing: Theoretical and Practical Perspectives,* edited by Marvin E. Goldberg, Martin Fishbein, and Susan E. Middlestadt, 3–19. Mahwah, NJ: Erlbaum.

Anonymous
1999. "New Hope with a New Start." *Global AIDSlink* 56:12–13.

Bouvier, Leon F., and Jane T. Bertrand
1999. *World Population: Challenges for the Twenty-First Century.* Santa Ana, CA: Seven Locks Press.

Brown, Christopher A.
1997a. "Social Marketing and Applied Anthropology: A Practitioner's View of the Similarities and Differences Between Two Research-Driven Disciplines." In *Practicing Anthropology in the South,* edited by James M. T. Wallace, 55–64. Athens, GA: University of Georgia Press.

1997b. "Anthropology and Social Marketing: A Powerful Combination." *Practicing Anthropology* 19 (4):27–29.

Bryant, Carol A., and Doraine F.C. Bailey
1991. "The Use of Focus Group Research in Program Development." In *Soundings: Rapid and Reliable Research Methods for Practicing Anthropologists,* edited by John van Willigen and Timothy L. Finan, 24–39. Washington, DC: American Anthropological Association.

Coreil, Jeannine
1990. "The Evolution of Anthropology in International Health." In *Anthropology and Primary Health Care,* edited by Jeannine Coreil and J. Dennis Mull, 3–27. Boulder, CO: Westview Press.

Currence, Cynthia
1997. "Demographic and Lifestyle Data: A Practical Application to Stimulating Compliance with Mammography Guidelines among Poor Women." In *Social Marketing: Theoretical and Practical Perspectives,* edited by Marvin E. Goldberg, Martin Fishbein, and Susan E. Middlestadt, 111–120. Mahwah, NJ: Erlbaum.

Dudley, Eric
1993. *The Critical Villager: Beyond Community Participation.* London: Routledge.

Fishbein, Martin, Carolyn Guenther-Grey, Wayne Johnson, et al.
1997. "Using a Theory-Based Community Intervention to Reduce AIDS Risk Behaviors: The CDC's AIDS Community Demonstration Projects." In *Social Marketing: Theoretical and Practical Perspectives,* edited by Marvin E. Goldberg, Martin Fishbein, and Susan E. Middlestadt, 123–146. Mahwah, NJ: Erlbaum.

Goldberg, Marvin E., Martin Fishbein, and Susan E. Middlestadt (eds.)
1997. *Social Marketing: Theoretical and Practical Perspectives.* Mahwah, NJ: Erlbaum.

Gwynne, Margaret A., Kennedy Roberts, and Norma Compton
1994. *National Health Insurance in St. Lucia.* St. Lucia, West Indies: USAID/OECS/HPMU.

Harvey, Philip D.
1997. "Advertising Affordable Contraceptives: The Social Marketing Experience." In *Social Marketing: Theoretical and Practical Perspectives,* edited by Marvin E. Goldberg, Martin Fishbein, and Susan E. Middlestadt, 147–169. Mahwah, NJ: Erlbaum.

Kernan, Jerome B., and Teresa J. Domzal
1997. "Hippocrates to Hermes: The Postmodern Turn in Public Health Advertising." In *Social Marketing: Theoretical and Practical Perspectives,* edited by Marvin E. Goldberg, Martin Fishbein, and Susan E. Middlestadt, 387–416. Mahwah, NJ: Erlbaum.

Kotler, Philip, and A. R. Andreason
1991. *Strategic Marketing for Non-Profit Organizations.* Englewood Cliffs, NJ: Prentice Hall.

Kotler, Philip, and Eduardo L. Roberto
1989. *Social Marketing: Strategies for Changing Public Behavior.* New York: The Free Press.

Krueger, Richard A., and Mary Anne Casey
2000. *Focus Groups: A Practical Guide for Applied Research* (3rd ed.). Thousand Oaks, CA: Sage Publications.

Morgan, David L.
1997. *Focus Groups as Qualitative Research* (2nd ed). Thousand Oaks, CA: Sage Publications.

Morgan, David L., and Richard A. Krueger (eds.)
1997. *The Focus Group Kit* (Vols. 1–6). Thousand Oaks, CA: Sage Publications.

Sherris, J. D., B. B. Ravenholt, R. Blackburn, R. H. Greenberg, N. Kak, and R. W. Porter
1985. "Contraceptive Social Marketing: Lessons from Experience." *Population Reports* (Series J, No. 30). Baltimore: Johns Hopkins School of Public Health, Population Information Program.

Smith, William A.
1997. "Social Marketing: Beyond the Nostalgia." In *Social Marketing: Theoretical and Practical Perspectives,* edited by Marvin E. Goldberg, Martin Fishbein, and Susan E. Middlestadt, 21–28. Mahwah, NJ: Erlbaum.

Stead, Martine, and Gerard Hastings
1997. "Advertising in the Social Marketing Mix: Getting the Balance Right." In *Social Marketing: Theoretical and Practical Perspectives,* edited by Marvin E. Goldberg, Martin Fishbein, and Susan E. Middlestadt, 29–43. Mahwah, NJ: Erlbaum.

Stewart, David W., and Prem N. Shamdasani
1998. "Focus Group Research: Exploration and Discovery." In *Handbook of Applied Social Research Methods,* edited by Leonard Bickman and Debra J. Rog, 505–526. Thousand Oaks, CA: Sage Publications.

Terry, Rhonda D.
1994. "Needed: A New Appreciation of Culture and Food Behavior." *Journal of the American Dietetic Association* 94 (5):501–503.

CHAPTER

11

APPLIED MEDICAL ANTHROPOLOGY

◇ ◇ ◇

INTRODUCTION

A thin young man of about twenty years of age enters a public health clinic in a city in the American Southwest, complaining of a persistent cough. Eventually he is taken to an examination room, where two doctors, "Dr. A" and "Dr. B," introduce themselves and interview the patient simultaneously. They learn that the patient's cough has been going on for several months. He is a heavy smoker and has therefore assumed that the cough is a result of smoking and will disappear if he were to quit or cut down on cigarettes. He thinks smoking probably also accounts for the general weakness he has been experiencing. This morning, however, he spat up some blood. He tells the two doctors that he is starting to get worried.

Dr. A immediately suspects tuberculosis. After listening to the young man's lungs through a stethoscope, she asks him to cough and then spit into a beaker. She then tests the patient's sputum for the presence of tuberculosis by looking for specific bacilli under a microscope. Dr. B also suspects tuberculosis, but he seems to have little interest in the sputum test. Instead, he begins to ask the young man a series of questions about his lifestyle. Where does the patient live, and with whom?

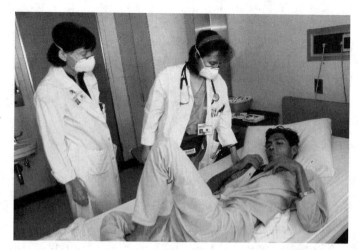

◇ *Professionals in medicine and applied medical anthropology approach serious illnesses such as tuberculosis from two different points of view, the biological and the cultural. Both viewpoints are important because the root causes of diseases lie in both realms. At New York's Bellevue Medical Center, health professionals interview a Mexican immigrant with contagious TB.*

How many people share how many rooms? Has he heard of tuberculosis? What does he think causes it? Does he know how it is spread? Does he know whether or not it can be prevented? Does he know anyone who has it?

Both Dr. A and Dr. B are well aware that tuberculosis—once thought by public health officials to be under control, thanks to powerful anti-TB medications—is making an unwelcome comeback all over the world. The reasons are many, including increased travel, increased migration, the rapid growth of cities (where overcrowded living conditions heighten the risk of spreading the disease), and the growing numbers of HIV/AIDS victims, who lack resistance to the TB bacillus. Today, worldwide, about eight million people become infected with TB each year, and three million people die, despite the fact that this is a curable disease (Farrell 1998: 8). The rise in the number of cases of TB among certain subgroups of people (including the inner-city poor, intravenous drug users, and people with HIV/AIDS) is especially alarming.

Why do the two health care professionals, confronted with a readily identifiable disease in a single patient, behave so very differently? Because one is a medical doctor; the other is a medical anthropologist. Their different lines of inquiry illustrate the point that human health, illness, and curing can be approached from two quite different points of view. Despite their considerable differences, the two approaches are both important to consider if one's goal is to understand, prevent, and treat tuberculosis, because the root causes of the disease are both biological and cultural.

One approach reflects the point of view of **biomedicine** (or **allopathy**), the contemporary Western system of health-related knowledge, beliefs, and practices. The primary concern of biomedical health practitioners is ill health, both physical and mental, and their primary goal is the prevention, diagnosis, and treatment of people's health problems. The other approach is that of **medical anthropology,** an academic discipline devoted to a comprehensive, cross-cultural, systemic understanding of human health, illness, illness prevention, and curing. Its major focus of interest and analysis is health-related knowledge, beliefs, and practices in the medical systems of both non-Western and westernized, industrialized societies.

Medical anthropology includes ethnographic, biological, and archaeological per-spectives, and medical anthropologists' philosophical orientations range from the cultural–ecological to the symbolic to the reflexive.[1]

Fundamental to medical anthropology is the premise that in every society, cul-ture is an important determinant of health, affecting both its material and symbolic dimensions (Sargent and Johnson 1996:xii). More specifically, various aspects of culture, both general (such as subsistence adaptations or religious beliefs and prac-tices) and particular (such as a patient's sex or dietary prescriptions and proscrip-tions) have been shown to have a profound effect on health-related behaviors. These include specific ways of experiencing and expressing illness, treatment choices, the reactions of community members to unwell individuals, and even ill-ness outcomes. This connection between health and culture is as important within Western biomedicine as it is in **ethnomedicine,** a collective term for the traditional medical systems found in non-Western societies (and also practiced in Westernized settings by members of various diasporas). Medical anthropologists view culture as the medium within which health-related beliefs and practices are generated and sustained.

FOOD FOR THOUGHT Chronic pain patients in the United States express and act out their suffering in very different ways, from stoic to emotional, depending on their cultural background (Zborowski 1969; Bates and Edwards 1992). These differences illustrate the intimate connection between health and culture. Based on your own experience, describe other examples of this linkage.

APPLYING MEDICAL ANTHROPOLOGY

Defining Applied Medical Anthropology

Like many anthropological subdisciplines, medical anthropology incorporates both theoretical and applied components. **Applied medical anthropology** can be de-fined as the use of the theories, methods, and accumulated data of medical anthro-pology to address specific health-related problems and achieve specific, practical health-related goals. These goals include promoting good health, preventing illness, helping to restore health, alleviating mental and physical suffering, ensuring pa-tients' access to appropriate care, and fostering communication between those who are ill and their caregivers.

Applied medical anthropology includes both applied research and hands-on practice. Practitioners usually work in the context of the Western biomedical system of health beliefs and practices, often in close association with health professionals, including not only those engaged in direct patient care but also health policy spe-cialists, health program planners, and the administrators of patient care facilities. However, applied medical anthropologists are only rarely involved directly in pa-tient therapy. Their roles are more apt to involve health-related research, advocacy, education, counseling, mediation, and program planning than patient care.

Some medical anthropologists argue that *all* medical anthropology is applied, since "the preponderance of research [in medical anthropology] . . . center[s] on pragmatic issues of improving the health and health care situations of contemporary people, both 'Western' and 'non-Western'" (Pelto and Pelto 1996:293; see also Sargent and Johnson 1996:xiv). However, the term *applied medical anthropology* is usually reserved for specifically goal-oriented medical anthropology practiced in nonacademic settings. One applied medical anthropologist, for example, works in the emergency room of a large urban hospital in a Southwestern city, where she helps the medical staff provide appropriate and sensitive care for Asian immigrants. Another is a health policy analyst who assists planners in the public health department of a Southern state to establish and improve outreach services in poor, rural communities, especially concerning early childhood immunizations and the control of sexually transmitted diseases. A third is employed by a subcontractor to the U.S. National Institutes of Health, where she helps select and prepare research subjects for clinical trials of potentially beneficial drugs to prevent the transmission of the AIDS virus from infected pregnant women to their unborn children. Another is employed as a program evaluator by a nationwide chain of nursing homes. Each of these career areas emphasizes the influence of culture on health, illness, and health-seeking behavior in both individuals and groups.[2]

Comparing Applied Medical Anthropology and Biomedicine

Some of the general goals of applied medical anthropologists, such as promoting good health and preventing illness, clearly overlap with those of biomedical professionals. For other, more specific goals—such as ensuring patients' access to culturally appropriate care and fostering effective communication between patients, patients' families, and caregivers—there is obviously less consonance. Despite the overlap in broad goals, however, representatives of these two disciplines approach patients and their health problems from quite different points of view. Biomedical health practitioners (including doctors, nurses, physicians' assistants, medical technicians, midwives, physical therapists, and mental health professionals) focus on the genetic, infectious, chemical, environmental, or traumatic causes of ill health; medical anthropologists, by contrast, focus on culture—the culture of patients, the culture of health care providers, the culture of facilities and institutions providing health care, and the culture of biomedicine itself. We might say, therefore, that the core concept for biomedical health practitioners is biology; for medical anthropologists, it is culture.

Another important difference lies in the primary interests of biomedical health practitioners and applied medical anthropologists. Whereas biomedical health practitioners focus on **disease,** which they define as any non-normal and therefore unwanted physical or mental condition, medical anthropologists distinguish between disease and **illness,** the collective—and hence culturally induced—responses of both unwell individuals and those around them to non-normal health conditions. A disease afflicts particular parts of the body, while illness afflicts a person as a member of society (Helman 2000:83). The distinction is a useful one. For example, because perceptions of what is "normal" differ from culture to culture, a condition identified as a disease in one cultural context may not necessarily be considered a disease in another. The implications for treatment are obvious.

Table 11.1 shows other significant differences between practitioners of the two disciplines. These differences are complementary and work to the advantage of both kinds of practitioners. Indeed, the presence of applied medical anthropologists among biomedical health practitioners is useful precisely because of these differences in perspective (Chrisman and Johnson 1996:90).

THE DEVELOPMENT OF APPLIED MEDICAL ANTHROPOLOGY

Cultural anthropologists have been interested in the cultural meanings inherent in medical systems, and in the impact of culture on human health, since the nineteenth-century inception of academic anthropology (Rubel and Hass 1996:113; Singer and Baer 1995:3). Thus most early fieldwork in cultural anthropology included some attention to the health-related beliefs and practices of the people under study. Early ethnographers discovered that in the small-scale, non-Western societies on which they focused, medicine is very often at one with religion and ritual, and medical practitioners are often religious functionaries as well. The ethnographies produced in the early decades of the twentieth century contain numerous descriptions of such medical and medico–religious systems.

Throughout these years, however, medical anthropology—as a discrete, formally recognized, theoretical subdiscipline of cultural anthropology devoted to the comparative study of human health, illness, illness prevention, and curing—did not exist. When medical anthropology did at last emerge as an academic subdiscipline,

◇ **TABLE 11.1** **Differences in Focus: Biomedicine and Applied Medical Anthropology**

	Biomedical Practitioner	Applied Medical Anthropologist
Core concept	Biology	Culture
Primary interest	Disease	Illness
Primary focus of interest	Individual	Community
Main research area	Specific pathogens	Health-related beliefs and behaviors
Major practical responsibility	Curative care	Preventive care
Time frame	Short term	Long term

beginning in the 1920s and 1930s, it was mainly a result of the interests of physical anthropologists in human biological variation, rather than an attempt to formalize the comparative study of health systems.

Stimulated after World War II by international public health efforts, the new subdiscipline grew slowly but steadily, widening well beyond comparative human biology to include the comparative study of health beliefs and practices. However, its

> emphasis tended to be on "folk beliefs" or on "alternative" delivery systems, reflecting an-
> thropologists' own cultural frameworks. . . . Western society and its sophisticated [medical]
> technologies, embedded within a powerful scientific paradigm, were . . . "off limits" to the
> kinds of investigations routinely performed on medical systems in other cultures. (Casper
> and Koenig 1996:525)

In 1971, the American Anthropological Association established a section de-voted to medical anthropology, the Society for Medical Anthropology. Its early membership was more interested in "blithely examin[ing] the exotic healing cere-monies and rituals of other cultures" than in any reflexive or critical examination of biomedicine (Margaret Lock, quoted in Casper and Koenig 1996:525). Beginning in the early 1980s, however, a more comprehensive and more critical orientation de-veloped, along with a new attention to theory building. Medical anthropology is now the largest subdiscipline of cultural anthropology, as evidenced by the mem-bership of the Society for Medical Anthropology.

As a distinct field of inquiry and endeavor, medical anthropology's *applied* component began to emerge at around the same time as its theoretical compo-nent—the late 1940s and early 1950s—in a public health context, remaining quite distinct from academic medical anthropology. Chapter 3 described how the United States, after the implementation in 1946 of the Marshall Plan to aid the recovery of war-torn Europe, subsequently joined with other westernized nations to create a number of international institutions broadly dedicated to economic, political, and social development. Human health soon emerged as an important aspect of devel-opment, and over the ensuing years a number of international institutions began to undertake health-related programs, with the specific goal of improving public health and relieving suffering in the less developed countries of the world. A few of them hired applied anthropologists, as early as the late 1940s and early 1950s, to do what would now be termed clinically applied medical anthropology (see p. 253). The first textbook on the subject of applied medical anthropology, Benjamin Paul's (edited) *Health, Culture, and Community*, was published in 1955. Subtitled *Case Studies of Public Reactions to Health Problems*, the book strongly reflected the public health ori-entation of applied medical anthropology as it then existed.

In North America, in the postwar years, existing government entities, such as the various branches of the military establishment, took on increasingly important roles in health services delivery. At the same time, new national-level institutions with health components, such as the U.S. Department of Health and Human Ser-vices (formerly the Department of Health, Education, and Welfare), were estab-lished. As the intellectual horizons of what is now known as academic medical an-thropology widened from a physical anthropology orientation to include health, illness, and curing in industrialized as well as non-Western societies, these governmental organizations began to draw upon the expertise of the new medical anthropologists in their efforts to improve the quality and efficiency of health services and the equity with which they were delivered.

Beginning in the 1970s, the number of academic jobs available each year in cultural anthropology was smaller than the number of cultural anthropologists receiving the Ph.D. degree, and in consequence cultural anthropologists more and more often accepted employment outside of academe (see Chapter 3, p. 71). Many of them, trained in the new subdiscipline of medical anthropology, took nonacademic jobs, especially in the public health sector, and found their nonacademic, more goal-oriented roles both socially beneficial and personally rewarding. Despite the steadily increasing involvement of trained medical anthropologists in nonacademic work, however, applied medical anthropology was not formally recognized as a specific subdiscipline of medical anthropology until the early 1980s (Chrisman and Johnson 1996:88).

ROLES FOR APPLIED MEDICAL ANTHROPOLOGISTS

The roles played by applied medical anthropologists are many and varied; indeed, applied medical anthropologists are involved in virtually all aspects of Western biomedical care. Most of their work falls into three major areas: (1) clinically applied medical anthropology, (2) health policy and planning, and (3) health education.

Clinically Applied Medical Anthropology

The term **clinically applied medical anthropology** refers to the application of medical anthropology in clinical settings, meaning places where patients receive health care. These settings include not only hospitals and ambulatory health care facilities (clinics and doctors' offices), but also other venues, such as nursing homes, police stations, jails, psychologists' offices, or courts, in which individuals with physical or mental health problems routinely encounter health care professionals (Rush 1996:199).

Clinically applied medical anthropologists are mainly involved in research, consultation, and teaching. Relatively few participate in actual therapeutic intervention (Miller 1997:119). Their major goal is to introduce, into the health system, anthropological principles and insights that will help biomedical professionals deliver effective and appropriate health care. Thus clinically applied medical anthropologists typically work as members of health teams that may also include one or more physicians, nurses, physical therapists, or social workers (Helman 2000:8). Although their work may be undertaken in any of a number of different health care settings, clinically applied medical anthropologists are most likely to be employed by relatively large public health departments or urban hospitals. Common work venues include community-based health facilities (such as family planning or substance abuse clinics) or hospital emergency rooms.

A few applied anthropologists began doing what would now be termed clinically applied medical anthropology in the 1950s, and the term *clinical anthropology* has been in use since the 1960s. However, clinically applied medical anthropology was not formally recognized as a specific kind of applied medical anthropology until the early 1980s, when the serendipitous combination of a decreasing number of academic jobs in medical anthropology, which began in the 1970s, and a growing awareness of cultural anthropology's potential for beneficial social change, encouraged the growth of this applied field (Chrisman and Johnson 1996:88). Since then, training programs in applied medical anthropology have increasingly emphasized the skills needed for collaboration with other kinds of health professionals and interaction with patients in clinical settings (Coreil and Mull 1990:8).

A major benefit resulting from the presence of medical anthropologists in clinical settings is their ability to mediate between patients and their caregivers—for example, helping to interpret a non-English-speaking immigrant's health-related complaints to her physician.[3] Not infrequently, bilingual clinically applied medical anthropologists serve as translators as well as mediators. Another benefit is their capacity for helping patients make difficult choices among alternative therapies. A third is their ability to educate and encourage patients to become partners in, rather than passive beneficiaries of, the therapeutic process. In any case, the purpose of clinically applied medical anthropology is to "help . . . health practitioners do their work better" (Chrisman and Johnson 1996:89).

In some of the relatively rare instances in which the clinically applied medical anthropologist's role is directly therapeutic, the anthropologist is also trained in one of the medical professions, such as nursing (Chrisman and Johnson 1996:91, 93). Otherwise, a hands-on role for anthropologists is somewhat controversial (Miller 1997:119), in part because of the general feeling, within the medical community, that only trained biomedical professionals are qualified to deliver medical care to patients. But medical anthropologist (and naturopathic physician) John A. Rush (1996) strongly encourages anthropologists to play a clinical role. Rush argues that Western biomedical practitioners tend to be overly focused on the individual and on

◇ *Few medical anthropologists— not even clinically applied medical anthropologists—are directly involved in patient care. The career of medical anthropologist Merrill Singer, shown here training public health workers in Inner Mongolia, China, has taken him from applied research to health program planning and operations to health education to the publication of papers and books about medical anthropology.*

the material manifestations of ill health, to the neglect of society and the social and emotional ramifications of illness. He believes that cultural anthropologists, because of their "information processing" skills (such as cross-cultural translation and the ability to appreciate multiple points of view) are eminently well suited to work in clinical settings.

FOOD FOR THOUGHT

Clowns, who share certain similarities (such as strange costumes, fool-the-eye tricks, and ventriloquism) with the shamans of small-scale, non-Western societies, are being used to improve the medical services provided to children in New York City hospitals (Van Blerkom 1995). Medical anthropologist John Rush (1996), a strong advocate of direct patient care roles for clinically applied medical anthropologists, suggests that certain therapeutic techniques practiced by shamans, such as hypnosis and the analysis of dreams, might also be used as adjuncts to more conventional biomedical therapies. In your opinion, would using shamanistic techniques be appropriate and effective with modern, adult, Western patients? Why or why not?

Some of the specialty areas in which clinically applied medical anthropologists work are cultural brokerage, reproductive health, infant and child health, and applied nutrition. These specialty areas by no means exhaust the range of possibilities for clinically applied medical anthropologists, but they broadly represent the roles these practitioners play.

Cultural Brokerage.   This term was defined in Chapter 6 (p. 134) as a specific kind of cultural advocacy, involving mediation or negotiation between community members and representatives of outside agencies. The cultural broker, with an understanding of the cultures of both parties, serves as an interpreter of each for members of the other.

In clinically applied medical anthropology, **cultural brokerage** usually involves mediation between patient and caregiver. Mediation may be desirable because a patient's ethnic or religious background differs from his or her caregiver's, but not all of a given patient's problems are the result of such obvious factors (Chrisman and Johnson 1996:99). Frequently, communication between these parties is made difficult by more subtle factors, such as gender, relative socioeconomic status, or differences in power and authority (such as a combination of professional presumption on the part of a caregiver and naiveté, resignation, or submissiveness on the part of a patient). When there are obvious cultural differences, clinically applied medical anthropologists serving as cultural brokers must be especially careful to differentiate between the cultural and the personal, explicitly avoiding the "ethnic cookbook" approach to cultural brokerage. It can by no means be assumed, for example, that all Hispanic patients will believe in *susto*—soul loss—as a cause of illness.

Some patients will be able to explain their symptoms in great detail; others will not, perhaps because of a lack of understanding of what sort of details caregivers need. Some will be forthcoming when they are in pain; others will suppress all expressions of pain. Some will hold alternative (that is, nonbiomedical) medical beliefs; others will not (and many will adhere to a combination of alternative and biomedical beliefs). Some will have tried alternative remedies before seeing a biomedical professional; others will not. Some will fully understand a physician's directives, and follow them to the letter; others will not, out of misunderstanding or resistance. Some will be content with whatever therapeutic regimen is prescribed; others will not consider themselves to have been well served unless some specific medication has been prescribed. The role of the clinically applied medical anthropologist as cultural broker is to recognize and help bridge such differences. He or she interviews patients, ideally in their own argot or language, in an attempt to gain a thorough understanding of their attitudes about illness in general, their beliefs about the causes of their specific illness, their degree of trust in biomedicine or other medical systems, their expectations regarding their diagnoses or illness outcomes, and their psychological states. The insights gleaned are communicated to caregivers; caregivers' explanations and instructions are likewise relayed to patients.

Cultural brokerage usually takes place in a clinical setting, but some applied medical anthropologists perform the same function outside the clinic. For example, they may help members of minority communities gain access to needed medical services that are culturally appropriate. No matter what the venue, the overall goals are the same: to provide support and empowerment for patients, and to foster productive communication between patients and their caregivers.

Reproductive Health.   Many clinically applied medical anthropologists work in the general area of health promotion, which involves working to encourage health-supporting practices among specific groups of people. Examples of health promotion arenas in which applied medical anthropologists work include geriatrics, epidemiology, school health, substance abuse, adolescent health, mental health, migrant and refugee health, and environmental health. Another important health promotion domain is **reproductive health,** the specialty area of biomedicine focusing on sex, pregnancy, and birth. Gynecology and obstetrics might appear to be mostly biological matters. However, these areas of biomedical practice are profoundly shaped by aspects of culture such as traditions, social relationships, and political and economic processes (Browner and Sargent 1996:225; see also Martin 1987).

To take one pervasive set of beliefs surrounding childbirth as an illustration, the "hot/cold theory of disease" may have an important effect on childbirth outcomes. This is the idea, rooted in the folk culture of Latin America and other parts of the world, that health is in part determined by the effects of heat and cold on the body (Helman 2000:19). Pregnancy is seen as a "hot" condition, while the postpartum period is viewed as a "cold" condition. "Hot" states are treated with "cold" substances, and vice versa. These beliefs can work either to the disadvantage or advantage of pregnant and newly postpartum women. While pregnant, women may compromise their health by avoiding certain healthful foods because they are classified as "hot." On the other hand, in the postpartum period, they may be helpfully encouraged to rest under warm blankets and consume hearty, "hot" foods.

While recognizing that a woman's cultural background is by no means the only determinant of her health-related beliefs and behavior, a clinically applied medical anthropologist, sensitive to and knowledgeable about both the general and specific implications of culture for reproductive health, may be better able than a physician or nurse to guide obstetrical patients toward safe, healthy behaviors. Other reproductive health issues, such as teen sexuality, women's reproductive rights, abortion, sex selection, and genetic screening are equally amenable to an anthropological approach, and clinically applied medical anthropologists can be found working in all of these areas.

Infant and Child Health.   Depending on parental cultural backgrounds, standards of care for infants and young children similarly incorporate a variety of beliefs and practices. Mothers with Middle Eastern or South Asian cultural backgrounds, for example, may believe that a smudge of charcoal on an infant's forehead will help to keep the baby safe by warding off the "evil eye"—a harmless and perhaps even a psychologically beneficial practice. The same mothers, however, may rim their babies' eyes with kohl, a cosmetic compound, in the belief that it makes children more beautiful. Kohl often contains lead sulfide, which may irritate or even infect the eye. A clinically applied medical anthropologist specializing in infant and child health care, who understands such customs and their cultural significance, can discuss specific health practices with parents and encourage them to choose those practices that are safe for their children.

FOOD FOR THOUGHT   What customs or traditions relating to childbirth and infant care are practiced by North American parents of western European ancestry? Are these helpful, harmful, or neither? Explain your answer.

Applied Nutrition.   Diet and nutrition are also heavily influenced by culture (see Quandt 1996; Rush 1996:211ff.; Helman 2000:32–49). The dietary choices people make from among available edibles, for example, are very largely culturally determined; the meat of horses is eaten in France, and dogs are consumed in China, but neither of these is found on menus in North America. Food preservation and preparation methods, too, are in part culturally determined. Moreover, as the "hot/cold theory" already described illustrates, many foods embody strong symbolic associations, and eating or avoiding them because of these associations may be either beneficial or deleterious to health. Food symbolism is by no means restricted to non-Westerners; many Westerners prefer less nutritious white bread to more nutritious whole-grain bread because of the general association of darker or coarser foods with poor people such as rural farmers (Helman 2000:38). Such culturally determined beliefs, values, and practices make diet and nutrition an appropriate area of practice for clinically applied medical anthropologists.

A genetic disease called phenylketonuria (PKU) provides an example of the link between culture and disease within the area of applied nutrition. Even though individuals are born with PKU, it is profoundly affected by diet—a cultural matter. If no action is taken, its victims become severely retarded. However, when their condition is diagnosed shortly after birth and their diet is modified accordingly, the degree of retardation can be greatly reduced (Romanucci-Ross et al. 1997:374–375). Thus, "cultural factors that influence diet and nutrition will directly influence whether this disease will be manifested in its most severe form" (ibid.:374).

An important subfield within the area of applied nutrition concerns the nutritional needs of the elderly, a growing field of inquiry given the increase in both the absolute and relative numbers of elderly individuals. Applied medical anthropologist Nancy Schoenberg, for instance, undertook research on the poor nutritional status of elderly, rural African Americans. Through interviews and telephone surveys, Schoenberg was able to identify specific factors, such as poverty, physical ailments, and eating alone, that put her research population at nutritional risk. Based on these data, she was then able to propose specific ways in which the diets of the elderly could be improved (Schoenberg 2000).

Miller (1997:119ff.) warns that clinically applied medical anthropology is at a "decisive" juncture at the moment. Two "core issues" face clinically applied medical anthropologists: "the need to examine the theoretical and technical foundation of clinical anthropology, and the disciplinary goals supporting its application" (ibid.). A special interest group of clinical anthropologists has recently been formed within the Society for Medical Anthropology to debate these and related issues.

Health Policy and Planning

Numerous applied medical anthropologists work not in direct patient care settings but in the policy arena—most of them in the public sector. Since all modern governments have the responsibility of ensuring that their citizens have adequate access to quality health care, delivered equitably, efficiently, and in sufficient quantity, government agencies at various levels (federal, state, and municipal) employ applied medical anthropologists. These research anthropologists analyze, plan for, regulate, and evaluate the quality and distribution of health care and health care resources, and help formulate policies to foster better health. (Resources, in this context, include not only necessities such as funding, health care facilities, drugs, medical equipment, and supplies, but also human resources—the trained personnel who actually deliver health care.) In the United States, for example, a number of applied medical anthropologists are employed by the Centers for Disease Control and Prevention (CDC), the National Institutes of Health (NIH), and other large health policy institutions.

The problems addressed by applied medical anthropologists employed by public sector institutions generally fall into three main areas: health care financing, the organization of health care (that is, how health systems are structured and what components are included to ensure that the public has adequate access to appropriate care), and the delivery of health care (how, where, and by whom health care is actually delivered to those who need it). These anthropologists collaborate with other professionals to answer questions such as: What is the cost of health care, who should pay for it, and who actually pays for it? What proportion of people are covered by health insurance, and how can insurance coverage be extended to those who lack it? What are the hidden costs of access to health services, in terms of the distance people must travel to reach a health care facility, the time spent in travel, and the time spent waiting for health services? How much demand is there for various kinds of care, what factors affect that demand, and is the supply of health care adequate to meet existing demand? What expectations and preferences do health care consumers have, and are these being met? What are the demographics of the various populations being served, in terms of age distribution, socioeconomic status, level of education, and preference for public or private care? Who is allowed to practice medicine, what kind of training must practitioners receive, and how should practitioners be licensed? Providing answers to such questions is made more challenging by the fact that governmental policies regarding health care financing, organization, and delivery change as different political parties, with differing philosophies and different constituencies, enter and leave office. Thus, public policy work in the area of health is quite literally never finished.

Applied medical anthropologists working in the policy arena are often involved in both research and operations. The activities of well-known applied medical anthropologist Merrill Singer provides an example. In his work for the Hispanic Health Council in Hartford, Connecticut, Singer has two major practical missions. First, he is directly involved in planning for, creating, and maintaining health programs, such as substance abuse and AIDS prevention programs, that are responsive to a specific constituency: the large population of people of Puerto Rican descent residing in Hartford. Second, Singer is also engaged in educating people outside this specific community about the relationship between the health problems encountered by the council's constituents and the conditions of poverty, undereducation, and unemployment in which many of them live (Singer 1995). In addition, Singer is also active in applied research. For example, he recently participated in a research study to define factors contributing to hunger and food insecurity among families with children in Hartford's Hispanic population (Himmelgreen et al. 2000).

A second example of anthropological involvement in health policy and planning, different from the first in that its focus is human resources rather than program planning or education, is provided by a recent anthropological research project to identify the attributes of a good family physician (Morrow 1997:128ff.). Study participants were U.S. family medical practitioners, patients, medical receptionists, and members of the general public. The research revealed a high level of consensus among physicians about the attributes of a good doctor, a consensus that is shared, in varying degrees, by patients, nonclinical health professionals, and the public. Thus the study demonstrated that a "culture of good medical practice" exists in the United States, and that this culture can be shared with nonphysician groups (ibid.:131). The implications of this finding for quality assurance in health services delivery are considerable.

Two important areas of public health policy and planning to which applied medical anthropologists contribute deserve special mention: environmental health and hospital administration. **Environmental health** is a catch-all term for a number of public health services including the provision of clean water, appropriate waste disposal, and pest control (see Boone 1991:27–28). Applied medical anthropologists are well prepared to "help . . . change [people's] values, develop policies, and construct social institutions which bring about behavioral change," which are needed to preserve and protect the public from environmental health threats (ibid.:28).

◇ *Environmental health, an important aspect of public health services, includes protecting the public from environmental hazards. In Niagara Falls, New York, environmental health officials closed a school situated near Love Canal, polluted by toxic waste.*

A number of applied medical anthropologists also work in hospital administration, a career area that is becoming increasingly challenging, thanks to the ever-growing costs of biomedical health care. Many public hospitals are finding it exceedingly difficult to balance their budgets while simultaneously providing high-quality health services to their constituents. Applied medical anthropologists are involved in an ongoing debate on the subject of greater autonomy for public hospitals, since it appears that granting public hospitals the authority to manage their own operations can result in cost savings, higher-quality care, increased community participation, and greater operational efficiency. Other applied medical anthropologists working in the policy and planning arena write grants, manage clinics, collect health statistics, follow health trends, oversee health insurance plans, regulate the production and distribution of pharmaceuticals, and conduct immunization campaigns.

Health Education

A third important role for applied medical anthropologists is to help promote and maintain good health and healthy lifestyles through educational programs, social marketing (see Chapter 10), and related efforts. The major beneficiaries of such efforts are biomedical health professionals and health care consumers.

Educating Health Professionals.   Applied medical anthropologists are becoming increasingly involved in educating clinicians about the importance of culture to human health, illness, and curing (Johnson 1991). Today, a number of enlightened medical schools offer training in medical anthropology, either in the classroom during medical students' first year, or during the third and fourth years when students rotate among specialty clinics (Joralemon 1999:93). Some nursing schools also now include medical anthropology in their curricula (Dougherty 1991).

The idea that future doctors and nurses should be exposed to the tenets of medical anthropology is by no means new, but has always been something of a "hard sell." One reason is the scientific orientation of clinical training; most of the instruction that future doctors, nurses, and other clinicians receive is in "hard science" areas, such as anatomy and microbiology, rather than in the social sciences. Many of these would-be health professionals are vaguely aware that culture—as expressed through patients' health-related beliefs, values, and behaviors—affects health. Yet because of their training priorities, they have tended to see culture as an intractable template governing health-related behavior, and hence a roadblock to health; medical anthropologists see it, more constructively, as a medium within which health-related beliefs and behaviors—some beneficial and some not—are played out, and health-related decisions are made (see ten Brummelhuis and Herdt 1995). Another reason for a reluctance to include the subject of culture in medical

AN APPLIED CULTURAL ANTHROPOLOGIST AT WORK

FRED BLOOM

In the 1970s, applied medical anthropologist Fred Bloom studied cultural anthropology and then nursing, receiving a Bachelor of Science degree in anthropology from the University of Illinois in 1974 and an Associate Degree in Nursing from Parkland College in Champaign, Illinois, in 1980. Embarking on a nursing career, he spent almost a decade working in a variety of hospital and community settings—often, as the AIDS crisis developed, with HIV-positive patients. In 1989, he returned to graduate school at Case Western Reserve University to become a medical anthropologist, a career in which he could combine his interests in both anthropology and nursing.

For his Ph.D. dissertation research, Dr. Bloom designed a research project that combined his anthropological expertise with his prior experience in working as a nurse with HIV-positive patients. He chose HIV-positive gay men in the United States as his research population, focusing on understanding the psychocultural basis for how the men in his study evaluated their own quality of life and its implications. He also became active in the AIDS and Anthropology Research Group, a special-interest group of the AAA's Society for Medical Anthropology.

After completing his doctoral work in 1995, Dr. Bloom—now a well-seasoned expert in the anthropology of AIDS—began working as a research anthropologist at the Center for AIDS Intervention Research (CAIR), an HIV/AIDS behavioral research center funded by the National Institute of Mental Health. This job, focused on HIV/AIDS prevention, involved him directly in applied work. He provided expertise on qualitative methodologies for applied research projects and proposals; trained and supervised faculty and staff in methodologies for qualitative data collection such as ethnographic observation, field notes, participant recruitment, semi-structured interviews, and ethnographic life story interviews; and conducted additional research on quality of life for HIV-positive gay men.

Three years later, Dr. Bloom moved to Atlanta to work for the National Center for HIV, STD (sexually transmitted disease), and Tuberculosis Prevention at the Centers for Disease Control and Prevention (CDC), where he now works in the Behavioral Intervention Research Branch of the Division of Prevention (Barone 1999). His work there focuses on rapid ethnographic assessment of community health care utilization, health knowledge, risk behavior, and disease outbreaks.[4]

curricula may be the already overwhelming amount of scientific and technical knowledge medical students are expected to absorb (see Joralemon 1999:92).

Yet a very good case can be made for introducing medical students and other would-be health professionals to the precepts of medical anthropology. The most important reason, of course, is the undisputed role of culture in illness. Another important reason for exposing future health professionals to medical anthropology is to foster an understanding of the cultural aspects of doctor–patient interactions, which almost always involve unequal relations of power and authority (see Joralemon 1999:92; Helman 2000:79–107). For example, it has been repeatedly pointed out that the traditional sexual division of labor in the medical and nursing professions mirrors the nuclear family, with the doctor as father, the nurse as mother, and the patient as child. Medical and nursing students who are aware of this are well prepared to understand the structural situation of patients (and also, perhaps, to avoid political pitfalls in their professional lives).

FOOD FOR THOUGHT

It has been observed that nursing and applied medical anthropology are natural allies; indeed, a number of applied medical anthropologists, like Fred Bloom (see p. 161), hold nursing degrees. The particular relevance of cultural anthropology to nursing is obvious: nurses are mainly responsible for those aspects of illness that reflect cultural patterns, such as pain, fatigue, fear, personal physical care, diet modification, and stigma (Dougherty and Tripp-Riemer 1990). (The main responsibility of medical doctors, in contrast, is to diagnose and treat illness.) What undergraduate anthropology courses would help prepare a person for a combined medical anthropology–nursing career, and why?

Educating Health Care Consumers.   Yet another aspect of medical education relevant to applied medical anthropology involves educating health care consumers rather than health professionals. A major goal of public health programs and the applied medical anthropologists who work in the public health education arena is to assist people to understand the factors that contribute to good health and to implement behavior changes that will promote it.

Health educators frequently encounter people—typically people with relatively low educational levels—who genuinely do not understand basic health principles, such as the need for hygiene, safe sex, and immunization. A great deal of thought and experimentation, on the part of both public health specialists and applied medical anthropologists, has been devoted to the problem of how best to identify and educate such people. Several effective techniques have been developed. One, a broad, media-based approach called social marketing, was described in Chapter 10. Another, termed **community-based education,** relies on the top-down education of community members, who then educate others in turn.

A related strategy for public health education that applied medical anthropologists currently use is called **peer health education,** in which education is accomplished not from the top down, by teachers, but by those being educated, who help educate each other. Conceptually, the model is based on the observation that traditional, institutionalized educational strategies frequently fail to foster a context for improving learners' feelings of empowerment and self-determination—often a necessary prerequisite for effective learning.[5]

The peer health education model varies depending on cultural context, but its basic steps remain the same. If implementing this model in HIV/AIDS education, for example, an applied medical anthropologist would first undertake background research on a group of people who are at risk of HIV infection, probably relying more heavily on ethnography than on quantitative instruments due to the subtlety and complexity of the social processes involved in negotiating sexual relationships. The anthropologist might identify this group himself or herself, but more typically it would be identified by the national- or local-level health organization, such as a public health service or a health-related PVO, for which the anthropologist works. This research would focus on the fundamental nature of sexual relationships among the group's members (which differs greatly with ethnic, socioeconomic, and occupational status) and the specific information needed (such as the behaviors that constitute risk for HIV infection, the ability to assess personal risk objectively, or the kinds of interpersonal skills necessary to negotiate sex in particular contexts).

The anthropologist would then organize several meetings of the group of participants. His or her main role in these meetings would not be to instruct the group but rather to foster feelings of safety and trust, ensure mutual respect, raise specific topics for discussion, and encourage group members to share their attitudes, beliefs, and insights in an atmosphere of informality and good humor. Topics might include group members' knowledge and perceptions about HIV/AIDS, their feelings of personal vulnerability, cultural norms governing gender relations in their social group, factors affecting the process of sexual negotiation, cultural expectations regarding

◇ *In the peer health education model, learners help to educate each other. At a college in Ruanda, Africa, students share with each other their insights and beliefs about human anatomy.*

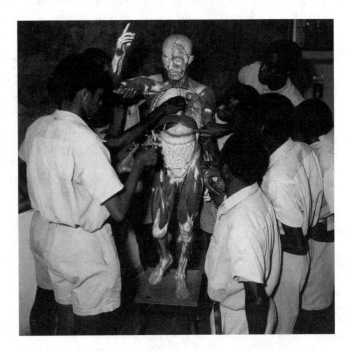

sexual behavior, and contraceptive knowledge and use. Role playing and storytelling might be used to facilitate the discussion and make participation more enjoyable. The anthropologist might introduce ideas such as "sexual self-defense strategies" (ways to protect oneself from HIV/AIDS regardless of what one's partner does or does not do) or the "universal precautions" approach to longer-term sexual risk management (Nelson 1991), allowing the group to discuss, revise, accept, or reject these ideas. The participants might practice verbal and nonverbal interpersonal communication to gain the skills necessary to make effective use of their insights and knowledge.[6]

The peer health education model is effective because it enhances people's feelings of self-esteem and empowerment, without which sustained behavior change is unlikely to occur. There are other benefits as well. It permits the participation of individuals with very little formal education; it provides a nonthreatening, small-group context in which people can make realistic assessments of their own risk (this is fundamental to future behavior change but is lacking in media-based approaches); it keeps the discussion focused on the actual problems with which people themselves are confronted, rather than the problems a health educator or researcher may assume to exist; it encourages mutual problem solving in an atmosphere of shared support and empowerment, which enhances people's ability to use their knowledge about risk reduction; and—perhaps most important—it takes the specific cultural context into account so that participants can examine both their personal practices and the social conditions in which these are embedded.

THE ETHICS OF APPLIED MEDICAL ANTHROPOLOGY

Chapter 4, on the ethics of applied cultural anthropology, mentioned that of the various kinds of applied anthropologists, applied medical anthropologists face a disproportionate share of ethical concerns, perhaps most especially in the area of human-subjects research. Some of these concerns arise because applied medical anthropologists are likely to be employed by institutions or organizations rather than acting as independent researchers. They must thus try to balance their accountability to the agency funding their research, the community in which the research takes place, and the research population, while treating them all with equal ethical consideration (Marshall 1991:215). Other concerns surround the issue of informed consent; for example, is there any such thing as truly *informed* consent on the part of people with low education and literacy levels? Additional problems include preserving research subjects' autonomy and confidentiality, determining the acceptable ratio of risk to potential benefit, and controlling the use of sensitive and personal research results.

FOOD FOR THOUGHT   Based on the information provided earlier in this chapter on clinically applied medical anthropology, describe a specific ethical problem that a clinically applied medical anthropologist might face in each of the following areas: cultural brokerage, reproductive health, infant and child health, and applied nutrition.

In general, applied medical anthropologists are well equipped to deal with such issues. First, they are guided by law. In the United States, for example, applied medical anthropologists are bound by the tenets of the National Research Act, which governs human-subjects research in both the biomedical and social-scientific disciplines and which mandates, among other things, that institutional review boards investigate and approve both research and treatment involving human subjects (see Chapter 4). Second, they are assisted by several sets of ethical guidelines established within the discipline of anthropology, such as the "Statement on Professional and Ethical Responsibilities" of the Society for Applied Anthropology (see Chapter 4). In addition, like all professionals involved in the human health arena, they are bound by a body of principles collectively termed **bioethics,** which originated in large part within the discipline of medicine and governs the moral and ethical considerations encountered in biomedical research and treatment.

Despite these ethical guidelines and strictures, however, applied medical anthropologists are "continually challenged to achieve a balance in meeting the requirements of [bioethical] principles and maintaining scientific rigor and integrity" (Marshall 1991:216). A good example is their participation in clinical trials of potentially beneficial drug-based therapies. Such trials are undertaken both by private sector organizations (primarily pharmaceuticals companies) and public sector organizations, such as the Centers for Disease Control and the National Institutes of Health. An applied medical anthropologist involved in clinical trials of a preventive AIDS drug might discover that trial participants felt protected from disease and were thus less inclined to practice safe sex. In a clinical trial to assess the potential value of a therapeutic AIDS drug, an applied medical anthropologist might face difficult choices about whom to include in and whom to exclude from the trials program, or an ethical quandary about further stigmatizing AIDS sufferers—already a socially marginalized group—included in the program.

There are no universally acceptable solutions to such issues. Marshall (1991: 229) reminds us that "ethical principles governing applied medical anthropological research are not unique to our discipline. Respect for persons, beneficence, and justice are overriding concerns for any scientist."

CRITICALLY APPLIED MEDICAL ANTHROPOLOGY

Beginning in the 1980s, in a climate of increasing reflexivity within anthropology as a whole, medical anthropologists began to reexamine and challenge the structure, goals, and methods of their discipline (see especially Singer 1986, 1989, 1995; Singer and Baer 1995). Medical anthropologists had long ago observed that socioeconomic conditions and political structures in the wider society have an important impact on health, but they became increasingly concerned about the many ways in which Western biomedicine mirrors and supports the Western capitalist social, economic, and political system, with its inequities related to gender, ethnicity, class, and age. This reality inevitably affects both the social structure of biomedicine and the treatment of patients, whose position within the biomedical system is always, to some degree, inferior and disempowered—more or less depending on a patient's status in society and specific relationships with his or her caregivers.

Those medical anthropologists who draw attention to the often inequitable relations of power and authority inherent in biomedicine, and the effect of these inequalities on patients, are said to practice **critically applied medical anthropology** (or, alternatively, **critical medical anthropology**). This is a kind of applied medical anthropology in which matters of health, illness, and curing are viewed within the context of "the larger political and economic forces that pattern human relationships, shape social behavior, and condition collective experience, including forces of institutional, national, and global scale" (Singer 1986:128). Critically applied medical anthropologists "attempt what is exceedingly problematic: to study biomedicine itself, recognizing that it is the product of [particular] social–historical forces" (Sargent and Johnson 1996:xv). The task of critical medical anthropologists is made even more difficult by the fact that they are members of the same societies in which the object of criticism, biomedicine, is the dominant medical ideology.

Critically applied medical anthropologists find fault with—and seek to change—three related elements affecting health care. One criticism is general in nature; one is somewhat more specific; and the third is unique to applied medical anthropology. The most general is the whole structure of modern Western society, in which social, economic, and political arrangements favor the potential for good health of some members of society over others. Somewhat more specific is the Western biomedical system, which itself is organized so as to promote—or at least to fail to identify and rectify—inequitable care. Additionally, critically applied medical anthropologists have sometimes very specifically challenged their clinically applied colleagues, on the grounds that their clinical work fails to sufficiently consider certain problematic social-structural implications of their role. They suggest, for instance, that clinically applied medical anthropologists should serve not just as cultural brokers but also as patient advocates, abandoning scientific objectivity in favor of working explicitly for (and, of course, with) patients.

One interesting proposition from these critics is based on the premise that social action can be a form of therapy. It is the notion that clinically applied medical anthropologists should continue to support biomedical health practitioners, while at the same time raising patients' awareness of their membership in groups defined by social, political, and economic status, and of the implications of such membership for individual patients' experience of illness (Chrisman and Johnson 1996:95). If widely implemented, this suggestion would, in effect, combine clinically applied and critically applied medical anthropology. It reflects the truism that the dividing line between clinical and critical medical anthropology has become less pronounced than it was twenty years ago.

Critically applied medical anthropology itself has not escaped criticism. Some applied medical anthropologists have censured critical medical anthropologists for being overly focused on issues of dominance and oppression in biomedicine (Johnson 1995:107). As Johnson points out, it would be a rare patient who would say to his doctor, "Forget the pain, Doc . . . let's talk about the sociopolitical impact of my illness" (ibid.:110). Critical medical anthropology has also been taken to task for having "much to say, but little to do" (ibid.:107). Despite such criticisms, however, applied medical anthropologists recognize that no discipline—perhaps most especially no applied discipline in which practitioners directly affect people's lives—can legitimately avoid taking a hard, introspective look at itself. Most would probably agree that critical medical anthropology is making an important contribution to applied medical anthropology by encouraging educators, researchers, and medical practitioners alike to address problematic issues (Singer 1995).

CONCLUSION

At first glance, the subject matter of medical anthropology—the impact of culture on human health, illness, illness prevention, and curing—may appear to be a far cry from the bacteria, viruses, faulty genes, environmental pathogens, and traumatic injuries on which biomedical practitioners focus. But the biomedical system of health services delivery includes many different roles and activities. In addition to the physicians, nurses, therapists, and other practitioners involved in direct patient care, biomedical health professionals serve as policy specialists, program planners, and administrators, not directly associated with patients but no less integral to the system. In addition to hands-on patient care, biomedical health professionals help prevent future ill health; plan for and regulate the production and distribution of health services in order to ensure equity, sufficiency, efficiency, and quality; produce the resources needed for health care (such as trained practitioners, facilities such as hospitals and clinics, drugs, and medical supplies); and engage in scientific research (Roemer 1985:19).

For the equitable and efficient delivery of high-quality biomedical health care, a fundamental understanding of culture is necessary to all of these roles and activities, because culture is a crucial determinant of human health. This reality lies at the heart of applied medical anthropology.

K E Y   T E R M S

allopathy   a synonym for *biomedicine*

applied medical anthropology   the use of the theories, methods, and accumulated data of medical anthropology to address specific health-related problems and achieve specific, practical health-related goals

bioethics   a body of principles governing the moral and ethical considerations encountered in biomedical research and treatment

biomedicine   the Western, "scientific" system of health-related knowledge, beliefs, and practices

clinically applied medical anthropology   applied medical anthropology practiced in clinical, or direct patient care, settings

community-based education   an education strategy based on the top-down education of community members, who then educate others in turn

critical medical anthropology   an alternative term for critically applied medical anthropology

critically applied medical anthropology   a kind of applied medical anthropology in which matters of illness, health, and curing are viewed within the context of the existing power structure

cultural brokerage   in medical anthropology, mediation between patient and caregiver

disease   a non-normal and therefore unwanted physical or mental condition

environmental health   a catch-all term for a number of public health services including the provision of clean water, appropriate waste disposal, and pest control

ethnomedicine   collectively, medical (or medico–religious) systems of health, illness, and curing found among non-Western peoples

illness   the collective response of both an unwell individual and those around him or her to the individual's non-normal physical or mental condition

medical anthropology   the comprehensive, cross-cultural, systemic study of human health, illness, illness prevention, and curing, with an emphasis on health-related knowledge, beliefs, and practices in the medical systems of both non-Western and westernized, industrialized societies

peer health education   education by those being educated, who help to educate each other, as opposed to education by teachers

reproductive health   a specialty area within biomedicine, focusing on health problems associated with sex, pregnancy, and birth

N O T E S

1. Useful introductions to medical anthropology, representing various approaches, include McElroy and Townsend 1989, Good 1994, Hahn 1995, Anderson 1996, Joralemon 1999, and Helman 2000. Case studies and topical discussions can be found in three edited volumes: Lindenbaum and Lock 1993, Sargent and Johnson 1996, and Romanucci-Ross et al. 1997.

2. Note that this chapter emphasizes the domestic roles and responsibilities of applied medical anthropologists. Their contributions in international settings are discussed in the following chapter on international health.

3. This kind of work shares a great deal in common with social work; see Chapter 7.

4. An ethical quandary emerging from Dr. Bloom's work with HIV-infected men is described in Chapter 4, pp. 79–80.

5. Peer health education is a variant of "popular education," the notion that people learn better when they teach each other than when learning is imposed on them by professional educators. The principles of this kind of education are perhaps most notably associated with Paolo Freire's work in nontraditional education in Latin America (Freire 1970), but they have also been successfully employed, more recently, in health promotion projects (for example, Wallerstein and Bernstein 1988).

6. A special issue of the journal *Practicing Anthropology* is devoted to HIV/AIDS prevention and education; see O'Connor and Leap (1993).

R E F E R E N C E S

Anderson, Robert
   1996. *Magic, Science, and Health*. Fort Worth, TX: Harcourt Brace College Publishers.

Barone, Timi
   1999. "Practical Advice from Practicing Anthropologists." *Anthropology Newsletter* 40 (3):37–38.

Bates, Maryann S., and W. T. Edwards
1992. "Ethnic Variations in the Chronic Pain Experience." *Ethnicity and Disease* 2:63–83.

Boone, Margaret S.
1991. "Policy and Praxis in the 1990s: Anthropology and the Domestic Health Policy Arena." In *Training Manual in Applied Medical Anthropology*, edited by Carole E. Hill, 23–53. Washington, DC: American Anthropological Association.

Browner, Carole H., and Carolyn F. Sargent
1996. "Anthropology and Studies of Human Reproduction." In *Handbook of Medical Anthropology: Contemporary Theory and Method* (rev. ed.), edited by Carolyn F. Sargent and Thomas M. Johnson, 219–234. Westport, CT: Greenwood Press.

Casper, Monica J., and Barbara A. Koenig
1996. "Reconfiguring Nature and Culture: Intersections of Medical Anthropology and Technoscience Studies." *Medical Anthropology Quarterly* 10 (4):523–536.

Chrisman, Noel J., and Thomas M. Johnson
1996. "Clinically Applied Anthropology." In *Handbook of Medical Anthropology: Contemporary Theory and Method* (rev. ed.), edited by Carolyn F. Sargent and Thomas M. Johnson, 88–109. Westport, CT: Greenwood Press.

Coreil, Jeannine, and J. Dennis Mull (eds.)
1990. *Anthropology and Primary Health Care*. Boulder, CO: Westview Press.

Dougherty, Molly C.
1991. "Anthropologists in Nursing-Education Programs." In *Training Manual in Applied Medical Anthropology*, edited by Carole E. Hill, 161–179. Washington, DC: American Anthropological Association.

Dougherty, Molly C., and Toni Tripp-Riemer
1990. "Nursing and Anthropology." In *Medical Anthropology: A Handbook of Theory and Method*, edited by Thomas M. Johnson and Carolyn F. Sargent, 175–186. Westport, CT: Greenwood Press.

Farrell, Karen
1998. "Stop Tuberculosis Now!" *Healthlink*, March/April 1998:1–8.

Freire, Paolo
1970. *Pedagogy of the Oppressed* (M. Bergman Ramos, trans.). New York: Herder and Herder.

Good, Byron J.
1994. *Medicine, Rationality, and Experience: An Anthropological Perspective*. Cambridge, UK: Cambridge University Press.

Hahn, Robert A.
1995. *Sickness and Healing: An Anthropological Perspective*. New Haven, CT: Yale University Press.

Helman, Cecil G.
2000. *Culture, Health, and Illness* (4th ed.). Oxford, UK: Butterworth Heinemann.

Himmelgreen, David A., et al.
2000. "Food Insecurity Among Low-Income Hispanics in Hartford, Connecticut: Implications for Public Health Policy." *Human Organization* 59 (3):334–342.

Johnson, Thomas M.
1991. "Anthropologists in Medical Education: Ethnographic Prescriptions." In *Training Manual in Applied Medical Anthropology*, edited by Carole E. Hill, 125–160. Washington, DC: American Anthropological Association.

1995. "Critical Praxis Beyond the Ivory Tower: A Critical Commentary." *Medical Anthropology Quarterly* 9 (1):107–110.

Johnson, Thomas M., and Carolyn F. Sargent (eds.)
1990. *Medical Anthropology: A Handbook of Theory and Method*. Westport, CT: Greenwood Press.

Joralemon, Donald
1999. *Exploring Medical Anthropology*. Boston: Allyn and Bacon.

Lindenbaum, Shirley, and Margaret Lock (eds.)
1993. *Knowledge, Power, and Practice: The Anthropology of Medicine and Everyday Life*. Berkeley: University of California Press.

Marshall, Patricia A.
1991. "Research Ethics in Applied Medical Anthropology." In *Training Manual in Applied Medical Anthropology*, edited by Carole E. Hill, 213–235. Washington, DC: American Anthropological Association.

Martin, Emily
1987. *The Woman in the Body: A Cultural Analysis of Reproduction*. Boston: Beacon Press.

McElroy, Ann, and Patricia K. Townsend
1989. *Medical Anthropology in Ecological Perspective* (2nd ed.). Boulder, CO: Westview Press.

Miller, Sharon Glick
1997. "The Development of Clinically Applied Anthropology: A Cautionary Tale." In *Practicing Anthropology in the South*, edited by James M. T. Wallace, 119–126. Athens, GA: University of Georgia Press.

Morrow, Robert C.
1997. "Anthropology in the Practice of Medicine." In *Practicing Anthropology in the South*, edited by James M. T. Wallace, 127–132. Athens, GA: University of Georgia Press.

Nelson, Edward W.
1991. "Sexual Self-Defense Versus the Liaison Dangereuse: A Strategy for AIDS Prevention in the '90s." *American Journal of Preventive Medicine* 7 (3):146–149.

O'Connor, Kathleen A., and William L. Leap (eds.)
1993. "AIDS Outreach, Education, and Prevention: Anthropological Contributions." *Practicing Anthropology* 15 (4):3–72.

Paul, Benjamin (ed.)
1955. *Health, Culture, and Community*. New York: Russell Sage Foundation.

Pelto, Pertti J., and Gretel H. Pelto
1996. "Research Designs in Medical Anthropology." In *Handbook of Medical Anthropology: Contemporary Theory and Method* (rev. ed.), edited by Carolyn F. Sargent and Thomas M. Johnson, 293–324. Westport, CT: Greenwood Press.

Quandt, Sara A.
1996. "Nutrition in Medical Anthropology." In *Handbook of Medical Anthropology: Contemporary Theory and Method* (rev. ed.), edited by Carolyn F. Sargent and Thomas M. Johnson, 272–289. Westport, CT: Greenwood Press.

Roemer, Milton I.
1985. *National Strategies for Health Care Organization: A World Overview*. Ann Arbor, MI: Health Administration Press.

Romanucci-Ross, Lola, D. E. Moerman, and L. R. Tancredi
1997. *The Anthropology of Medicine* (3rd ed.). Westport, CT: Bergin and Garvey.

Rubel, Arthur J., and Michael R. Hass
1996. "Ethnomedicine." In *Handbook of Medical Anthropology: Contemporary Theory and Method* (rev. ed.), edited by Carolyn F. Sargent and Thomas M. Johnson, 113–130. Westport, CT: Greenwood Press.

Rush, John A.
1996. *Clinical Anthropology: An Application of Anthropological Concepts Within Clinical Settings*. Westport, CT: Praeger.

Sargent, Carolyn F., and Thomas M. Johnson (eds.)
1996. *Handbook of Medical Anthropology: Contemporary Theory and Method* (rev. ed.). Westport, CT: Greenwood Press.

Schoenberg, Nancy E.
2000. "Patterns, Factors, and Pathways Contributing to Nutritional Risk Among Rural African American Elders." *Human Organization* 59 (2):234–244.

Singer, Merrill
1986. "Developing a Critical Perspective in Medical Anthropology." *Medical Anthropology Quarterly* 17 (5):128–129.

1989. "The Coming of Age of Critical Medical Anthropology." *Social Science and Medicine* 28:1193–1203.

1995. "Beyond the Ivory Tower: Critical Praxis in Medical Anthropology." *Medical Anthropology Quarterly* 9 (1):80–106.

Singer, Merrill, and Hans Baer
1995. *Critical Medical Anthropology*. Amityville, NY: Baywood Publishing.

ten Brummelhuis, Han, and Gilbert Herdt (eds.)
1995. *Culture and Sexual Risk: Anthropological Perspectives on AIDS*. Amsterdam: Gordon and Breach Publishers.

Van Blerkom, Linda Miller
1995. "Clown Doctors: Shaman Healers of Western Medicine." *Medical Anthropology Quarterly* 9 (4):462–475.

Wallerstein, N., and E. Bernstein
1988. "Empowerment Education: Freire's Ideas Adapted to Health Education." *Health Education Quarterly* 15 (4):379–394.

Zborowski, Mark
1969. *People in Pain*. San Francisco: Jossey-Bass.

CHAPTER

12 INTERNATIONAL HEALTH

INTRODUCTION

Chapter 5 described the field of international development, aimed at helping to bring about beneficial economic, social, political, educational, and other changes in the lives of disenfranchised people in the developing nations of the world. International development efforts are based on the premise that every human being on earth is entitled to certain basic rights, among them the rights to sufficient nourishing food, clean water, adequate shelter, and economic and educational opportunities. Another of these basic human rights is the right to health. Acknowledging this right is not the same as saying that every human being has the right to be disease-free; to attempt to secure universal good health as a basic human right would be to pursue an unrealistic and hence frustrating goal. The right to health does mean that every human being should have the opportunity to live a healthful lifestyle in a safe, healthful environment, with access to basic health services when unwell.

International health (or, alternatively, **global health**) is a multidisciplinary specialty within the international development arena, dedicated to securing people's right to health. In theory, the term should refer to health promotion efforts anywhere in the world. In practice, however, it usually refers to the use of First

World resources—human, financial, or technological—to help address health problems in developing countries in Asia, Africa, Latin America, and—more recently—eastern Europe (Lane and Rubinstein 1996:397). Often these are specific health problems afflicting specific population groups (Pillsbury 1991:54): the failure of a government-sponsored vaccination program in a Central American country, a lack of access to information about birth control in West Africa, a budget insufficient for a Caribbean ministry of health to carry out its mandate, a need for environmental sanitation measures in a city neighborhood in Honduras, or rural women's inability to protect themselves against AIDS in India.

Problems such as these derive from complex cultural, historical, biological, and ecological factors, and finding solutions to them requires information and techniques from many different disciplines (Lane and Rubinstein 1996:396). The international health arena thus includes specialists in biomedicine, health economics, health policy analysis, health education, health administration, environmental sanitation, nutrition, biostatistics, cultural anthropology, and other fields. Whatever their professional discipline, however, the fundamental objective of international health specialists, including applied cultural anthropologists, is to help address contemporary health problems (see Table 12.1) and satisfy the health-related needs of the billions of people around the world who, for many reasons, are unable to answer these needs satisfactorily on their own.

International health traces its roots back to the colonial era, with missionaries' efforts to contribute to the well-being of indigenes and colonizers' efforts to safeguard themselves from disease and reap the economic rewards of healthy indigenous populations (Lane and Rubinstein 1996:397). Cultural anthropologists did not become institutionally involved in the international health arena until the middle of the twentieth century, when the idea of large-scale foreign assistance that emerged following World War II included assistance related to health problems (see Chapter 3, p. 65). The first cultural anthropologist to be employed by a major, multilateral international health organization was Cora DuBois. Better known for her earlier work on culture and personality, based on fieldwork on the island of Alor in the (then) Dutch East Indies, DuBois was hired as an international health specialist by the newly established World Health Organization in 1950 (Hill 1991:15). Cultural anthropologists have been contributing to this field ever since. Their involvement has recently been accelerated by developments within anthropology itself, such as the growing number of graduate programs in medical anthropology and public health and the decrease in academic opportunities for cultural anthropologists (Coreil 1990:9).

FOOD FOR THOUGHT Chapter 3 described a number of significant events of the mid–twentieth century that greatly influenced applied cultural anthropology. These included a resurgence of academic anthropology in a climate of intradisciplinary skepticism and even criticism; the establishment of the United Nations' International Bank for Reconstruction and Development; President Truman's Point Four program; the beginning of the Korean War; and—within anthropology—the founding of the SfAA. How might the World Health Organization's early (1950) employment of cultural anthropologist Cora DuBois, an academic and a theoretician, relate to these events?

◇ **TABLE 12.1** **Major International Public Health Issues, 2002**

Issue	Evidence
Bioterrorism	Recent anthrax and saran gas attacks in the United States and Japan
Child health and nutrition	Worldwide, 250,000 deaths of infants and children per week, from pneumonia, diarrhea, malaria, malnutrition, and measles
Environmental health	Approximately 25 percent of all preventable illness, worldwide, due to poor quality of environment
Health care financing	Per capita expenditures for health: in industrialized nations, $2,000; in sub-Saharan Africa, $20
HIV/AIDS	Worldwide, 36 million people currently infected; 6,500 new infections daily; 3 million deaths/year
New and reemerging infectious diseases	Increasing number of cases of ebola, hantavirus, anthrax, treatment-resistant tuberculosis, and pneumonia
Refugee health	Currently almost 12 million refugees, worldwide, at major risk of malnutrition, intestinal parasites, hepatitis B, and tuberculosis
Reproductive and maternal health	585,000 deaths per year from complications of pregnancy and childbirth

Sources: World Health Organization; Global Health Council; UNHCR.

If the international health field, as described above, appears to be purely humanitarian, it is more realistically portrayed by applied medical anthropologist Barbara Pillsbury as a "blend of self-interest and altruism" (Pillsbury 1991:57). Certainly the desire to help improve the health of disenfranchised people around the world motivates many individuals involved in this field. Governments providing international health assistance, however, may be equally motivated by "a desire for good will, prestige, . . . political influence, [or] national protection and defense against communicable diseases" (ibid.). International health efforts are also driven, in part, by the profit motive: this career field employs many thousands of people through hundreds of organizations, from huge multilaterals such as the World Health Organization to tiny, local NGOs. The total budget for international health efforts amounts to many hundreds of millions of dollars per year.

International health work is a natural fit for applied cultural anthropologists. Its **public health** orientation, emphasizing the health of populations rather than individuals, mirrors anthropology's emphasis on the culture and behavior of people in groups (Overbey 1998:7). Most applied cultural anthropologists who have chosen this domain of application find themselves drawing frequently on anthropological theories, field methods, and comparative ethnographic information about health, illness, and curing. Many supplement their anthropological training with expertise in some field of public health, such as maternal and child health, epidemiology, or environmental sanitation. The overall point of their work is to help find culturally appropriate solutions to four different kinds of health problems facing people in developing countries.

GLOBAL HEALTH PROBLEMS

Four Categories of Global Health Problems

The health problems most commonly addressed by international health specialists fall into several broad, overlapping, and frequently interconnected categories. One category is specific diseases, such as AIDS or tuberculosis. Since the discovery of the role of microorganisms in disease and the advent of modern medicine, and perhaps most especially since the discovery of antibiotics, many of the ailments that once plagued human communities have become either avoidable or controllable, yet numerous life-threatening diseases still exist. Some of these, such as tuberculosis, were once thought to be nearly eradicated but have reemerged—in some cases developing resistance to the medications that previously held them at bay. Others are diseases previously unknown in humans, such as AIDS, Ebola virus, and hantavirus, for which effective strategies for prevention or cure have yet to be developed. In addition, diseases that are in theory controllable, such as measles or cholera, sometimes afflict populations because of insufficient financial resources with which to control them, or a lack of appropriate vigilance. Thanks to rapid intercontinental transportation, even those diseases endemic to only one area of the world—tropical diseases, for instance—now threaten public health worldwide. Tracking, preventing, and attempting to control them amount to an enormous global public health burden.

A second category of health problems addressed by international health specialists consists of socioeconomic conditions that threaten the overall health of whole populations. Despite slow worldwide improvements in per capita income and living standards over the last half of the twentieth century, certain intractable, systemic problems continue to characterize the cultural climate in which many of the world's people, particularly those in developing countries, live. Most important among these are poverty, social inequality, and low levels of education, which are directly related to health problems such as malnutrition, unwanted pregnancy, and infectious diseases that thrive in unsanitary conditions.

A third category of global health problems of concern to international health specialists consists of human-made, and often lifestyle-related or economically or politically inspired, events or behaviors that pose a threat to good health. Traffic accidents and substance abuse are examples. In developing countries, many of these problems can be related to increasing Westernization. The devastating effects on public health of warfare, interpersonal violence, and migration are often included in this category by public health specialists.

Finally, global health is continually threatened by environmental problems, both natural and human-made. Both industrialized and developing countries are at risk. Perhaps of greatest concern is the ongoing degradation of the natural environment caused by humans' immoderate and unsustainable use of natural resources. Industrial pollution, untreated wastewater, and the unsafe storage or disposal of nuclear wastes have rendered the air, soil, and water unsafe in many parts of the world. Likewise, unregulated population growth has, in some areas, outstripped the carrying capacity of local environments.

Urban Growth as a Factor in Global Health

Since the Industrial Revolution, and especially since the middle of the twentieth century, these four global health problems have been greatly exacerbated by the growth of **megacities,** urban centers that are enormous both in terms of population numbers (ten million or more) and geographical extent.[1] Many of these cities are located in developing countries: São Paulo, Shanghai, Mexico City, Jakarta, and Bombay are examples. All are characterized by large populations of impoverished, malnourished, underemployed, and undereducated people, who continually create new squatter settlements on a city's ever-expanding periphery to accommodate their ever-increasing numbers. An astonishing 44 percent of all the people in the world now live in such cities, where they suffer disproportionately from the many health problems attributable, directly or indirectly, to urban poverty.

Some of the health problems plaguing megacities are the result of specific diseases that are transmitted through air or water pollution, or which flourish in conditions of inadequate sanitation; 23 percent of the world's urban dwellers do not have adequate sanitary facilities in their homes (WHO 1998:125). Other problems include adverse health conditions related to diet and reproductive health, most especially malnutrition and lack of birth control information and devices. The urban poor also suffer disproportionately from the negative health effects of lifestyle problems such as drug use, alcoholism, prostitution, and interpersonal violence. In short, the poor inhabitants of the world's megacities suffer the most perilous health conditions of anyone in the world.

Cultural anthropologists have made important theoretical contributions to the international health community's understanding of the negative health implications of unrelenting urban growth. The subdiscipline of **urban anthropology,** which focuses on cultural features characterizing city life (such as rural-to-urban migration, social networks among city dwellers, and the adaptation of ethnic minorities to urban environments), has proven particularly relevant (Southall 1973; Leeds 1994). Urban anthropologist Oscar Lewis, for example, identified a useful association of features he collectively termed the **culture of poverty** (Lewis 1966), elements of which include social disorganization, a weakening of kinship ties, and—at the level of the individual—chronic depression. Anthropologists' understanding of the sociocultural ramifications of an impoverished urban lifestyle have thus provided a foundation for the work of international health specialists targeting specific health conditions that commonly afflict city dwellers, such as tuberculosis, acute respiratory infections, and certain vector-borne diseases.

APPLIED MEDICAL ANTHROPOLOGY AND INTERNATIONAL HEALTH: A COMPARISON

Medical anthropology was described in Chapter 11 as a subdiscipline of cultural anthropology focusing on human health, illness, illness prevention, and curing. The applied component of medical anthropology may appear to overlap considerably with international health as a field of professional endeavor, and in fact most applied cultural anthropologists specializing in international health have backgrounds in medical anthropology. In both disciplines, the primary focus is health-related beliefs and behaviors rather than germs and genes. Both disciplines are oriented mainly toward the preventive aspects of health care, leaving direct curative care to biomedical professionals. In both, practitioners acknowledge the efficacy of biomedicine and work mainly with biomedical professionals, while at the same time taking ethnomedical belief systems into account (see Lane and Rubinstein 1996). Because of these similarities, some anthropologists specializing in international health view their area of expertise as one kind of applied medical anthropology (see Pillsbury 1991; Lane and Rubinstein 1996), and indeed much of what they do, such as health education, health policy analysis, and health planning, is essentially applied medical anthropology undertaken in international contexts.

Despite these similarities, however, there are some significant differences— mainly differences in emphasis—between the two disciplines. First, because international health is an aspect of the more comprehensive field of international development, its practitioners take a global perspective that tends to be wider in scope than that of medical anthropologists (Coreil 1990:4). International health specialists are very much concerned with broad issues of human and economic development in the less developed countries of the world. One of these issues, already mentioned, is the linkage between health and development, and especially between ill health and systemic problems of underdevelopment such as poverty and illiteracy. Applied medical anthropology, in contrast, lacks international health's development orientation, although medical anthropologists do sometimes play important roles in international health projects.

A second difference, following from the first, is that the intended beneficiaries of international health efforts are mainly poor people in developing countries. Most Western-educated applied medical anthropologists work in North America and the other industrialized countries.

FOOD FOR THOUGHT In many developing countries, health care is provided to all citizens at no charge, by government-employed health practitioners at government-run hospitals and clinics. In industrialized countries, by contrast, most individuals are expected to pay private health care providers for their health care or purchase health insurance. If access to health care is considered by development specialists to be a basic human right, how can the private provision of health care be justified?

Third, international health, because of its broad concern with the social, political, and economic factors that contribute to public health problems, is less explicitly "medical" than medical anthropology. This difference is reflected in the different kinds of work and different workplaces that characterize the two disciplines. International health specialists do not typically engage in clinical work, as do some applied medical anthropologists; they are much more apt to be involved in research than in hands-on practice. While an applied medical anthropologist would be likely to work in an inner-city clinic, helping non–English-speaking immigrants to understand when and how to take their TB medication, an international health specialist would be likely to work in an office, either at home or abroad, helping the water and sanitation ministry of a developing country to implement a plan for installing modern wells in order to bring clean water to rural areas.

Another difference between applied medical anthropology and international health can be attributed to political factors. While much of the work of specialists in both fields is ultimately humanitarian, international health concerns and efforts are sometimes shaped or steered by local or global political concerns in a way that the domestic efforts of applied medical anthropologists are not. As an example of how political pressure can affect international health efforts, funding provided by USAID for reproductive health in developing countries has been restricted for many years because of the lobbying efforts of anti-abortion activists in the United States.[2]

Even the diseases of interest to practitioners of the two disciplines differ. The specific health problems that garner most of the international health community's attention and dollars—such as diarrheal disease and upper respiratory infections in children, measles, and the major parasitic diseases such as onchocerciasis and malaria—disproportionately afflict people in developing countries. The applied medical anthropologist's interests are much more likely to focus on diseases that commonly afflict Westerners, such as cancer and heart disease. (Today, practitioners of both disciplines are of course heavily invested in helping to find solutions to the problem of HIV/AIDS; see p. 284.)

In addition to their somewhat different emphases, other differences exist between the two disciplines. Health care financing is a major aspect of international health work but not of applied medical anthropology. The funding of the two disciplines differs: funding for international health efforts comes mostly from public and private agencies in the industrialized nations and is spent on improving the health of people in developing nations, but no such flow of funding from rich nations to poor ones supports work in applied medical anthropology. Sponsorship also differs: international health work is often sponsored, whether in the form of money or technical assistance, by multilateral organizations or by bilateral organizations in donor countries, in addition to the national-level organizations, nongovernmental organizations, universities, and private businesses providing support for applied medical anthropology. Finally, while international health is sometimes self-critical, it lacks the reflexive component of applied medical anthropology, with its critical focus on the Western capitalist social, economic, and political system.

FUNDAMENTAL CONCEPTS IN INTERNATIONAL HEALTH

The Health–Development Link

Especially in the developing world, the basic causes of ill health—specific diseases, unhealthy socioeconomic conditions, lifestyle-related choices and behaviors such as smoking or certain sexual practices, and environmental degradation—are inextricably linked, since diseases flourish wherever poverty, social inequality, lack of education, or misuse of the environment result in inadequate housing, deficient sanitation, poor nutrition, unemployment, or a lack of understanding about the causes of ill health. Today, defining the linkages, both negative and positive, among economic development, the environment, and human health represents a major focus of international health specialists (Rodriguez-Garcia and Goldman 1994; Bradford and Gwynne 1995).

The linkages are subtle. One of the major, overall objectives of international development is to raise the standard of living of poor people in developing countries (see Chapter 5). In any given developing country, this may be accomplished in many different ways, but it almost always includes an overall economic goal: increasing individual and household income by increasing the country's industrial production. In many developing countries, however, moving toward that goal has come at a price: even as industrial production and income (as well as the availability of modern health care) increase, so do people's access to commodities, technologies, and lifestyles with negative health effects. As inevitable concomitants to Western-style economic development, factories create jobs and produce desirable consumer goods, but also spew air pollution. Technological advances permit people the leisure time to indulge in sedentary activities such as watching television, which means they get less and less physical exercise. Processed, canned, and frozen foods—often imported— offer convenience and variety, but they replace fresh, home-grown, high-fiber foods, and often contain more calories, sugar, animal fats, and sodium than locally produced foods. New roads, rail lines, and airports permit more and easier travel, but travel exacerbates disease transmission and exposes people to transportation accidents. Alcohol, tobacco, and recreational drugs become more available. In short, the modern Westernized lifestyle, wherever in the world it is pursued, can be hazardous to human health.

The health problems to which the lifestyle changes accompanying economic development contribute are collectively termed **the diseases of affluence.** They include both chronic degenerative diseases (such as cancer, heart disease, diabetes, and hypertension) and lifestyle-associated health problems (such as alcoholism and traffic fatalities). Of course, one need not be affluent or Westernized to suffer from these health problems; even in small-scale, traditional societies, people sometimes succumb to cancer or heart disease or die in transportation accidents. But people in societies that have enjoyed Western-style development are much more apt to suffer from this particular group of ailments than people in nonindustrialized societies. Taken together, the diseases of affluence are by far the commonest causes of morbidity and mortality in the West, and their incidence is growing rapidly in the developing world.

Increases in the health problems attributable to Westernization result in changes in a country's **national health profile,** a summary of the kinds and rates of sickness and death from which the population of a given country suffers. These changes are both positive and negative, but the more Westernized a developing country becomes, the more dramatic the changeover in its national health profile. On the positive side, life expectancy goes up, and infant mortality decreases. In some cases, nutrition improves. People no longer routinely die of measles and infected wounds; however, they are more likely than previously to suffer from obesity and alcoholism and to die of cancer and in traffic accidents. This inevitable linkage between development and health, for better and for worse, is perhaps the most fundamental concept in international health.

◇ *Residents of developing countries suffer increasingly from "diseases of affluence," health problems caused mainly by lifestyle changes accompanying economic development. The proportion of teenagers who smoke is even higher in China than it is in the Unites States.*

The Primary Health Care Concept

In 1978, in the city of Alma Ata in what was then the Soviet Union, health officials representing most of the nations of the world gathered at a conference organized by the World Health Organization and UNICEF, two branches of the United Nations. Their goal was to identify what could be done, worldwide, to improve public health, especially in developing countries. For decades, Western nations and charitable organizations had been donating money, high-tech medical equipment, and even whole hospitals to developing countries, with an emphasis on curative rather than preventive care, but people's health in these countries was improving only slowly. The Alma Ata conferees realized that the best way to make significant and lasting improvements in world health would be to shift the developing countries' focus away from costly, high-tech facilities and equipment, in favor of concentrating on the basics. They agreed on an ambitious goal: to ensure that by the year 2000, all people, no matter where in the world they lived, would have access to minimal but crucial biomedical health services.

The Alma Ata conferees agreed on a package of health services they considered essential, which they termed **primary health care** or **PHC** (see Macdonald 1993). PHC is an assortment of relatively simple procedures for preventing or curing common medical conditions—the kinds of procedures one would expect to access at a clinic or doctor's office as opposed to a hospital. Providers of PHC need not be physicians; members of local communities with only minimal medical training can provide most services. Included are first aid for injuries or sudden illnesses; growth monitoring and vaccinations for young children; routine gynecological and obstetrical care for women (such as breast exams, Pap tests, prenatal care, and normal deliveries); and routine monitoring and treatment of chronic conditions such as diabetes and high blood pressure. PHC also includes several other services—"public health" services in that they are directed at the health of whole populations rather than individuals—such as sanitary waste disposal, water quality assurance, and a basic level of health education for schoolchildren.

The Alma Ata conference attendees drew up and signed a document, the "Alma Ata Convention," which proclaimed their intention to work toward the goal of "Health For All by the Year 2000" (HFA/2000). This slogan did not mean that the conferees expected that disease would be eradicated and everyone in the world would be healthy by the year 2000. It did mean that ideally, by the year 2000, basic health services would be available to everyone in the world, giving them the opportunity to remain or to become healthy.

Obviously, this goal has not been fully realized; some proportion of the world's population still lacks access to basic health services and suffers from preventable diseases (see Table 12.1 on page 273). Children are at particular risk: around the world, some 250,000 infants and children die per week, most of them from infantile diarrhea or upper respiratory tract infections, because they lack access to primary health care. However, improvements implemented over the past twenty-odd years in the name of HFA/2000 have helped bring better health to millions, if not billions, of people around the world, and most international health specialists would agree that the PHC concept has been a success. At the time of the Alma Ata Convention, only 60 percent of the world's people could expect to live beyond the age of sixty; today, 86 percent do. At the time of Alma Ata, 70 percent of all countries in the world suffered infant mortality rates above fifty per one thousand births; now, only 40 percent do (WHO 1998:39). Polio immunization coverage has gone from fewer than a third of infants to over 80 percent (ibid.:156). Dozens of additional health indicators show similar levels of improvement, thanks in large part to PHC.

Despite improvements over the years, the concept of primary health care has been occasionally criticized as too ambitious, too expensive, or too labor-intensive (Pillsbury 1991:58). Defenders of PHC now acknowledge that progress has been slow and that they may have been overly optimistic about the extent to which local people would actually participate in rectifying their own health problems; some are reluctant since the gains realized from the PHC approach are long term and thus less visible than short-term gains (ibid.). Such considerations have led, in recent years, to a more focused approach to global health, in which funding and expertise are dedicated to a narrow range of specific interventions such as child health and population control programs. These refinements to the idea of HFA/2000 are subsumed under the umbrella term **GOBI-FFF**, which stands for Growth monitoring, Oral rehydration therapy, Breast-feeding, Immunization, Female education, Family spacing, and Food supplements. Programs dedicated to realizing gains in these specific areas now account for a major proportion of international health funding.

Health Services as "Public Goods" and "Merit Goods"

A third concept basic to international health—a concept fundamental to the economics of health care—is that many of the goods and services that are vital for the health of populations fall into two categories: public goods or merit goods. The term *public goods* was defined in Chapter 10 as goods (or services) that benefit society as a whole, and to which individual access cannot be restricted. Clean air is a frequently cited example. **Merit goods** are goods (or services) that in theory could be bought and sold like other commodities, but—if left to the private sector to produce—would not be purchased in sufficient quantity to make production financially worthwhile. Public health education is an example. Since neither public goods nor merit goods respond to the laws of supply and demand affecting other kinds of goods and services, the private sector has no incentive to produce them. In most modern societies, therefore, they are provided by public sector or not-for-profit institutions.

Sometimes what is or is not a public good is not at all clear, which greatly complicates the ethics of public health. For example, there is no doubt that malaria, a mosquito-borne disease, is a serious threat to public health, killing some 2.7 million people a year, mostly in developing countries (Stolberg 1999:1). Neither is there any doubt that the cheapest and most effective way to prevent malaria is to use the pesticide DDT; other pesticides cost so much more than DDT that developing countries cannot afford to buy them. And there is absolutely no doubt that DDT is an environmental poison, traveling through the food chain from sprayed trees to farm animals to humans, and turning up, for example, in the breast milk of nursing mothers (ibid.:8). Should the governments of developing countries spray mosquito-infested areas with DDT or—in the name of environmental protection—stand by as their citizens die from malaria? International health professionals struggle constantly with such quandaries.

FOOD FOR THOUGHT

Using pesticides on food crops greatly improves their yield, and consequently increases the profits earned per acre of crop land. In the industrialized countries of the world, therefore, large-scale agribusinesses have a strong incentive to use pesticides. But some pesticides, such as DDT, are known to be extremely harmful to human health. Can you think of any reasons why private sector food producers would be motivated to regulate pesticide use themselves? If self-regulation fails, who should be responsible for regulating pesticide use? Why?

Community Participation and Sustainability

Finally, two principles that were described in detail in Chapter 5—community participation and sustainability—are as important in international health as they are in other areas of development. A solution to a public health problem that is imposed on a group of people in a developing country from the top down, without their wholehearted involvement in identifying the problem and then selecting and implementing a solution, is practically guaranteed to be unsustainable, even if the international health specialists who implemented it have the best of intentions. Such solutions are very likely, for example, to be unacceptable to their intended beneficiaries for cultural reasons; or they may be too difficult or too expensive to maintain after foreign assistance ends.

To prevent this frustrating and wasteful outcome, it is vitally important that all international health projects include host-country counterparts from the outset. Sometimes these are representatives of the government of a developing country, such as employees of the ministry of health; sometimes they are health professionals—doctors, nurses, pharmacists, environmental health specialists, or health educators; sometimes they are local people—for instance, the residents of a village or district in which a health plan is to be implemented. If health improvements are to be sustained, the importance of including the intended beneficiaries of international health projects, at every level, can be neither overestimated nor overemphasized.

An international health project recently undertaken in forty-eight small villages in rural Gujarat, a state in northwestern India, owes a large part of its success to its implementation of the notions of community participation and sustainability. The residents of the forty-eight villages were universally poor and uneducated, and they suffered inadequate sanitation and housing in addition to their lack of access to biomedical health care. Employing a KAP (knowledge, attitudes, and practices) survey (defined in Chapter 1, p. 19), a methodological tool frequently used in international health research, international health researcher Aziz Popatiya found that village residents suffered high rates of preventable illnesses, and background research revealed why: there were significant gaps in residents' knowledge about how to maintain good health (Popatiya 2000).[3]

With funding from the Aga Khan Health Service, Popatiya and his colleagues set out to establish a sustainable, financially viable health system to answer village residents' needs—a daunting challenge, given the number of times similar efforts to provide health facilities and practitioners for impoverished communities have proven unsustainable. Rather than planning the project, constructing local health facilities, and hiring staff themselves, project planners encouraged the participation of community members throughout all phases of the project. The villagers were unable to contribute financially to constructing, equipping, and staffing health facilities, but their ideas, opinions, and volunteer labor were encouraged and relied upon throughout the project, which ensured that the new health system would be truly need based and demand driven. Once it was in place, the community assumed full responsibility for it through community-based governance. The extent to which members of the beneficiary villages participated in the project, at all levels, fostered feelings of empowerment, pride, and ownership that are expected to sustain the new system indefinitely.

ROLES FOR APPLIED CULTURAL ANTHROPOLOGISTS IN INTERNATIONAL HEALTH

In any country or culture, the many activities required to secure and maintain people's health can be classified into several types (see Roemer 1985:19). Perhaps the most obvious is treating individuals who are ill, but other activities, undertaken on a societywide rather than an individual level, are just as important: appraising health conditions to identify problems; preventing future illness; educating populations about healthy behaviors; planning for, acquiring, and financing the resources needed for health care; evaluating efforts to improve health; and organizing and regulating the health care system. In modern societies, there is yet another important task: doing scientific research on which to base future solutions to health-related problems.

Applied cultural anthropologists specializing in international health are involved in all these activities except for the actual treatment of the sick (which they leave to physicians)—in other words, all health-related activities above the level of

⟡ *In many places in developing countries, like this rural village in Northwestern India, modern health services are nonexistent or rudimentary, yet international health workers' experience has shown that the top-down imposition of health services on impoverished communities is usually unsustainable.*

the individual. They may specialize in the health of specific groups of people, defined by ethnicity, social status, age, or illness (for example, pastoralists in East Africa, refugees, infants delivered by midwives in developing countries, or AIDS patients). Alternatively, they may specialize in the organization and operations of health-related institutions in specific cultural settings (for example, hospitals, ministries of health, or health insurance plans). The following examples of the different types of health-related activities with which international health specialists are concerned will provide a broad picture of the work of these applied cultural anthropologists.

Preventing Illness

It was noted at the beginning of this chapter that the causes of ill health range from the specific and clinically defined (bacteria, viruses, faulty genes) to the general and socially defined (poverty, malnutrition, unsanitary living conditions). Although some international health specialists, mainly scientists and physicians, are concerned with the former (for example, helping to identify specific microbes or specific pollutants causing ill health), most—including most applied cultural anthropologists working in this field—focus on the latter: the systemic social and behavioral factors that cause or contribute to ill health. Some of them help ensure that people in developing countries have nutritious food, clean water, clean air, and sanitary waste-disposal facilities. Others work to create and maintain healthy environments, free not only of pollution but also of war, crime, and interpersonal violence. Others, concerned about the linkages among overpopulation, poverty, and illness, specialize in reproductive health (defined in Chapter 11). Other areas of illness prevention to which anthropologists

contribute include child health services (such as immunization and growth monitoring); vector control (to prevent the spread of parasitic, communicable, and infectious diseases); occupational health and safety (to ensure healthy, safe workplaces);
diet and nutrition (see Chapter 11, p. 257); and the modification of behaviors that
increase the risk of ill health—all in specific cultural settings.

FOOD FOR THOUGHT Imagine an international health project aimed at discouraging smoking
among school-age males in Thailand, whose high incidence of tobacco use
is seriously jeopardizing their health and that of those around them. How
would you go about learning why members of this particular group used
tobacco so heavily? Based on the information presented in Chapter 10 on
social marketing, how could this approach be used to "sell" beneficial ideas
to this particular group? What other strategies might be used to discourage
young Thai males from smoking? How would you evaluate the success
of the project, one year after implementation? If a given strategy, once
implemented, proved successful, how could it best be sustained?

The war against AIDS provides an example of cultural anthropologists' role in
illness prevention (Reid 1995; ten Brummelhuis and Herdt 1995). The most threatening of all new diseases in public health terms, AIDS claims astonishing numbers of
victims worldwide (see Figure 12.1), despite the efforts of many thousands of international health workers striving to reduce its spread. Over 36 million people, of
whom 1.5 million are children, are estimated to be currently infected with the
human immunodeficiency virus (HIV), which causes AIDS. In the year 2000 alone,
some 3 million people worldwide, including half a million children, died of
HIV/AIDS-associated illnesses, and 6,500 people a day contracted the infection
(ibid.). More than 95 percent of these new infections were in developing countries—two thirds of them in Africa, which by the year 2010 may have lost a quarter
of its labor force to AIDS (WHO 1998:93). Young people and women are particularly
at risk: 60 percent of new cases, worldwide, occur in the 15–24 age group, and the
rate of increase of AIDS in women is much greater than it is in men.

Given that AIDS is essentially the same biological disease wherever it occurs,
what help can applied cultural anthropologists provide in the global war against this
disease? One anthropologist who specializes in AIDS has identified three crucial
contributions: (1) anthropologists can help prevent new cases through attempts to
change people's high-risk behaviors; (2) they can help those already living with HIV
or AIDS to improve the quality of their lives; and (3) they can work to overcome obstacles to the achievement of the first two tasks (Bolton 1995:289).

The first of the three contributions engages the largest proportion of anthropologists working in AIDS prevention. Since the virus is transmitted through certain
behaviors, persuading people to change those behaviors can help control its spread.
This requires an understanding of the particular factors, in a given cultural context,
that affect health-related behavior. Indonesian culture, for example, incorporates
the idea that medicine should be taken by injection rather than by mouth. Because
needle reuse is an important mode of transmission of the AIDS virus, Indonesians

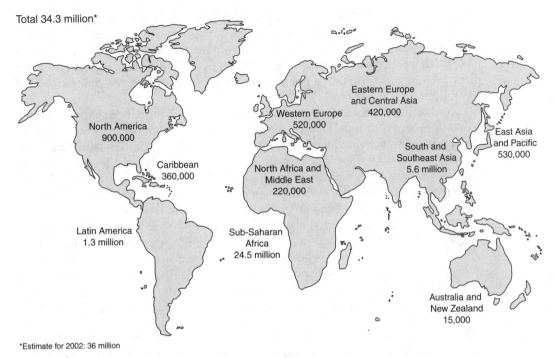

Total 34.3 million*

North America
900,000

Caribbean
360,000

Latin America
1.3 million

Western Europe
520,000

Eastern Europe
and Central Asia
420,000

North Africa and
Middle East
220,000

Sub-Saharan
Africa
24.5 million

South and
Southeast Asia
5.6 million

East Asia
and Pacific
530,000

Australia and
New Zealand
15,000

*Estimate for 2002: 36 million

◇ **FIGURE 12.1   Global Distribution of HIV/AIDS as of January 1, 2000**

Source: UNAIDS, NIAID

may be more at risk from this disease than people living in a cultural context in which taking medications by mouth is preferred.

Persuading a group of people to change their behavior somehow is more than just a matter of educating them about risk. Many people smoke even though they know they are risking future lung cancer. Likewise, many people engage in behavior that puts them at risk of AIDS, even though they understand the ways in which AIDS is transmitted. One can advise an at-risk group to abstain from sex, use condoms, and avoid sharing needles, but whether they will heed this advice or not depends very largely on the culture or subculture in which they are immersed. Youth subcultures, for example, are apt to incorporate the idea that risky sexual or drug-related behavior is glamorous or macho. In certain religious contexts, people may fail to take precautions against AIDS because they believe God will protect them. In patriarchal cultures, women may be afraid to say no to their male sex partners. Anthropologists' understanding of these cultural contexts is a crucial aspect of AIDs prevention.

Stemming Overpopulation

In many countries around the world, there has been a dramatic increase in population over the past two or three generations, thanks mainly to the introduction of modern medicine. The rate of world population growth has been nothing short of astonishing. It took 173 years, from 1801 to 1974, for the world's human population to grow from 1 billion to 4 billion people—an average growth rate of a little less than 1 billion people every 50 years. By 1992, less than 20 years later, world population had grown by another billion, to over 5 billion. In 1999, less than 10 years later, we topped 6 billion. By 2050, the population of the planet may be 9.3 billion (Moffett 1994; Bouvier and Bertrand 1999:4).

Today, the number of people being born exceeds the number dying by about a million people every four days. In some countries, the *rate* of growth is falling, but the population is still growing in absolute terms. In a few countries—all of them industrialized ones—fertility has actually fallen below replacement levels, but those falling rates have been insufficient to offset worldwide growth.

This is considered a health problem because of the indisputable linkages among rapid population growth, poverty, and ill health, as reflected in national health status indicators in rapidly growing countries—indicators such as life expectancy, the infant mortality rate, and the average daily number of calories consumed per person. The most rapid population growth is taking place in the developing countries of the world, poor countries whose health systems are already failing to answer people's basic health needs and provide basic health services (Bouvier and Bertrand 1999:4). The implications are obvious. Unless rapid population growth is slowed in the developing world, the incidence of ill health will greatly increase.

A rapidly growing population is often an overwhelming burden for a developing country's government, which must be responsible for providing public goods and merit goods (including health services) to more and more people every year—not to mention other expensive social services, such as housing and education, that people cannot afford to pay for themselves. For many developing countries—including some with long traditions of religious objection to artificial means of birth control—slowing population growth has become nothing short of an economic imperative.

The most effective way to control population growth is through the use of contraceptives, and worldwide, contraceptive use has increased greatly over the last generation. But this increase has not always taken place in the countries with the worst problems of overpopulation, poverty, and ill health. For example, in the United States, 71 percent of sexually active women of reproductive age (ages 15–45) use some form of contraception, but only 3 percent of women in the impoverished African country of Mauritania do (Bouvier and Bertrand 1999:75–76).

Thus family planning has become an important part of the international health field, and numerous applied cultural anthropologists, together with host-country counterparts (most often public health officials), are working to encourage the distribution of family-planning information and aids (such as condoms, contraceptive pills, and IUDs) in Third World countries. Much of the funding for their projects is supplied by USAID. Projects targeting specific countries or regions are usually implemented by small NGOs dedicated exclusively to population control.

In recent years, international development professionals have realized that the empowerment of women—providing them with the resources needed for greater autonomy and greater participation in social and economic life, above the level of the household—is highly correlated with the acceptance of family planning. In general, women who are happily and fruitfully employed choose to bear fewer children than unemployed women do. For this reason, many family-planning projects now include education, training in specific skills, or income-generating activities for women.

The family-planning efforts of international health agencies have long been criticized, for several reasons. Primary among them, of course, is the idea that artificial contraception is immoral from a religious point of view. Second, in some settings, the idea of birth control is unacceptable for cultural reasons—for example, a big family may convey high status. Third, members of some ethnic minorities view birth control suspiciously, as a possible ruse intended mainly to reduce the size of their groups. Fourth, there has been widespread objection to the way contraceptive products have been tested for safety and effectiveness; some drug companies have made virtual guinea pigs of women in developing countries by offering them free contraceptives that have not yet been approved for use in the West. Finally, human rights advocates insist on **reproductive rights**—the right of individuals to decide for themselves the number of children they wish to have, without pressure from outsiders (Dixon-Mueller 1993). For all these reasons, it is important for those working to control overpopulation around the world to understand that there are circumstances in which such efforts will be inappropriate or unsuccessful.

Organizing and Regulating Health Care Systems

In any country, health services, because they fall into the category of public or merit goods (see p. 280), must be subject to government oversight instead of being allowed to be driven entirely by market forces. Some applied anthropologists specializing in international health help organize the provision of health care in developing countries and then help these countries regulate their health systems to ensure that health services are of sufficient quantity and high quality, are distributed equitably among the population, and are delivered efficiently.

The most fundamental health-related organizational decision is whether a country's health services should be provided and funded mainly by the government or by private entities. Modern health care for the citizens of any country can be organized, financed, and delivered through either the public or private economic sectors, or a combination of both. For most countries, a "mixed" health care system, in which both sectors are players, is ideal, based on considerations of quantity, quality, equity, and efficiency. In most developing countries, however, relatively little private health care is available; the government is, in effect, the owner, operator, and financier of most health services. Many governments would like to cut back on this role, but no responsible government can withdraw from the health care arena without first ensuring that satisfactory private sector alternatives to government services are available. Thus an important area of international health today is helping developing nations determine—and achieve—the right balance between publicly provided and privately provided health care.

Persuasive arguments can be made for the public provision of at least some health services (see, for example, Roth 1987:130). But there are a number of compelling reasons for increased privatization of health services (Griffin 1989:1), and in fact the international development policy of the United States and other donor countries now stresses the value of privatization. Public health systems typically

LILY P. KAK

Lily Patir Kak was born and raised in Assam, India, where she earned a B.A. in English and a Master's degree in linguistics. In 1979, never envisioning a future career in international health, she came to the United States to study anthropology, eventually earning a second Master's degree as well as a Ph.D. in cultural anthropology. At the time, her university did not offer graduate courses in either applied or medical anthropology, so even if she had been interested in a career in health, specializing in the subject would not have been possible. Her Ph.D. dissertation, based on ten months of fieldwork in India, explored social change among members of a northeastern Indian hill tribe.

While still in graduate school, Dr. Kak married, and when her husband (also an anthropologist) was awarded a postdoctoral position at the Johns Hopkins School of Public Health, she applied for and won a similar postdoc in the university's Department of Behavioral Science and Health Education. Hopkins postdocs are permitted to audit courses, so Dr. Kak attended classes in international health, including health education, epidemiology, biostatistics, and research methods. "It really grabbed my interest," she now recalls. "I felt international health was very meaningful."

A short time later, with two babies in tow, the Kaks left the United States for jobs in Indonesia. The University of Indonesia had received funding from a private U.S.-based charitable institution, the Ford Foundation, to serve as the secretariat for the Indonesian Epidemiology Network, which linked foundation grantees working mainly on child health projects. As a long-term consultant for the foundation, Dr. Kak was charged with setting up the network. The job made public health "very real" for her, because "I was working on real projects. I had a good time learning—and giving as well. I just got more and more into public health."

After three years in Indonesia and a great deal of experience in the international health field, Dr. Kak decided it was time to change jobs. "If you want to move up the international health career ladder," she advises, "don't spend too long in one country; you become branded as an expert in that country. I didn't want to be known as an Indonesia expert; I wanted to learn more about other countries." She soon found a job as an evaluation specialist at the Center for Development and Population Activities (CEDPA), in Washington, D.C. A nonprofit organization specializing in population and women's issues, CEDPA conducts international health projects (many of them funded by USAID) all over the world.

Dr. Kak remained with CEDPA for eight years, traveling the globe to participate in numerous overseas projects and moving from evaluation specialist to deputy director for Asia to senior program adviser. For this last position, she was stationed in Delhi, India, where she provided technical assistance to the largest family-planning effort in the world—USAID's Innovations in Family Planning Services project. This job, in which she helped build the capacity of NGOs to develop and implement community-based reproductive health programs, was particularly rewarding. "Here was my chance to show my children (then seven and nine) where I was born and raised," Dr. Kak says.

Eventually, once again feeling "the itch to move on," Dr. Kak left CEDPA. She worked briefly as a consultant for a consortium of PVOs that needed a standardized evaluation manual to help build the capacity of NGOs around the world. Developing this manual occupied her for two months. She discovered, however, that "I'm not cut out to be a consultant. I like the camaraderie of the office." As soon as the consultancy ended, she accepted a job at a major consulting firm, Abt Associates, where she served as Asia–Near East regional manager for eighteen months, working on a global, USAID-funded reproductive health project.

In 2001, Dr. Kak changed jobs again, becoming senior maternal and child health adviser at USAID's Asia–Near East bureau. This job involves considerable travel, a definite advantage to Dr. Kak: "The day the travel stops, I will have to quit this job and look for another one. The real programs are being implemented out in the field. What you do here [in Washington]—planning, report writing—is necessary, but I just wait for those trips overseas, because that's where it all comes together." Being able to travel every couple of months, and having friends all over the world "make the whole world feel like a global village."

Recent trips have taken Dr. Kak to Egypt, where she worked on the country's long-term population and health strategy, and also to Cambodia. In each country she worked with senior-level public health specialists, USAID staff, and consultants. "I like teaming up with experienced people; I learn a lot from them, and we have a lot of fun together. I feel good about being part of a team working to develop a strategy that lays a foundation for the long-term USAID program for a country. Even though I don't actually implement the pro-gram, I help envision a strategy that will have an important impact on women and children."

Dr. Kak feels her anthropology background has influenced her in a very basic way. "Anthropology becomes a part of you, like a philosophy; you have it in you, and it frames your whole thought process." Probably because of her anthropological training, she favors community-based approaches to international health. "In the low-income countries where we work, it is the community that has the greatest impact. To have any impact on people's health, you have to understand their culture and belief system. If you don't, trying to improve health is like putting another Band-Aid on a huge wound."

Dr. Kak has developed a distinguished career in international health as a specialist in the health of poor people in Asia and the Near East, managing to combine her work with marriage and parenthood. In a few years, when her children are both in college, she would like to work in a USAID mission in another country, because "that's where you can really do the most to make a difference."

Working in foreign countries is common in the international health arena. In 1997, applied cultural anthropologists and international health expert Lily Kak (center, with Indian colleagues) participated in a health awareness seminar in India.

consume a relatively large (and constantly escalating) proportion of what it costs the government of a developing country to run the country. These systems also tend to be inefficient, which increases costs; the quality of care tends to be poorer than in mixed systems; provider morale and consumer satisfaction tend to be lower; and consumers' choices are usually more limited. Finally, in any country, the demand for health services increases, over time, with increasing population and technological advances. No government can realistically expect to meet this constantly rising demand indefinitely. Sooner or later, the government will no longer be able to provide adequate health care for everyone, so some people will either have to pay for private health services or do without.

A government can take a number of steps to encourage privatization. For example, it can create a hospitable regulatory environment by making it relatively easy for private medical practices and hospitals to get licenses; it can provide tax incentives by lowering taxes on private health services, pharmaceuticals, or medical supplies; it can lower interest rates to encourage borrowing for purposes of investment in the private health sector; or it can stimulate the demand for private care by making medical expenditures tax deductible (Berman and Rannan-Eliya 1993:63). Comparing its own situation with that of other countries, with the help of applied cultural anthropologists, can help a developing country achieve an appropriately balanced health care system.

Planning for, Securing, and Financing Health Care Resources

The term *health care resources* refers to any and all of the components required for modern biomedical health care, including funds, practitioners, facilities such as hospitals and clinics, medical equipment and supplies, pharmaceuticals, and health-related programs such as environmental sanitation or health education programs. For a country's health system to meet its citizens' health needs responsibly, health care resources must first be obtained in sufficient quantity; then they must be organized and administered efficiently and equitably, and maintained at adequate levels into the future.

FOOD FOR THOUGHT   In the United States and other industrialized countries, the burden on the public health sector is greatly alleviated by private health insurance. Over the past generation, however, private health insurance has increasingly meant *managed care*—to the general dissatisfaction of both patients and their health care providers. Should Western health care financing specialists working in developing countries encourage the growth of private health insurance? If so, should managed care be encouraged or discouraged? Why?

International health specialists working in this area help host-country public health officials determine what resources are needed in a given country and how best to ensure that all needed components—public and private—are available. They may help decide, for example, how many public and private hospitals and clinics, doctors, nurses, traditional healers, and pieces of diagnostic and therapeutic equipment (such as x-ray and dialysis machines) are needed to serve a given population, how many are currently available, how additional resources can be obtained, and how resources can best be organized and managed to ensure a smoothly functioning system.

A crucial issue confronting any developing country's health system is financing. How much do health services cost? Who should pay for them—the government, private employers, private health insurers, or individuals? In most developing countries, as noted above, the government attempts to provide health services for all citizens who cannot pay for them, but in many of these countries the government's budget for health is insufficient to meet this goal. One possibility for rectifying this problem is for a government to impose modest fees on visitors to public sector health facilities. This has the effect of creating demand for private care, which helps offset the burden on the public sector. It may also help decrease unnecessary utilization of public facilities, improve consumers' perception of the quality of care, and—if the revenues collected are allowed to remain at the local level—improve providers' morale. Governments are often reluctant to institute such fees for fear of depriving the poor of health care, but the evidence for whether or not this will actually result is conflicting. In some developing countries, instituting user fees has not discouraged utilization; in others, utilization has dropped significantly at government facilities. Helping to determine ahead of time which is likely to happen in a particular cultural setting is one way applied cultural anthropologists can help solve systemic health care financing problems.

An international health project undertaken in the early 1990s provides an example. Funded over the course of one year by a U.S.-based private charitable foundation, the project was intended to help the governments of three small Caribbean countries to improve the way their national health systems were organized and financed.[4] As is typical in international health projects, the project included both American researchers and host-country counterparts: economists, medical doctors, statisticians, employees of the ministries of health and finance in the three countries, insurance specialists, and an applied cultural anthropologist, all working together toward a common goal (Zschock et al. 1991).

In each of the three countries, the national health system was severely handicapped by insufficient funding. Thus a major goal of the project was to help identify additional sources of revenue, so that the three ministries of health involved could continue providing free health care to all poor citizens. Government health officials in all three countries were interested in obtaining any information that could help them understand the health-related beliefs, expectations, and values of citizens, so that any reforms they instituted would be acceptable to the population and hence sustainable over the long run.

The applied anthropologist's primary role in this project was to investigate whether or not beneficiaries of free, government-provided health services would be willing to pay a small amount for these same services. In all three countries, her research into this question included semistructured interviews and focus group sessions with both public and private health services consumers, selected to reflect each country's population both demographically and socioeconomically. Based on this

work, the project team was able to report to the three ministries of health that requiring patients to shoulder a small proportion of the cost of government-provided
health care would be acceptable, provided that health services improved in quality.

The examples above by no means exhaust the possible roles of applied cultural
anthropologists in international health. Other roles include serving on the faculties
of schools of public health, medicine, and nursing; working for national or multinational agencies such as the U.S. Centers for Disease Control and Prevention or the
World Health Organization; and working for community health organizations
(Overbey 1998:7).

CONCLUSION

The substantial and growing involvement of applied cultural anthropologists in international health seems particularly apt, given the close relationship between
health and culture: there is no profession or academic specialty whose practitioners
are better qualified to evaluate and help address the health-related problems of
needy population groups, large or small, in the light of ethnicity, gender, residence,
socioeconomic circumstances, or other cultural factors. For most anthropologists
engaged in international health, this confluence of interests and needs makes their
work both intellectually challenging and personally rewarding.

As Lane and Rubinstein (1996:396) point out, however, the fact that international health was born—and still exists—in a climate of unequal power relations between international health specialists and beneficiaries is problematic to some
(ibid.:398). Moreover, international health work can be frustrating, because "the interaction of the broader political and economic contexts in which international
health and development work is situated and the culture of the community of international health workers often leads to perverse outcomes" (ibid.). Millions of children in developing countries still die from preventable diseases such as measles.
Massive amounts of foreign assistance for health result in only paltry gains. Bureaucratic problems stall progress.

Yet even though such criticism is valid and worthy of continued attention, the
efforts of applied cultural anthropologists in the international health arena—working in multidisciplinary teams with Western and host-country medical professionals,
government officials, health economists, biostatisticians, and others—are indisputably, if slowly, paying off. Most of the world's children are now immunized
against the major childhood diseases. Except for the possibility of terrorism, small-
pox has been eradicated as an international health threat. Infant and child mortality
rates are still too high, but are lower than at any time in human history. There are
more healthy senior citizens than ever, more people than ever have safe drinking
water supplies and sanitation facilities, and more people than ever have access to at
least a minimum level of health care (WHO 1998). It is doubtful that such significant gains in global health could have been realized, much less sustained, without
the dedicated participation of applied cultural anthropologists.

◇ ◇ ◇

KEY TERMS

culture of poverty   an association of features, including social disorganization, a weakening of kinship ties, and chronic depression, characterizing the lives of the urban poor

diseases of affluence   the health problems largely brought about by the lifestyle changes accompanying economic development

global health   a synonym for *international health*

GOBI-FFF   Growth monitoring, Oral rehydration therapy, Breast-feeding, Immunization, Female education, Family spacing, and Food supplements; a refinement of the PHC concept, targeting a series of specific health needs

international health   a multidisciplinary specialty within the field of international development, dedicated generally to addressing public health-related issues and specifically to helping attain specific health-related goals

megacities   huge and still-growing cities, in both the industrialized and developing worlds

merit goods   goods or services that—if left to the private sector to produce—would not be purchased in sufficient quantity to make production financially worthwhile

national health profile   a summary of the kinds and rates of sickness and death from which a country's population suffers

primary health care (PHC)   an assortment of relatively simple items and procedures for preventing or curing common medical conditions

public health   a career field focusing on the health of whole populations, as opposed to individuals

reproductive rights   a general term for the right of individuals to decide when to have children and how many to have

urban anthropology   a subdiscipline of cultural anthropology, focusing on the culture of city dwellers

NOTES

1. In 1950, only two megacities existed: London and New York. By the year 2010, it is predicted that there will be twenty-six megacities, of which twenty-one will be in developing countries (Bradford and Gwynne 1995:13).
2. Abortion is illegal in most countries, but self-induced abortion is nevertheless common, killing an estimated 100,000 to 200,000 women per year. In countries in which sexually active adults have access to contraception, the rate of self-induced abortion is dramatically lower than in countries that ban the dissemination of contraceptive information and devices (Rahman et al. 2001).
3. KAP surveys unearth information on the health-related lore, behavior, and values of a study population—what people know about health and health care, what they think and feel about these subjects, and what they actually do about them.
4. This project was carried out jointly by the State University of New York at Stony Brook and the Pan American Health Organization, with grant support provided by the Pew Charitable Trusts.

REFERENCES

Berman, Peter, and Ravindra Rannan-Eliya
1993. *Factors Affecting the Development of Private Health Care Provision in Developing Countries* (Health Financing and Sustainability Project, Major Applied Research Paper No. 9). Washington, DC: USAID.

Bolton, Ralph
1995. "Rethinking Anthropology: The Study of AIDS." In *Culture and Sexual Risk: Anthropological Perspectives on AIDS*, edited by Han ten Brummelhuis and Gilbert Herdt, 285–313. Amsterdam: Gordon and Breach Publishers.

Bouvier, Leon F., and Jane T. Bertrand
1999. *World Population: Challenges for the Twenty-First Century*. Santa Ana, CA: Seven Locks Press.

Bradford, Bonnie, and Margaret A. Gwynne (eds.)
1995. *Down to Earth: Community Perspectives on Health, Development, and the Environment*. West Hartford, CT: Kumarian Press.

Coreil, Jeannine
1990. "The Evolution of Anthropology in International Health." In *Anthropology and Primary Health Care*, edited by Jeannine Coreil and J. Dennis Mull, 3–27. Boulder, CO: Westview Press.

Dixon-Mueller, Ruth
1993. *Population Policy and Women's Rights: Transforming Reproductive Choice*. Westport, CT: Praeger.

Griffin , Charles C.
1989. "The Private Sector and Health Care Policy in Developing Countries." In *Strengthening Health Services in Developing Countries Through the Private Sector* (International Finance Corporation Discussion Paper No. 4). Washington, DC: The World Bank.

Hill, Carole E.
1991: "Continuities and Differences in the Old and the New Applied Medical Anthropology." In *Training Manual in Applied Medical Anthropology*, edited by Carole E. Hill, 14–22, Washington, DC: American Anthropological Association.

Lane, Sandra D., and Robert A. Rubinstein
1996. "International Health: Problems and Programs in Anthropological Perspective." In *Handbook of Medical Anthropology: Contemporary Theory and Method* (rev. ed.), edited by Carolyn F. Sargent and Thomas M. Johnson, 396–423. Westport, CT: Greenwood Press.

Leeds, Anthony
1994. *Cities, Classes, and the Social Order*. Ithaca, NY: Cornell University Press.

Lewis, Oscar
1966. "The Culture of Poverty." *Scientific American* 215 (4):19–25.

Macdonald, John J.
1993. *Primary Health Care: Medicine in Its Place*. West Hartford, CT: Kumarian Press.

Moffett, George D.
1994. *Critical Masses: The Global Population Challenge*. New York: Viking.

National Institute of Allergy and Infectious Diseases (NIAID)
2001. "Fact Sheet: HIV/AIDS Statistics." Retrieved 10/25/01 from www.niaid.nih.gov

Overbey, Mary Margaret
1998. "Anthropology's Relevance to Public Health." *Anthropology Newsletter* 39 (7):7.

Pillsbury, Barbara L. K.
1991. "International Health Overview and Opportunities." In *Training Manual in Applied Medical Anthropology*, edited by Carole E. Hill, 54–87. Washington, DC: American Anthropological Association.

Popatiya, Aziz
2000. "Community-Managed Health Systems: Improved Health Status." Paper presented June 14, 2000, at the annual meeting of the Global Health Council, Arlington, VA.

Rahman, Mizanur, Julie DaVanzo, and Abdur Razzaque
2001. "Do Family Planning Services Reduce Abortion in Bangladesh?" *The Lancet* 358 (9287). Retrieved November 2001 from www.thelancet.com

Reid, Elizabeth (ed.)
1995. *HIV and AIDS: The Global Inter-Connection*. West Hartford, CT: Kumarian Press.

Rodriguez-Garcia, Rosalia, and Ann Goldman (eds.)
1994. *The Health-Development Link*. Washington, DC: Pan American Health Organization.

Roemer, Milton I.
1985. *National Strategies for Health Care Organization: A World Overview*. Ann Arbor, MI: Health Administration Press.

Roth, Gabriel
1987. *The Private Provision of Public Services in Developing Countries*. New York: Oxford University Press.

Southall, Aidan
1973. *Urban Anthropology: Cross-Cultural Studies of Urbanization*. New York: Oxford University Press.

Stolberg, Sheryl G.
1999. "DDT, Target of Global Ban, Finds Defenders in Experts on Malaria." *New York Times*, August 29, 1999, 1, 8.

ten Brummelhuis, Han, and Gilbert Herdt
1995. *Culture and Sexual Risk: Anthropological Perspectives on AIDS*. Amsterdam: Gordon and Breach Publishers.

World Health Organization (WHO)
1998. *The World Health Report 1998*. Geneva: World Health Organization.

Zschock, Dieter, Margaret A. Gwynne, Barry Wint, and Jorge Castellanos Robayo
1991. *Comparative Health Care Financing in St. Lucia, Grenada, and Dominica*. Needham Heights, MA: Ginn Press.

CHAPTER

13 FINDING A JOB

INTRODUCTION

Every successful applied anthropologist has a unique story to tell about securing a first job. Some entered this career field with only a B.A. in hand; others first earned Master's degrees or Ph.D.s. Some developed their interest in applied anthropology while still undergraduates; others not until much later. Some went directly into applied anthropology from preparatory academic programs; others earned "life credits" first. Some planned their careers carefully; others fell serendipitously into their careers in applied anthropology.

James W. decided on a career as an applied cultural anthropologist during the summer after his sophomore year, when a major hurricane struck Guatemala. News reports of this storm and its aftermath—death, property destruction, devastating crop losses, and epidemic disease—affected him profoundly, and he decided to focus his career on the health and welfare of the poor in Central America. Already an anthropology major, James rounded out his undergraduate education with relevant courses, including Spanish and Latin American history, and became a student member of an international health advocacy organization. After graduation, not yet ready for graduate school, he reasoned that an entry-level job with an organization involved in international development would provide him with experience and opportunities for advancement. He moved to Washington, D.C., to be near USAID and the many consulting firms that help USAID carry out its mission. Soon James landed a job as a lowly office manager at a consulting firm specializing in international health, where he spent the next eight months doing clerical chores and learning everything he could about the problems of the poor in developing countries. When his firm won a USAID contract to help the Honduran Ministry of Health conduct a survey of vaccination compliance, James applied for the on-site office manager's slot on the project. Soon he was living and working in Honduras, where he found an opportunity to describe his anthropological expertise to the project director and to explain how it could contribute to the success of the survey. Within months, James was working as an applied cultural anthropologist, participating in ethnographic research in the barrios of Tegucigalpa.

Wendie L.'s experience was quite different. In college, Wendie was initially attracted to the hard sciences, but (perhaps not too surprisingly for a "people person" whose avocation was writing poetry) she found biology, zoology, and geology "sterile" and yearned for a course of study with a specifically human focus. In her sophomore year, she discovered anthropology, although with little thought of putting her newfound interest to use in a future career. Shortly after graduation, Wendie got married and went to work as a bank teller. Within a few years, she was the mother

◇ *Academic training in applied cultural anthropology is useful in many entry-level jobs, yet few employers insert "Wanted: Applied Anthropologist" advertisements in the help wanted sections of newspapers. Entry-level jobs for which newly-minted cultural anthropologists might apply include "interviewer," "assistant policy analyst," or "assistant human services administrator."*

of three young children. During these years of motherhood, she occasionally had the opportunity to accompany her husband, a police officer, on "ride-alongs," as he patrolled the streets in his squad car. In talking with him about police work, Wendie realized the extent to which "he saw his role as being a facilitator and an advocate for citizens." It was an exciting discovery, she recalls. "I could see that my anthropological training could be of real benefit in law enforcement." When her children reached school age, she applied for police training at the Center for Criminal Justice and Law Enforcement in St. Paul, Minnesota. After receiving her certificate and going through a rigorous police academy training program, she went to work for the St. Paul Police Department, putting her anthropological interests and expertise to use as a member of the patrol division on St. Paul's East Side.

Other applied anthropologists—those profiled in each chapter of Parts Two through Five of this book—found their way to applied work via other routes. Soheir Stolba (Chapter 5) drew on her own ethnic background and study of linguistics to get a start on her career in international development. Leslie Raneri (Chapter 7), who decided on a social work career while still in high school, studied anthropology in college and entered a two-year graduate program in social work immediately after receiving her B.A. She has been working with HIV-infected women and children ever since. John Sherry (Chapter 9), doing Ph.D. dissertation research among the Navajo, wondered whether some technology company would be interested in a detailed understanding of how various groups of people who were not yet fully engaged in the world of high tech might profitably use its products. Today he does "design ethnography," helping a computer company identify new uses for computing power by understanding the needs of potential users. Fred Bloom (Chapter 11) came to anthropology through nursing; working with HIV-positive patients inspired his desire to become an applied medical anthropologist, a career in which he could combine his interests in both anthropology and nursing.

The purpose of this chapter is to give you some specific ideas about nonacademic employment for people who are interested and trained in cultural anthropology, and how to find such employment. The study of cultural anthropology will qualify you for literally hundreds of different jobs —in international agencies; in federal, state, and local government offices; in private businesses and charitable organizations. Almost any of these organizations would benefit from having an employee with an educational specialty in how people in groups think and behave, and why. Few of them, however, advertise for employees under the job title "applied cultural anthropologist" (Singer et al. 1994:5).

Most jobs in applied cultural anthropology require at least some additional training beyond a B.A. degree with a major in anthropology (Singer et al. 1994:2). This chapter, therefore, is not primarily about getting a rewarding job immediately after graduation. Even James W., who went from college graduate to applied anthropologist in only a little over a year, spent some time in on-the-job training and independent study before he was ready for applied anthropological work in the international health field. Instead, this chapter is about the possibilities that exist—and there are many (Kahn 2000:G1)—for building toward a satisfying future career in which the study of cultural anthropology proves to be a strong asset.

ASSESSING YOUR ANTHROPOLOGICAL POTENTIAL

If you are thinking about a possible career in applied cultural anthropology, your first step—no matter what your grade level at present—should be to survey the field to get a broad sense of the many kinds of work applied anthropologists do. This book has described a number of major fields of anthropological practice, but it has by no means exhausted the possibilities. Three recent publications, each entitled *Careers in Anthropology,* will widen your perspective (Omohundra 1998; Sabloff 2000; Stephens 2002).

Second, take stock of the anthropological *interests, knowledge, skills,* and *experience* you have already accumulated. It might help to make systematic written lists of all four of these (you should expect some overlap). Consider not just the academic subjects you have taken, but also extracurricular activities, such as club or sports team memberships; your life at home and as a member of your community, summer jobs, and travel.

Beginning with your *interests,* make a note of both your academic interests and any others you may have developed outside the classroom—for example, as a member of any on-campus or off-campus organizations. Perhaps you have always been interested in West African art and culture; perhaps your own heritage is eastern European and you would like to learn more about it; perhaps you got great personal satisfaction out of tutoring children as a volunteer for the campus Big Brothers organization. As you list your interests, ask yourself whether they are strong enough to underpin a career.

Next, consider the *knowledge* you already have amassed, first by reviewing the college courses you have taken so far, not only in anthropology but in other relevant fields as well. Perhaps you particularly enjoyed a course in gender theory or medical anthropology or did especially well in French or statistics. Include knowledge gained in any academic area in which you feel you have some expertise. Then add to your list any knowledge, relevant to anthropology, gained in nonacademic ways, such as an understanding of Jewish religious traditions or familiarity with a particular country or region of the world.

Next, list the specific *skills* you already have that might be relevant to the work of an applied cultural anthropologist. Consider your academic skills (such as analytical ability, writing competence, facility with computers, foreign language skills, or specific skills learned in methods courses). Include any relevant skills you may have developed as a result of membership in on-campus or off-campus organizations. Perhaps you learned photographic techniques as a member of a photography club, taught Sunday school, or served as a volunteer docent in a museum. If you were a member of the debating club, list "ability to present and defend a position publicly." If you were a summer camp counselor, list "teaching crafts skills to children." Consider also the jobs you have held, both paid and volunteer, and list the specific skills you developed as a result of these jobs: for example, office management, fund raising, or interacting with the public in a retail sales position. Include talents and personal qualities you have always taken for granted: maturity, leadership ability, good judgment, or the capacity to adjust rapidly to new surroundings.

Finally, under *experience*, list any and all practical, hands-on accomplishments that would enable you to say, to a prospective employer, "I've done this." Consider the specific experiences you gained while working at paid or volunteer jobs ("I did a phone survey for the Young Republicans Club"); your travel or vacation experiences ("I mapped out a four-day biking tour of Vermont"); any relevant academic experiences ("I presented a research paper in front of an audience"); team sports participation ("I learned to interact with and support others as a member of a team"); any relevant methods courses you have taken ("I studied ethnographic field methods"); and experience gained from academic assistantships ("I worked as a lab assistant in an archaeology lab") or work-study jobs ("I maintained a computer database of classroom assignments for the registrar's office").

Additionally, try to imagine the career area in which you would like to work and the specific job you would like to hold ten years from now. Make a separate list of the interests, academic degrees, specific kinds of knowledge, specific skills, and experience or work history you would need to enter this career area, be hired for a particular job, and be successful at it. In your mind, "subtract" the items on your first list from those on your second. This will help you identify the gaps, both in your formal résumé and life experience, you will need to fill in order to reach your goals.

IMPROVING YOUR ANTHROPOLOGICAL SKILLS

Steps to Take Now

No matter what your current grade level, there is much you can do, starting immediately, to close any career-related gaps you have identified and to prepare yourself for a career in applied cultural anthropology.

Your first step, if you have not taken it already, should be to declare a major in anthropology. Depending on what courses are available to you and how close you are to graduation, consider a combination of an anthropology major and a minor in some other relevant discipline—international studies, economics, or Spanish language and literature, for example. If you have already accumulated too many credits in another major to change majors at this point, consider an anthropology minor.

Another important step is to narrow down your interests by choosing an area of specialization within cultural anthropology. Important factors to consider, in addition to your own talents and inclinations, include the availability of upper-division courses in cultural anthropology and any positive relationships you have already developed with anthropology professors whose courses you have particularly enjoyed. If possible, your choice should combine a theoretical with a geographical focus (for example, gender relations in Japan; ethnomedical systems in sub-Saharan Africa). If you are undecided, pick two or even three areas. It is not too soon to begin to develop some very specific expertise; indeed, the sooner you do, the sooner you will reach your career goals.

Tell anthropology faculty members that you are planning on a career in applied cultural anthropology. Make a particular effort to get to know faculty members who have done applied work or whose professional interests coincide with yours. You might think up specific questions to put to these faculty members during their office hours. Consider asking one or more of them to guide you in a directed readings or independent research course. This is an excellent way either to sample areas of possible long-term interest or to gain in-depth knowledge in specific career-related areas. Focused, directed research projects can be cited later to demonstrate your genuine interest in anthropology to graduate school admissions committees or future employers.

In addition to taking independent readings courses with professors who are knowledgeable in your area of interest, you can develop expertise in a particular subject by choosing courses—in anthropology or other disciplines—related to that subject, and of course, by reading independently. You can also devise research paper topics that relate to your area of interest; it is often possible to tailor the topics of required papers for your own benefit, even in courses in which your area of interest is only peripheral. Continue, each semester, to let your professors know of your area(s) of special interest. If you want to work internationally, begin or continue language training. (Arabic-speaking applied cultural anthropologist Daniel Varisco says his language ability is his "single most important skill.") You should be fluent in one of the "world" languages, such as Spanish or French, and if you can speak and read a more parochial language—Tagalog or Urdu or Shona or Vietnamese—so much the better.

FOOD FOR THOUGHT College students who are the children of recent immigrants, or are immigrants themselves, often enjoy the significant advantage of fluency in a non-English language spoken in their homes. Besides language proficiency, what other specific skills or experiences, relevant to a career in applied cultural anthropology, might derive from growing up in a bicultural home or neighborhood?

Plan your course of study over your remaining semesters to fill in specific educational gaps. After all academic requirements have been satisfied, take other anthropology courses as your schedule permits—in any of the four fields of the discipline. Search your college's course catalog for courses in other departments that might relate to your interests. Depending on your career goal, you might find language, economics, history, psychology, or women's studies courses—even art or music courses—relevant to your area of interest. At the campus library or on the Internet, search course offerings at other colleges and universities for relevant subjects you might be able to study during summer sessions, or during a semester away from your home campus. And if you have not done so already, take some basic courses in statistics, computer science, or even (depending on your career goals) art or women's studies or business management. Learn to use anthropology-specific computer programs, such as SPSS and ANTHROPAK.

◇ *Applied anthropology students with family ties to other cultures have a natural advantage when developing regional or ethnic specialties. At right, an American college student of South Asian descent greets Indian family members at an airport in India.*

If time permits, become a volunteer. Employers hire applicants with hands-on experience. College graduates looking for their first jobs often discover that—as one frustrated recent graduate put it—"to do a particular job, it seems you have to have done it already." You cannot expect an employer to pay you to get experience, so consider any on-the-job training you can get to be a form of "payment." Explore the possibility of an internship; a short-term, institutionalized (even if unpaid) apprenticeship with a corporation, nongovernmental organization (NGO), or private voluntary organization (PVO) would be a worthwhile addition to your résumé and would enable you to learn about the organization from the inside (see Schlotter 1993; Kushner and Wolfe 1993; Joseph 1999). One good way to find an internship is to search the Web; if your career goal is medical anthropology and you live in Connecticut, for example, you will find information about internships at the Hispanic Health Council at this organization's website (Singer et al. 1994:3). The "Finding a Job" section of the *Anthropology Career Resources Handbook* lists several generic sites that provide information on internships. If you cannot identify an appropriate internship, volunteer your services in a law office, hospital, or accounting firm—any organization whose work has some relevance to your career goal. Remember that while a paying job is immediately attractive, you are wasting time in the long run if you cannot use the experience you gain as a stepping-stone toward your career goal.

Finally, begin networking (Stone 1993). Try to find people, on campus or off, who are knowledgeable about your area of interest or who are working in your field of interest. These people might be fellow students who have specific skills, who have held interesting summer jobs or internships, or who were born and raised in another culture. They might be members of your own family who have interesting careers or have lived in other cultures, or professors or researchers involved in projects that interest you. If your focus is international and your campus has a residential college for students interested in international relations, consider joining it. Ultimately you will want to develop as extensive as possible a network of professionals in your area of interest. Applied anthropologist John Stone has found the "topically focused professional network" to be "an extremely valuable thread linking professional development and disciplinary advancement" (ibid.:25).

Graduate Education

Even if, like James W., you are fortunate enough to find work in applied cultural anthropology shortly after earning a B.A. with a major in anthropology, it is highly likely that for a lifetime career in any subfield of applied cultural anthropology you will need additional formal education. For some kinds of applied anthropology, a Master's degree will be sufficient (Quirk and Jenakovich 1997).[1] Some universities now offer specifically career-oriented Master's degree programs (Singer et al. 1994:2). For other kinds of applied anthropology, you will need to earn a Ph.D.

The growing number of universities in the United States now offering Master's and Ph.D. programs in applied anthropology is a relatively recent development. Anthropology graduate programs

> have always been focussed, overtly or not, on training for employment in museums, research institutions, and academia . . . [but] it has only been in the past several decades that we have seen that full-time employment in roles other than that of professor can be not only legitimate, but also deserving of special training. (Kushner 1994:187)

You will find a list of graduate programs in applied anthropology in the *Anthropology Career Resources Handbook;* alternatively, the reference librarian at your campus library can direct you to this information. Be aware, however, that in some cases, a "glaring incongruity" exists between the needs of future applied anthropologists and the graduate programs they attend (Price 2001:57). Be careful, therefore, to ensure that any graduate program in which you consider enrolling will actually provide you with the resources you will need in your future career. And do not limit your exploration of the possibilities for graduate education to anthropology departments. It may be that a combination of specialties—for example, a B.A. in anthropology plus a Master's degree in social work or public administration, or a B.A. in anthropology, an M.A. in public health, and a Ph.D. in psychology—will be the best route to your goal.

Not all education is formal education; some kinds of nonacademic experience, too, can be considered a form of "higher education." If you are interested in international work, consider volunteering for the Peace Corps, an agency of the U.S. government headquartered in Washington, D.C. After intensive training, Peace Corps volunteers serve for two years in a developing country. Most work in African or Latin American countries, but some are stationed in Asia, eastern Europe, or the western Pacific. Volunteers' roles involve helping local people address economic, social, educational, health, agricultural, and refugee problems. Applied anthropologist and international health specialist Lily Kak (Chapter 12, p. 288) comments, "I see a lot of people in my field with a Peace Corps background. Particularly for Americans who have never been overseas, this is a chance to really learn what it is like to live and work abroad. For many of them, it's a life-changing experience." There are also opportunities for relevant volunteer work in the United States—for example, with AmeriCorps, Citizen Corps, or Teach for America.

Professional Organizations for Applied Anthropologists

A number of professional organizations in the United States exist to support and promote applied anthropology, and most applied cultural anthropologists belong to one or more of them. The main functions of these organizations include helping applied anthropologists keep abreast of new developments in the field, providing opportunities for applied anthropologists to meet and share their knowledge and experiences, and encouraging colleges and universities to offer applied anthropology courses and create graduate programs. While helping students find jobs is not one of their primary functions, these organizations can nevertheless be very useful to you.

The Society for Applied Anthropology. The oldest professional organization for applied anthropologists, the Society for Applied Anthropology (SfAA), was formed at Harvard University in 1941, to "promote the investigation of the principles of human behavior and the application of these principles to contemporary issues and problems" (see Chapters 1 and 3). It now has over two thousand members. The SfAA publishes two well-respected journals, *Human Organization* and *Practicing Anthropology*. Perusing the last few years' worth of these publications will give you an excellent idea of what applied anthropologists do. SfAA's address and website (where you will find a link to a site designed especially for students), as well as a website for *Human Organization*, are listed in the *Anthropology Career Resources Handbook.*

The National Association for the Practice of Anthropology. The other major U.S.-based membership organization for applied anthropologists is the National Association for the Practice of Anthropology (NAPA), a unit of the American Anthropological Association established in 1983 (see Chapters 1 and 3). Thanks to a sharp increase in the number of applied anthropologists in recent years, NAPA now represents around 10 percent of the membership of the AAA.

Membership in this organization might be particularly helpful to first-time job-seekers, since NAPA—in addition to the networking opportunities and publications that are benefits of membership in any practitioner organization—also conducts professional development workshops and a mentoring program in which professional applied anthropologists, called "councilors," provide students with guidance and career-related information (Singer et al. 1994:1). NAPA is currently running an on-line résumé workshop. You can become a student member of NAPA for only $15, but you must also be a member of AAA. Student membership in both NAPA and

AAA is $50. This may seem like a daunting sum to some students, but if you are serious about a career in applied cultural anthropology, membership in these two organizations will entitle you to a number of benefits directly related to your career goal, and you can list your memberships on your résumé, which will suggest to potential employers how determined you are to find an anthropological job. NAPA's address and website are listed in the *Anthropology Career Resources Handbook*.

NAPA and SfAA have joined together to publish a comprehensive directory of applied anthropologists, which includes not only their names and addresses but also their areas of expertise and their qualifications. This directory is available from the AAA.

The National Association of Student Anthropologists.   Like NAPA, the National Association of Student Anthropologists is an arm of the American Anthropological Association. It is not specifically aimed at students who plan to become applied cultural anthropologists, but membership—especially if you attend AAA meetings—will surely bring you into contact with other students who share your interest in applied work.

Local Practitioner Organizations.   In addition to SfAA and NAPA, a number of **local practitioner organizations** (LPOs) exist to support and promote applied anthropology at the regional level. Examples are the Great Lakes Association of Practicing Anthropologists, the North Florida Network of Practicing Anthropologists, the Southern California Applied Anthropology Network, the High Plains Society for Applied Anthropology, and, on the west coast of Florida, the Sun Coast

◇ *Attending conventions of anthropologists, such as the annual meeting of the Society for Applied Anthropology, can provide students with important career development activities.*

Organization of Practicing Anthropologists (SCOPA). A list of LPOs, with contact information, can be found in the *Anthropology Career Resources Handbook*. In addition, since these professional organizations are affiliates of NAPA, information about them can be found on the NAPA website.

FOOD FOR THOUGHT

The point has been made, throughout this book, that applied cultural anthropologists are likely to work mainly with professionals representing disciplines other than anthropology. This being the case, what specific advantages might an applied cultural anthropologist derive from meeting, from time to time, with other applied cultural anthropologists?

SELLING YOUR ANTHROPOLOGICAL SKILLS

First Jobs for College Graduates

As you know from Chapter 1, most employment in applied cultural anthropology takes place in nonacademic institutions—private and public, national and international, profit-making and not-for-profit.[2] Many of the institutions requiring the expertise of applied cultural anthropologists employ them on a temporary basis, either short-term or long-term, as independent consultants. The advantages of this kind of employment are many, including much greater variety and job flexibility than permanent employment offers. However, it is almost unheard of for an applied anthropologist to win a consulting assignment without prior work experience. Your first few years of employment, at the very least, should be in permanent, full-time employment. If your eventual goal is consulting work, use these early career years to develop a résumé that suggests both depth and breadth in experience and specific skills.

   Trying to convey, to potential employers, some sense of the relevance of the knowledge and skills you gained in an academic context "requires some legwork" (Kuehnast 1999:32)—perhaps more legwork than is required in searching for other kinds of jobs, since most potential employers probably do not have an accurate appreciation of what cultural anthropology is. Indeed, employers' concepts of what anthropologists actually do are apt to be at best narrow, and at worst erroneous. Be prepared for jokes about Indiana Jones. Part of the problem is that news stories about cultural anthropologists' activities are as likely to be of the tabloid type ("Anthropologist Finds Lost Jungle Tribe!") as they are to be accurate accounts of the myriad ways cultural anthropology can provide useful information, discourage ethnocentrism, and contribute to intercultural understanding. Job hunters, therefore, "must creatively interpret job announcements, then construct a cover letter and [résumé] aimed at communicating how their versatility and special skills meet the employer's needs" (Kuehnast 1999:32; see also Owens 1993).

When searching for a job, applied anthropologist Walter Owens discovered that "most prospective employers had no idea what applied anthropology was. I had to explain repeatedly what [it was] all about, and that, no, I did not sit around all day studying bones" (Owens 1993:23). In two or three sentences, define and describe cultural anthropology for someone who thinks the discipline consists of "studying bones."

Want Ads.   When looking for your first full-time job, a daily search of the Internet (CareerBuilder.com is a good site) and the Help Wanted sections of the classified pages of newspapers may be a good place to start. Do not, however, waste time looking under *A* for *applied anthropologist.* With much of the general public still ignorant of cultural anthropologists' many areas of expertise, you are unlikely to find any entry-level jobs that even mention anthropological training as a criterion for application. Look instead for job descriptions for entry-level jobs for which anthropology would be relevant, such as poll-taker, interviewer, assistant policy analyst, or assistant human services administrator.

Besides searching the want ads for specific jobs, another way to approach your search is to make a list of those businesses, foundations, consulting firms, or NGOs for which you would like to work, and then search the want ads for any openings in these organizations for which you would be qualified as a recent college graduate. Do not set your sights too high; look for listings, for example, for "gal/guy Friday," or "administrative assistant," or even "secretary" or "data entry clerk" (as James W. did). The first step is just to get your foot in the door of an organization that interests you. After you have been hired, have had a chance to get to know the organization, and have proven yourself to be an intelligent, hardworking, reliable employee, you can more easily identify the kinds of contributions you could make, as a cultural anthropologist, to the organization. For example, one anthropology major who loved both cultural anthropology and books landed an entry-level job doing word processing in the electronics and engineering texts department of a major textbook publisher. At just the right time, she made a strong case for what an anthropology major could contribute to the editorial process in the social sciences department. She is now an assistant to the social sciences editor, with the long-term goal of eventually replacing her boss as editor.

Networking.   Mari Clarke, former president of an LPO, the Washington Association for the Practice of Anthropology (WAPA), suggests that networking is the key to learning about nonacademic jobs in anthropology (quoted in Stone 1993). Attending meetings of practitioner organizations, national or local, is an excellent way to "meet professional anthropologists, arrange informational interviews, and begin to learn about the multitude of job possibilities that exist for anthropologists outside the academy" (Kuehnast 1999:32).

The most important anthropological convention—and the biggest, in terms of the number of attendees—is the annual meeting of the American Anthropological

Association. Sessions on applied anthropology are included every year. However, the annual meeting of the Society for Applied Anthropology may prove a better investment of your time and resources. The SfAA meeting is specifically focused on applied anthropology. It is also smaller than the AAA meeting and thus is more manageable and less overwhelming. Moreover, attendees at the SfAA meeting may be more willing than AAA attendees to take the time to meet with and counsel students. Both conventions are held annually in major North American cities and last for several days.

Medical anthropologist Fred Bloom (see Chapter 11, p. 261) advises taking a slightly different approach to networking. "Talk to people doing work you think you might want to do," says Bloom. "Interview them about what their job is like, how they got their job, do they like their job, and how they would recommend you get this kind of job. Do they know of two people you might talk to who might be interested in hiring you in the future? Ask if you can use their name when introducing yourself to them. Don't forget to send a thank-you note after you talk to people" (quoted in Barone 1999:38).

Résumés.   A résumé or **curriculum vitae** is a description, written with potential employers in mind, of a professional's job-related educational background, experience, and skills.[3] You can get advice on résumé writing from your college's career placement office. In addition, you will find instruction books on how to prepare an effective résumé in almost any bookstore (see also Skreija 1998). Most of these books contain the same excellent—if generic—advice: be sure your résumé is clear, well-organized, neatly printed, and visually attractive; emphasize your actual experience (especially specific skills) over your theoretical knowledge; gear your résumé specifically to its potential reader(s) by emphasizing particular job-related qualities.

In addition to consulting how-to manuals and career placement professionals, ask any applied anthropologists you know—for instance, members of a local practitioner organization you have joined, or professors who do applied work—for copies of their résumés. Study these for ideas on how to put your best foot forward on paper.

As you try to summarize what you can bring to a job as an anthropology major, bear in mind the following points. First, in describing your anthropology major and the skills it has taught you, remember that many prospective employers will not respond with immediate understanding to words like *ethnography, qualitative analysis,* or *structural-functionalism;* to highly specific upper-division course titles; or to the abstruse-sounding title of your senior thesis. Use easily understood terms to describe your past experience—phrases such as "different roles of men and women," "Chinese languages" or "three-person research project"—wherever you can.

Second, phrase any relevant summer jobs, internships, or campus positions you have held in terms of specific experience rather than job title. For example, if you interned at your local Planned Parenthood office as an assistant to the office manager, describe yourself as "receptionist, typist, and assistant appointments coordinator" instead of "administrative assistant." This will give your reader a much better idea about your actual experience and training.

And third, include any information you can to show that you are serious, diligent, disciplined, and have had experience working with others. Perhaps, for example, you did volunteer work or held a part-time job in addition to maintaining a high grade-point average; perhaps you were a member of the Anthropology Club or participated in a joint research project. Any of these attributes and experiences would be meaningful to a prospective employer and should be included on your résumé. Sample résumés are included in most job-search books.

Interviews.   You can learn the job interview basics—demeanor, appropriate dress, and so on—from any job-search how-to book. Obviously you will not want to be late to your interview, or neglect common courtesies such as smiling, offering your hand, and introducing yourself by name; do not arrive dripping with ethnic jewelry to emphasize your background in cultural anthropology. Do be prepared to explain to your prospective employer why he or she would do well to hire an anthropology major, as distinct from other applicants with B.A. degrees. All college graduates (in theory, at least) can think logically, write clearly, and use a computer, but your anthropology degree has given you two kinds of special proficiency that no applicant (other than another anthropology major) will have: a repertoire of specific skills, many of them readily translatable into a professional context, and a body of specific knowledge about human behavior. You might find it useful to list mentally your proficiencies in these two areas ahead of time, and to practice describing them in a way that will make clear what each would contribute to a prospective employer's overall mission or goals.

The skills acquired in your study of anthropology will—or should—include the following. First, you are a trained observer of culture and human behavior; you can unearth, synthesize, and analyze data, most especially qualitative data, about people. Second, you have learned to think holistically, to apply a "systems perspective"—to figure out "how all the pieces fit together" (Kuehnast 1999:32). And third, you are a "people person." You are interested in other people and their behavior, you are understanding and objective rather than ethnocentric, you can talk with and learn from others in one-on-one interviews or focus groups, and you enjoy working with others. Taken together, these skills will help you perform successfully in almost any professional context.[4]

In addition to specific skills, your anthropological education has imparted to you various kinds of knowledge and areas of expertise. Which of these you will emphasize in a job interview depends entirely on the job for which you are applying. You might want to stress your broad understanding of how people behave in groups: "I understand hierarchical relationships in the workplace," or "I know how both simple and complex political systems work," or "I've studied health-seeking behavior." You might want to focus on your in-depth knowledge of a particular culture, subculture, or group: "I understand the culture of urban African Americans," or "I've worked with troubled young people," or "I speak Greek." Or you might want to stress some topical area: "I know the cross-cultural literature on domestic violence," or "I spent a whole semester researching how human groups adapt to different natural environments," or "I used my knowledge of legal anthropology as an intern in a law office."

FOOD FOR THOUGHT As an exercise to help prepare you for a job interview, try to devise a list of as many words as possible that accurately describe traits you feel you will be able to bring to your future job. Use the alphabet as a guide. You might begin, for example, with analytical, broad-minded, caring, dependable . . . and so on.

Figure 13.1 outlines one possible strategy that could help you get started in a career in some branch of applied cultural anthropology.

Domestic Jobs for Applied Cultural Anthropologists

More American-trained applied cultural anthropologists work domestically than internationally. The reasons are many: there are more domestic jobs available; working domestically may be preferred because it is usually more compatible with family life than working internationally or because one is apt to feel more comfortable in familiar surroundings; and most domestic jobs do not require proficiency in a foreign language.

If you grew up in the United States or Canada and would like to work as an applied cultural anthropologist in the country in which you were raised and with which you are familiar, you should first define the general arena in which you would like to work—business, the legal profession, law enforcement, health care, social

◇ **FIGURE 13.1   Career Development: One Possible Scenario**

1. Save up $1,000.

2. Consult any recent issue of *Anthropology Newsletter,* a monthly publication of the American Anthropological Association, for announcements of the place and date of future annual meetings of the AAA or SfAA.

3. Use your savings to cover the costs of attending the next annual meeting of one of these organizations.

4. As a conference registrant, you will receive a program listing all presentations and other meeting events. Read this program carefully, and identify all sessions related—even peripherally—to your particular field(s) of interest.

5. Attend these sessions, and listen for information or ideas you find fascinating.

6. After each session, approach the presenter of the most interesting presentation. Thank him or her for an informative talk, say you are very interested in the subject, and ask for advice on how to learn more.

7. Later, write this person a thank-you note.

8. Try to maintain a dialogue with this person so that you can ask for career advice and information when you are ready. There are very few professional anthropologists who will not respond helpfully to a sincerely interested student.

work, or something else—and whether you would prefer the private or public sector. Private sector employment is likely to earn you more money in the long run, but public sector jobs tend to be more secure and may provide superior pension and other benefits. Another consideration may be urban versus rural residence. For most domestic jobs in applied cultural anthropology, you will be working in a city, for the simple reason that most companies or government agencies large enough to hire an applied cultural anthropologist are located in urban rather than rural areas. After you have made these fundamental decisions, you can actively begin your job search.

National, State, and Local Governments.   The opportunities to work for a government agency at some level are many, although not all government agencies have slots earmarked for applied cultural anthropologists. You will probably need to sell yourself and your skills. If you take a job with the federal government, you may or may not be stationed in the national capital; many federal bureaus have regional or state branches. Among the branches of the U.S. federal government you might consider are the Departments of Defense, Veterans Affairs, Health and Human Services, or Housing and Urban Development (all of these departments have state offices), or perhaps the National Park Service, the Immigration and Naturalization Service, the Social Security Administration, the National Institutes of Health, the Federal Emergency Management Agency (FEMA), or the Bureau of Indian Affairs. You will find web addresses where you can get more information on these offices in the *Anthropology Career Resources Handbook.*

State or local government agencies can also benefit from anthropological expertise. Most state governments have a division of family services, a department of education, an office of mental health, and a veterans affairs department, plus departments or offices intended specifically to address issues facing the elderly, prisoners, alcoholics, abused children, the mentally retarded, and so on. At the local level, you might work for a city or county hospital, an education department or school district, an urban planning department, a social services department, a drug abuse agency, or a county legal aid society. Your job possibilities are almost as numerous as your imagination, intelligence, training, creativity, and determination are broad.

Corporations and Consulting Firms.   You are much more apt to find a niche doing applied cultural anthropology domestically in a large rather than in a small business organization—or, if your employer is a for-profit consulting firm, *for* a large business or social services agency. Chapter 9 provides examples of the kinds of businesses that hire applied cultural anthropologists and what these anthropologists do. Many are tasked with assessing consumers' values, preferences, and behavior patterns in order to help a company or social services agency identify its market and develop and sell its products or ideas. But remember that anthropological training can be useful (both to you and your employer) in other ways as well. For example, an undergraduate degree in cultural anthropology would qualify you for work in a large corporation's human resources department, where you might be a personnel or employment manager, director of community relations, or health and pension benefits coordinator. Additionally, you might oversee the company's compliance with equal opportunity guidelines or serve as a liaison between the company and its retirees' organization. Private hospitals and educational institutions also hire human resources specialists. Private consulting firms, most of them relatively small, rarely have applied anthropologists on staff but often arrange for anthropologists to work for big corporations or social services agencies on a consulting basis. James W.'s experience as an employee of a consulting firm (see the chapter introduction) is typical.

FOOD FOR THOUGHT   For those whose goal is business anthropology, one obvious choice for an advanced degree is a Master's in Business Administration (MBA). Based on the range of possibilities for business anthropologists described in Chapter 9, what other degrees, at either the Master's or Ph.D. level, in combination with a cultural anthropology B.A., might make you especially attractive to a major corporation?

Museums and Other Cultural Institutions.   If your major interest, as an anthropology major, was indigenous art or culture history, and especially if you minored in art, history, or education, consider looking for a job at a museum, art institute, historical society, or other cultural institution. Most such institutions are interested not just in displaying the works of art and artifacts that form their collections but also in interpreting them in terms of their cultural context. For higher-level jobs in these organizations (for example, director or curator), you will undoubtedly need a graduate degree. However, you could gain entry into a cultural institution by starting out with an internship or trainee position. One anthropology major whose family heritage was South Asian and who wrote a senior honors thesis

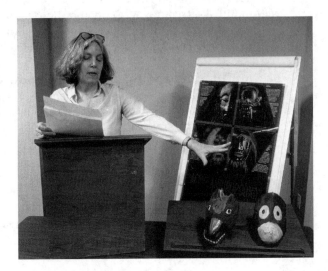

◇ Museums—particularly major museums of art, history, or folklore—employ applied cultural anthropologists because of these anthropologists' ability to interpret objects in terms of their cultural context.

entitled "Symbolism in Indian Art of the Gupta Period" found his first job as a curatorial assistant at a major museum of Asian art located in New York City. There he is working on developing artistic and curatorial expertise to parallel his anthropological expertise. After graduate school, he will be well on his way to achieving his professional goal, to be an art museum director.

The Private, Nonprofit Sector.   Many of the NGOs, PVOs, and charitable foundations whose work is done internationally are based in the United States or Canada. It is therefore quite possible to work domestically while serving the needs of people in developing countries. In addition, there are numerous NGOs, PVOs, and foundations whose work is purely domestic. You might find a particularly rewarding career with one of the many advocacy organizations dedicated to serving the needs of minority groups in either the United States or Canada.

International Jobs for Applied Cultural Anthropologists

Working internationally is mind expanding, exciting, and sometimes even adventurous, and—if you are so inclined—it provides the opportunity to make a significant difference in the lives of the "poorest of the poor." If you like the idea of international work, your first step should be to decide what specific arena you would most like to work in, such as business, economic development, WID/GAD (see Chapter 5, p. 120ff), or cultural advocacy. This decision may steer you to either private or public sector employers (although in some areas of international work, you might work in either sector, or even alternate between sectors). The next step is to decide where you would like to live and work, and whether you would prefer working on a permanent, semi-permanent, or short-term consulting basis (meaning, respectively: indefinitely; for a couple of years; or for a couple of weeks—or at most a couple of months—at a time). Most organizations involved in international work, both private and public, rely on short-term, medium-term, and long-term employees. With these decisions made, you can begin actively researching potential employers.

Multilateral and Bilateral Aid Organizations.   If you are looking for an international job in which you can make a difference in the lives of poor people in developing countries, consider working for an international aid organization. These organizations are headquartered in both industrialized and developing countries, and they typically have branches (sometimes called missions or regional development offices) in developing countries.

As you know from Chapter 1, there are two main types of aid organization. Multilateral organizations, so called because aid is both funded by and distributed to many countries, have a worldwide reach. Examples are the United Nations and its various arms—the World Bank, the World Health Organization, the United Nations Development Program (UNDP), the United Nations Food and Agricultural Organization (FAO), UNICEF (the United Nations children's organization), or the United

Nations High Commission on Refugees (UNHCR). Bilateral organizations, so called because aid flows, on a country-by-country basis, from one country to another, are branches of national governments, such as the U.S. Agency for International Development (USAID), Britain's Overseas Development Agency (ODA), or Japan's Japanese International Cooperation Agency (JICA). All of these organizations have websites (see the *Anthropology Career Resources Handbook*).

International NGOs, PVOs, and Private Foundations. While the multilateral and bilateral aid organizations are large, complex bureaucracies, most nongovernmental organizations (NGOs), private voluntary organizations (PVOs), and private charitable foundations are smaller in both size and scope of work. Many have a particular focus or specialize in a particular type of assistance. International Planned Parenthood, for example, specializes in the distribution of family-planning information and devices around the world, while the Global Health Council lobbies for health improvements worldwide, and La Leche League International promotes breast-feeding. Most of the major charitable foundations (such as the Rockefeller, Pew, Ford, or Kellogg Foundations) are divided into separate departments and further divided into programs, each dedicated to providing assistance in a specific area. A website where you can access major NGOs, PVOs, and private charitable foundations is listed in the *Anthropology Career Resources Handbook.*

International Businesses and Consulting Firms. Chapter 9, on business anthropology, addressed the roles of applied anthropologists in international corporations, which are increasingly hiring cultural anthropologists to work in areas such as marketing and cross-cultural orientation. That chapter will give you a good idea of the kinds of jobs most applied anthropologists do for international corporations. But in addition to hiring applied cultural anthropologists to assist in their for-profit ventures, some international businesses—especially those involved in commercial ventures in developing countries—have whole departments dedicated to charitable assistance. If your interest in a career in applied anthropology includes the goal of helping the world's poor in some way, do not overlook the possibility of reaching that goal in the context of a for-profit business. For example, Bristol-Meyers Squibb, a large pharmaceuticals company, has recently donated one hundred million dollars to improve HIV/AIDS research and foster AIDS education in five southern African countries. While much of the actual work done under bequests of this kind is farmed out to social services professionals, donor corporations do hire in-house staff to develop and administer their assistance programs.

Another private sector alternative would be a job with a consulting firm that does international development work. There are literally hundreds of these firms in the United States alone, employing thousands of people. Most of them are located in or near Washington, D.C., because so many of the contracts that fund their work are with USAID or the World Bank, both headquartered in Washington. Some are headquartered in other major cities, including New York, Boston, and San Francisco. You will find a list of these firms in Vickery 1988.

CONCLUSION

Choosing a career is a complex and difficult decision. A primary consideration, of course, is the need to make a comfortable living; indeed, for many of today's undergraduates—perhaps most especially now, in a time of worldwide economic stagnation—future economic security is the main point of getting a college education (Hoffman 2001). Additional factors, such as family expectations and hopes, preferences about residence, or the availability of funding for further education, complicate the decision-making process.

This book has described a number of career fields and specific jobs in applied cultural anthropology in which employment is available and, with experience and usually with additional education, relatively secure. But if you have read this book mainly in terms of preparation for a good job (or, more broadly, if view your undergraduate experience in this way), you will have failed to take advantage of what is perhaps the most important promise, as well as the greatest challenge, of higher education: the opportunity to explore any and all possibilities, not just for a secure job but for a lifetime of satisfying—even passionate—intellectual and professional activity.

This is a good time in your life to think as broadly and creatively as possible about a future career in anthropology—more specifically, in one of cultural anthropology's many professional applications. Applied anthropologist Riall W. Nolan calls this "developing a personal vision" (Nolan 2001:60); Jeffrey Schlotter refers to it as "creating an identity" as a practicing anthropologist (Schlotter 1993:16). "My advice to anthropologists entering the applied field," writes a third applied cultural anthropologist, Karin Tice, "is to think about how you want to make a difference, find people who have similar concerns, and *create an opportunity for yourself*" (Tice 2000:33; emphasis added). Creating opportunity for yourself out of your personal interests and current skills is undoubtedly "a formidable developmental task" (Hoffman 2001:32), but your efforts will be rewarded over the long term.

Dream, plan, study, learn, explore. Do not allow yourself to be limited by the possibilities for work in applied cultural anthropology presented in this book. Numerous other opportunities exist in addition to the jobs—mainly jobs in institutional settings—on which this book has focused (Kahn 2000:G1). Many applied cultural anthropologists have defined unique areas of specialization, using their training creatively and usefully in careers as priests, ministers, and rabbis; public opinion pollsters; documentary filmmakers; journal, magazine, or book editors; fiction writers; hospital or school administrators; second-language or adult literacy educators; or urban planners. Indeed, an understanding of how people in groups behave, and why, is relevant to almost any career you might choose. Spending some time and effort on planning your future, starting now, may be the best investment you will ever make.

KEY TERMS

curriculum vitae   a synonym for *résumé*

local practitioner organization (LPO)   a membership organization of applied anthropologists that exists to support and promote applied anthropology at the regional level

NOTES

1. Vol. 19, no. 2 of the journal *Practicing Anthropology* is a special issue devoted to practicing anthropology with a Master's degree. Vol. 20, no. 4 of the same journal is a special issue devoted to graduate students doing applied anthropology.
2. A list of the kinds of organizations employing applied cultural anthropologists can be found in Chapter 1, pp. 13–14.
3. In academics, the Latin term **curriculum vitae** is used instead of résumé; the two terms are synonymous.
4. Although its subject is a specific kind of applied anthropology (international development work), Nolan 2001 contains an informative chart, "Functional and Technical Skills," which would be helpful in many other areas.

REFERENCES

Barone, Timi
   1999. "Practical Advice from Practicing Anthropologists." *Anthropology Newsletter* 40 (3):37–38.

Hoffman, Nancy
   2001. "The Career Conundrum." *Brown Alumni Magazine* 101 (6):32–7.

Joseph, Rebecca M.
   1999. "Making the Most of Your Internship." *Anthropology Newsletter* 40 (2):33.

Kahn, Virginia Munger
   2000. "Higher Degrees of Occupation." *New York Times*, June 7, 2000, G1.

Kuehnast, Kathleen
   1999. "Career Options Outside the Academy." *Anthropology Newsletter* 40 (2):32.

Kushner, Gilbert
   1994. "Training Programs for the Practice of Applied Anthropology." Human Organization 53:186–192.

Kushner, Gilbert, and Alvin Wolfe (eds.)
   1993. "Internship and Practice in Applied Anthropology." *Practicing Anthropology* 15 (1):3–33 (special issue).

Nolan, Riall W.
   2001. "Teaching Anthropology As If Jobs Mattered." *Practicing Anthropology* 23 (1):58–60.

Omohundra, John
   1998. *Careers in Anthropology.* MountainView, CA: Mayfield Press.

Owens, Walter
   1993. "Competing in the Market Place." *Practicing Anthropology* 15 (1):22–24.

Price, Laurie J.
   2001. "The Mismatch Between Anthropology Graduate Training and the Work Lives of Graduates." *Practicing Anthropology* 23 (1):55–60.

Quirk, Kathleen, and Marsha Jenakovich
   1997. "Anthropologists Practicing with Master's Degrees: Introduction." *Practicing Anthropology* 19 (2):2–6.

Sabloff, Paula L. W. (ed.)
   2000. *Careers in Anthropology: Profiles of Practitioner Anthropologists.* Washington, DC: National Association for the Practice of Anthropology.

Schlotter, Jeffrey
   1993. "The Internship as a Vehicle to Identity." *Practicing Anthropology* 15 (1):16–18.

Singer, Merrill et al. (eds.)
   1994. *Anthropologists at Work: Responses to Student Questions About Anthropology Careers.* Washington, DC: NAPA.

Skreija, Andris
1998. "Tips for Job Hunters: The Vita and Cover Letter." *Anthropology Newsletter* 39 (7):29.

Stephens, W. Richard
2002. *Careers in Anthropology: What an Anthropology Degree Can Do For You.* Boston: Allyn and Bacon.

Stone, John V.
1993. "Professional Networks." *Practicing Anthropology* 15 (1):25–27.

Tice, Karin E.
2000. "Engaging Anthropology in the Nonprofit Sector." In *Careers in Anthropology: Profiles of Practi-tioner Anthropologists,* edited by Paula L. W. Sabloff, 31–33. Washington, DC: National Association for the Practice of Anthropology.

Vickery, William E. (ed.)
1988. *Internet 1988 Profiles of International Development Contractors and Grantees, Vol I: United States.* Chapel Hill, NC: Network for International Technical Assistance.

Wilson, Ruth P.
1998. "The Role of Anthropologists as Short-Term Consultants." *Human Organization* 57 (2):245–252.

APPENDIX 1

REVIEW: ANTHROPOLOGY'S FOUR TRADITIONAL FIELDS

Anthropology, broadly speaking, is the study of human beings as both natural and social creatures, from the time of our prehuman ancestors' earliest appearance on earth to the present. As an academic discipline, anthropology overlaps with many other disciplines, among both the sciences and the humanities. Examples include primatology, human physical morphology, human psychology, and sociology. However, anthropology differs from all other disciplines in the inclusiveness of its interests in all aspects of the human story, in its multiplicity of perspectives from which to view human existence, and in some of the methods it calls upon in its search for knowledge about humankind.

The study of human beings as both natural and social creatures is so broad a subject that a number of different vantage points are required. Thus, different kinds of anthropologists focus on different aspects of what it means—or meant—to be human. Some anthropologists are primarily interested in the ideas and lifeways of contemporary human beings. Others study human beings of the past, as revealed through physical objects and other clues left behind when ancestral groups died out or migrated. Still others focus on human beings' physical evolution, from the first appearance of prehuman creatures of the taxonomic order **Primates** to the present day; on human beings' contemporary physical status; and on their relationship with other members of their taxonomic order. A relatively small number of anthropologists study human beings' many languages, past and present. In short, anything and everything that sheds light on the existence, development, appearance, behavior, and beliefs of human beings is of interest to anthropologists.

Reflecting the diversity of anthropologists' interests in human beings, anthropology is traditionally divided into four major branches, called its four fields, each of which focuses on a different aspect of human life:

1. Cultural (sometimes called sociocultural) anthropology
2. Archaeology
3. Physical (sometimes called biological) anthropology
4. Anthropological linguistics

Despite the single academic umbrella beneath which these anthropological topics all cluster, and also despite the considerable overlap among them, they differ considerably in terms of their knowledge bases and methodologies. The traditional division of anthropology into four fields both acknowledges and perpetuates these intellectual "turf" distinctions. Most anthropologists have some graduate training in each of the four fields, but specialize, for the entirety of their careers, in only one.

CULTURAL ANTHROPOLOGY

The largest field of anthropology, in terms of relative numbers of practitioners, is **cultural anthropology.** This field is concerned with the behavior of human beings in social groups ("societies"). Its focus is **culture,** defined for purposes of this book as all the behaviors, ideas, manufactured objects, and systems of expression that characterize life in human social groups. These elements of culture are repeated in the present and handed down through the generations, rendering the lifeways of a group of people meaningful, both to themselves and to others. (The term *culture* has been defined and redefined frequently. For those unfamiliar with its complex and controversial meanings, see Appendix 2.) More specifically, the term *cultural anthropology* usually refers to the study of the cultures of contemporary peoples (those living today) or of peoples who lived recently enough to have left written records of their lives. These cultures include those of people in traditional, small-scale societies as well as large-scale, highly industrialized societies.

Over the years since cultural anthropology's nineteenth-century inception as a discrete academic discipline, its practitioners have studied literally thousands of different cultures, including not only those currently extant but also many that are now either extinct or so altered as to be quite different from their ancestral forms. Anthropology's one-hundred-plus years' worth of information and ideas about all these cultures, presented from a number of different viewpoints as anthropological perspectives changed through time, now form an enormous compendium of data about people, past and present, all over the world. This body of knowledge is so wide ranging that it has enabled the field of cultural anthropology to become highly comparative. Today's cultural anthropologists, in their pursuit of knowledge about human beings, often compare the behaviors, ideas, manufactured objects, and languages of the people of one culture with those of others.

To study the culture of a group of people, a cultural anthropologist usually lives and works among them for an extended period of time. (For those who are unfamiliar with this major anthropological research method, termed *participant observation,* see Appendix 2.) The data gathered are then compared with data about other cultures to gain a clearer understanding of how human beings as members of social groups mirror, and also differ from, one another.

Because its core concept and major learning principle—culture—has been called into question (see Appendix 2), cultural anthropology today is a discipline in flux. It remains to be seen whether there really is, or can be, a "science of culture" (see below), as anthropological traditionalists believe, or instead a humanistic compendium of data about people all over the world, as postmodern anthropologists believe—or some combination of the two.

ARCHAEOLOGY

Archaeology is the study of the cultures of people who (mainly) lived in the past, through analysis of their material remains. The specific ways in which its practitioners, termed *archaeologists*, pursue the answers to questions about people of the past are necessarily quite different from the methods used by cultural anthropologists, since the human beings who are the target of archaeological research are usually long gone.

Archaeologists find, analyze, and interpret materials that were discarded or left behind when their makers died or moved away. These remains, termed **artifacts**, include everything from stone tools to cooking pots made of baked clay to ancient city walls—or small fragments of any of these. Since artifacts are apt to be buried under layer upon layer of soil by the passage of time, the primary research method of archaeologists involves excavation.

Archaeology is divided into subfields, and most archaeologists specialize in one or more of them. Some are most interested in the prehistoric period, the time before human beings kept written records; others in the historic period, the time after the invention of writing. (The periods of time designated by these two terms vary in absolute terms, depending on the specific culture under discussion.) Some specialize in the archaeology of a particular group of people (for example, Neanderthals, Bronze Age Greeks, or Native Americans); others specialize in a particular part of the world (for example, Oceania, northern Europe, or the American Southwest). Many archaeologists specialize in cultural resources management: archaeological research in support of the effective implementation of laws intended to protecting humans' prehistoric and historical legacy (see Appendix 3).

PHYSICAL ANTHROPOLOGY

A third field of anthropology is **physical anthropology,** whose practitioners study the biological development and current physical status of human beings and their direct ancestors.

Like archaeology, physical anthropology is divided into subfields. One is **primatology,** the study of nonhuman primates (such as apes and monkeys)—human beings' closest animal relatives. Another is **paleoanthropology** (or **human evolution**), the study of how and when human beings evolved from earlier forms of life. A third is **biological anthropology** (or **human variation**), the study of physical differences among human beings. A fourth is **forensic anthropology,** the use of data on human variation to help law enforcement agencies solve crimes, investigate fatal transportation accidents, or identify murder or accident victims. Paleoanthropology, biological anthropology, and forensic anthropology are grouped under the rubric "human evolution and variation" (see Appendix 4). Some physical anthropologists are specialists in more than one of these subfields.

ANTHROPOLOGICAL LINGUISTICS

The fourth traditional field of anthropology is **linguistic anthropology** (sometimes called **anthropological linguistics**). This is the study of languages, ancient and modern, written and unwritten, and of how languages develop, diffuse, and are used. Linguistic anthropologists attempt to reconstruct now-extinct languages, study how languages spread and change through time and space, and explore and explain the connections between language and other aspects of culture.

ANTHROPOLOGY AS NATURAL OR SOCIAL SCIENCE

Although many now view it as fitting more appropriately among the humanities, anthropology has historically been considered a **science**—a body of knowledge gained from studying, learning about, and testing phenomena and ideas within a particular subject area using agreed-upon data-collection and testing methods (see Kuznar 1997). Most sciences are designated either *natural* or *social*, depending on their subject matter. The natural sciences are a group of disciplines, including botany, geology, and astronomy, that are concerned with physical phenomena such as the evolution, current status, and future of plants, rocks, or stars. The social sciences are a group of disciplines, including political science, economics, history, psychology, and sociology, that are concerned with social phenomena—social in that their focus is some aspect of the behavior of human beings as they live with and relate to each other in social groups.

Anthropology is unusual for a science in that it straddles the natural science–social science divide. On the one hand, its object of inquiry, like that of the other social sciences, is human beings; on the other hand, it is concerned with human beings as creatures of nature as well as society.

Persuasive arguments have been put forward for considering cultural anthropology as one of the humanities rather than one of the sciences. Indeed, "even those scholars who acknowledge science as cultural anthropology's 'dominant parental strain,' intellectually speaking, often do not recognize it as the only strain" (Kuklick 1997:47). Practitioners of a more humanistic cultural anthropology refer to it by a number of different names; its leading proponent, Clifford Geertz, labels this kind of cultural anthropology *interpretive anthropology,* but it has also been termed hermeneutic, symbolic, deconstructionist, postmodern, critical, and reflexive, among other appellations (Lett 1997:5).

No matter what the designation, however, defenders of this view see the search for cultural anthropological knowledge as more appropriately a search for meaning than fact, always subject to change and reinterpretation and specific to particular times, places, and even researchers rather than universal (Lett 1997:5). Moreover, these champions of a more humanistic anthropology hold that cultural anthropologists' "scientific quest for objective knowledge is unavoidably doomed, because the subject matter of [cultural] anthropology defies objective description" (ibid.:14).

The disagreement about cultural anthropology's appropriate academic placement is ongoing, with interpretive anthropologists viewing traditional anthropologists' attempts to be scientific as "naive and unrealistic," and scientific anthropologists' view of the goals of interpretive anthropology as "trivial and unworthy"(Lett 1997:14). This book takes the time-tested view that whatever else it may be, cultural anthropology is a science, and that therefore the principles of scientific inquiry can and should apply to the greatest extent possible, given the variability and mutability of the discipline's object of inquiry.

If cultural anthropology is a science, then it is indisputably a social science, since its focus is the behavior and beliefs of human beings in social groups. Linguistic anthropology is customarily placed in the same category. Archaeology, with its interest in understanding the cultures of past peoples through sophisticated analyses of physical remains (analyses which often take place in the laboratory), combines social and natural science. Physical anthropology is the field of anthropology that is most clearly affiliated with the natural sciences.

It is important to note that in anthropology, the distinction between natural and social science is by no means clear-cut. Many aspects of being human are neither wholly products of social life nor of biology. Examples include human beings' historical and linguistic development and their cognitive and symbolic abilities.

KEY TERMS

anthropology   the study of human beings as both natural and social creatures, from the first appearance of prehuman creatures to the present

anthropological linguistics   an alternate term for *linguistic anthropology*

archaeology   the study, through material remains, of the cultures of people who lived in the past

artifacts   material remains of people of the past

biological anthropology   the study of physical differences among human beings

cultural anthropology   the study of culture

culture   collectively, all the behaviors, ideas, artifacts, and systems of expression that characterize life in human social groups and are repeated in the present and handed down through the generations, rendering the lifeways of a group of people meaningful, both to themselves and to others

forensic anthropology   a branch of physical anthropology; the use of data on human variation to help law enforcement agencies solve crimes, investigate fatal transportation accidents, or identify murder or accident victims

human evolution   an alternate term for *paleoanthropology*

human variation   an alternate term for *biological anthropology*

linguistic anthropology   the anthropological study of languages, ancient and modern, written and unwritten

paleoanthropology   the study of how and when human beings evolved from earlier forms of life

physical anthropology   the study of the biological development and current physical status of human beings

Primates   the taxonomic group to which humans and related creatures, past and present, belong

primatology   a branch of physical anthropology; the study of nonhuman primates

science   a body of knowledge gained from studying, learning about, and testing ideas within a particular subject area, using agreed-upon data-collection methods

R E F E R E N C E S

Kuklick, Henrika
  1997. "After Ishmael: The Fieldwork Tradition and its Future." In *Anthropological Locations: Boundaries and Grounds of a Field Science*, edited by Akhil Gupta and James Ferguson, 47–65. Berkeley: University of California Press.

Kuznar, Lawrence A.
  1997. *Reclaiming a Scientific Anthropology*. Walnut Creek, CA: Altamira Press.

Lett, James
  1997. *Science, Reason, and Anthropology*. Lanham, MD: Rowman and Littlefield.

APPENDIX 2

REVIEW: THEORY AND METHOD IN CULTURAL ANTHROPOLOGY

Academic cultural anthropologists call upon two important kinds of tools in their work: conceptual and methodological. Their conceptual tools include not only certain specific concepts often referred to as anthropology's "theories," but also various perspectives or viewpoints. Their methodological tools include a number of data-gathering techniques, most of which yield qualitative, as opposed to quantitative, data. This appendix provides a brief review of the most important (and most familiar) of cultural anthropology's tools. Many of them have proven as useful to applied cultural anthropologists, as they search for practical solutions to real-world problems, as they are to academic anthropologists.[1]

THEORIES

A **theory,** in any science, is an idea that is believed to explain some observed phenomenon, or the constant relationships between two or more phenomena. There should be no exceptions to a theory. It should always hold true, or it cannot be considered a theory; nor can it be summoned in the defense of new findings. Theory is the bedrock of scientific knowledge. The major motivation behind most of the scientific research undertaken by college- or university-based scholars, no matter what their academic discipline, is to find that bedrock; that is, their research is *theoretical* (also termed *basic,* or *pure*), done mainly for the purpose of contributing to human knowledge. It should be borne in mind that there is no clear-cut, black-and-white distinction between this kind of research and more practically oriented applied research. However, the *primary* impetus behind theoretical research is a quest for knowledge rather than for specific solutions to specific problems.

Compared with other scientists, cultural anthropologists have discovered few if any genuine theories, primarily because human beings are so infinitely variable (see Bennett 1996; Layton 1997; Moore 1999:1). Nevertheless, they have identified a number of ideas that have proven useful for understanding aspects of what it means to be human, and these ideas are often referred to as cultural anthropology's "theories." Not all of them are unique to cultural anthropology; some were borrowed, with or without alteration, from other disciplines, including philosophy, psychology, biology, biomedicine, and even literature.

Cultural anthropology's "theories" are unlike those that underpin most other sciences (for example, the theory of gravity in physics) in that they are employed somewhat differently in cultural anthropology's different subdisciplinary arenas (symbolic anthropology, cognitive anthropology, cultural ecology, and so on). Thus they convey different meanings to different anthropologists. Moreover, none is static; each "theory" continues to be the subject of debate and revision.[2] Despite their variability, however, cultural anthropology's "theories" remain the primary tools cultural anthropologists use "to give meaning to their data . . . and to sort significant from meaningless information" (McGee and Warms 2000:1; see also Bernard 1998:696).

The Culture Concept

The specific focus of cultural anthropology is culture. Historically, the concept of culture has been touted as cultural anthropology's linchpin, yet it has been defined and refined so frequently as to suggest both complexity and controversy. Some cultural anthropologists view culture as a comprehensive system consisting of a complex of interlocking human behaviors, ideas, artifacts, and means of expression that are produced, and reproduced through time, by the members of a given social group. Others prefer to see culture as a set of rules for how to behave in a particular society—an ensemble meaningful to that society's members but not necessarily to the members of other societies. Still others prefer the even broader heuristic image of a lens, or prism, through which meaning is revealed and through which the lives of a particular group of people can be viewed and understood.

These definitions are not mutually exclusive, and most cultural anthropologists would probably agree with Wolcott (1999:248) that "one or a combination of many different conceptions of 'culture' . . . serves as the bonding agent that allows disparate bits of data to be formed into a cohesive whole." Yet there is enough difference among the meanings of the term to make it clear that cultural anthropologists do not agree on the constitution of their primary research focus. This book takes the view that culture is a complex whole (to use late nineteenth-century anthropologist E. B. Tylor's famous term) consisting of all the behaviors, ideas, manufactured objects ("artifacts"), and systems of expression that characterize life in human social groups. These elements of culture are repeated in the present and handed down through the generations. Collectively, they render the lifeways of a group of people meaningful, both to the people themselves and to others.

Whatever their preferred definition, most cultural anthropologists draw a distinction between *culture* and *a culture*. Culture is a general concept that helps anthropologists and others interested in human beings as objects of research to distinguish between those aspects of being human that are biological and those that are not. *A culture* is the particular behaviors, ideas, artifacts, and systems of expression that characterize life in a particular human group and are recognized as meaningful and repeated within that group—and through which the lives of members of that group can be studied and appreciated. *Culture* in the generic sense is thus the more abstract concept; *a culture* or *the culture of society X* is more specific, referring to the sum total of all the cultural elements that characterize that particular society.

Perhaps unfortunately for cultural anthropology, the culture concept has become increasingly problematic as a guide for the conduct of anthropological research (Gupta and Ferguson 1997:2). This is true for several reasons. First, over the past twenty years or so, the notion that there are "wholes," prisms, road maps, or sets of rules that somehow define and delimit specific groups of people has gradually changed, within anthropology, into a more global idea. Today many cultural anthropologists hold that globalization (the increasing homogeneity of the world's people), and in particular various social and economic processes that now link people in every part of the world, are more useful foci for research than the elements that separate "cultures" from one another (ibid.). The point is well taken: it is difficult to conceive of a global phenomenon—the Internet, for example, or air transportation—in terms of either *culture* or *a culture*. Thus contemporary anthropology "appears determined to give up its old ideas of ... stable, localized cultures, and to apprehend an interconnected world in which people, objects, and ideas are rapidly shifting and refuse to stay in place" (ibid.: 4).

A second reason why many contemporary anthropologists see "culture," in the sense of a guiding anthropological concept, as problematic is the growing realization that it does not and cannot mean any one particular thing. This is because cultures are impermanent, ephemeral, and evanescent. Moreover, any given element of culture can have multiple meanings, both from the point of view of those whose lives are embedded in a particular culture and those who are looking into it from the outside.

And third, some contemporary anthropologists believe that a description or analysis of any given culture may be more an artifact of a particular ethnographer's preconceived notions and imagination than a reflection of reality (see, for example, Fabian 1983; Clifford and Marcus 1986). Particularly if ethnographers describe the cultures of "the other" based on their own culture's predispositions regarding ethnicity, class, and gender, their descriptions may be so skewed as to be worthless—or worse.

Society

A **society** is a group of people who describe themselves as sharing a common identity and hence as distinguishable from the members of all other groups. The sense of common identity of members of a society is usually based on their shared customs, beliefs, values, and language, and sometimes on certain more or less similar physical attributes.

In the past, some societies were associated with particular territories, cultures, and languages. Today, however, there can be no one-to-one relationship between societies and specific territories, cultures, or languages, since a given individual can be a member of more than one society at a time and since many societies are multicultural and multilingual. Thus the concept is less precise and therefore less useful today than it was in the past, and many contemporary anthropologists avoid it in favor of more neutral terms, such as *group*. Nevertheless, it remains important for an understanding of earlier anthropological work.

Holism

An Indian poet, A. K. Ramanujan, once said, "Things are clear only when looked at from a distance." This observation holds true whether the thing in question is a culture or a car engine. To fully understand either, one must step back and look at it as an aggregate of interrelated and interdependent parts, all functioning together to make up a whole. This is the idea behind **holism.** To look at something holistically means to understand its parts individually, to comprehend the ways in which the parts are interrelated, and to understand that—because the parts are interrelated—to change one of them is to change the whole.

The concept of holism is difficult for some Western students to understand, probably because our own postindustrial, information-age Western culture is less integrated than many others. Westerners tend to separate and compartmentalize different aspects of culture, such as health care and religion. But this compartmentalization is not characteristic of many societies, especially small-scale ones. In a culture in which ancestors are worshipped as gods, for example, religion and kinship are thoroughly intertwined, and one cannot fully understand one without also studying the other.

The idea of holism is used in anthropology not only to convey the idea that cultures are made up of interlocking parts but also to integrate the different aspects of what it means to be human. If one's goal is to forge a comprehensive understanding of a group of people, one cannot study any one feature that characterizes them—their physical morphology, or the effects of the natural environment in which they live, or their social system, or their language—in a vacuum. This, too, is holism.

Cultural Evolution

The earliest anthropologists noted that gathering-and-hunting societies, with very simple subsistence technologies, tended to evolve into agricultural societies with more complex subsistence technologies; nonliterate societies tended eventually to become literate or to be incorporated into literate societies; simple political organizations, run by one powerful individual, tended to evolve into multilayered governmental bureaucracies. They concluded, logically, that cultures inevitably change through time, and that the changes tend to be from relative simplicity toward relative complexity.[3]

Broadly speaking, this is the notion behind **cultural evolution.** Throughout the history of cultural anthropology, numerous ideas have been put forth to explain it, among them population growth, environmental adaptation, technological innovation, the increasingly efficient use of energy, increasingly complex social organization, and contact with other cultures. The process is by no means inevitable; noteworthy exceptions to evolutionary tendencies exist, and cultures differ in the extent to which they embrace or resist change. Moreover, sometimes cultural evolution seems to imply progress, in the sense of betterment; sometimes it does not. Thus there is no consensus among anthropologists as to why or how cultural evolution actually takes place. Perhaps not surprisingly, then, various "theories" of cultural evolution have arisen over the years, found favor, attracted criticism, and faded from popularity.

It is important to note that the idea of cultural evolution is no more a genuine theory than the idea of culture itself. Indeed, some anthropologists would dispute the premise that any functional model, including cultural evolution, opens doors onto social realities. But as a general observation, cultural evolution does help some anthropologists comprehend the why and how of both past and contemporary human behavior.

Functionalism

The term **functionalism** means different things to different anthropologists. Some employ it as a virtual synonym for one kind of holism, the idea that cultures consist of individual elements that function both individually and together. For other anthropologists, functionalism is the idea that aspects of culture, far from being random or irrational, are functional—their function is to answer individuals' biological and psychological needs. Since cultures other than a given anthropologist's own culture are very likely to incorporate aspects that at first seem irrational and hence inexplicable, this has proven to be a useful notion. Finally, some cultural anthropologists use the term *functional* in a narrower sense, to refer to the ways in which social relationships between members of a group function to maintain the social structure of the group. This idea is more accurately termed *structural-functionalism* because aspects of culture are viewed in terms of the part they play in maintaining the social structure.

There are a number of other ideas, sometimes referred to as theories, that help cultural anthropologists understand and explain their subject. Those briefly reviewed here are only examples, albeit important ones, of the kinds of ideas that cultural anthropology has devised for the theoretical understanding of the behavior of people in groups. Applied cultural anthropologists can and do appropriate these ideas for their own, more practical, work, blurring the line between "pure" and applied research.

CULTURAL ANTHROPOLOGICAL PERSPECTIVES

In addition to its "theories," cultural anthropology has devised a second, distinct, set of ideas over the years, which might be termed perspectives or philosophical stances. These are broad, intellectual organizing principles representing alternative ways of approaching cultural anthropological data. They cannot be termed theories under even the loosest of definitions, but they have indisputably helped to shape the discipline. Two of them, cultural relativism and the emic point of view, have particular relevance for applied anthropology.

Cultural Relativism

One of cultural anthropology's most important contributions to social science, **cultural relativism** originated in the idea that to understand other people, an anthropologist must view their culture through their eyes. Some still view it in these terms, as a straightforward research strategy that allows the anthropologist a more accurate glimpse into another culture. For others, however, cultural relativism incorporates an ethical principle: that every culture should be evaluated in terms of its own shared precepts and values, not those of any other culture (including a fieldworker's). Employed in this sense, the concept has occasionally been criticized because, if taken to its logical extreme, it seems to imply that there are no universal human values (Gert 1995:30), that "anything goes" so long as a particular behavior is viewed within its cultural context (Wolcott 1999:140–141). It has also been criticized as "no longer appropriate to the world in which we live," on the grounds that today's anthropology should attempt to promote socially beneficial change (Scheper-Hughes 1995:409). However, cultural relativism by no means suggests that cultural anthropologists should not have opinions about what is right or wrong, that they must uncritically accept any behavior, no matter how reprehensible, on the part of individual members of other cultures, or that they should make no attempt to right wrongs. It does mean that they should be cautious about making value judgments concerning the customs, behaviors, or opinions that are widely shared by members of a society under study.

Cultural relativism is basic to theoretical cultural anthropology. Fieldworkers trying to learn as much as possible about cultures would find it virtually impossible to understand certain unfamiliar customs, behaviors, or ideas if they evaluated these according to their own, usually Western, preconceptions. Cultural anthropologists are fond of pointing out that the idea of cultural relativism accounts for their lack of ethnocentrism, the belief that one's own society is superior to others. Both notions have important ethical ramifications for applied anthropology (see Chapter 4).

The Emic Viewpoint

The **emic view** of a human group is the native, or "insider," view; its opposite, the "outsider" point of view, is termed the **etic view** (Harris 1968:571). The emic view reflects cultural categories and understandings that have meaning for members of a given culture, while the etic view reflects categories and understandings imposed by outsiders in order to create meaning for themselves, and might or might not be recognized by members of the culture under consideration (Adams 1998:329). Some cultural anthropologists would argue that, as quintessential outsiders, they can hope only to approximate the emic viewpoint. Others believe that by exploring the temperaments, feelings, motivations, interests, and problems of a society's members, they can indeed understand not only what is obvious about a human group but also what is going on under the surface.

Today, the degree to which an anthropological fieldworker is able to tease out the emic viewpoint is often viewed as one measure of his or her success in the field. The notion that insider knowledge is attainable and useful in social analysis constitutes a major contribution of cultural anthropological fieldwork to the social sciences. It is especially useful to applied cultural anthropologists because "the best way to solve human problems and understand the issues is to include the perspective of the people being affected by change" (Sabloff 2000:3).

Cultural Ecology

Different societies view and use the natural environment in different ways. Western concepts about the environment, which have historically tended toward the romantic, prevailed for many years in anthropology. Beginning in the late 1960s, however, **cultural ecology,** the study of the ways in which human groups view and interact with their natural environment, arose. Cultural ecologists highlight the role of culture in human adaptations to different environments (see, for example, Vayda 1969), explaining various aspects of culture in terms of their contribution to humans' adaptation to various environmental settings. The cultural ecological approach is a holistic one, in which culture, the environment, and human interactions with the landscape and its flora and fauna are viewed as inseparable. This approach is particularly important for applied cultural anthropologists involved in development (see Chapter 5), whose work (especially in Third World countries) often combines economic development with cultural and environmental conservation.

Cultural Materialism

Cultural anthropologists have never achieved consensus on the relative influence, on cultures, of the many factors presumed to shape them. To what extent, for example, is culture influenced by the human intellect, custom and tradition, or social arrangements? Cultural materialism is a way of looking at cultures that presumes a seminal role for the material aspects of life. In this view, culture is best understood and explained in terms of tangible, measurable, quantifiable things, as opposed to ideas. Thus, for example, a given society's natural environment, level of technological expertise and work organization (its "mode of production"), and demographic factors such as marriage patterns, fertility, and mortality (its "mode of reproduction") are heavily weighted in cultural materialists' explanations (see Harris 1979).

STANDARD CULTURAL ANTHROPOLOGICAL METHODS

Just as academic anthropologists, over the years, have devised (or in some instances, adopted) certain ideas and perspectives to guide and aid the task of understanding and interpreting the existence, development, appearance, behavior, and beliefs of human beings, so too have they invented (or in some instances, borrowed) a number of specific methods for the thorough and efficient collection of data about human beings in groups (see especially Ellen 1984; Bernard 1994, 2000; Grills 1998; Wolcott 1999; Schensul and LeCompte 1999). And just as the conceptual tools developed by academic cultural anthropologists have proven invaluable to their applied counterparts, so too have the methodological ones.

Qualitative versus Quantitative Approaches

In general, the methodological tools traditionally used by cultural anthropologists produce data that are more qualitative than quantitative; that is, the data are somewhat less easily expressed in absolute or numerical terms than the data other kinds of scientists collect. A fundamental reason is the ephemeral and transitory nature of the variables with which cultural anthropologists work, such as human beliefs and behaviors. It is always difficult—and sometimes impossible—to establish concrete, testable, replicable, cause-and-effect linkages among such variables. In contrast, the methodological tools used in most other sciences, including the other social sciences, produce data that tend to be more quantitative than most cultural anthropological data.

Scientists, especially social scientists, have disagreed about the scientific validity of data produced through the use of qualitative techniques. Some have argued that qualitative methods, by definition, produce data that are impressionistic and subjective, and hence not as amenable to rigorous analysis and theory formulation as data produced by quantitative methods. Others firmly believe that data produced using qualitative techniques can be as objective and scientifically valid as quantitative data.

The last decades of the twentieth century saw increasing movement toward the use of quantitative methods on the part of cultural anthropologists—not as a replacement for, but as an addition to, the qualitative approach. One reason stems from anthropology's increasing self-criticism and self-awareness. Today's ethnographers realize that no matter how they might strive for objectivity, the training, intellectual proclivities, and persona of the fieldworker together conspire to bias his or her data, as collaborators' information and views are fitted into the fieldworker's own frame of reference. The result may be an unintentionally skewed portrait of a human group. A second reason is the explosion in computer technology over the past generation, which has made large quantities of quantitative data much easier to assemble and manipulate.

The debate is ongoing, with many cultural anthropologists choosing to combine quantitative and qualitative methods. Thus many ethnographers have added techniques yielding replicable and in many cases numerically quantifiable data, amenable to statistical analysis, to their repertoires. These include surveys and questionnaires, genealogies (essential in studies of descent and marriage), case studies (frequently used, for example, in studies of legal systems), network analysis (useful for establishing patterns of association among people), and focus groups. (Social network analysis and focus group research are described in Chapter 2.)

A brief review of cultural anthropology's traditional, and still most frequently used, ethnographic methods will help contrast these methods with the quantitative methods described in Chapter 2. Despite the increasing use of quantitative methods by academic anthropologists, such methods are still more commonly used in applied than theoretical work (see Chapter 2).

Fieldwork

The process of collecting data about human beings, in any of the subdisciplines of anthropology, is called **fieldwork,** a generic term for a number of data-collecting strategies that differ according to what kind of information about people is being collected. Fieldwork in cultural anthropology—collecting data from living people— is termed **ethnographic fieldwork;** the cultural anthropologist in the process of collecting ethnographic data is called an **ethnographer,** and the resulting data about a particular culture—compiled, analyzed, digested, and written down—constitute an **ethnography.** When cultural anthropologists compare and synthesize ethnographic data in order to discern broad generalizations about the behavior of human beings in groups, this effort is termed **ethnology.**

Participant Observation

Foremost among the methodological tools used by academic ethnographers is **participant observation,** the cultural anthropologist's total immersion in the culture he or she is interested in studying. Usually for many months or even years, the ethnographer lives and works among a group of people from whom ethnographic data are to be collected, observing their behavior, learning from them, sharing in their activities, and communicating with them in their own language. Those from whom the anthropologist collects specific information are called **informants.** The ethnographer not only studies the group but also participates in its members' lives to the greatest extent possible.

There are, of course, other ways of studying people in groups besides participant observation. One might make one or more short-term visits to a group of people as an outsider, read about them in books, or interview others who have visited the group. However, through multiple generations of academic cultural anthropologists who have undertaken ethnographic research in literally hundreds of cultures with the same goal in mind—learning as much about the lifeways of a particular group of people as possible—participant observation has proven to be by far the most effective strategy for achieving the goal of understanding people in groups. Some cultural anthropologists view long-term, intensive fieldwork, involving total immersion in the context of the "other," as the *sine qua non* of cultural anthropology (Gupta and Ferguson 1997:1).

The Comparative Method

It would be impossible to develop an understanding of the wide range of human behavior—to learn what is possible and what is not, what works when people interact and what does not, what is common to all cultures and what varies from culture to culture—by studying a single group. Another traditional methodological tool in cultural anthropology, the comparative method, provides cultural anthropologists with a broad, cross-cultural view encompassing the whole range of human behavior. Culture-specific information is interesting and useful, but ethnology—the process of comparing and synthesizing ethnographic data in order to discern broad generalizations about the behavior of human beings in groups—is even more so.

Ultimately, cultural anthropologists hope to forge a thorough understanding of which features of human social life are shared among cultures and which are unique to particular cultures. The comparative method has been criticized, with undoubted justification, as overly reliant on the notion that discrete, bounded cultures actually exist and can be compared, yet because of its utility it continues to underpin both traditional and more recent anthropological thinking.

The "New Ethnography"

In academic cultural anthropology, the ongoing debate about the scientific relevance of quantitative as opposed to qualitative data (see above) has resulted, over the past generation or so, in the introduction of a range of new, more objective, and more quantitative field methods, ultimately derived from the discipline of linguistics. These new methods, a reaction to the subjectivity of traditional anthropological fieldwork, are now used by some, but by no means all, ethnographers; many prefer to rely on more traditional field methods.

The new ethnography can be defined as a set of field techniques designed to produce an understanding of cultural categories and distinctions meaningful to the members of a given society (Adams 1998:330) and also to yield very accurate, language-based, numerically quantifiable field data. Its underlying principle is that people in all societies mentally categorize everything in their world (albeit in different ways, depending on their culture) and express their culture's particular categories through language. Thus, eliciting the words and terms referable to specific categories of thought in a specific society should open a window into that society's culture (Wolcott 1999:35).

A classic example, drawn from applied medical anthropology (see Chapter 11), is the "free listing" technique used by Frake (1961) to elicit a folk taxonomy from Filipino collaborators (see Anderson 1996:104ff.). Frake was interested in collecting thorough, unbiased data about skin conditions. By repeatedly pointing to people's skin problems and asking for the terms by which each problem was known and described, he developed a list of all the terms associated with skin diseases. Some were general terms (the local equivalents of "itchy rash" or "skin eruption"); some were more specific (the local equivalents of "acne" or "hives"). Not surprisingly, Frake's collaborators sometimes supplied different terms for the same skin ailment. His subsequent manipulation of these terms, distinguishing the general or abstract from the specific, yielded a thorough folk taxonomy of skin ailments as perceived by his research population. The result was greater insight into how the members of this population categorized and thought about this particular aspect of their lives.

Postmodernism

If the new ethnography was a reaction against the subjectivity of traditional field methods, postmodernism—among other things, yet another philosophy of fieldwork—was a reaction against the new ethnography. Postmodernists believe that the information an ethnographer collects in the field is more a product of the ethnographer's own experiences, personality, and worldview, and those of his or her collaborators, than of objective social reality. Standard field methods introduce distortion caused by anthropologists' hidden agendas. Because there is no discrete entity called a culture, the best the ethnographer can do is interpret and then report on what he or she saw and heard in a particular place at a particular point in time.

Postmodern ethnography is **reflexive,** meaning that it reflects its author. This is intentional: postmodern ethnographers include, in addition to information from collaborators, information on their own thoughts and feelings, assuming that these will color the data. They may also fictionalize their ethnographies, on the assumption that the complexity of real life obscures the truth, and that fiction can sometimes paint a truer portrait of a culture than a litany of facts. The results, postmodernists hope, are portraits of cultures that convey reality better than classic ethnographic writing does (Mitchell and Charmaz 1998).

The conceptual and methodological tools briefly reviewed here were developed primarily for use by scholars whose overall goal is to attain as broad a theoretical understanding as possible about the behavior of human beings as members of social groups. The practical problems on which applied cultural anthropologists focus are amenable to investigation by means of these tools, but they often require different tools as well. Thus, although applied cultural anthropology is fundamentally informed by the ideas and methods of classic anthropological research, applied cultural anthropologists have altered some of anthropology's tools to help accomplish their often shorter-term, more narrowly focused, more practical goals. The theories and methods most commonly used by applied anthropologists are discussed in Chapter 2 and are exemplified throughout the chapters of this book.

KEY TERMS

cultural ecology   the study of the ways in which human groups view and interact with their natural environment, with an emphasis on the role of culture in adaptations to different environments

cultural evolution   the notion that with the passage of time, aspects of culture tend to move from relative simplicity toward relative complexity

cultural relativism   the idea that every culture should be evaluated in terms of its own shared precepts and values, not those of any other culture

emic view   the native, or "insider," view of a culture

ethnocentrism   the belief that one's own society is superior to others

ethnographer   a cultural anthropologist in the process of collecting ethnographic data

ethnographic fieldwork   fieldwork in cultural anthropology; the collection of data from living people

ethnography   data about a particular culture, compiled, analyzed, digested, and written down

ethnology   the process of comparing and synthesizing ethnographic data in order to discern broad generalizations about the behavior of human beings in groups

etic view   the non-native, or "outsider" view of a culture

fieldwork   a generic term for a number of anthropological data-collecting strategies that differ according to what kind of information about people is being collected

functionalism   a word with three anthropological meanings: the idea that cultures consist of individual elements that function individually and together; the idea that aspects of culture are useful rather than random or irrational; or the idea that the relationships between a group's members function to maintain the social structure of the group

holism   the idea that cultures are best viewed as integrated systems

informant   a member of a culture under study by a cultural anthropologist, who provides the anthropologist with information

participant observation   the primary data-collecting method of cultural anthropologists, involving total immersion in a culture under study

qualitative data   data that are subjective and hence not expressible in numerical terms

quantitative data   data that are objective and hence easily expressed in numerical terms

reflexive   as used in anthropological fieldwork, reflecting the views and experience of the fieldworker

society   a group of people who describe themselves as sharing a common identity and hence distinguishable from the members of all other groups

theory   an idea that is believed to explain some observed phenomenon or the constant relationships between two or more phenomena

N O T E S

1. For further information on any of the anthropological concepts, approaches, and methods described here, consult any standard introductory cultural anthropology textbook.
2. Some of this debate and revision has been spurred by the work of applied anthropologists, whose new ways of conceiving of traditional ideas helps to account for much of applied anthropology's feedback into theory formulation (see Chapter 2).
3. A further conclusion on the part of the earliest anthropologists was the ethnocentric notion that cultural evolution had propelled Western culture faster and further than other cultures.

R E F E R E N C E S

Adams, William Y.
  1998. *The Philosophical Roots of Anthropology.* Stanford, CA: Center for the Study of Language and Information.

Anderson, Robert
  1996. *Magic, Science, and Health.* Fort Worth: Harcourt Brace.

Bennett, John
  1996. "Applied Anthropology: Ideological and Conceptual Aspects." *Current Anthropology* 36:S23–S53.

Bernard, H. Russell
  1994. *Research Methods in Anthropology: Qualitative and Quantitative Approaches* (2nd ed.). Thousand Oaks, CA: Sage Publications.

  2000 (ed.). *Handbook of Methods in Cultural Anthropology.* Walnut Creek, CA: Altamira Press.

Clifford, James, and George E. Marcus (eds.)
  1986. *Writing Culture: The Poetics and Politics of Ethnography.* Berkeley: University of California Press.

Ellen, Roy F.
  1984. *Ethnographic Research: A Guide to General Conduct* (ASA Research Methods in Social Anthropology No. 1). London: Academic Press.

Fabian, Johannes
  1983. *Time and the Other: How Anthropology Makes Its Object.* New York: Columbia University Press.

Frake, C. O.
  1961. "The Diagnosis of Disease Among the Subanum of Mindanao." *American Anthropolgist* 63 (1): 113–132.

Gert, Bernard
  1995. "Universal Values and Professional Codes of Ethics." *Anthropology Newsletter* 36 (7):30–31.

Grills, Scott (ed.)
  1998. *Doing Ethnographic Research.* Thousand Oaks, CA: Sage Publications.

Gupta, Akhil, and James Ferguson (eds.)
  1997. *Culture, Power, Place: Explorations in Critical Anthropology.* Durham, NC: Duke University Press.

Harris, Marvin
  1979. *Cultural Materialism: The Struggle for a Science of Culture.* New York: Random House.

  1968. *The Rise of Anthropological Theory.* New York: Crowell.

Layton, Robert
  1997. *An Introduction to Theory in Anthropology.* Cambridge, UK: Cambridge University Press.

McGee, R. Jon, and Richard L. Warms
  2000. *Anthropological Theory: An Introductory History* (2nd ed.). Mountain View, CA: Mayfield.

Mitchell, Richard G., Jr., and Kathy Charmaz
  1998. "Telling Tales and Writing Stories: Postmodernist Visions and Realist Images in Ethnographic Writing." In *Doing Ethnographic Research,* edited by Scott Grills, 228–248. Thousand Oaks, CA: Sage Publications.

Moore, Henrietta L.
  1999. "Anthropological Theory at the Turn of the Century." In *Anthropological Theory Today,* edited by Henrietta L. Moore, 1–23. Cambridge, UK: Polity Press.

Sabloff, Paula L. W. (ed.)
  2000. *Careers in Anthropology* (NAPA Bulletin No. 20). Washington, DC: American Anthropological Association.

Schensul, Jean J., and Margaret LeCompte (eds.)
  1999. *The Ethnographer's Toolkit* (Vols.1–7). Walnut Creek, CA: Altamira Press.

Scheper-Hughes, Nancy
  1995. "The Primacy of the Ethical: Propositions for a Militant Anthropology." *Current Anthropology* 36 (3):409–420.

Vayda, Andrew P. (ed.)
  1969. *Environment and Cultural Behavior: Ecological Studies in Cultural Anthropology.* New York: Natural History Press.

Wolcott, Harry F.
  1999. *Ethnography: A Way of Seeing.* Walnut Creek, CA: Altamira Press.

CAREERS IN APPLIED ARCHAEOLOGY

Archaeology, one of the four traditional subfields of anthropology (see Appendix 1), is similar to cultural anthropology in that its subject, broadly speaking, is human beings and their cultures. In the case of archaeology, however, the human beings of interest are mainly people who lived in the past. Since the inception of archaeology as a recognized discipline in the eighteenth century, archaeologists have developed a number of theories that help explain the behavior of people in the past. They have also devised numerous field and analytical methods to support their study of people of the past and have assembled an enormous amount of information about them.

The principal field method used for studying the peoples of the past is **excavation**—digging carefully through the soil at the places where people once lived or worked. Over the past half-century or so, this fundamental archaeological activity has become increasingly sophisticated, and today it is often supplemented with a variety of highly technical—and in many cases still-evolving—methods for locating, recording, dating, preserving, and analyzing archaeological objects. A good example is GPS (Global Positioning System) technology, which, through the use of earth-orbiting satellites, permits archaeologists a much broader view of significant human-made patterns on the ground than was possible even a few years ago (Kelly 2002:4).[1]

In the process of archaeological excavation, **material remains,** the physical objects left behind by people of the past, are revealed and unearthed. The material remains of past cultures range from simple, temporary campsites to huge walled cities, from roughly flaked stone arrowheads to highly sophisticated tools and weapons of exquisite design, from crude pottery utensils to magnificent urns, from casually deposited garbage heaps to carefully prepared grave sites. Some remains—for instance, dark charcoal stains in the soil where an ancient campfire once burned—cannot even properly be called objects and cannot be retrieved from the ground; they can only be observed and recorded. Archaeologists refer to physical objects that were made by human hands as **artifacts;** other, nonartifactual, kinds of evidence of human activity in the past, such as soil stains, are termed **features.** Floral or faunal remains found in archaeological contexts (for example, charred animal bones indicating that a meal was cooked in the past) are referred to as **ecofacts.**

Many of the ancient people whom archaeologists study were nonliterate; they lacked a tradition of reading and writing and therefore left no written records of their lives. Learning about them and their cultures, therefore, depends entirely on studying their material remains. Other groups of people who lived in the past were literate and did leave some written documentation of their lives, on materials ranging from stone to clay to paper. In most cases, however, these written documents contain only an incomplete picture of ancient lifeways, so archaeology complements the ethnographic record. Archaeological remains from both nonliterate and literate groups, therefore, are of great interest and value for the light they can shed on the cultures of our ancestors. Collectively, these valuable human-made artifacts, together with features and ecofacts suggesting human activity, are termed **cultural resources.**[2]

The archaeology of nonliterate human groups who lived in the past is referred to as **prehistoric archaeology.** No specific dates can be assigned to the prehistoric phase of human existence because written documents were first produced at different times in different places around the world. The archaeology of literate human groups who left written records of their lives is termed **historical archaeology.** Again, this phase of human history began at different times in different places. Most archaeologists focus on either prehistoric or historical archaeology. A few, however, focus on contemporary people, using the study of modern material remains to supplement the ethnographic and documentary record of contemporary lifeways.

Second only to cultural anthropology in terms of numbers of advanced degrees awarded in anthropology, archaeology is divided into many different areas of specialization. Major distinctions are made between the prehistoric and historic periods and between archaeological cultures in the Old World and the New World. Many archaeologists specialize in the study of a particular group of people, such as the ancient peoples of the American Southwest. Others specialize in a particular ecological adaptation, such as hunting and gathering; a particular activity, such as stone tool making; or the archaeology of a particular region of the world.

The term **applied archaeology** refers to the use of archaeological theories and methods to achieve specific, practical, archaeological goals. Examples of applied archaeologists' goals include recovering archaeological remains, preserving archaeological remains, and managing archaeological sites.

Applied archaeology differs considerably from basic or theoretical archaeological research, which involves studying the people of the past not to achieve specific, practical goals, but rather for the sake of learning something new about the cultures and behaviors of human beings who lived in the past. The major motivation behind applied archaeology is the desire to prevent the disappearance of the material remains of past people, valuable to all contemporary (and future) people for the light these remains shed on the physical and especially the cultural evolution of the human species.

THREATS TO ARCHAEOLOGICAL SITES

An archeological **site** can be defined as a place where people of the past once lived or worked. Archaeological sites are nonrenewable. Unlike certain natural resources (like forests), which may reconstitute themselves over time, the information a site contains can never be retrieved once the site has been dug, because a significant component of that information comes from the location of archaeological remains, relative to each other, in the ground, and also from features that cannot be removed from the ground. Around the world, however, archaeological sites, both prehistoric and historic, are rapidly disappearing or—almost as detrimental to our understanding of the past—being dug into and disrupted ("disturbed"). The three main causes of this loss are the detrimental effects of natural processes; the theft of archaeological remains from sites, either for monetary gain or for recreation; and economic development. (A fourth problem, accounting for fewer instances of cultural resources destruction, is warfare. In times of armed conflict, military priorities often interfere with the need to protect ancient remains. During the Vietnam War, for example, the site of Angkor Wat, the ancient capital of the Khmers, the aboriginal people of Cambodia, was heavily damaged.)

Natural Processes

Some archaeological sites are threatened by natural processes, such as rising sea levels or erosion due to the action of wind or water. While numerous ancient sites have been "drowned" by rising sea levels, gradually eroded by wind, or covered up by these processes, collectively natural processes are probably the least threatening of the three major causes of the destruction of archaeological sites.

Theft

Of greater concern than natural processes, in terms of the amount of damage caused to archaeological remains, is the illicit removal of cultural resources from archaeological sites. This occurs for two reasons, both of which are driven by the monetary or interest value of archaeological artifacts. In some cases, knowledgeable amateur archaeologists, or even unethical professionals, locate, unearth, and steal archaeological remains for profit, an activity termed **looting.** Ancient Native American sites in the southwestern United States, for example, occasionally yield unbroken pottery vessels (called pots, although—based on their design and craftsmanship—these objects more strongly resemble attractive vases) for which collectors of art and antiques are willing to pay many thousands of dollars. In the process of unearthing these valuable objects, looters literally destroy archaeological sites and all of the information about the past they contain.

Other miscreants, mostly untrained amateurs, search out, dig up, and collect artifacts more for the enjoyment of the quest than out of any expectation of financial gain. This kind of nonprofessional activity is termed **pot hunting.** For example, even though prehistoric Native American archaeological sites along the eastern seaboard contain virtually nothing of monetary value, pot-hunters continually destroy these sites because searching for them and unearthing the archaeological remains they contain is, for them, a highly enjoyable pastime.

Infrastructure Development

Perhaps the greatest threat to archaeological sites results from development—mainly infrastructure development. Unceasing infrastructure development is made necessary by constant (and in many places, accelerating) human population growth, and the consequent need, worldwide, to create additional places for people to live and work, to increase the supplies of energy and food on which human populations depend, and to develop ever more efficient modes of transportation and communication. Developers thus continually erect new homes, lay new oil and gas pipelines, build nuclear reactors, dig mines, clear new farmland, build additional highways, railroads, and airports, and establish more and better communications networks. One cost of these projects is the continual loss of nonrenewable archaeological sites and, along with them, irreplaceable archaeological information.

CULTURAL RESOURCES MANAGEMENT

Much of the work of applied archaeologists centers on the attempt to manage the world's remaining archaeological resources wisely, an effort termed **cultural resources management (CRM)** (Kerber 1994; Pastron 1994; King 1998; Stapp 1998; Ferguson 2000; Neumann and Sanford 2001a, 2001b). Most applied archaeologists involved in cultural resources management work to prevent the destruction of archaeological sites directly, either by excavating them before they are destroyed or by taking steps to ensure that destruction will not occur and the sites will be preserved. As an alternative, some work as the managers or administrators of government agencies or private firms involved in cultural resources management.

Salvage and Preservation of Archaeological Sites

The destruction of archaeological sites and the consequent loss of irreplaceable information about human beings of the past can be directly prevented in one of two main ways: preservation or salvage. **Archaeological preservation** is the attempt to preserve archaeological remains threatened with destruction, usually by ensuring that the remains are neither disturbed nor removed from the ground. Instead, they are left untouched, for excavation and study by future generations of archaeologists whose techniques for recovery and analysis may be better than those in use today.

It often happens that preservation of an archaeological site for future excavation proves impractical or even impossible. Common reasons include ongoing or threatened erosion, looting, pot-hunting, or impending infrastructure development. In such cases, applied archaeologists undertake **data recovery** (alternatively, **salvage archaeology**), the attempt to rescue the information and artifacts the site contains before the site is destroyed. The usual method is to remove the remains from the ground, under controlled circumstances, as quickly as possible.

Legislation to Protect Archaeological Remains

Prior to the 1960s, federal or state funding was occasionally provided for salvaging important archaeological sites before they were obliterated by major infrastructure development projects such as highways or pipelines. In addition, wealthy individuals or institutions occasionally underwrote archaeological research (Pastron 1994:

87). However, the idea that both natural and cultural resources—including not only forests and rivers but also, for example, historic buildings and archaeological sites—should be considered "public goods" (see Chapter 10, p. 230), and should therefore be legally protected from destruction, has been incorporated into law only within the past forty years or so. In the 1960s, in response to growing public concern about environmental, historical, and architectural preservation, the U.S. Congress passed two important laws, the National Historic Preservation Act of 1966 and the National Environmental Policy Act of 1969. State and local governments also passed laws to prevent the loss of archaeological remains.

The National Historic Preservation Act of 1966.   This law inaugurated the National Register of Historic Places, an ever-growing list of protected sites that has been consistently interpreted by the law as including both historic and prehistoric places (Tylor 1999; King 2000). Sites of recognized cultural and historic value have been continually added to this list ever since. In addition, the act mandated that certain infrastructure development projects must undergo an **archeological survey**—a systematic search for hidden remains—to detect the presence of as-yet-undiscovered sites. Development projects requiring a survey include those funded even in part by the federal government, those taking place on federal or tribal lands, and those requiring federal licenses or permits. Any significant sites found in the course of an archaeological survey must be either preserved (if they are eligible for the National Register of Historic Places) or salvaged. Preservation is sometimes accomplished by changing the scope or location of the planned development to avoid the site. To date, approximately 74,000 sites have been listed on the National Register of Historic Places.

The National Environmental Policy Act of 1969.   Three years after the passage of its first archaeologically important act, Congress passed a second, the National Environmental Policy Act of 1969 (customarily abbreviated as NEPA 1969). The primary intent of NEPA 1969 is to protect natural resources such as forests, rivers, seacoasts, and wetlands, but cultural resources are included as well. This act requires that before any infrastructure development involving federal land, funding, or permits takes place, developers must consider any potential damage to both the natural and cultural environments. They must then submit an "environmental impact statement" detailing all resources present at the development location and what will be done to salvage or preserve them.

Since their original passage, both of these acts have been strengthened by the addition of numerous amendments. In 1979, they were supplemented with the passage of the Archaeological Resources Protection Act, which specifically protects archaeological resources on both public and tribal lands. In addition, individual states, counties, and municipalities have passed legislation protecting cultural resources lying within their borders. The cumulative impact of these laws has been the salvage or preservation of literally thousands of archaeological sites, although since the laws do not apply to development on most privately held land, some sites do continue to be lost (see Carnett 1991).

These laws have also had a profound impact on the profession of archaeology, virtually creating the subdiscipline of applied archaeology. In the United States, applied archaeology underwritten by the federal and state governments and private industry now represents the bulk of all archaeological research.

Complying with Cultural Resources Legislation.   To comply with the laws governing cultural resources management, applied archaeologists undertake one or more of three separate phases of investigation at locations where development has been scheduled. In Phase I, the survey phase, the landscape is studied and an archaeological survey is undertaken. The purposes of Phase I are to understand the potential of the area for prehistoric or early historic human habitation or other use; to identify the location of subsurface sites, if possible, from surface manifestations such as mounds or the presence of bits of pottery; and to assess the extent of any remains discovered and the time period during which they were deposited. (Subsurface surveys may also be undertaken in this phase, especially in the eastern part of the United States.)

If anything of archaeological significance is located during Phase I, a second phase of work commences. The purpose of Phase II, the evaluation phase, is to examine the archaeological remains discovered in Phase I more thoroughly, often by undertaking limited test excavations, and to document the presence, extent, and significance of the remains. Phase II usually involves the preparation of a formal report on the archaeologists' findings, which is filed with the appropriate federal or state office.

Phase III, termed the mitigation phase ("to mitigate" means "to alleviate a problem"), is undertaken only if warranted by Phases I and II. Used in an archaeological context, the term refers to the problem of the imminent destruction of a site, which can be mitigated in one of two ways: either the site can be protected for posterity or the information it contains can be salvaged through archaeological excavation.

EMPLOYMENT IN APPLIED ARCHAEOLOGY

The numerous pieces of legislation passed since the 1960s have resulted in jobs for thousands of applied archaeologists. Some work as field researchers or lab analysts; others as owners or administrators of archaeological consulting firms; still others as government bureaucrats "primarily concerned with ensuring that development projects maintain compliance with the expanding, and sometimes confusing, body of laws and directives pertaining to the treatment and disposition of cultural resources" (Pastron 1994:87).

One major advantage of applied archaeology as a career field is that—thanks to cultural resources legislation—jobs are readily available and presumably will continue to be available in the future. Another advantage is that a bachelor's degree alone may suffice for an entry-level job in this field. Students with a B.A., a major in anthropology, several courses in archaeology, and some archaeological field experience usually have no trouble finding jobs immediately after graduation, as "dig bums" or "shovel hounds" on projects undertaken to comply with CRM legislation. Field experience is usually gained by attending a summer-session archaeological field school. Job applicants who have taken specialty archaeology courses (such as lithic or faunal analysis) or who have other relevant skills (such as writing, photographic, or computer skills) may be especially valuable new employees. According to the Society for American Archaeology, there are some six thousand contract archaeologists currently working in the United States, many of them "dig bums" without advanced degrees.

Since most jobs in applied archaeology exist thanks to the federal and state regulations mandating archaeological survey and salvage prior to infrastructure development, government agencies, either federal or state, are an excellent place to seek employment. In the United States, for example, a number of federal agencies (including the U.S. Forest Service, National Park Service, Bureau of Land Management, Army Corps of Engineers, and Bureau of Indian Affairs) hire applied archaeologists. The National Park Service is especially active in archaeology, since national parks in over half all states contain archaeological remains.[3] Most state departments of parks and recreation also hire archaeologists, as do many departments of historic preservation or environmental conservation and some highway agencies (see Pastron 1994; McManamon 2000).

The private sector, too, employs applied archaeologists. Most of them work for the hundreds of small consulting firms that have sprung up since the 1960s to provide contract archaeologists to the individuals and organizations that are obliged to comply with cultural resources laws. In addition, some work for environmental planning firms, which "prepare the copious environmental impact documents that nowadays almost always accompany applications for both public and private development projects" (Pastron 1994:87). Still other applied archaeologists own their own private consulting firms.[4]

The main disadvantages of an entry-level job doing applied archaeology are that such jobs pay poorly and often do not include any fringe benefits. For a rewarding lifetime career in cultural resources management, a Ph.D. in archaeology, or in anthropology with an archaeology focus, is virtually mandatory. Also obligatory is the accumulation of skills more often thought of as characterizing entrepreneurship than scholarship, such as "engaging in competitive bidding" and "doing research in accordance within exacting constraints of schedule and budget" (Pastron 1994:89). Earning a Ph.D. in archaeology requires the expenditure of considerable time (on average, about seven years), although—because scholarships and assistantships are widely available—it need not be costly. It almost always involves doing original field research.

Another way to "apply" archaeology is to teach the subject. Since the initial passage of cultural resources legislation in the 1960s, numerous public school districts in the United States have incorporated archaeology into their curricula, at both the primary and secondary levels (see, for example, Rogge and Bell 1989; BLM 2000). Museums, too—in particular, local history museums, children's museums, and science museums—often run archaeology education programs for both children and adults. Applied archaeology may soon be routinely taught in law schools. The National Park Service, which has a substantial archaeology component, recently began to press for the inclusion of cultural resources law in programs and courses on environmental law.

Another applied archaeological career possibility, and one that could be fruitfully combined with museum teaching, would be a curatorial position in a museum featuring archaeological collections. Archaeology's focus on material culture—the objects humans create—makes it "an important bridge between anthropology and museums" (Kelly 2002:4). Relatively few artifacts unearthed from archaeological sites actually wind up on display in museums, but those that do must be analyzed and compared, and their meaning interpreted for museum goers (see Sullivan 1992). A Master's degree in museum science is usually required for a curatorial job.

A final note: one important consideration for students who are planning to earn a Ph.D. in anthropology is their probable future lifestyle. For a Ph.D. in any subfield of anthropology, one must ordinarily do original field research. Many if not most students in cultural anthropology do this research in foreign countries rather than in the United States. Archaeological research, however, can often be done locally. Moreover, because of the availability of jobs in applied archaeology in the United States, most of those trained in this subfield of applied anthropology work domestically rather than internationally. Applied archaeology is thus a career field that may be more compatible with family obligations than some other kinds of applied anthropology.

KEY TERMS

applied archaeology   the use of archaeological theories and methods to achieve specific, practical archaeological goals

archaeological preservation   the attempt to preserve archaeological remains threatened with destruction, usually by ensuring that the remains are not removed from the ground

archaeological survey   a systematic search for hidden archaeological remains

archaeology   a subfield of anthropology focusing mainly on the cultures of people who lived in the past

artifact   a physical object made by human hands

cultural resources   collectively, human-made objects plus features and ecofacts suggesting human activity

cultural resources management (CRM)   the effort to manage the world's remaining archaeological resources wisely

data recovery   in archaeology, the attempt to rescue the information and artifacts an archaeological site contains before the site is destroyed

ecofact   floral or faunal material found in an archaeological context

excavation   the primary research method of archaeologists, involving digging carefully through the soil at the places where peoples of the past once lived or worked

feature   nonartifact evidence of human activity in the past, such as a soil stain

historical archaeology   the archaeology of literate human groups who left written records of their lives

looting   locating, unearthing, and stealing archaeological remains for profit

material remains   the physical objects left behind by peoples of the past

pot hunting   digging up artifacts more for the enjoyment of the quest than for any expectation of financial gain

prehistoric archaeology   the archaeology of nonliterate human groups

salvage archaeology   an alternative term for archaeological *data recovery*

site   a place where people of the past once lived or worked

NOTES

1. GPS technology is sometimes referred to as GIS, or *Global Imaging Satellite* technology; however, the acronym *GPS* is preferred, since *GIS* can also stand for a broader concept, Geographic Information Systems.

2. Cultural resources also include other meritorious products of human cultures, such as works of art and architecture.

3. The National Park Service maintains the National Archaeological Database, a computer network that provides information to those interested in archaeology.

4. The requirements of the new cultural resources preservation laws have prompted discussions, and some differences of opinion, between scholars and entrepreneurs over ethical issues (Garrow 1993; Vitelli 1996). For example, with so many archaeological sites currently threatened with obliteration, are academic archaeologists justified in spending time and money excavating sites that are *not* threatened?

REFERENCES

Bureau of Land Management (BLM)
2000. *Intrigue of the Past: Investigating Archaeology (An Archaeology Education Program for Fourth Through Twelfth Grades). Salt Lake City:* Bureau of Land Management.

Carnett, Carol
1991. *Legal Background of Archeological Resources Protection* (National Park Service Technical Brief No. 11). Washington, DC: National Park Service.

Ferguson, T. J.
2000. "Applied Anthropology in the Management of Native American Cultural Resources: Archaeology, Ethnography, and History of Traditional Cultural Places." In *Careers in Anthropology: Profiles of Practitioner Anthropologists* (NAPA Bulletin No. 20), edited by Paula L. W. Sabloff, 15–17. Washington, DC: American Anthropological Association.

Garrow, Patrick H.
1993. "Ethics and Contract Archaeology." *Practicing Anthropology* 15 (3):10–13.

Kelly, Robert L.
2002. "American Archeology in Thirty Years." *Anthropology News* 43 (1):4.

Kerber, Jordan E. (ed.)
1994. *Cultural Resource Management: Archaeological Research, Preservation Planning, and Public Education in the Northeastern United States.* Westport, CT: Bergin and Garvey.

King, Thomas F.
1998. *Cultural Resource Laws and Practice: An Introductory Guide.* Walnut Creek, CA: Altamira Press.

2000. *Federal Planning and Historical Places: The Section 106 Process.* Walnut Creek, CA: Altamira Press.

McManamon, Francis P.
2000. "A Public Archaeologist in a Public Agency." In *Careers in Anthropology: Profiles of Practitioner Anthropologists* (NAPA Bulletin No. 20), edited by Paula L. W. Sabloff, 58–63. Washington, DC: American Anthropological Association.

Neumann, Thomas W., and Robert M. Sanford
2001a. *Cultural Resources Archaeology: An Introduction.* Walnut Creek, CA: Altamira Press.

2001b. *Practicing Archaeology: A Training Manual for Cultural Resources Archaeology.* Walnut Creek, CA: Altamira Press.

Pastron, Allen G.

1994 (orig. 1988). "Opportunities in Cultural Resources Management." In *Applying Anthropology* (3rd ed.), edited by Aaron Podolefsky and Peter J. Brown, 86–89. Mountain View, CA: Mayfield.

Rogge, A. E., and Patti Bell

1989. *Archaeology in the Classroom: A Case Study from Arizona* (National Park Service Technical Brief No. 4). Washington, DC: National Park Service.

Stapp, Darby (ed.)

1998. Changing Paradigms in Cultural Resource Management. *Practicing Anthropology* 20 (3):1–33 (special issue).

Sullivan, Lynne

1992. *Managing Archaeological Resources from the Museum Perspective* (National Park Service Technical Brief No. 13). Washington, DC: National Park Service.

Tylor, Norman

1999. *Historic Preservation: An Introduction to Its History Principles, and Practice*. New York: Norton.

Vitelli, Karen D. (ed.)

1996. *Archaeological Ethics*. Walnut Creek, CA: Altamira Press.

CAREERS IN APPLIED PHYSICAL ANTHROPOLOGY

Physical (or **biological**) **anthropology** is the branch of anthropology that addresses the biological characteristics of humans, as well as their closest relatives (prosimians, monkeys, and apes), both past and present (see Appendix 1). Most physical anthropologists specialize in one of two broad yet interrelated topical areas. The first, **human evolution and variation,** encompasses the study of the gradual evolution of anatomically modern human beings from our more archaic forebears, as well as the study of the physical differences among contemporary people. The second, **primatology,** is the comparative study, generally from an ecological perspective, of members of the order **Primates,** the taxonomic group to which humans and their closest relatives belong.

Numerous subfields of physical anthropology—some of them previously established fields of inquiry that have only recently been welcomed under the rubric of physical anthropology, and some of them newly established subfields dependent on highly technical methods (such as DNA analysis)—have emerged in the past few decades. These include human genetics, nutritional anthropology, human ecology, and certain kinds of population studies (such as population genetics, which measures and tracks genetic changes in human populations).

These fields of interest and expertise are primarily theoretical. Some physical anthropologists, for example, study the evolution of somatic (bodily) changes that occurred as hominids (early humans) became anatomically modern; others focus on the behavior of primates in the wild; still others are interested in comparative anatomy, the study of the complex of characteristics that distinguishes us from other members of the hominoid superfamily (which includes the great and lesser apes in addition to humans). More recently, physical anthropologists have widened their interests to include subjects as varied as the relationship between humans' genetic makeup and the environments in which they live; the nutritional effects of foods consumed in different societies, past and present; and the constraints that human anatomy places on the design of the material objects humans make and use, from cars to computers (an area of inquiry called ergonomics or human factors research).

In addition to these theoretical considerations, however, physical anthropology also provides practitioners with numerous opportunities to make use of their discipline's theories, methods, and accumulated data in order to address real-world issues and solve real-world problems. This appendix describes three of the most interesting kinds of applied physical anthropology: clinically applied physical anthropology and medical research, forensic anthropology, and applied primatology.

CLINICALLY APPLIED PHYSICAL ANTHROPOLOGY AND MEDICAL RESEARCH

Because of their training in areas such as human growth and development, human genetics, and human skeletal morphology, physical anthropologists are finding more and more applications for their expertise in clinical settings. Helping physicians screen for genetic diseases, such as the fatal neurological disorder Huntington's chorea (for which the precise genetic cause was only recently discovered), is an example.

Physical anthropologists also participate in the health sector by contributing to the diagnosis and treatment of maladies of abnormal physical growth and development (Harris 2002). For example, specialists in craniofacial biology, many of them physical anthropologists, now serve as members of "craniofacial anomalies teams," which diagnose and treat abnormalities of the head. The physical anthropologist "is often the team member who is best equipped, in terms of training, to define the range of normalcy, and thus diagnose . . . which structures are abnormal, how far outside of 'normal' they are, and how much treatment is needed" to restore the victim of a craniofacial disorder to a condition as close to normalcy as possible (ibid.:32). Other clinically applied physical anthropologists help pediatricians to determine whether children who have been exposed to certain adverse circumstances (such as malnutrition or premature birth), or who are suffering from specific diseases (such as Down syndrome or sickle cell anemia), are growing and developing normally (ibid.:34). Still others, because of their familiarity with human anatomy, work in the area of physical rehabilitation, often as physical therapists.

Other physical anthropologists, specialists in the effects of nutrition on human growth and development, are employed either as nutritionists in clinical settings or by private sector corporations interested in nutritional research and product development (Ryan 2000:33). Dr. Alan S. Ryan, for example, is employed in the pediatric nutrition product industry, where he monitors trends in infant feeding practices (such as breast-feeding prevalence), conducts nutritional studies of potential changes to the composition of infant formulas, and helps the industry develop baby foods that optimize infants' and children's healthy growth and development.[1]

FORENSIC ANTHROPOLOGY

Many physical anthropologists whose overall field of interest is human variation are experts in **human skeletal morphology,** the study of the size, shape, and interrelationship of the elements of the human skeleton, and **biomechanics,** the study of the ways in which the physical parts of the bodies of humans or other primates work together—for example, to support locomotion. Combined, these two areas of expertise lend themselves to **forensic anthropology,** the practical application of certain principles of physical anthropology (especially those governing the study of human variation) to the solution of legal problems—usually involving the identification and analysis of human remains (Rathbun and Buikstra 1984; Haglund 1993; Evans 1996; Rhine 1998; Fairgrieve 1999; Nafte 2000).

Forensic anthropology originated in the nineteenth century, with the development of an anthropological technique called **anthropometry,** the precise measurement of the parts of the human body. Originally used in forensics as a technique for identifying criminals, anthropometry was soon replaced by superior methods of identification, such as photography and fingerprinting, but can be said to be the ancestor of today's modern forensic anthropology.

The term **forensic** is a broad one, meaning "pertaining to the law and legal affairs," and experts in numerous professional fields besides physical anthropology—such as pathologists, dentists, radiologists, other biomedical health professionals, and law enforcement officials—are involved in forensic work. Forensic anthropologists, however, bring a special expertise to the task of identifying those whose identity is unknown because they have both knowledge of human variation and skeletal morphology and an understanding of culture. Thus a forensic anthropologist would be able to determine the sex, age, and sometimes even the ethnic affiliation of an individual whose unidentified remains had been found buried in an unmarked grave; this profession could also help interpret the remains by contributing information on, for example, the cultural ramifications of the clothing of the deceased, the state of his or her dentition, the particular type of burial, and any items or materials found in the grave.

Most forensic anthropologists specialize in one of two areas: the identification of the dead through an examination of physical remains (the largest forensic specialty) or facial reconstruction, also for identification purposes.[2] The latter is much less widely used than the former, but often garners greater popular interest. The need to identify human remains arises in various circumstances, including missing persons cases, murders, transportation accidents, wars, and terrorist attacks. A major role for forensic anthropologists in recent decades has been the identification of victims of warfare, political violence, or "ethnic cleansing," whose remains have been recovered from burial sites in El Salvador, Guatemala, Chile, Argentina, Uganda, Rwanda, Bosnia, Croatia, East Timor, and elsewhere. Recently, for example, the government of Guatemala hired forensic anthropologist Carlos Federico Reyes Lopez to help identify the recovered bodies of "the disappeared," victims of the country's bitter counter-insurgency war in the early 1980s (Edelman 1996:13). In some cases, attempts are made to hide or obliterate human remains by reburying them, dusting them with lime, or burning them, but in most cases, enough bones remain for identification (Mydans 2001:A10).

Identifying Human Remains

Now as in the past, people sometimes die under circumstances in which no form of personal identification, such as an identification card, membership cards, or a driver's license carried in a purse, wallet, or pocket, is clearly associated with the remains. In the absence of such identification, the identity of the deceased may be difficult to prove to the satisfaction of both family members and the law. Yet without proof that a given individual has died, that individual's monetary assets cannot be distributed to heirs, nor can his or her spouse remarry. If a murder has been committed, it is very difficult to prosecute the suspected murderer without a securely identified victim.

Forensic anthropologists possess the skills needed to identify the physical remains of people who have died under such circumstances, as well as to determine the cause and the time of death when these are also unknown (Huyghe 2002). Thus they are called upon when remains are discovered that may be human or non-human, are incomplete, have been burned, have decomposed, or—in the case of multiple deaths—are mixed together, as may happen in the case of transportation accidents or large-scale terrorist attacks. The methods used in these circumstances differ, depending on the completeness and state of preservation of the remains, and whether they are believed to be those of one individual, several, or many.

The forensic anthropologist's specific goal also varies, depending on the suspected time of death and the consequent age of the remains. For a skeleton that appears to be very old, the anthropologist attempts to determine the cause and approximate date of death, as well as the sex, age, physical condition, and (in many cases) ethnic identity of the deceased. After examination and analysis of the remains, for example, he or she may be able to state with confidence that the deceased was a robust Native American male who died five hundred years ago, at the age of about fifteen, from a blow to the head. (In the case of ancient remains, archaeologists may also be called upon to determine the date of death using archaeological techniques such as carbon-14 dating.) In most cases of ancient remains, more specific identity is not possible. If, on the other hand, the remains represent an individual who has only recently died—in a plane crash, for example—the forensic anthropologist attempts to discover the individual's specific identity.

A knowledge of culture often helps the forensic anthropologist add information to the search for identification that goes well beyond what a medical doctor, dentist, or radiologist can contribute. A doctor, for example, could probably determine, from studying a corpse, that the deceased was a middle-aged female; a dentist or radiologist could determine, from studying the teeth or x-rays of the head, that the individual had untreated dental cavities. A forensic anthropologist, upon examining the same corpse, teeth, and x-rays, would be much more apt to suggest, for example, that the observed pattern of tooth decay and tooth loss might reflect a life of prolonged poverty—a cultural phenomenon. This kind of information can contribute significantly to the identification of specific individuals.

Biological Profiles. If the forensic anthropologist is attempting to verify the identity of a specific person and the remains are well preserved, the evidence needed for identification (such as the individual's fingerprints, pattern of dental work, or distinguishing birthmarks or scars) is often easily visible. However, the remains may be burned, deteriorated, partial, or mixed together with the remains of others. In this case, the forensic anthropologist attempts to establish a **biological profile** of the individual, consisting of all the information he or she can recover from the remains, including sex, approximate age, approximate height, physical condition, nutritional health, cause of death, and—if the remains are those of a female—whether or not she ever gave birth. Ethnic affiliation can also sometimes be specified, although if the remains are identified as to race, this term is more apt to reflect the cultural label likely to have been applied to the person during his or her life, rather than any biologically meaningful complex of physical characteristics.

Indicators on Bones.   In many cases, the remains of an unknown individual will consist only of bones, but these are often sufficient to establish a biological profile. Mathematical formulas, based on the careful analysis of large numbers of human skeletons, help the forensic anthropologist determine the sex, age, stature, physical condition, and ethnicity of the deceased, based solely on osteological analysis. (Two large, mixed collections of nineteenth-century human skeletons, one located at the Cleveland Museum and the other at the Smithsonian, provided the bases for these formulas.)

The sex of a skeleton is based on its size, stature, and—most reliably—on the shape, size, and condition of the pelvic bones. There are also some suggestive differences between male and female skulls; the male eyebrow ridge is more prominent, for example, and the male jaw heavier.

Approximate age is indicated by the relative size of the bones; the presence or absence of baby teeth; whether or not the wisdom teeth have erupted; whether or not the seams between the major bones of the skull—open at birth—are fully fused; whether or not the long bones of the arms and legs are fully developed; and the presence or absence of degenerative conditions such as arthritis or osteoporosis.

Stature, if the skeleton is incomplete, can be determined by applying a mathematical formula to measurements of arm and leg bones. The physical robustness of the bones and their muscle attachment points may also suggest the stature, in life, of the deceased.

It may also be possible for a forensic anthropologist to make a positive identification based on physical condition, specifically, the presence of certain diseases and disorders of the bones or teeth (Chamberlain 1994:26–39). If an individual suffered a bone fracture during life and lived for some period of time afterwards, the healed fracture will be evident. Chronic joint diseases also leave visible clues on bones; a common form of arthritis, osteoarthritis, is observable in the major joints of the body, such as the hip and knee; a less common form, rheumatoid arthritis, affects the joints of the hands and feet (Chamberlain 1994:31). Nutritional deficiencies, chronic bone infections, congenital abnormalities, and dental diseases such as cavities and periodontal disease may also aid the forensic anthropologist in identifying human remains.

Finally, for those increasingly rare individuals whose ancestry is relatively unmixed, ethnicity can sometimes be established on the basis of certain diagnostic traits of the skull and dentition. In the past, some anthropologists distinguished various human groups (which they called "races") from one another on the basis of certain physical characteristics, produced by geographical (and hence genetic) isolation in particular environments. Arctic peoples, for example, tended to have stocky (and thus more heat-retaining) torsos in response to living in a very cold environment. However, beginning with the age of exploration and continuing through colonial times until the present, humans groups have interbred all over the world.

Most humans today are the descendants of multiple ethnic or "racial" groups. Thus, although teeth are occasionally diagnostic, and several multivariate statistical tests for ethnicity, based on skull measurements, exist, distinguishing ethnicity based on physical characteristics is problematic and can only become more so over time.

Facial Reconstruction

Relative to the number of forensic anthropologists involved in identifying human remains, only a small number specialize in **facial reconstruction.** If a skull is available, it is possible for a skilled forensic specialist to create a reasonably accurate portrait of the deceased as he or she appeared in life, based on the size and shape of various skull features, especially muscle attachment points (Prag and Neave 1997). A facial reconstruction can be a drawing, sometimes computer-assisted but is more apt to be a three-dimensional model. Layers of modeling clay, representing the features and underlying facial musculature that once existed, are added to the actual skull of a crime or accident victim until a likeness of the victim emerges. In a recent, well-publicized case of facial modeling, a forensic anthropologist helped determine the identities of skeletons suspected to be those of members of the Russian royal family, murdered in the former Soviet Union during the Bolshevik Revolution of 1918. When facial reconstructions, prepared by the anthropologist, were compared with old photographs of family members, the reconstructions strongly suggested that the remains were indeed those of the Romanovs. The conclusion was later confirmed using DNA evidence.

APPLIED PRIMATOLOGY

In conjunction with research on the evolution and contemporary physical variation of humans, some physical anthropologists specialize in primatology, the comparative study of human beings and the other primates. As mentioned above, primates are a taxonomic group of animals that includes humans and their closest relatives: apes, monkeys and prosimians (lemurs, lorises, tarsiers, and related species). Genetically, humans are 98 percent similar to certain of our "great ape" relatives, such as the chimpanzees of Africa.

Like other subfields of anthropology, primatology is mainly a theoretical discipline, pursued in universities and research institutes. However, theories and methods developed within this discipline are sometimes put to specific, practical use, an effort termed **applied primatology.** Most applied primatologists work in one of two main arenas: environmental conservation of primate habitats (especially in places where nonhuman primates and humans interact) and the study and care of captive primate populations.

Environmental Conservation

About half of all nonhuman primates, some 250 species in all, are considered endangered. The most common reason is habitat loss due to logging, road building, or other human activity. An additional problem is that some primates, mostly in

Central and West Africa, are hunted by indigenes who rely on "bush meat" (primarily chimpanzee flesh) as a food source. The need to conserve threatened primate species is urgent: primates promote forest regeneration and plant diversity (particularly important given the potential of plants as sources of useful drugs) by consuming and excreting seeds; they help prevent the loss of other species by contributing to the maintenance of predator–prey systems; they are a major source of information on human evolution; and, through ecotourism, they help bring much-needed tourist dollars into the developing countries where most of them are found. A number of applied primatologists have thus found roles working with environmental conservationists and members of local communities to protect endangered primate species.

Over the years, creating nature preserves, erecting protective barriers, and passing laws forbidding the hunting of primates have all proven largely ineffective. Far more successful have been various efforts in which indigenous people, conservationists, and applied anthropologists have worked together to improve the overall relationship, in a given natural area, between humans, animals, and the environment. An example of such efforts is the linkage of environmental conservation (including the protection of primates) with local development concerns (such as indigenous people's need for jobs, educational opportunities, or health care). Today this development model is supported by numerous multilateral organizations, governments, and NGOs. Programs intended to package environmental conservation education with development issues, and which encourage the participation of local communities, are termed **integrated conservation and development plans (ICDPs)**. Where these have been implemented, they have often proven highly successful.

Captive Primates

The second area in which primatology is commonly applied revolves around colonies of captive primates. Such colonies exist, in the United States and many other countries, for three main reasons: for research (mainly medical research), for the preservation of endangered species, and for the education and entertainment of the public.

Because they are genetically so similar to humans, primates—especially chimpanzees—are excellent analogs to humans for purposes of medical research into certain diseases. (Unfortunately, AIDS is not among these diseases; the so-called simian immunodeficiency virus has proven unsuitable in the search for ways to prevent or cure HIV/AIDS in humans.) Only a few decades ago, tens of thousands of primates were routinely captured in the wild and imported into the West for biomedical research, a practice widely criticized as inhumane. Today this practice has been drastically curtailed; research animals now come largely from captive colonies. Two advantages of using captive animals are that they are less expensive to procure and healthier than wild animals.

Captive animals are also used to preserve endangered species. For example, using captive populations, gene banks have been established to ensure that particular species do not become extinct. Captive animals are preferable to wild animals for purposes of species preservation, since they are generally healthier, thanks to their ample and nutritious diets and veterinary care. In some cases, captives—usually housed in zoos—have been used to build up population numbers for eventual reintroduction into the wild.

Applied primatologists help in species preservation efforts by using their knowledge of primate behaviors in the wild—for example, primates' feeding and mating strategies—to help design appropriate captive care. They are also involved in "environmental enrichment" projects, intended to ensure that captive animals are physically and psychologically healthy, in compliance with the requirements of the U.S. Animal Welfare Act. Some applied primatologists are actively engaged in preparing captive animals for life in the wild by, for example, creating naturalistic enclosures, hiding primates' food in order to promote foraging behavior, and teaching primates to fear their natural predators.

Modern zoos have three main objectives: entertainment and education of the public; the conservation of endangered species through the maintenance of genetic diversity; [3] and husbandry (the facilitation of reproduction in captivity). A number of applied primatologists have found rewarding careers as zookeepers or curators. In addition, some are zoo-based research scientists, engaged either in behavioral research on captive animals or in fieldwork in primate habitats. Many primates have never been adequately studied in their natural habitats, so information about their behaviors and diets is almost entirely lacking.

EMPLOYMENT IN APPLIED PHYSICAL ANTHROPOLOGY

Applied physical anthropologists seeking to enter the area of clinically applied physical anthropology are most likely to find employment in hospitals or physical rehabilitation facilities attached to major university medical centers. Some of those engaged in medical research are employed by private sector corporations—for example, companies producing foods or prostheses or whose products incorporate principles of ergonomics. Advanced degrees are required for these jobs.

Forensic anthropologists, who must have considerable additional training beyond the B.A. degree, are employed by local and state law enforcement agencies, by branches of the federal government (including the National Transportation Safety Board; the FBI; the Bureau of Alcohol, Tobacco and Firearms; and the Defense Department), and by international organizations, including the United Nations.

A county coroner might require positive identification of suspected human remains discovered in the course of a construction project. A state medical examiner might need this kind of information in the prosecution of a crime or the search for a missing person. (Both state and federal laws require that when human remains are found, they must be identified.) The federal government is responsible for identifying the remains of war casualties and victims of terrorist attacks such as the attacks on the World Trade Center and Pentagon in September, 2001. The specific government agencies tasked with identifying victims of terrorist attacks in any of the fifty states are the FBI and the Bureau of Alcohol, Tobacco, and Firearms; if an attack occurs in a foreign country, such as the 1998 bombing of U.S. embassies in Nairobi, Kenya, and Dar es Salaam, Tanzania, the Department of Defense is responsible. Victims of war crimes are investigated by individual governments or by the International War Crimes Tribunal (an arm of the United Nations), located in The Hague, Netherlands.

Forensic anthropology is a very small field. It is estimated that there are only about fifteen full-time forensic anthropologists in the United States, and perhaps 150 others, associated with universities, museums, or research institutes, practicing part time (Stephens 2002:75). Since only a few graduate programs offer courses in forensics (see *Anthropology Career Resources Handbook*), most forensic anthropologists learn their skills in Master's or Ph.D. programs in physical anthropology and then receive mentoring and on-the-job training. One way to establish a career in this area is through law enforcement (Chapter 8); one forensic anthropologist, for example, entered the field by first becoming a crime scene technician with a state police department of forensic services (Stephens 2002:76). Practicing forensic anthropologists may gain certification by the American Board of Forensic Anthropology, and many are members of the anthropology section of the American Academy of Forensic Sciences.

Career opportunities in applied primatology are available with conservation organizations, university primate laboratories where animals are kept for research purposes, and zoos. Both zoos and laboratories offer internships, often a sensible first career step, and some accept—and train—volunteers. Zoos require staff, and some zoo jobs, such as keeper or environmental enrichment technician, require only a bachelor's degree. At a research institution, an entry level job as field assistant to a primatologist would require only a B.A. Many more career areas, including field research positions and management or educational positions in labs or zoos, are open to those with a Master's degree in physical anthropology with a specialty in primatology. Most top primatological research scientists employed by research institutes, and most animal curators employed by zoos, have Ph.D. degrees plus a great deal of experience.

KEY TERMS

anthropometry   the precise measurement of the parts of the human body and their relationship to one another

applied primatology   the use of theories and methods developed within primatology to achieve specific, practical purposes

biological anthropology   a synonym for *physical anthropology*

biological profile   all the information a forensic anthropologist recovers from the remains of a given deceased individual

biomechanics   the ways in which the physical parts of the bodies of humans or other primates work together

facial reconstruction   a drawing or three-dimensional clay model, based on a skull, portraying a deceased person as he or she appeared in life

forensic   pertaining to the law and legal affairs

forensic anthropology   the practical application of the principles of physical anthropology to the solution of legal problems

human skeletal morphology the study of the size, shape, and interrelationship of the elements of the human skeleton

human evolution and variation the study of the gradual evolution of anatomically modern human beings from our more archaic forebears, as well as the study of the physical differences among contemporary people

integrated conservation and development plans (ICDPs) development programs combining environmental conservation education and development issues, and incorporating local community members

physical anthropology the branch of anthropology that addresses the biological aspects of being human, past and present

Primates the taxonomic group to which humans and their closest relatives, the prosimians, monkeys, and apes belong

primatology a subfield of human evolution; the comparative study of human beings and the other primates

NOTES

1. See especially Ryan 2000.
2. Volume 34, no. 2 of the journal *Social Science and Medicine*, published in 1992, contains a special section devoted to forensic anthropology.

3. At present, approximately eighty to ninety primate genetic-diversity maintenance programs exist, a number far exceeded by the number of threatened primate species.

REFERENCES

Chamberlain, Andres
1994. *Human Remains.* Berkeley, CA: University of California Press.

Edelman, Marc
1996. "Death Threats Against Forensic Anthropologist." *Anthropology Newsletter* 37 (6):13–17.

Evans, Colin
1996. *The Casebook of Forensic Detection: How Science Solved 100 of the World's Most Baffling Crimes.* New York: Wiley.

Fairgrieve, Scott I. (ed.)
1999. *Forensic Osteological Analysis: A Book of Case Studies* . Springfield, IL: Thomas.

Haglund, William D.
1993. "Beyond the Bare Bones: Recent Developments in Forensic Anthropology." *Practicing Anthropology* 15 (3):17–19.

Harris, Edward F.
2002. "The Physical Anthropologist as Craniofacial Biologist." *Practicing Anthropology* 24 (2):32–34.

Huyghe, Patrick
2002 (orig. 1988). "Profile of an Anthropologist: No Bone Unturned." In *Physical Anthropology 02/03*, 202–206 Guilford, CT: McGraw-Hill/Dushkin.

Mydans, Seth
2001. "Bones Offer Testimony of Killings in East Timor." *New York Times*, Sept. 30, 2001, A10.

Nafte, Myriam
2000. *Flesh and Bone: An Introduction to Forensic Anthropology.* Durham, NC: Carolina Academic Press.

Prag, John, and Richard Neave
1997. *Making Faces: Using Forensic and Archaeological Evidence.* College Station, TX: Texas A&M University Press.

Rathbun, Ted A., and Jane E. Buikstra (eds.)
1984. *Human Identification: Case Studies in Forensic Anthropology.* Springfield, IL: Thomas.

Rhine, Stanley
1998. *Bone Voyage: A Journey in Forensic Anthropology.* Albuquerque: University of New Mexico Press.

Ryan, Alan S.
2000. "Practicing Physical Anthropology in the Pediatric Nutrition Industry." *Practicing Anthropology* 22 (4):33–36.

Stephens, W. Richard
2002. "Forensic Anthropology." In *Careers in Anthropology,* edited by W. Richard Stephens, 75–78. Boston: Allyn and Bacon.

INDEX

◇ ◇ ◇